Handbook of
War Studies III

Handbook of War Studies III

THE INTRASTATE DIMENSION

EDITED BY

Manus I. Midlarsky

THE UNIVERSITY OF MICHIGAN PRESS

ANN ARBOR

Copyright © by the University of Michigan 2009
Published in the United States of America by
The University of Michigan Press
Manufactured in the United States of America
⊗ Printed on acid-free paper

2012   2011   2010   2009   4   3   2   1

A CIP catalog record for this book is available from the British Library.

U.S. CIP data is on file.

ISBN: 978-0-472-07057-2 (cloth : alk. paper)
ISBN: 978-0-472-05057-4 (pbk. : alk. paper)
ISBN: 978-0-472-02217-5 (e-book)

Contents

Part III. Ethnic Conflict, International Relations, and Genocide

Contributors

Bruce Bueno de Mesquita is the Julius Silver Professor of Politics at New York University, Director of NYU's Alexander Hamilton Center for Political Economy, and a senior fellow at the Hoover Institution, Stanford University. Bueno de Mesquita received his Ph.D. in political science from the University of Michigan in 1971 and a doctorate (Honorus Causa) from the University of Groningen in the Netherlands in 1999. He is the author of 14 books and more than 100 articles primarily on political conflict, the political economy of governance, and policy forecasting. His most recent books include *The Logic of Political Survival* (coauthored with Alastair Smith, Randolph Siverson, and James Morrow, MIT Press, 2003) and *The Strategy of Campaigning* (coauthored with Kiron Skinner, Serhiy Kudelia, and Condoleezza Rice, University of Michigan Press, 2007). Bueno de Mesquita is a former Guggenheim fellow, former president of the International Studies Association, recipient of the 1985 Karl Deutsch Award, the 2007 DMZ Peace Prize, the 2007 Lifetime Achievement Award from the Conflict Processes Section of the American Political Science Association, the 2008 recipient of the Distinguished Foreign Policy Analysis Award given by the Foreign Policy Analysis Section of the International Studies Association, a member of the Council on Foreign Relations and a member of the American Academy of Arts and Sciences. He is also a partner in Mesquita & Roundell, LLC, a consultancy based in New York that uses game theory models he developed to assist government and business in complex negotiations.

Nils Petter Gleditsch is research professor at the International Peace Research Institute, Oslo (PRIO), professor of political science at the Norwegian University of Science and Technology (NTNU) in Trondheim, and editor of *Journal of Peace Research*. He is president of the International Studies Association (2008–9). He has published on democracy and peace, environmental factors in conflict, arms races, the peace dividend, and other topics related to the study of war and peace. He has guest-edited (2007, with Ragnhild Nordås) a special issue of *Political Geography* on climate change and conflict, and he has edited several books, including *Globalization and Armed Conflict* (2003, with Gerald Schneider and Katherine Barbieri) and *Environmental Conflict* (2001, with Paul Diehl).

Håvard Hegre is Professor of political science at the University of Oslo and research professor at the International Peace Research Institute, Oslo (PRIO). He has also worked for the World Bank and is a coauthor of its report on civil war (*Breaking the Conflict Trap*, 2003). He is coeditor of the Norwegian national political science journal *(Norsk statsvitenskapelig tidsskrift)* and serves on the editorial committee of *Journal of Peace Research*. He has guest-edited special issues of World Bank studies on civil war for *Journal of Peace Research* (2004, 2008) and *Defence and Peace Economics* (2002).

Erin K. Jenne is an associate professor at the International Relations and European Studies Department at Central European University in Budapest, where she teaches masters and Ph.D. courses on qualitative and quantitative methods, ethnic conflict, international relations theory, nationalism and civil war, and international security. She has received numerous grants and fellowships, including a MacArthur Predoctoral Fellowship at the Center for International Security and Cooperation at Stanford; a two-year postdoctoral fellowship at the Belfer Center for Science and International Affairs and the World Peace Foundation at Harvard University, and a two-year Carnegie Corporation Scholarship for a book project that compares the League of Nations regional security regime with that of postcommunist Europe to determine which instruments have been most effective in managing ethnic conflict. Recent or forthcoming publications include a book with Cornell University Press and articles in *International Studies Quarterly, Security Studies,* and *Journal of Peace Research.*

Mark Irving Lichbach is professor and chair of Government and Politics at the University of Maryland. He received a B.A. (1973) from Brooklyn College of the City University of New York, an M.A. (1975) from Brown University, and a Ph.D. (1978) in political science from Northwestern

University. A theorist interested in social choice and a comparativist interested in globalization, Lichbach explores the connections between collective action theories and political conflict as well as the connections between collective choice theories and democratic institutions. He is the author or editor of many books, including the award-winning *The Rebel's Dilemma,* and of numerous articles that have appeared in scholarly journals in political science, economics, and sociology. His work has been supported by the National Science Foundation and private foundations. Lichbach, who was book review editor of the *American Political Science Review* (1994–2001) and editor of the University of Michigan Press's series Interests, Identities, and Institutions, served as chair of two other political science departments: the University of Colorado (1995–98) and the University of California–Riverside (1998–2001).

Roy Licklider is professor of political science at Rutgers University in New Brunswick. His recent research has been on how people who have been killing one another in civil wars can form working political communities with one another (not all the time, but more often than you might think). He has edited two books on the subject *(Stopping the Killing: How Civil Wars End* and, with Mia Bloom, *Living Together after Ethnic Killing: Exploring the Chaim Kaufmann Argument)* and has published articles in the *American Political Science Review, International Studies Quarterly,* and the *Journal of Peace Research* among other periodicals, as well as edited books. He is currently studying how competing military forces can be integrated after negotiated settlements of civil wars.

T. David Mason (Ph.D., University of Georgia, 1982) is the Johnie Christian Family Professor of Peace Studies at the University of North Texas. He is the author *Caught in the Crossfire: Revolution, Repression, and the Rational Peasant* (Rowman and Littlefield, 2004) and coeditor (with James Meernik) of *Conflict Prevention and Peace-Building in Post-war Societies: Sustaining the Peace* (Routledge, 2007). His research on civil conflict has appeared in journals such as *Journal of Politics, Journal of Conflict Resolution, Political Research Quarterly, Journal of Peace Research, International Studies Quarterly,* and *American Political Science Review.* He is currently Editor of *International Studies Quarterly.*

Rose McDermott holds a Ph.D. in political science and an M.A. in Experimental social psychology, both from Stanford University. She held a National Institute on Drug Abuse Post Doctoral Fellowship in Substance Abuse Treatment Outcome Research at the San Francisco VA through the University of San Francisco Psychiatry Department. Professor McDermott's main area of research revolves around political psychology in international relations. She is the author of *Risk Taking in International Relations: Prospect Theory in American Foreign Policy* (University of Michigan Press, 1998), *Political Psychology in International Relations* (University of Michigan Press, 2004), and *Presidential Leadership, Illness, and Decision Making* (Cambridge University Press, 2007). She is coeditor of *Measuring Identity: A Guide for Social Science Research*, with R. Abdelal, Y. Herrera and A. I. Johnston (Cambridge University Press, 2009). Professor McDermott has held fellowships at the John M. Olin Institute for Strategic Studies and the Women and Public Policy Program, both at Harvard University. She has written numerous articles and book chapters on experimentation, the impact of emotion on decision making, and evolutionary and neuroscientific models of political science.

Manus I. Midlarsky is the Moses and Annuta Back Professor of International Peace and Conflict Resolution at Rutgers University, New Brunswick. He is the founding past president of the Conflict Processes Section of the American Political Science Association and a past vice president of the International Studies Association. He is currently working on *The Origins of Political Extremism* (Cambridge University Press, forthcoming); his most recent book is *The Killing Trap: Genocide in the Twentieth Century* (Cambridge University Press, 2005). He published *The Evolution of Inequality: War, State Survival, and Democracy in Comparative Perspective* (Stanford University Press, 1999); the *Handbook of War Studies III* is the third in the sequence of *Handbooks of War Studies*. An earlier edited volume is *Inequality, Democracy, and Economic Development* (Cambridge University Press, 1997). In all, he has published over 65 articles and book chapters in venues such as the *American Political Science Review, American Journal of Political Science, Journal of Politics, International Studies Quarterly, Journal of Conflict Resolution, Journal of Peace Research*, and *Journal of Personality*. He has served as a consultant to the governments of the United States, Canada, and the Netherlands. Most recently, he was a keynote speaker at the Religion and Identity in Global Governance conference at the University of Southern California in October 2007, a speaker in the Inaugural Series of Lectures on Genocide and Human Rights of the Division of Global Affairs at Rutgers University, Newark, March 2008, and was an invited participant at the Conference on War Crimes sponsored by the U.S. Department of State and Central Intelligence Agency in March 2006, where *The Killing Trap* was featured.

Stephen Saideman is Canada Research Chair in International Security and Ethnic Conflict and associate professor of political science at McGill University. In addition to his books, *The Ties That Divide: Ethnic Politics, Foreign Policy, and International Conflict* and *For Kin or Country: Xenophobia, Nationalism, and War* (with R. William Ayres), he has coedited *Intra-state Conflict, Governments, and Security: Dilemmas of Deterrence and Assurance* and published articles on the international relations and comparative politics of ethnic conflict in *International Organization, International Studies Quarterly, Comparative Political Studies, Journal of Peace Research,* and *Security Studies.* Saideman spent 2001–2 on the U.S. Joint Staff working in the Strategic Planning and Policy Directorate as part of a Council on Foreign Relations International Affairs Fellowship. As a consequence of that experience, Saideman is now trying to understand the complexities facing military officers in multilateral operations in places like Bosnia and Afghanistan.

Håvard Strand holds a Ph.D. in political science from the University of Oslo and is senior researcher at the International Peace Research Institute, Oslo (PRIO). His articles have appeared in *American Journal of Political Science, International Studies Perspectives, Journal of Conflict Resolution,* and *Journal of Peace Research.* His main research interests are the study of democracy, civil war, and the relationship between elections and civil violence.

Monica Duffy Toft is associate professor of public policy at the John F. Kennedy School of Government. She holds a Ph.D. and M.A. from the University of Chicago and a B.A. in Political Science and Slavic Languages and Literatures from the University of California, Santa Barbara. Professor Toft was a research intern at the RAND Corporation and served in the U.S. Army in southern Germany as a Russian voice interceptor. She was the assistant director of the John M. Olin Institute for Strategic Studies from 1999 to 2006. Her research interests include international relations, religion, nationalism and ethnic conflict, civil and interstate wars, the relationship between demography and national security, and military and strategic planning. Professor Toft is the author of *The Geography of Ethnic Conflict: Identity, Interests, and Territory* (Princeton, 2003) and coeditor of *The Fog of Peace: Strategic and Military Planning under Uncertainty* (Routledge, 2006). Her second monograph on civil war termination, *Securing the Peace: The Durable Settlement of Civil Wars* is forthcoming. She is finishing a coauthored book on religion in global politics, *God's Century* (Norton, 2009) and beginning a monograph on religion and violence, tentatively titled *Faith as Reason: The Role of Religion in Civil Wars*. Professor Toft is director of the Belfer Center's Initiative on Religion in International Affairs, which was established with a generous grant from the Henry Luce Foundation. The Carnegie Foundation of New York recently named her a Carnegie Scholar for her research on religion, Islam, and civil war.

Introduction: Interstate and Civil Strife

Not too long a time has passed since publication of the *Handbook of War Studies II,* yet much has happened in that period. The prevalence of civil war, the mass killing, even genocide, of noncombatants, and other forms of brutality not typically associated with interstate war have increasingly occupied the attention of researchers. At the same time, interstate war, especially between major powers, now appears to be too costly a venture for the vast majority of states. Even superpowers such as the United States have hesitated to enter that arena, except on a limited basis, as exemplified by the Gulf War of 1991. The United States did undertake the invasion of another sovereign entity in 2003—its entry into Iraq—but it was civil strife of the most intense variety that ultimately forced sectors of the United States government and society to recognize the high cost and limited benefit, if any, of this policy. Thus, much of this volume is devoted to an examination of the systematic study of civil strife and its sometime correlate, genocide. Although infrequent, genocide can yield many times the number of dead resulting from most interstate or civil conflicts. It is therefore deserving of our attention.

Because interstate war is still with us, albeit less frequently, it is examined along with civil strife in Part I of this volume. Analyses of the onset and termination of civil wars are found in Part II. The book concludes with an examination of ethnic conflict, international relations, and genocide in Part III.

The main reason for publishing this volume is found in the increasing reluctance of developed states to engage in interstate war, a development first seriously examined by John Mueller in the post–World War II period, and the simultaneous emergence of the largely unexpected civil conflicts of various sorts. Although around the turn of the twentieth century, earlier observers had predicted the end of interstate warfare and in midcentury were roundly castigated for their naïveté, the current state of the international system suggests that these commentators were simply premature in their judgments. There are many sources of this newer reluctance to wage war among developed states. Among them are the increased antiwar sentiments in the aftermath of World War I that World War II magnified enormously, the emphasis on economic well-being that precludes the onset of highly destructive wars, and the existence of international structures such as the European Union that explicitly prohibit warfare among their constituent units. One can also add the democratic peace that virtually eliminates the possibility of war between democracies, and the emergence of a fundamental though embryonic ethic prohibiting the large-scale killing of human beings in the name of political goals.

In Part I, Bruce Bueno de Mesquita reviews one of the most prominent analytic approaches to understanding the origins of war—rational choice. As we shall see in later chapters, rational choice can help us understand the origins of civil strife as well. Beginning with the basics of rational choice as a starting point for constructing theory, Bueno de Mesquita principally examines the game-theoretic literature and rational choice behavior against the backdrop of domestic politics. Challenging the more venerable claims that either a balance of power or a serious imbalance of power leads to war, Bueno de Mesquita finds greater explanatory power in his game-theoretic approach. Neorealist theories also are found wanting. Ultimately, he settles on a selectorate theory of politics in which audience costs are paramount. The vaunted theory of the democratic peace then becomes one in which the audience costs of making war are far higher in democracies than in autocracies. The selectorates for each are different.

The chapter on emotions and war by Rose McDermott provides a very different perspective on issues of war and peace. Included here is a presentation of theories that go beyond interstate and civil war, even to the perpetration of genocide. McDermott reviews prospect theory at length, as a theory of cognition that provides an alternative to the conventional uses of expected utility theory examined in the preceding chapter. Because of the asymmetry between gains and losses, a central prediction of prospect theory is that people within the domain of losses are risk acceptant in their decision making, while those in the domain of gains are risk averse. These predictions are important for understanding the onset of genocide, among other violent phenomena. McDermott also finds that prospect theory is importantly linked to theories of the emotions, and reviews theories that take as their starting point emotion instead of cognition. Although many of these perspectives are oriented to voting behavior, especially in the United States, others can help us understand international crises, such as that of Suez in 1956. The relationship between fear and war is another area usefully examined by theories of the emotions.

Part II turns to the onset and termination of civil wars. In his chapter, T. David Mason details the evolution of theory on civil war and revolution. Carefully distinguishing among civil wars and other forms of conflict that can occur within the state, such as genocide or politicide, Mason reviews the existing theories. Among them are models of the deprived actor and rational actor, as well as theories based on resource mobilization. State-centric models also receive a fair share of attention. Mason concludes his chapter with empirical studies that systematically test these models and theoretical orientations. The availability of data is, of course, a problem in any such empirical investigation. GDP per capita emerges as the most significant negative correlate of the onset of civil war. Some support exists for the proposition that ethnic division affects the probability of civil war, while evidence for the potentially important relationship between democracy and civil war is mixed. This latter relationship is taken up in more detail in the subsequent chapter, by Nils Petter Gleditsch, Håvard Hegre, and Håvard Strand.

The state also occupies a significant position in Mark Lichbach's review of bargaining theory in contentious politics. Timing of state formation is, of course, important, if only because of the consequent variability in genuine independence of the newer sovereign entities. This condition, in turn, can affect the applicability of theoretical approaches. Lichbach reviews in detail the dynamics of contention and sequential bargaining theories of war. Game theory is the principal mode of presentation in the latter instance. For that reason, the discovery of stable Nash equilibria is a major purpose of Lichbach's analysis. A principal substantive finding is that incomplete information, mutual uncertainty, and erroneous expectations are significantly more important as causes of civil war than are the traditional emphases on the anarchy inherent in the security dilemma. Social contracts among contending parties and stable institutions as equilibria are important implications of Lichbach's analysis, as are changes in equilibria as harbingers of regime change.

Because of the salience of the democratic peace in the international relations literature and its implications for peaceful relations between groups within democracies, the nature of the association, if any, between democracy and civil war is a topic eminently worthy of attention. In the chapter by Gleditsch, Hegre, and Strand, the relationship between the two variables is carefully examined empirically. These authors find some support for an inverse U-curve relationship between democracy and the onset of civil war, and more substantial support for a lower magnitude of civil-war-related violence when it occurs in democracies. However, if one uses a different measure of democracy than the widely used Polity IV measure, the U-curve finding is not replicated. As implied in the chapter by Mason, when the GDP per capita variable is introduced, the impact of democracy on civil war declines. The authors also present other interesting and provocative findings. As a careful empirical examination of an important area of inquiry, this chapter is an exemplary contribution.

Last, but not least in this examination of civil wars is the matter of their termination. Here, as in preceding chapters, the author, Roy Licklider, carefully examines the issues and findings. Defining terms is important, especially the meaning of the "ending" of civil wars. The role of external actors is often crucial, for they frequently are the only agencies with significant force capability (or the threat of its usage) to direct the warring parties to the negotiations table. Of course, not all civil wars end in negotiations hosted by external parties. Military victories ending the war clearly in favor of one party to the conflict, or the "hurting stalemate" that can lead both protagonists to seek a negotiated settlement, also can end civil wars. Licklider examines the prevalence of these modes of ending civil conflict. Outcomes of settlements have included partition, and the institution of democracy, with each solution presenting its own unique difficulties. Licklider wisely discusses not only the empirical issues of the success or failure of the several alternative possible outcomes in rendering a stable peace, but also the ethical issues associated with each.

Part III deals explicitly with ethnic conflict, its origins, the impact of international relations, and the occasional but nevertheless important degeneration of ethnic conflict into genocide. Monica Duffy Toft reviews this literature with careful attention to both theory and dimensions of international relations. One of her most important findings is that concentration of a single ethnicity in a homeland dominated by a stronger power—for example Chechnya within the Russian Federation—greatly increases the probability of ethnic war. Toft also critically evaluates the four theoretical strands she identifies in the systematic literature. These are the security dilemma, the culpability of elites, collapsed or flawed political institutions, and material-based (economic development and distribution) theories. She finds positive and negative elements in each, but in the end advocates a syncretic approach that, for example, unites issues of wealth, identity, and fear as necessary pieces of the puzzle of why ethnic violence persists. It is clear that future studies need to pay close attention to this recommendation.

Stephen Saideman and Erin Jenne explicitly investigate the association between international relations and ethnic conflict. A natural point of departure for their analysis is the contagion and diffusion of conflict that has a relatively long history in the literature. Diasporas too are important as external sources of ethnic conflict. The authors rightly mention the role of Irish Americans in the recent "troubles" in Northern Ireland. Yet the impact of this Irish Diaspora is deeper still, for it originated largely from the Irish famine of the mid-nineteenth century and mass emigration to the United States. Thereafter, until the twentieth century, the organization of Irish nationalism against Britain (and the consequent ethnic conflict within Ireland) took place mainly on U.S. soil. Saideman and Jenne explore irredentism and cross-border violence as sources of ethnic conflict. They conclude their chapter with recommendations for future research on the internal dynamics of ethnic organizations, the differentiation among various consequences of external interventions, and the distinction, if any, between ethnic conflict and civil war.

Because of the absence of agreement among scholars on whether such a distinction exists, I have tended to use the term *civil strife* to denote a more generic category that subsumes both civil war and ethnic conflict. Yet this is only a semantic solution to a more fundamental problem. The correlates of both civil war and ethnic conflict need to be examined carefully to see if the domains of explanation differ substantially between the two cases. On the other hand, areas of overlap actually may be found that could intimate the robust nature of certain variables in explaining civil strife as a generic category.

Finally, my own chapter is concerned with the explanation of genocide and the policy recommendations that follow. Although initially I had not intended this outcome, much of the chapter is devoted to a comparison between large-N and small-N approaches to the study of genocide, especially regarding the suitability of each in generating policy-relevant conclusions. As it turns out, the findings of both types of investigation can be relevant to policy; it simply depends on how the studies are organized. The large-N studies require a specific comparison among alternative policies. Because of the inherent need for process tracing in determining causality in small-N studies, they can somewhat more readily yield policy-relevant findings, but only if the theory is precisely examined by means of clearly stipulated real-world operational measures. Territorial loss is one such measure of a diminished authority space that requires sensitivity by policymakers in other countries in dealing with the actor who loses. The potential uncompensated territorial losses by Sudan in the south of the country resulting from governmental defeats in ethnic strife and consequent international agreements, in part generated the Darfur genocidal crisis in the west. In pushing for the 2004 settlement likely leading to independence only of the Christian and animist south, and thoroughly ignoring Darfur, the U.S. government opened the door to ethnic cleansing and genocidal behavior in Darfur in an effort by the Khartoum government to at least retain that territory.

One can even understand the desire of larger states to avoid such territorial losses in the future by tolerating ethnic strife in a contested territory, and not agreeing to its secession. Indian policies in Kashmir are driven at least in part by its desire to avoid any future secessions from its federated system by disallowing that possibility in Kashmir. Without the force capability available to states such as India, and in the absence of international agreements that would firmly and effectively guarantee compensation for Sudan in the event of independence of the south, the ethnic cleansing, even genocide, in Darfur persists.

This third in the series *Handbook of War Studies* has once again responded to international events that have driven the research interests of scholars in the field. As we know, despite the decreased prevalence of interstate war, it is still extraordinarily difficult to predict the future of interstate and civil conflict in the midst of technological revolutions that can place the weapons of mass destruction in the hands of leaders of the smallest states, even of terrorist groups. Only time will tell if this and other eventualities will lead the discipline of international relations to rival economics as the "dismal science." Yet if like the economists and other empirically oriented social scientists we persist in the effort to disclose the often hidden relationships among variables and those with policy relevance, then we may be able to avoid being saddled with that dubious distinction.

MANUS I. MIDLARSKY

PART I

Perspectives on Interstate and Civil Strife

War and Rationality

BRUCE BUENO DE MESQUITA

Any appraisal of the state of knowledge about conflict and war is both a daunting task and a challenging one. Much progress is being made through the design and testing of rational actor models that investigate the state as a unitary actor, and through political economy models that look within states at citizen and leadership interests and institutionally induced incentives. Still, vastly more remains to be learned than has thus far been learned, and much confusion remains to be overcome. In examining this topic I take as my charge to reflect on what we know, how we might improve our knowledge, and what we think we know that now seems more limited in usefulness than we previously believed. Before addressing this task and advancing some claims, however, let me begin by clarifying what I do and do not mean by the rational actor approach. Then it will be sensible to specify the boundaries of what I include within this review.

What Is a Rational Actor Model?

Although the rational actor perspective as applied to international conflict has been around for several decades (some early examples include Russett 1967; Brams 1975; Zagare 1977; Altfeld and Bueno de Mesquita 1979; Wittman 1979), misunderstandings and misplaced critiques of the approach persist. Perhaps a better understanding of the approach will lead to more thoughtful and informed discussion. With that in mind, I begin with what the rational actor model is *not* before explaining briefly what it is, at least as I understand it.

What a Rational Actor Model *Is Not*

A recent, otherwise superb study by the historian H. A. Drake states concisely common misconceptions or caricatures of the rational actor model. He writes:

> In its purest form, the Rational Actor approach presumes that such a figure [as the Emperor Constantine] has complete freedom of action to achieve goals that he or she has articulated through a careful process of rational analysis involving full and objective study of all pertinent information and alternatives. At the same time, it presumes that this central actor is so fully in control of the apparatus of government that a decision once made is as good as implemented. There are no staffs on which to rely, no constituencies to placate, no generals or governors to cajole. By attributing all decision making to one central figure who is always fully in control and who acts only after carefully weighing all options, the Rational Actor method allows scholars to filter out extraneous details and focus attention on central issues. (2000, 24)

This description might have been appropriate—if ever—forty or more years ago. It reflects what Simon (1976) called procedural rationality, as distinct from instrumental rationality (Zagare 1990; Jackman 1993) which is the form that virtually all rational actor models adopt, whether they assume that the state is a unitary actor or take a political economy point of view that looks within states. There are reasons this caricature persists among some critics in international security studies. The multiple domestic interests that Drake mentions are overlooked in much international relations research because so much of that literature, especially when concerned with conflict, has taken as axiomatic that the state is the relevant unit of analysis and that the state is beneficially viewed as a rational, unitary actor. As a consequence, many conflate rational actor models and the notion of the state as a unitary rational actor.

Rarely do scholars pause to reflect on the significance of the term *uni-*

tary when speaking of the state as a rational actor. Most rational actor models in virtually all other fields, and of late in international relations as well, do not take an aggregate like the state as the relevant actor but rather explore the microfoundations of individual choices by individual decision makers. An exception might be early incarnations of the theory of the firm in economics, which inspired much of the theorizing behind realist theories. In the international conflict literature the shift toward an internal, political economy focus is, to a significant degree, the consequence of the discoveries made by many of the formal, game-theoretic models of state interactions reviewed later in this chapter, in which states are treated as unitary actors.

It is the state-centrism of much international relations scholarship that is behind the survival of caricatures of rational actor models. Since realists drew their core insights by examining the history of European monarchies in the post-Westphalian era, they described a political process that emphasizes the national interest in a way that is reasonably in accord with leadership incentives in fairly centralized monarchies, but not in accord with incentives either in rigged-election autocracies or in democracies, the most common forms of government in the contemporary world (Acemoglu and Robinson 2001; Bueno de Mesquita et al. 2003). That is, they assumed that the desires of the monarch could be equated with the national interest, following the logic of Louis XIV's famous declaration, *l'État c'est moi*. This implicit assumption tends to result in deductions that turn out to be inconsistent with observed patterns of action in contemporary international politics. In contrast, political economy rational actor models that look within as well as between states provide insights into international affairs that are supported empirically across all regime types. Many of these insights do not follow logically if a state-centric perspective is adopted. A critical purpose of this chapter is to present evidence regarding this claim.

What a Rational Actor Model *Is*

From the perspective of rational choice theorists, any rational actor model assumes that actors (such as decision makers) make choices that the actors believe will lead to the best feasible outcomes for them as defined by their personal values or preferences. The interests of the decision makers may or may not include enhancing something called the national interest. Decision makers connect alternatives consistently (i.e., transitively) in relations of preference or indifference, take constraints, such as impediments in nature (e.g., where they are located geographically) and the anticipated actions of others, into account, and act in a manner that is consistent with their desires and beliefs. Such models, for instance, examine the past actions and anticipated actions of staffs, constituencies, generals, and governors in trying to understand international conflict choices. This literature, focused on the principal-agent problem, is at the core of diversionary war theories (Levy 1989; Russett 1990; Morgan and Bickers 1992; Morrow 1991b; Smith 1996; Leeds and Davis 1997) and bureaucratic or interest group analyses (Allison 1972; Goldstein and Freeman 1991) of international conflict.

These and other rational actor literatures make clear that decision makers—even central decision makers—do not have complete freedom of action and they are not in full control. They must consider whatever constraints block the path to the outcome they desire and adjust their behavior accordingly, often abandoning their most preferred goal in favor of an attainable second or third best. Sometimes they end up with their least preferred outcome even though they chose rationally at every step along the way (Bueno de Mesquita 2006). Furthermore, rational decision makers do not exhaustively consider all possible alternatives if the cost of doing so exceeds the marginal gain. To do so, in fact, would be irrational, as they would knowingly be wasting resources without a reasonable expectation of their recovery (Riker and Ordeshook 1973).

The assumption of rationality is not a theory of international conflict. Rather, it is a starting point for constructing theories. The rationality condition sets out the theorist's view of how people are likely to select actions given their motivations or preferences; it says nothing about the content of those preferences (Bueno de Mesquita 1981; Zagare 1990; Jackman 1993). That is the sense in which such models consider instrumental, rather than procedural, rationality. Rational choice models are models of action. The contents of assumed preferences vary from theory to theory. Sometimes critics mistakenly believe that the assumption of rationality means that self-interested actors must want to maximize their income or wealth, a condition commonly (but certainly not universally) assumed in models of individual or firm behavior in market economics but uncommon in political science rational actor models, even oligopoly models of international relations (Powell 1993, 1999).

International relations models vary in what they assume as the ultimate goal or set of goals of their actors. These goals may be national security, national power, personal wealth, control over international rules, norms, or policies, personal power, survival in office, decision-making discretion, or a host of other possibilities. The actors may be individual citizens, elites, leaders, states, nongovernmental organizations, international governmental organizations, multinational corporations, or many other entities. Thus, the assumption of rationality neither limits the goals to be studied nor the identity of the actors pursuing those goals. It only limits how actors choose actions given their desires and beliefs. It certainly does not require—nor does it disallow—the notion that the state is a rational, unitary actor.

Decision-Making Choice Frameworks

Theories about how people choose are as diverse as the theorists who develop them, but they tend to follow a limited variety of conceptual strategies and basic assumptions. These conceptual strategies tend to be limited to principles concerning bounded rationality (Simon 1955), such as satisficing behavior; the framing assumptions of prospect theory (Kahneman and Tversky 1984; Tversky and Kahneman 1986) and its close cousin, minimax regret decision making (Riker 1996); expected utility maximization; and evolutionary selection models. Each of these conditions provides a different way to think about how calculating actors select their tactics (i.e., individual moves or actions) and strategies (i.e., their complete plan of action).

Furthermore, models of calculated choices tend to divide between those that address individual decision making in the face of natural, nonstrategic constraints and those that look at strategic, game-theoretic problems in which choices of tactics and strategies are not only constrained by nature (e.g., geography, natural resources), but also by the expected actions of other decision makers (at home and abroad). The former are the domain of decision theory models such as are offered by prospect theory or simple expected utility models. The latter are the domain of game theory or evolutionary models. I will primarily examine game-theoretic models here, especially noncooperative, extensive form games (represented as trees of choices involving two or more players) that rely on expected utility maximization. This means that I will overlook the literature that applies satisficing criteria or that relies on prospect theory arguments, and omit spatial models of bargaining and evolutionary, computational modeling.[1]

I divide my review along two dimensions: (1) game-theoretic studies that treat states as rational unitary actors and (2) studies that look within states at rational choices against the backdrop of domestic politics. On the empirical side, I consider some of the challenges that must be confronted when testing propositions derived from game theory models of international affairs.

Modeling the State as a Rational Unitary Actor

Throughout most of the history of research on international conflict, states have been conceived of as rational unitary actors seeking—depending on the theory in question—to maximize national power (Morgenthau 1978); maximize control over the rules thought to govern international interactions (Organski 1958); maximize cooperation and economic exchange (Keohane and Nye 1977); or maximize national security (Waltz 1979). Of course, the developers of these theories understood that domestic politics—Drake's staffs, generals, bureaucrats, and governors—play a part in international politics. They assumed away that component to filter out "extraneous details and focus attention on central issues," in Drake's terms, thus simplifying analysis.

Every theory, whether grounded in rational choice, constructivism, cognitive psychology, or something else, makes simplifying assumptions. The rational unitary actor assumption is an example of such a simplification. Indeed, Waltz (1959) explicitly divided international affairs into three images, arguing that the most helpful simplification for understanding international interactions was to examine what happens at the level of the international system where states interact, avoiding what he saw as the reductionism of the first image (concerned with individuals) and the second image (concerned with domestic political factors). Waltz, like many other system-level theorists, concluded that one could not understand international relations without understanding the constraints that the system's structure imposes on strategic choices.

Structuralists do not conceive of Waltz's first two images as providing a foundation for building a theory that could explain the international system's structure and changes in that structure over time. Instead, they take the structure (e.g., bipolar or multipolar, balanced or imbalanced, with offense dominance or defense dominance) as given. They justify a system-level approach and a focus on unitary state-interactions by dismissing the possibility that state actions and system characteristics are the aggregated, strategic consequence of individual choices within each state, constrained by domestic institutions, resources, geography, and the choices within other states.

Unitary, rational-actor theories represent an important advance in understanding. As an explanation of international interactions they provide testable hypotheses about important phenomena like war and peace or the survival or demise of states. They also have helped draw attention to which of their assumptions are limiting factors that impede further explanation and which shall endure because they continue to advance our ability to grasp the complexities of international relations. An objective of research is to build on strengths in prior work and to overturn, when possible, contending theories, narrowing the range of accounts that are candidates for being a correct understanding of how the world works. In that spirit, there has been lively debate regarding the efficacy of unitary actor models and political economy, new institutionalist models (Milner 1998; Powell 1994; Vasquez 1997).

War and Rationalist Explanations of State Action

Loosely speaking, we can think of war from the perspective of states in two analytic contexts. We can examine the initiation, escalation, and termination of disputes from the perspective of the war-of-attrition model or from the viewpoint of models that see war and peace as choices over risky lotteries. In a war of attrition, the good in dispute often is indivisible. In these winner-take-all contests, one party either quits at the outset or the combatants face a problem akin to an ascending price auction. When do you stop bidding if each bid incurs a sunk cost? The answer, of course, is to bid as long as the expected benefit is greater than or equal to the marginal expected cost. Naturally, this can lead to a war that persists until one or the other side has exhausted its resources.

Such models provide one way to look at problems of deterrence. When, for instance, the anticipated costs of attack exceed the expected gains, the would-be belligerent is deterred from attacking. The problems of deterrence are, therefore, inherently problems about uncertainty. If the price each side is prepared to pay were known, then the prospective contest would end instantly. The problem of deterrence is to find the price at which a prospective belligerent can be persuaded to back down rather than attack or escalate a crisis.

Schelling (1960) addressed these issues from a rational actor perspective, with many of his insights helping to formulate American deterrence policy during the Cold War. Powell (1990) augmented Schelling's analysis, identifying the principle that deterrence is most likely to be effective if there is "something left to chance," that is, a risk of error sufficiently large that it makes opting for peaceful coexistence relatively attractive compared to risking the consequences of escalation. Downs and Rocke (1990, 1995) show the benefits and importance of uncertainty in shaping and containing both arms races and negotiable international disputes.

Zagare and Kilgour (2000) further advanced our understanding of deterrence issues by making clear that effective deterrence requires not only sufficient capabilities to inflict unacceptable costs in response to the initiation of belligerency, but also sufficient will to do so such that threats of retaliation are credible. Here they emphasize that a deterrent threat, to be credible, must be (at least) subgame perfect; that is, a deterrence posture must be (believed to be) a best reply to the anticipated actions of other actors from each point in the game—the strategic interaction—forward. The insights from this basic noncooperative game-theoretic solution concept help solve many of the dilemmas present in the earlier research on deterrence that built on Schelling's use of the game of chicken. The notion of subgame perfection eliminates strategies that rely upon threats that are not credible such as retaliatory nuclear strikes even when doing so means national suicide. It recognizes that decision makers not only consider whether adversaries have the wherewithal to inflict unacceptable costs, but whether it is in the adversary's interest to do so down the road when it might be confronted with the need to act.

Lottery Models of War or Lesser Conflict

In lottery models of war or lesser conflict, the parties face a probability of victory and of defeat, a setting also more akin to Zagare and Kilgour's approach to deterrence. In variants that include ongoing bargaining, beliefs about those probabilities presumably change endogenously as a function of what is learned on the battlefield (Gartner 1997; Wagner 2000; Smith and Stam 2004), and so the range of bargains that are acceptable changes as well (Wittman 1979).

Taking a simple view within the lottery perspective, suppose that state A's probability of winning a war is known to be p and B's probability of victory is, therefore, known to be $1 - p$.[2] Suppose war costs equal k for each side and A and B are fighting over X so that the victor gets all of X and

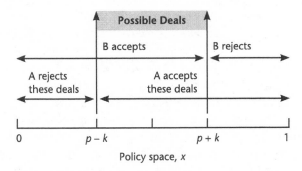

Fig. 1. Bargaining, war, and ex post inefficiency

the defeated state gets none. Let A's utility be increasing in the proportion of X it gets so that if it gets all of X through victory or in a negotiated settlement its utility equals 1 (without loss of generality) and B's utility is decreasing in the quantity of X A gets so that B's utility equals 1 when A gets 0 of X (and B gets all of X) and B's utility increases as A's share of X in a negotiated settlement decreases. Then A's expected utility for victory in war is $p - k$ and B's is $1 - p - k$. What if a settlement is proposed that divides the good in dispute between A and B such that A's value for the proposed settlement is x, that is, a fraction of X, and B's value for the proposed settlement is $1 - x$. Then, as shown in figure 1, a range of acceptable negotiated settlements exists to avoid war while satisfying both A's and B's expectations. With complete and perfect information—a demanding condition—A accepts offers made such that $x > p - k$ and B accepts offers if $x < p + k$. We will return to this figure from time to time, as it helps sort out some interesting features of conflict.

Although the opportunity for a negotiated agreement exists, many disputes become wars. This seems puzzling, much as labor strikes or lawsuits seem puzzling. Of course, from the perspective of the welfare of a nation-state, by which I mean the welfare of the majority of the citizenry, war, like strikes and litigation, is always ex post inefficient. That is, knowing how a war turned out, there must have existed an ex ante, Pareto-improving outcome, an outcome that at least could have avoided the transaction costs for each side associated with conducting and concluding the war.

As James Fearon (1995) has argued, war, looked at from the perspective of states, can only arise rationally if at least one of three conditions exists: an asymmetry of information,[3] a commitment problem, or a dispute over an indivisible good. Recent research by Slantchev (2003), building on earlier studies (Taylor 1976; Axelrod 1984; Powell 1993, 1999), adds a fourth rationalist condition that can lead to war: impatience.

An asymmetry of information, of course, can mean that one or both parties miscalculate the bargaining range seen in figure 1, and so offers are made that result in war rather than agreement. Asymmetric information is seen by some as so important a contributor to the danger of war that it is sometimes argued that all the other rationalist explanations are just special cases of this condition, that war is, in Gartzke's (1999) memorable phrase, in the error term.

Bueno de Mesquita and Lalman (1992) and Slantchev (2003), in a more general setting, provide models in which war can arise without uncertainty because of commitment problems. Commitment problems arise when one or the other party cannot trust the rival's statements because the rival has incentives to renege on promises. Indivisibility means that the contest is necessarily a winner-take-all affair, so that there is no room for compromise, probably leaving the dispute to devolve into a war of attrition. Civil wars and other disputes over governing a given territory sometimes are indivisible. Naturally if there is not some way to compensate a player for a loss of this sort, the problem does not have a bargaining range. One side wins and the other loses. Impatience comes into play if the expected future stream of benefits from behaving aggressively now is sufficiently large that it is worth tolerating the short-term costs of war (Powell 1993, 1999). It remains an open question whether this consideration of impatience, or the discounted value of anticipated future costs and benefits, is a unique rational factor that can lead to war or is a special case of asymmetric information or commitment problems.

The insight that war cannot arise between states unless at least one of the rationalist conditions arises is an important advancement in knowledge. It narrows the range of pathologies we as researchers must look for to understand classes of events or even individual cases. It helps point the way for policymakers seeking to reduce the risk of war. Since these are collectively necessary conditions, removing all of them would make war impossible. Of course, removing them is more easily said than done, as they often reflect fundamental policy concerns. These rationalist explanations stand in contrast to more venerable views, such as that a balance of power (Morgenthau 1978; Waltz 1979; Gulick 1955) or an imbalance of power (Organski 1958) promotes peace and stability. To the extent that the distribution of power is known to all and all know it is known (that is, the distribution of power is common knowledge, in game theory jargon), its degree of balance or imbalance should not determine the likelihood of peace or war. Rather it should only matter in terms of locating the bargaining range in figure 1.

If contending sides in a dispute know their chance of victory (presumably that is what is dictated by the distribution of power) and what is at stake in a war they should find a bargaining solution (as in fig. 1) that is at least as good—and possibly even better—for each of them than would be realized through fighting. They could, for instance, negotiate a settlement on the same terms as the outcome expected after a war, given the balance of power between them, while avoiding the costs of fighting. That is what Fearon (1995) means when he argues that war is ex post inefficient.

The distribution of power may dictate what the bargain will look like, but it should not, by itself, determine the likelihood of fighting. Uncertainty about the balance of power may be a factor, but not the balance per se. But then uncertainty is one of the rationalist explanations of war.

The rationalist explanations of war when considered in terms of state action rely on at least one implicit assumption. Implicit in the claim that war is always ex post inefficient is the idea that the welfare of the citizenry—generally referred to as the national interest—is the same as (or at least highly correlated with) the well-being of those making war and peace choices. That is not to say that war is ever ex post efficient or that the rationalist factors are not critical, but rather to suggest that the source of uncertainty or of commitment problems may be relatively remote from decisions about war and peace when those choices are not correlated with the national interest (Maoz 1990; Goemans 2000; Chiozza and Goemans 2003, 2004). The sources of uncertainty, indivisibility, impatience, or commitment problems may reside in the disconnection between the interests of leaders and those in whose name they lead (Bueno de Mesquita and Siverson 1995; Werner 1996). Leaders may knowingly make choices that harm national welfare but improve their own well-being. Stalin's decision to purge his generals may be an example in point, as may John Kennedy's decision to risk nuclear war over Soviet missiles in Cuba rather than risk impeachment for failing to act even though he knew the missiles did not appreciably alter the strategic situation between the United States and the USSR (Kennedy 1969; Allison 1972).

Realist Models and the Balance of Power

The most prominent and influential theorizing about international conflict is broadly wrapped up in the realist and neorealist views. Realist theorizing is dominated by the idea that uncertainty about the distribution of power and the reliability of commitments between states is essential to understanding how politics unfolds at the international level (Thucydides 1959; Morgenthau 1978; Gulick 1955; Waltz 1979; Mearsheimer 1990a; Elman and Elman 1997). For realists, the primary subject matter of international affairs is the balance of power and efforts by states to maximize their security in the face of anarchy. I have already argued that a known balance of power cannot be a rationalist explanation of war, although, in conjunction with other variables, it may create a commitment problem or another necessary rationalist condition. Now I summarize limitations of the balance-of-power perspective identified by formal rational choice models that accept the assumption of the state as the essential unit of analysis.

Geoffrey Blainey (1988) and others have argued that war follows from what might be termed mutual optimism. That is, the contending sides under uncertainty collectively overestimate their individual prospects of victory, so that the sum of the subjective probabilities of sides A and B winning is greater than 1. Fey and Ramsay (2007) investigate this claim, showing with a provocative model that even if decision makers process information inefficiently, it is not possible to support war as part of a Bayesian perfect equilibrium based on their mutual optimism. Such an outcome can arise only if the actors start with different prior beliefs about each other's prospects, ignoring all previous actions that signal those beliefs even when it is in the interest of the actors or unavoidable for the actors to signal reliable information.

Niou and coauthors (Niou, Ordeshook, and Rose 1989; Niou and Ordeshook 1990, 1991) explore closely the neorealist version of balance of power. They provide formal, game-theoretic examinations of neorealism's assumptions. By making the theory's logic fully explicit they provide the means to determine what propositions follow logically from the theory's argument, thereby making it possible to discern whether the more loosely argued claims of neorealism can be derived from neorealist assumptions. They show that the logic of neorealist theory does not point to any particular distribution of power as being uniquely privileged in promoting international stability. In fact, they show that an infinitely large set of power distributions are consistent with the neorealist notion that stability means the survival of states. They demonstrate that balance-of-power arguments about the conditions under which states survive or cease existing lead to empirical generalizations that are inconsistent with the record of history. In particular, they show that the following four propositions follow from a rigorous exploration of neorealist assumptions about the international system as a self-help system: (1) essential states[4] never cease to exist; (2) essential states never become inessential; (3) inessential states never become essential; and (4) inessential states are eliminated from the international system.[5]

The first proposition is falsified by the disappearances of the Soviet Union and Austria-Hungary. The second proposition is falsified by the decline of Spain, the Netherlands, Portugal, and countless other formerly essential states that probably no longer qualify as essential. The rise of the United States and Japan in the late nineteenth and early twentieth centuries contradicts the third proposition, while the fourth proposition is contradicted by the existence of vast expanses of the contemporary world.

Kim and Morrow (1992) and Powell (1996) further demonstrate that neither equality nor preponderance of power is either necessary or sufficient for war and may not even probabilistically influence the likelihood of war. Wittman (1979) shows that, because the price at which rivals will settle a dispute changes as battlefield performance changes, establishing a substantial military power advantage does not inherently make conflict resolution easier as long as demands are endogenously dependent on expectations regarding the probability of victory (or defeat). Indeed, Downs and Rocke (1994) highlight how a high probability of defeat can embolden individual leaders to take risks in war that would be unwarranted by a state-centric, balance-of-power perspective, while Bueno de Mesquita and Lalman (1992) identify specific conditions under which unusually weak states—or weak actors like terrorist groups—are particularly likely to rationally initiate violence against stronger adversaries, seemingly in contradiction of standard balance-of-power tenets.

Powell (1991, 1993) further explores the essential features of neorealist theory. He investigates the notion that the distinction between relative and absolute gains is a critical feature of international relations. He also probes the neorealist idea that in anarchy war is the natural state of affairs and that war can only be thwarted by concerted efforts at balancing while taking into account whether military offense or defense is favored in the event of a dispute. His 1993 model depicts a world with two players that could be thought of as two states or as a bipolar international environment. The two states or players allocate resources between guns and butter; that is, between war-fighting ability and domestic consumption. Powell demonstrates that there is a unique, Pareto-dominant equilibrium in which peace prevails and a minimal amount is spent on guns, leaving most resources for butter. He shows how the location of this equilibrium shifts as a function of the risk-acceptance or risk-aversion of the players as well as when the offense-defense balance shifts. Powell assumes, in neorealist fashion, that there is a conflict of interest between the two rational unitary states and that each state prefers to attack an unarmed adversary now even at the expense of current consumption, thereby gaining a long-term improvement in consumption prospects.

Powell's analysis, designed as a faithful representation of neorealism, challenges neorealist thinking. Rather than security dominating resource allocations given the omnipresent threat of war, in equilibrium most resources go to butter. Powell also shows that, contrary to the claim that anarchy is what makes international politics distinctive, anarchy, in either of its prevalent meanings, is not distinctive to international politics.

Anarchy means either that states are engaged in noncooperative, self-help games solved by subgame perfect equilibria or that anarchy incorporates this meaning plus incorporating the idea of a continuous, ongoing threat of the use of force (war as the natural state of affairs). If anarchy takes on just the simple notion of a self-help system, then it is not distinctive to international politics since a variety of problems in economics and politics are usefully characterized and solved through the application of subgame perfect equilibrium. If the second, more demanding assumption that includes the omnipresent threat of war is adopted, then, Powell shows, it is the threat of coercion and not the absence of a supernational authority capable of enforcing contracts that is fundamental to international politics. But coercion is common in a host of political settings and is certainly not unique to international affairs. Thus Powell shows that it is neither the case that security dominates state spending nor that the concept of anarchy is a distinctive feature of international politics.

Powell's critique continues as he analyzes his infinite-horizon game designed to capture the essence of neorealist theorizing. He shows that the debate about relative and absolute gains (Waltz 1979; Grieco 1988; Snidal 1991; Mercer 1995) is misguided. In Powell's (1993) model, states' utilities are stated strictly in terms of absolute gains, yet their actions are driven by the threat that another state will use force against them. Thus he shows that neorealism is perfectly compatible with an absolute-gains view of international politics. Elsewhere (Powell 1994) he elaborates on this theme, noting that the literature confuses relative gains as a cause of action in the international environment and relative gains as an effect of strategic interactions that is to be explained.

The intellectual force of Powell's analysis raises doubts about state-centric investigations as uniquely characterizing the essential features of strategic interaction in international relations. In doing so he also raises doubts about structural critiques of so-called reductionist approaches that look within states at individual behavior and domestic institutional arrangements. One may deny the importance of logical consistency, arguing that it thwarts creativity (Walt 1999), but as Powell's and other studies intimate, to do so is to risk formulating policies on the basis of whim or personal predilection rather than the logic of situations over which life and death choices must be made.

The Political Economy of Conflict: Models Looking within the State

The focus on states as the central actors in international politics leads to the view that what happens within states is of little consequence for understanding what happens between states. Although there have always been those who argued against these claims, the view of the state as the central player in the international arena is so strong that the English language does not provide a common word or phrase to describe inter*national* relations without invoking the *nation* as the key unit of analysis. Indeed, this is also true of languages at least as diverse as Chinese, French, German, Japanese, and Urdu. I believe that this linguistic limitation—this compulsion to think in terms of nations or states—reflects a mistaken central focus in conflict research. Anthropomorphizing the state may work as rhetoric, but states do not make war, people do, and states do not have preferences or choose policies, people do.

Strategic political economy models, in contrast to system-level theories, assess policy choices as equilibrium behavior induced by domestic political interests and domestic institutional structures and often see the choice of foreign policy interactions as incentive compatible with the motivations of national leaders to maintain their personal hold on political power. Domestic institutional structures—such as the inclusiveness or

exclusiveness of governance, the extent to which government is account-
able and transparent or personalist and opaque, and so forth—help
shape the domestic and international interplay of leaders, elites, and ordinary citizens, resulting in domestic and foreign policies that create the
contours of the international environment. From many of these rational-
actor, political economy perspectives, leaders act to maximize their
prospects of staying in office rather than acting to maximize national security, national wealth, or some collective notion of the national interest
(Bueno de Mesquita and Lalman 1992; Fearon 1994a; Schultz 2001a;
Bueno de Mesquita et al. 1999, 2003; Werner 1996).

If our attention is turned to national political leaders rather than to
states, then it becomes apparent that fundamental policy choices—even
war and peace choices—may be made without any regard for citizen welfare or the national interest. One has only to reflect on Myanmar's ruling
junta, North Korea's Kim Jong Il, or Zaire's late Mobutu Sese Seko to recognize that many leaders govern for their own benefit at the cost of the
welfare of their subjects. So many nations have been beggared by their
leaders that it is difficult to see how we can maintain the fiction that the
national interest dictates even the most important foreign policy choices.

Bueno de Mesquita and Lalman (1992) suggested an early model of international conflict that attempted to begin to unravel the role that domestic politics plays in international affairs. They proposed two variants
of what they called the international interaction game (hereafter IIG).
One, the realpolitik version, attempts to capture the essential features of
neorealist thought. The other, the domestic variant, in a preliminary and
simple way allows for the possibility that national foreign policy goals are
set by a domestic political process—without specifying that process—
that takes the international setting into account but also is subject to domestic pressures and domestic political costs. Later, Bueno de Mesquita
and others developed a more elaborated theory of the interplay between
domestic politics, domestic institutions of governance, and international
politics (Bueno de Mesquita et al. 1999, 2003) that endogenizes resource
allocations and policy choices, including war and peace decisions within
a model of domestic institutional constraints.

The realpolitik IIG led to three central propositions: (1) a state will not
wage war if its subjective probability of winning is less than .5; (2) uncertainty increases the likelihood of war, with war being impossible in the
absence of uncertainty; and (3) there are no information conditions under which one state will acquiesce to the policy demands of another state

without resistance. The first echoes a familiar balance-of-power argument as well as the mutual optimism hypothesis. The second is a more general statement of the neorealist hypothesis that bipolar systems, because of their low level of uncertainty, are more stable and peaceful than multipolar systems. The third proposition had not previously been articulated but follows directly from neorealist logic. The three propositions were tested and each failed to find empirical support.

In contrast, the domestic variant produces numerous propositions, and, based on Bueno de Mesquita and Lalman's European sample of dyads and their operational procedures, all were supported. Especially noteworthy is a core prediction that provides a critical test of the competing neorealist and domestic variant perspectives.

The second realpolitik proposition predicts that uncertainty always makes both war and instability more likely and that reducing uncertainty is stabilizing and peace-promoting. This is, as noted previously, a general form of Waltz's proposition that bipolar systems are more stable and peaceful than multipolar systems. The important dividing line between these two types of systems in neorealism is that bipolar systems contain substantially less uncertainty than multipolar systems (Waltz 1964; Deutsch and Singer 1964). The domestic IIG, however, predicts specific conditions that, in the absence of uncertainty, lead to war and that in the presence of uncertainty reduce the likelihood of war. Likewise, the domestic IIG identifies specific equilibrium conditions under which the absence of uncertainty diminishes the risk of war and shows that the same equilibrium conditions in the presence of uncertainty increase the risk of war. Empirical tests support these domestic propositions (Bueno de Mesquita and Lalman 1992).

These findings, if correct, help separate the neorealist account from the domestic account. Both theories make the same prediction in two of the four circumstances just outlined. But the domestic IIG separates from neorealism when it predicts conditions under which war is made more likely by the absence of uncertainty (the condition involves a problem with credible commitment, one of Fearon's rationalist explanations for war) and when it predicts conditions that make peace and stability more likely under uncertainty than in its absence. In this example, when the neorealist proposition is supported, the proposition also follows from a theory that combines Waltz's first and second images (individual choice and domestic constraints) rather than relying on his third image (the effects of the international system), and when the proposition is not supported, the empirical results seem consistent with predictions from the domestic IIG. That is not to say that we should embrace the domestic IIG, which contains important theoretical limitations, but rather that we should be skeptical that neorealism is distinctive or advantaged in its explanatory power. Indeed, in a later section, when I discuss some important challenges in testing game-theoretic models, I will discuss the mixed results that arise in replications of tests of the domestic IIG.

The Political Economy of Regime Type and Conflict

Of course, the IIG was only a primitive, early attempt to evaluate the role of domestic politics in influencing international conflict. A substantial body of political economy research has grown up around the distinction between democratic and nondemocratic governing institutions, in part because of the empirical discoveries collectively known as the democratic peace and in part as a natural outgrowth of the lessons learned from structural realist investigations.

Gaubatz (1999), Fordham (1998a, 1998b), and Smith (2004) show that war-timing by democratic leaders is strongly influenced by the election cycle and electoral rules. They provide a nuanced perspective on the links between foreign policy adventures and a rally-round-the-flag effect. These findings raise fundamental questions about the reliability of unitary-actor models that see war as being provoked by circumstances within the international system. Since timing may involve hastening or delaying war by years, with issues waxing and waning over such time periods, it is difficult to see how the system's structure can be determinative of the fundamental decision to fight or not.

Fearon (1994a) suggests that democratic leaders are more constrained than autocrats to act on threats they make because of domestic audience costs if the rival fails to back down. In his model, when democratic governments issue threats of war these threats are seen as more credible by targets than comparable threats from autocrats who have low audience costs. The reason is straightforward. There are costs to going to war, but, particularly in democracies, there are also domestic political costs for threatening action to correct a perceived wrong and then failing to act on the threat. Thus, the distribution of disputes that escalate to violence should be different when a democrat is involved compared to when the parties are all nondemocratic. This leads to an interesting selection effect. Threats from democrats should increase the likelihood that rivals back down. If the rival is not expected to back down, then democrats who are reluctant to escalate should negotiate rather than make threats. But if a threat is made when the adversary is mistakenly expected to back down, democrats should be more likely to carry out their threats than are autocrats because of the audience cost tied to not doing so.

The audience costs concept has an important impact on how scholars think about conflict decision making across regime types, but, as with any model, it makes some important simplifying assumptions. In particular, the model assumes that audience costs are higher in democracies than in autocracies for interpretive purposes rather than deriving this claim as an endogenous property of domestic institutions. Bueno de Mesquita et al. (2003) expand on Fearon's idea by showing that political loyalty to incumbents is weaker in democratic systems than in autocratic systems and that this means democratic leaders must try harder to satisfy their constituents than must nondemocratic leaders, thereby making audience costs endogenous. Smith's (1996) study of diversionary war also raises concerns about whether the effect of audience costs on conflict decisions is subgame perfect; that is, whether the domestic threat to punish the leader for failing to follow through on a foreign policy threat is credible at the time the audience must choose to act.

Schultz (1998, 2001b) further expands the ideas behind audience costs by constructing a model in which there are two domestic players in one state, the incumbent government and a legitimate opposition. He shows that the existence of a legitimate domestic political opposition—a characteristic inherent in democracy—significantly constrains and narrows the range of foreign policy adventurism of democratic leaders in ways not experienced by nondemocrats. This should lead to a selection effect against conflict choices by democrats that is different from, perhaps complementary to, that captured by Fearon's idea of audience costs.

Bueno de Mesquita and various coauthors (Bueno de Mesquita and Siverson 1995; Bueno de Mesquita et al. 1999, 2003) develop a two-dimensional "selectorate" theory of institutional arrangements and show how variations in the size of a polity's selectorate and the winning coalition help explain such phenomena as the empirical regularities known as the democratic peace, while also explaining the preparedness of democracies to fight wars of imperial and colonial expansion or the preparedness of democracies to overthrow foreign rivals more often than do nondemocratic interveners.[6] This theory identifies still other selection effects that complement those found by Schultz and by Fearon. In particular, the selectorate perspective supports the ideas that democracies are highly selective about the conflicts they enter, requiring a near-certain expectation of victory before escalating to war. Bueno de Mesquita and Smith (2009) have developed a more generalized version of the selectorate theory that, in passing, also helps explain civil war and revolutions and the impact that foreign aid has on endogenous institution change.

Nowhere has the role played by domestic political institutions been more important a topic of inquiry than in the study of the impact these institutions have on war and peace. If there is one area in which it can be unequivocally stated that the political economy of international conflict has become central to policy debate it is in the arena of the empirical regularities collectively known as the democratic peace. It is to the study of the democratic peace, then, that I now turn.

The Democratic Peace

State-centric, unitary rational actor theories lack an explanation of perhaps the most significant empirical discovery in international relations over the past several decades (Levy 1988). That is the widely accepted observation that democracies tend not to fight wars with one another even though they are not especially reluctant to fight with autocratic regimes.

By looking within states at their domestic politics and institutionally induced behavior, the political economy perspective provides explanations of the democratic peace and associated empirical regularities while also offering a cautionary tale for those who leap too easily to the inference that since pairs of democracies tend to interact peacefully, therefore it follows that they have strong normative incentives to promote democratic reform around the world (Bueno de Mesquita and Downs 2006).

Democratic leaders cannot afford to pursue overly risky foreign policies because they are judged by their voters primarily in terms of how good a job they do in providing public benefits, including foreign policy benefits (Lake 1992; Lake and Baum 2001; Bueno de Mesquita et al. 2003). Defeat in war is always costly for society and for democratic leaders (Bueno de Mesquita and Siverson 1995; Werner 1996; Schultz 2001a, 2001b; Chiozza and Goemans 2004). Given the political costs of defeat, democrats are only prepared to become involved in wars when they believe at the outset that their chance of victory is high or when all efforts at negotiation (as in the period 1938–39) fail (Bueno de Mesquita et al. 1999, 2003; Powell 1996, 1999).

Autocrats, in contrast, are not retained or deposed by their essential domestic supporters primarily because of the job they do in providing successful public policies. Rather, they are judged by their ability to deliver private benefits to their winning coalition members, their cronies. Defeat in war is often less costly politically for autocrats than it is for democrats. Few autocrats are overthrown and executed (though they might be sent into exile) by their coalition even after defeat in war, and they are also unlikely to be executed by foreign autocratic victors. Democratic victors pose the greatest risk to autocrats following war. For autocrats, winning a war—especially against nondemocrats—by spending on the war effort money they could have used to bribe cronies jeopardizes their hold on power because their cronies have no reason to remain loyal if they are deprived of their private rewards. Autocrats are more likely to be deposed—and executed—by disgruntled domestic backers for their failure to pay off key military officers or bureaucrats than they are by victorious external powers following military defeat. As a result, autocrats do not commit as many marginal resources to improving their prospects for victory in war as do democrats, nor do they try as hard to find negotiated settlements of their disputes. Quite to the contrary, to survive in office, autocrats need to be sure that they can pay their essential supporters enough that they do not defect.

For autocrats, extra money that goes into trying to win a war is usually better spent buying the loyalty of cronies. For democrats, saving money to bribe backers is not nearly as politically beneficial as is spending money to assure policy success, including victory in war (Bueno de Mesquita et al. 2003, 2004; Chiozza and Goemans 2004; Morrow et al. 2006).

Because democrats are selective about the circumstances under which they are prepared to fight, they almost always win the wars they initiate. In fact, recent research shows that democracies have won 93 percent of the wars they initiated over the past two centuries, while autocrats won only about 60 percent of the time (Reiter and Stam 2002). Allowing for the small advantage gained by striking first, autocrats basically have even odds of winning when they start a war while for democrats victory is practically certain. But if two democrats are at loggerheads, then war is unlikely. Each democratic leader has similar, institutionally induced incentives (Mintz and Nehemia 1993), including an incentive to try hard if war ensues (Bueno de Mesquita et al. 1999, 2003). Each must provide policy success in order to be retained by his or her constituents. Each must believe ex ante that the probability of winning the war is a near certainty. The likelihood is practically naught that leaders of two rival democracies each believes at the same time about the same dispute that their prospects of victory are nearly certain. When democrats do not think they are nearly certain of victory, they choose negotiations over fighting. This way, they cut their losses and reduce the risk of deposition. Thus leaders of two democracies are unlikely to find that the circumstances are right for them to gamble on war rather than negotiate. Autocrats do not face the same constraints theoretically except when at the outset an autocrat thinks that defeat means being deposed by the victor, a circumstance that is especially unusual when the adversary does not represent a democratic government.

In the account of the so-called democratic peace just summarized, democratic leaders are not more civic minded; their actions are not shaped by superior social norms or values (Maoz and Russett 1993); and they are not inherently better at fighting wars than other types of political leaders (Morgan and Campbell 1991). As a result, the selectorate perspective allows us to explain not only the apparently jointly pacific behavior of democracies, but also such less attractive characteristics as the preparedness of democracies to engage in wars of colonial or imperial expansion and even the willingness of a powerful democracy to force a much weaker democracy to capitulate to its demands rather than pay the price of fighting back.[7] Instead, their desire to stay in office and their dependence on a large constituency shapes their choices and makes them highly selective about escalating disputes. Likewise, autocrats are not assumed to have different motivations than democrats; they just face different institutional constraints and incentives (Mintz and Nehemia 1993). State-centric approaches to international relations simply have no basis for explaining the pattern of behavior I just described, and yet historical, case study, and statistical analyses support the implications just reviewed.

These studies tie war and peace choices to a theoretic framework that places international politics squarely within the logic of domestic politics while producing propositions that confirm some system-level hypotheses while refuting others. They come at the problem with different models, but all in a common political economy framework that shares a conviction that policy decisions are strategic, taking into account expected responses by both foreign and domestic adversaries and supporters, and designed to maximize the leader's (not the state's) welfare. Each leads to some conclusions that cannot be true according to theories of international politics that treat states as undifferentiated wholes. Each has mustered empirical evidence that indicates support for the propositions that cannot hold if system-structural accounts are correct. Each bridges the divide that has in the past distinguished international politics analysis from investigations of comparative politics (Werner, Davis, and Bueno de Mesquita 2003), thereby highlighting the possibility of a more integrated theory of politics.

Empirical Challenges

There is now a fairly substantial empirical literature concerned with testing propositions derived from political economy models of conflict processes. As my task is to examine the rational actor formal literature, I will not summarize many specific empirical studies here. Rather I will draw attention to some of the challenges that are inherent in constructing properly specified tests.

Most statistical techniques assume right-hand-side variables—the independent variables—are, well, independent of each other. This often is a significant issue in empirical studies regardless of what motivates the tests. Multicollinearity is, of course, the best-known problem related to nonzero correlations among independent variables. The problem is compounded in tests of game-theoretic models. The nature of such models is to render many of the factors shaping outcomes as endogenously dependent on each other. That is, the values for some variables that are thought to influence the dependent variable are themselves the product of strategic influences from other explanatory variables, including expectations about the dependent variable. Without correcting for this endogeneity, statistical models are inherently incorrectly specified. For instance, in asking questions about the effect of alliances and international threats on the likelihood of war, one cannot treat the existence or absence of an alliance between states as independent of the threat of entanglement in war. The decision to form an alliance is endogenous to the threat (and the threat's magnitude may be endogenous to the alliance), and the likelihood of war is dependent both on the existence of a threat and on the existence or absence of reliable allies, creating simultaneity. A statistical model that specifies the likelihood of war as an additive function of the level of threat between two states and the presence or absence of an alliance between a target and another state is problematic because it overlooks the likelihood that the presence or depth of an alliance commitment is itself dependent on the level of threat (as well as a possible shaper of that threat level). Smith (1998), Signorino (1999), and Ward, Siverson, and Cao (2007) propose statistical methods to address concerns about endogeneity and related matters.

In addition to the challenges created by endogeneity, game theory models uncover selection effects that create contingent predictions. This means that the impact of critical theoretical variables on outcome variables is complex. Continuing with the alliance example, if one asks whether alliances make war more or less likely, game-theoretic assessments tell us that there cannot be a straightforward yes or no answer (Morrow 1991a, 1994; Smith 1995); the answer depends on selection effects. For instance, when prospective defenders have alliances and prospective attackers believe the defender's allies are capable and their commitment to defend their ally is credible, then the would-be attacker is likely not to attack. This is exactly an instance of Zagare and Kilgour's (2000) notion of perfect deterrence discussed earlier. In this case—conditioned by capability and credibility—alliances make war less likely. But if the would-be attacker believes the target's allies lack capability or credibility, then attack is more likely. This means, for instance, that if we examine the reliability of alliances by observing what happens following an attack, we are selecting a biased sample. The attacker has also contemplated whether to attack in part as a function of the anticipated reliability of allies. So it is likely that the most reliable alliances are never tested with an attack, thereby biasing upward the apparent unreliability of alliances by examining only cases in which an attack took place and deterrence failed.

The contingent aspect of game theory predictions is, of course, one of the great strengths of the method, but it can bedevil empirical efforts. Earlier I discussed predictions from Bueno de Mesquita and Lalman's international interaction game. There I noted that the presence or absence or magnitude of uncertainty has different effects on the likelihood of war in their domestic IIG, depending on the specific interaction of preferences of contending sides in the strategic setting. When certain preference configurations arise and there is no uncertainty, the domestic IIG predicts war will occur. When those same preference configurations arise but there is uncertainty that affects one or both side's beliefs about the preferences and payoffs expected by the other side, the likelihood of war diminishes and the likelihood of some other outcome events increases. Tests that fail to control for the interaction between uncertainty and the preference configurations or that treat the equilibrium expectations as unaltered by uncertainty fail to capitalize on the contingent nature of the predictions, so that one would have no expectations about what the empirical results might look like. While many (but certainly not all) comparative static predictions are monotone—that is, as X increases, holding everything else constant (a big ceteris paribus), Y increases (decreases)—few equilibrium strategy predictions are.

Finally, it is worth noting that game theory models, like all means of generating hypotheses, rarely produce predictions based on readily and directly observable factors. This is especially true of game-theoretic models, as utilities and subjective probabilities—often core concepts—are virtually never directly observable. This means that the empiricist must be clever in devising instruments or proxies that capture the essential features of the theoretically interesting variables. Fearon's audience costs, for instance, are not directly observable. They also create selection effects that make observed war choices biased samples. This means that testing Fearon's audience costs predictions is exceedingly difficult (Schultz 2001b).

Bueno de Mesquita and Lalman (1992) use similarities in dyadic military alliance portfolios to tests parts of the IIG in the context of strategic interactions among European states, but this same instrument is much less reliable in regions or in time periods when military alliances either were not used to signal mutual interests or simply did not vary, as has been true in much of the contemporary world outside of Europe. In these cases, other indicators must be developed to test their theory in times and places where alliances do not vary sufficiently or are less indicative of the underlying theoretical concept. Gartzke (2000), for instance, has constructed a similar instrument based on United Nations General Assembly voting records.

The challenges in testing game-theoretic, political economy arguments are, as I have noted, significant, but then so too are the potential rewards for sorting out which among the contending theories are most helpful in advancing knowledge and which are not. In the end we have greatest confidence in those theories, whether based on rational actors, constructivism, cognition, group-think, or some other intellectual construct, when we see that predictions withstand numerous careful, well-specified empirical investigations. There is no substitute for logic and evidence in the quest for understanding how to advance the prospects of peace.

Conclusion

The rational-actor, political economy perspective offers an explanation of international relations significantly different from that suggested by unitary rational actor theories such as realism, neorealism, liberalism, and other state-centric viewpoints. All of us should be cautious about dismissing received wisdom in favor of alternative accounts of history or alternative predictions about the future. Presumably there are reasons to believe state-centric views, or they would not have so many adherents and such a long history. Yet neither should we be so wedded to these ideas that we refuse to confront their lapses in logic or their empirical failures.

Logic and empirical evidence are growing in favor of the rational-actor, political economy accounts. They are consistent with those aspects of received wisdom that are also consistent with the record of history. Yet political economy models also provide reliable explanations for facts that seem anomalous in the context of state-centric perspectives. The coming years of debate, testing, and retesting will help reveal whether the rational-actor, political economy outlook supplants its older "rivals" or whether it falls by the wayside in the face of superior alternative explanations of key features of the struggle for international peace, justice, and cooperation. For now, I conclude that those who want to understand and advance knowledge about conflict should not continue to anthropomorphize the state. Instead, I believe we should look at domestic institutions, regulations, endowments, and the ease with which citizens opposed to government policies can coordinate. Then we will better grasp how domestic conditions shape the incentives of political leaders to pursue war and impose misery on their subjects or to pursue peace and advance prosperity.

NOTES

1. See Riker and Ordeshook (1973) for an explanation of satisficing behavior as a rational process of search until the expected cost of the continued search for better actions equals the expected gain. See Sargent (1993) for a formal demonstration that bounded rationality models make problems computationally and cognitively more complex rather than less complex. He shows that satisficing, bounded-rationality models expand the range of possible equilibrium choices of action. Alternatives can crop up in almost any sequence, so a satisficing perspective makes it all but impossible to make concrete predictions, whereas a maximiz-

ing perspective reduces the possible set of predicted actions to a usually manageable and falsifiable set. See Levy (1992a) for a review of the prospect theory literature in international relations. See Bueno de Mesquita and McDermott (2004) for a discussion of the close ties between prospect theory and rational choice models. For a comprehensive view of prospect theory in the subfield of international relations see McDermott (2004c). For the claim that prospect theory is generally not applicable to international relations or other complex, strategic choices, see Kahneman (2000, xi), in which he acknowledges that prospect theory is in the family of utility models and says that "it is futile to 'test' prospect theory against utility theory in the domain of international relations." On the reasons why prospect theory cannot presently accommodate a strategic choice environment see also Bueno de Mesquita, McDermott, and Cope (2001) and Langlois and Langlois (2006).

2. For convenience, I exclude the possibility of a draw.

3. Asymmetric information indicates that information is incomplete or imperfect or both; that is, A or B or both do not know the history of prior moves made by their rival, or do not know the value their rival or they themselves attach to alternative outcomes, or they know neither.

4. States are essential if they can convert at least one coalition or alliance of states that can be defeated into a coalition or alliance that cannot be defeated. This is similar to Gulick's (1955) notion of key states.

5. In their 1989 formulation, the game is cooperative, but the system is, as in Waltz's (1979) theory of international politics, a self-help system. In Niou and Ordeshook's subsequent, noncooperative versions of the theory, there are modest modifications to the preceding results. They find that with stationary strategies, essential states are not eliminated and inessential states may be.

6. The selectorate is the set of people with a formal say in the selection of leaders and, more importantly, with the possibility of becoming members of a winning coalition. The winning coalition is the set of people whose support is essential for an incumbent leader to remain in power.

7. Consider, for instance, the preparedness of the United States to intervene in the Dominican Republic in 1965 to overthrow its democratically elected leader, Juan Bosh, and the inability of the Dominican military to credibly resist.

Emotions and War: An Evolutionary Model of Motivation

ROSE MCDERMOTT

In Jack Levy's excellent chapter on prospect theory in the *Handbook of War Studies II* (Midlarsky 2000a), he discusses the implications of loss aversion and framing effects for foreign policy decision making and bargaining. In so doing, he writes that the "process of framing undoubtedly involves cognitive and affective variables and this is inherently 'psychological' in nature" (Levy 2000, 218). Most of the theoretical and empirical discussion of framing effects has focused on the more cognitive aspects of this phenomenon. Yet clearly both losses and gains evoke powerful emotional components, specifically fear and anger or happiness and joy. Although such emotional elements have received less attention, this does not mean they are necessarily less important. In fact, emotional forces are often undertheorized in international relations—ignored altogether, assumed to exert only negative effects on outcomes, or assumed away as having little causal influence on variables of interest, such as war. This approach seems mistaken because emotions clearly play a powerful role in human discourse and interactions, especially in situations involving conflict and cooperation. This chapter is designed to directly address these inconsistent and often confusing approaches to the impact of emotion on processes relating to the conduct of war.

Popular analyses of war often assume that feelings of hate, anger, revenge, and greed remain inextricably linked with fighting and war. For example, several explanations for the current American war in Iraq mention President Bush's desire to avenge Saddam Hussein's assassination plot against the senior President Bush, or note the personal animosity that existed between the two leaders prior to the war. Yet such perspectives hold less sway in traditional academic discourse. Factors that seem more objective, such as territorial drives, strategic needs and threats, alliance structures, or the distribution of resources, dominate discussions of the causes of wars and other conflicts. Certainly part of the reason for this tendency lies in the fact that the psychological literature is full of controversy and confusion over the nature and measurement of emotion. In addition, emotions are often ephemeral and transient, making it all the more difficult to ascertain cause and effect. But their impact should not therefore be partitioned out or waved aside.

This chapter argues that specific, albeit different and discrete, emotions can contribute to processes of both war and peace. Further, emotional processes should not be understood solely as the source of conflict; instead, they can encourage peace and reconciliation as well. In fact, neurocognitive findings demonstrate that emotions serve as a primary motivating force for both conflict and cooperation. These processes likely evolved as part of human collective history, helping people effectively respond to repeated challenges posed by conflicts over resources, mates, and territory. This chapter will focus on the way in which specific emotions can inspire three dynamics central to the instigation, coordination, and termination of war: the formation and maintenance of coalitions; small group identification and unit cohesion among soldiers; and the social and punitive sanctioning of free riders, especially draft evaders. The important effects of emotion on war are not limited to these factors, but they provide an important start in any evolutionary approach to the processes underlying war.

This chapter proceeds as follows. The first section briefly reviews prospect theory's psychological understanding of risk taking in times of crisis, including war. This discussion proceeds to examine how emotions might influence framing. The second section surveys models for the impact of emotion on conflict, focusing on an evolutionary model for emotional motivation in conflict. The third section explores the ways in which emotion influences the three central dynamics already introduced. And the final part briefly illustrates how a specific emotion, fear, influences human responses in situations of threat.

Prospect Theory

Prospect theory provides an experimentally valid model of decision making under conditions of risk, developed by psychologists Daniel Kahneman and Amos Tversky (1979, 1984, 1992). Kahneman won the 2004 Nobel Prize in Economics for these theoretical and empirical insights into the psychological processes underlying choice. Prospect theory has become very influential in a wide variety of fields, including economics, medicine, mathematics, statistics, and law. Prospect theory has also made modest inroads into analyses of international relations (for reviews, see Levy 1992a, 1992b, 1996, 1997; McDermott 1998, 2004b).

First and foremost, prospect theory is a theory of decision making, meaning that choices are based on prior judgments about the likelihood or frequency of particular outcomes or events. Briefly, the theory posits two phases in the decision-making process. The first involves editing, or framing, options for choice; the second encompasses an evaluation across these prospects. Much of the criticism of prospect theory in political science has centered on the lack of a general theory of framing effects. This lacuna represents a theoretical challenge similar to that posed by the lack of a suitable explanation for the origin of preferences in rational choice models. This point remains important not only for the suggestions it provides concerning the relative strengths and weaknesses of these sometimes opposing models, but also because a more widespread appreciation of emotional motivation may point to at least part of the solution to each of these limitations (Bueno de Mesquita and McDermott 2004). For now, as with rational choice models, it nonetheless remains possible to make predictions based on prospect theory despite these theoretical deficiencies.

The second phase involves an evaluation of prospects. Rather than assess prospects according to utility and probability, as expected utility models do, prospect theory presents a value and weighting function that accomplish the task of evaluation in relatively simple and straightforward cognitive calculations. The value function supposes that individuals evaluate options based on how far each choice will take the person from his or her reference point, which typically is represented by the current status quo position, although, importantly, sometimes this assessment takes place in terms of a particular level of expectation or social comparison. These values manifest diminishing marginal utility similar to classical economic models, such that changes in value closer to the origin hold more psychological power. The intuition behind this remains clear: adding $100 to $1 means a lot more than adding $100 to $1,000. To be clear, such a model would not validate liberal perspectives of conflict that might argue that as long as everyone does better, relative position is not as important as absolute outcomes. From this perspective, relative outcomes do hold weight, for two important psychological reasons. First, human perception is designed to recognize and react to change more than stasis; shifts from the status quo position garner more attention than a steady state of affairs. Second, status concerns, including one's relative place in a hierarchy, appear to be ubiquitously and pervasively important to people, especially men. Importantly, this concern with status does not appear limited to humans; many primates share similar concerns, and will fight hard to maintain or improve their relative position in the social hierarchy, most likely because prospects of survival and access to reproduction increase as a direct consequence of improvements in social status (Wrangham and Peterson 1996). These status concerns render relative position central to the evaluation of changing conditions, environments, and physical responses.

There are two important additional components of the value function. Indeed, the central prediction of prospect theory derives from the value function: people in the domain of gains tend to be more risk averse, while those in a domain of loss tend to be more risk seeking. The consequence and evaluation of gains and losses offers an important way in which emotion might influence and enlighten the evaluation of options as well. Specifically, what constitutes an obvious loss for one person may represent a gain for another, independent of framing effects. To take one simple example, most Westerners have a hard time understanding the motivation behind suicide bombers because the cost seems so high and so permanent. Part of this failure of comprehension no doubt lies in the difficulty of appreciating what an utterly hopeless future feels like, and how desperation can drive individuals to take tremendous risks to potentially improve their communal lot, even if the chances of failure appear high, and the likelihood of benefit infinitesimally small. But part of the difficulty may also rest in the psychological discomfort of experiencing oneself or one's nation as the target of such intense hatred when we believe ourselves to be good and kind. Such emotional assessments may appear peripheral to those who prefer more rational evaluations of terrorist action, but rather than dismiss them out of hand, recall that such assessments remain central to public policy choices and mass public opinion on such issues as the extent, conduct, duration, and justification for war, torture, and surveillance. These evaluations proceed not only from the construction of options in framing but also from the estimation of social comparison in evaluating payoffs.

Furthermore, the value curve in the domain of loss remains much steeper than in the domain of gains, indicating that losses hurt more than equal gains please. This asymmetry derives directly from the psychophysics underlying hedonic experience. The mirror of introspection should inform any observer that it takes a lot for others to make you happy for a brief period, but not much for others to make you miserable for a long time; such discrepancies exist to motivate individuals to attempt to rapidly change those circumst ances that may endanger their survival. This phenomenon of loss aversion has been used to help explain the stickiness of historical grievances over lost territory, for example, because people tend to renormalize to gains almost instantaneously, while taking a very long time indeed to accept losses (Jervis 1992; Levy 2000).

Victors immediately prove willing to sacrifice for newfound gains, while losers remain entrenched in their willingness to suffer greatly to recoup previous losses. Anyone observing the long-standing territorial disputes in places like Northern Ireland or the Middle East recognizes the power of history and memory for the evaluation of current rights. Indeed, in such conflicts it is not unusual for participants to discuss events that occurred a thousand years ago in justifying their current claims for land or resources. Those who lost rights ages ago have not accepted their loss and are willing to fight to the death to regain them; while those who more recently secured control feel equally entitled, and equally willing, to sacrifice to retain their rights.

Manus Midlarsky (2005b) invokes prospect theory as part of his explanation for the underlying causes of genocide. In discussing the importance of loss, and in particular, the memory of loss, on decision making under conditions of uncertainty, Midlarsky brilliantly illuminates the way in which human propensities to minimize risk and compensate for loss can escalate individual acts of brutality and killing into genocide. Midlarsky persuasively argues that the experience of loss links leaders and their followers in ways that exacerbate the impact of loss on public opinion. For example, the loss experienced by Germany in World War I predisposed the population to take greater political risks in embracing National Socialism in order to recapture their previous feelings of pride, strength, and nationalism.

The weighting function provides the psychological allegory to the probability function in expected utility models. But this function is not linear. For one thing, people have a strong preference for choices that appear certain, as opposed to probable, and often treat highly probable events as though they were certain, while treating low-probability events as though they were impossible. In addition, people tend to psychologically overweight low-probability prospects while similarly underweighting moderate and high-probability choices.

Prospect Theory and Emotion

In many ways, prospect theory represents the apex of the cognitive revolution in psychology. As such, it presents a heavily cognitive view of decision making. However, this does not mean that emotion finds no place in the model. It remains noteworthy that the original label that Kahneman and Tversky gave to prospect theory was "value theory" (Kahneman 2000). Indeed, Kahneman's recent work on well-being and happiness has centered on the importance of emotion (Kahneman, Diener, and Schwarz 2003). Indeed, emotion remained central to the generation of the theory in two ways. First, the original work (Kahneman and Tversky 1979) touched on the distinction between decision utility and experienced utility, recognizing the important difference between what individuals might think is best and what they expect will make them feel best. Anyone who craves cookies while on a diet will have an intuitive appreciation of this conundrum.

Second, as Richard Thaler suggested (1980, 1999), processes of mental accounting form an intrinsic part of framing effects. In particular, mental accounting offers an explanation for how people organize, trade off, combine, and justify various experiences in their lives, financial as well as personal. As Kahneman notes:

> a particularly significant feature of this accounting metaphor is that mental accounts are eventually closed and that strong emotions can be experienced at those times of reckoning. An implication of this insight is that people can to some extent control their own rewards and punishments by choosing whether to close an account or keep it open as well as deciding when to evaluate it. (2000, xiv)

At an individual level, such choice in accounting will seem painfully clear to those who have contemplated divorce: should the marriage be closed, or should the line of personal credit be endlessly extended? The political manifestations of this system of accounting should be obvious to anyone who has witnessed leaders justify continued fighting on the basis of sunk costs. Continuing a battle for the sake of those already lost cannot bring back the dead, but will certainly result in further casualties, whose loss can be similarly leveraged to justify escalation. This pattern clearly characterized at least three American administrations' response to casualties in the war in Vietnam, for example. In whatever circumstance, the critical personal or political question revolves around the appropriate point at which to cut losses and tally the costs and benefits. The normative response always suggests that sunk costs should not be considered in deciding future action; but emotional considerations often pull in the opposite direction. Determining the best moment at which to evaluate a given person or policy often remains challenging as long as hope for the recovery of past losses, or the prospect of a better future, remains; for one thing, continuing the battle forestalls the closing of mental accounts, thus delaying the reckoning associated with having to accept past failures.

In this light, it becomes clear how emotion might provide a basis for a more comprehensive understanding not only of framing effects, but also the origin of preferences as well. As will be discussed at greater length subsequently, emotions can provide an evolutionarily viable model for motivation. As such, emotions can provide a source for preferences, as well as a foundation upon which the framing of particular options might be based. In particular, framing effects may provide a powerful way in which politicians and others can strategically influence and manipulate mass publics through the use of emotional appeals, symbols, and other mechanisms, encouraging automatic association between powerful signs or labels, such as flags or calls to patriotism, with desired behavior, such as support for favored public policy choices, including war.

Emotion

The influence of emotion in psychology has waxed and waned over the last hundred years or so. Early Freudian models posited powerful instinctual drives toward sex and aggression, giving way to more behavioral understandings of human action. Humanist models that dominated psychology in the 1960s brought emotion back to the center, only to have it replaced by cognitive models in the 1990s. More recent neurocognitive discoveries have brought emotion back to the fore, suggesting that the brain privileges affective information in both speed and import (for a review, see McDermott 2004a).

The influence of emotion in political science models has remained more consistent and, by and large, less influential and more wholly negative. The political models into which emotional processes have been incorporated have usually been analyses of voting behavior and campaign strategies in the realm of American politics (for a good review, see Marcus, Neuman, and MacKuen 2000). This relative lack of importance appears surprising in the realm of international relations and war, at least in part because of the clear, persistent, and obvious discrepancy between the public and academic understanding of the motives for war and conflict. This breach can begin to be bridged through a more comprehensive scholarly understanding and appreciation of the motivational force of emotion in generating processes of both war and peace. Emotions contribute to both conflict and cooperation, and their impact should be recognized and properly acknowledged and contextualized in order to better understand their specific operation and impact.

Types of Emotion

A few scholars have made notable advances in systematically examining the impact of emotion on international relations. Several examples will be discussed later. However, before proceeding, I should note that definitions and measurements of emotion differ across disciplines and individual researchers. Such differences can cause both meaningful and silly divides in interpretation, but should not discourage further research. As Jervis's (1993) analogy of the drunkard's search usefully indicates, we should not only look under the light for our keys.

Earlier work examining the impact of "hot" motivational factors, such as emotion, as opposed to "cold" more cognitive processes, included the classic study by Janis and Mann (1977). Early work by Lasswell (1930, 1948) and the seminal psychobiography of Woodrow Wilson by George and George (1955) were heavily influenced by traditional psychodynamic notions of emotion. Such interesting and valuable studies tended to examine the personality of leaders and the impact of their emotions on political outcomes. More recent work has tended to stress the biological and neurocognitive aspects of emotional experience, such as those described later in this chapter.

Neta Crawford (2000) offers a series of propositions on emotion in world politics in the context of realist and liberal models of international relations. Her comprehensive analysis argues that emotions remain pervasive but largely implicit in extant models and that, as a result, they are often incorrect and always undertheorized. She notes that the consequences are an emphasis on cognition in foreign policy decision making and a failure to articulate and explore the impact of emotions such as fear and hate, which are accepted but never fully explored, or empathy and love, which are ignored altogether. She suggests that a more explicit consideration of these latter emotions might facilitate analysis of the art as well as the practice of diplomacy, confidence building, and postconflict peacebuilding efforts. She proposes that while emotions are ubiquitous, they vary in form and intensity, depending on such factors as culture and learning. Further, she suggests that emotion can affect perception, in ways that can shift the interpretation of reality, relationships, and threats. In addition, she argues that emotion can directly impact cognition by altering information gathering and processing; evaluations of risk, costs, and benefits; and the selection of analogy and argument. Finally, she emphasizes the importance of emotion, relatively unrecognized, in central features of international relations, including deterrence, peacebuilding, persuasion, and the maintenance of norms.

George Marcus, Russell Neuman, and Michael MacKuen (2000) have presented perhaps the most comprehensive theoretical attempt to incorporate emotion into political analysis with their theory of affective intelligence. This model, based in part on Jeffrey Gray's neural-behavioral theories, remains concerned with voting behavior in particular. The authors suggest that anxiety provokes voters to seek out new information, which in turn increases political learning and attention, while enthusiasm encourages voters to rely on habits such as party identification to determine their vote choice. More recent renditions of the model suggest a place for the independent action of aversion in determining vote choice. In suggesting a causal role for emotions in mediating the effect of habit and reason on behavior, Marcus and his coauthors suggest that emotions serve a positive purpose in increasing the efficiency and accuracy of political judgments.

In a separate article concerning the impact of emotion on politics, Marcus (2000) notes that scholars who study emotion can be divided into those who focus on leaders, and those who concentrate on followers, or mass publics. Although Marcus does not use these terms, such scholars can be categorized into those who use emotion as a "trait"-based explanation, suggesting that emotions developed in childhood help structure later political attitudes and behaviors through the influence of memory, and those who analyze emotion as a "state"-based contemporaneous explanation, exploring how mood can interact with current environments and circumstances to affect outcomes.

In his trait-based discussion, Marcus notes the several ways in which emotions provide a basis for behavior and attitudes. These appraisals include the more traditionally psychodynamic models of personality and politics pioneered by such leaders as Lasswell (1930, 1948) and James David Barber (1985). Another approach that concentrates on affect as evaluation assumes emotional responses underlie coherent public dispositions on a variety of political factors. The classic model in this vein is represented by Campbell and colleagues' (1960) classic work on *The American Voter,* which posited an affective attachment between parent and child that translated into the socialization of the child into the parent's political party identification. A third perspective notes how overall evaluations can be affective in nature. This notion regards emotion as a recipient of various cognitive evaluations. Such reactions can then be elicited or manipulated through framing or priming manipulations by others. This often occurs by invoking powerful political institutions or concepts.

The state-based approach examines the ways in which emotions may exert an independent influence on contemporaneous evaluations. In this mode, Marcus mentions Schwarz and Clore's (1983) affect-as-information model. As Marcus notes, one important implication of this theory lies in the suggestion that social categorization (including "us" vs. "them" evaluations) becomes linked to affective responses. Thus, knowing that a person is "white," "old," "Catholic," "fat," or "female" provides all the information someone needs in order to know how to feel about that person. The category itself proves sufficient to trigger a positive or negative emotional response.

Marcus also notes the historical controversy in psychology over the primacy of cognition versus affect. Recent neurocognitive findings pretty definitively resolve this issue in favor of the primacy of affect in terms of speed (for a review, see McDermott 2004a). However, such a dichotomy seems false in conception, a point to which I will return. Finally, Marcus reviews models that posit that affective reactions affect how information is processed and can influence responses. This process remains significant because emotional responses to a particular group can influence how individuals respond to public policy that affects that group. Current debates surrounding immigration exemplify this dynamic. So, for example, if politicians evoke stereotypes about a religious or cultural group that individuals find hostile or threatening, particularly if these evocations make individuals angry, men in particular seem to become more likely to support punitive measures against the group (Gault and Sabini 2000). Marcus concludes by advocating a more constructive understanding and appreciation of the impact of emotion on politics. In this volume on war and conflict, I should note that his analysis is restricted to American public opinion and voting behavior.

Jonathan Mercer (2006) has also written on the impact of emotion on international relations, examining in particular the relationship between emotion and rationality. Dividing the literature into four categories, Mercer suggests that the influence of emotion has typically been ignored. The most common view in international relations sees emotion as epiphenomenal. In Mercer's words, "in this view, emotion is all consequence and rarely cause" (2006, 4).

The second approach sees emotion as a mistake, a source for error and irrationality. This approach recognizes that emotion may have an impact, but suggests that its influence can only prove negative in outcome. Studies that see emotion as instigating misperception and bias are in this vein, for example. From this perspective, emotions can only get leaders into trouble, with anxiety, fear, or stress leading them into conflicts and wars they may not want.

The third perspective considers emotion as a rational strategy, which may cause problems in the short run but benefit leaders in the long run. Schelling's (1960) "rationality of irrationality" argument falls under this category. The final category suggests that emotion represents an intrinsic component of any rational action. Recent experimental evidence provided by D'Amasio (1994) and others supports this contention, noting that so-called rational decisions and actions depend on emotional processing. D'Amasio's somatic marker hypothesis in particular suggests that the physical body, and the feelings that run through it and emanate from it, provide the physiological basis upon which are based quick and efficient decisions about what is right and wrong. Without access to such a feeling marker, individuals prove unable to successfully negotiate the social world, failing to attach the emotional consequences of bad behavior to current actions, thereby losing jobs, relationships, and other important resources.

Mercer suggests that emotion can be employed to advantage in all three of the central dynamics on which this chapter focuses. Most importantly, he suggests that emotion can prove essential for group identification, and serve as a mechanism by which to understand and evaluate the relationship between individual and group behavior. This important theme will be discussed at greater length later in the chapter.

Finally, in an article I wrote on the meaning of neuroscientific advances for political science, I posed several theories of emotion, as well as several ways in which emotion might specifically impact decision making (McDermott 2004a). Most of those theories I have already mentioned in one guise or another. Here it may prove helpful to briefly review the four ways in which emotion can influence decision making.

First, emotion can influence decision making during the course of the actual choice. Important influences in this regard include stress and fatigue, each of which can render time-sensitive decisions more difficult. Extremely stressful events can produce odd effects on memory, as anyone will attest who, having moved residences, can't remember where an item is. Specifically, stress produces chemicals that aid in memory consolidation for the stressful event, but memory loss for unrelated events (Arnsten 1998). Such biochemical markers may help explain how posttraumatic stress in battle sears traumatic events into memories that can last for decades.

In addition to the immediate experience of emotion, which can be intense and compelling, mood also has an impact on memory, resulting, for example, in strong conviction. The very authenticity of such conviction often proves persuasive to others; individuals captured by the power of their own emotions can be charismatic leaders precisely because others find their passion convincing and appealing. This is so even when the leader's motives derive from socially undesirable goals, as in the case of Hitler. People are much more likely to remember events that are consonant in mood to the feeling they experience in the moment of decision; panic recalls experiences of fear and terror, while anger reminds people of occasions of past rage.

Note that the intensity and consistency of the emotional state evokes the memory, not the frequency or duration of its occurrence, or the success or failure of the outcome. This dynamic heavily influences the selection of historical analogies more than do relevant strategic aspects of a situation. For example, when British and French leaders compared Nasser to Hitler after the Egyptian president nationalized the Suez Canal, they may have been responding as much to the feelings of impotence and humiliation that Nasser aroused in them as to his strategic bid for power and territory. Clearly, a manipulative facet enters into such analogies as well. Those listening to them are meant to draw the intended lesson: people did not respond to Hitler when they should have because they did not immediately recognize him for the ruthless dictator he was; the mistake must not be repeated with another potential dictator, whether Nasser, Saddam Hussein, Kim Jong Il, or someone else.

As noted earlier in the discussion of prospect theory, another way in which memory can impact mood is through framing effects, and the evaluation of gains and losses. Needing an explanation for Germany's loss in World War I, Himmler and other Nazi leaders placed blame on the Jews, arguing that it was necessary to eliminate them if the larger German state was to survive and prosper. Midlarsky (2005) makes a compelling case that Himmler's inconsistent behavior—a man who disliked violence yet orchestrated one of the greatest acts of violence in human history—can be explained from the perspective of altruistic punishment. This concept, drawn from evolutionary models, argues that individuals will make sacrifices in order to punish defectors. Some of the original experimental work in this regard, conducted by Ernst Fehr and colleagues (Fehr and Gachter 2000), showed that negative emotions provide the mechanism that instigates such punishment, and that opportunities for punishment prove critical in establishing and maintaining large cooperative enterprises. Midlarsky demonstrates that Hitler, Himmler, and other Nazi leaders asked ordinary Germans to join in altruistic punishment against the Jews, arguing that such sacrifice was necessary to punish those who were uncooperative with the larger purpose of the state. The fact that Jews were not in fact defectors from the German regime during World War I, for example, received less attention.

This concept can also help explain why Jewish fighters engaged in an organized revolt against their German oppressors in Warsaw, but not in the Vilna or Lodz ghettos. Midlarsky (2005a) details how the Zionist leaders in Warsaw modeled altruistic punishment in an earlier fight with the Germans in January, while preventing some Jews from deportation. Such acts by individual partisans on behalf of the larger community, for the survival of the collective, spurred others to fight in the later, larger uprising. This uprising served as a model for Israelis fighting Arab countries in the early days of their republic.

For as Paul Slovic (1999) argues, emotion can affect perception of risk as well as reward, because people tend to see threat and value as perceptually, albeit not logically, linked. Thus, people tend to see risk and benefit in opposition. If they have a positive feeling about an act or issue, like nuclear power, they tend to see the risks as low and the benefits as high, whereas the reverse holds true if they have a negative feeling. A government that wants to generate support for a war needs to minimize perceived costs, heighten perceived benefits, and diminish perceived risks. Since people also tend to overestimate the likelihood of a good outcome when they are happy, and overestimate the likelihood of a bad outcome when they are sad (Johnson and Tversky 1983), bad news from a war front does not appear self-limiting. Not only do high casualties or bad actions hurt on their own account, but they are likely to make people feel sad, thus diminishing perceived success and benefit, and lowering support in the process. Such outcomes may also raise empathy for the victims, further encouraging more lenient policy choices, with heightened concern for victims.

Gender differences can affect this evaluation process as well, since men are more likely to respond to challenge or threat with anger, and women with empathy (Gault and Sabini 2000). This is important in the context of foreign policy because angry people are much more likely to support punitive and retributive policies, such as attack and execution. Empathic people are much more likely to support lenient public policy choices and victims' rights organizations. Second, the emotions people expect to feel after decision making can have an impact on choice. These influences mostly relate to regret and disappointment about making the wrong choice. Third, anticipated emotion can influence decision making as well. Most significant in this regard is the fact that people tend to be atrociously bad at predicting how they will feel in the future (Gilbert et al. 1998). In particular, when they are in a "hot" state, people appear to be particularly inept at judging how they will feel in a "cold" state and vice versa. The classic example is the person waking up next to a stranger after a drunken binge, and wondering what he or she was thinking the night before, but this inability to predict one's own future feelings also encourages decisions to make an untoward threat or a precipitous attack before thinking through all the implications in the cold light of day. Attack can feel very good when an angry person seeks vengeance, but seem less advisable after one's nose is broken by the opponent.

Last, emotion can impact memory, such that people tend to recall the peak emotional intensity of an experience and its endpoint, but not its duration (Frederickson 2000). This information proves useful because it allows people to learn how many resources they need to summon when confronting a similar challenge in the future, and also allows a closing of a mental account, so that an assessment of meaning can begin, as discussed previously. However, it also means that people often make choices to endure more pain rather than less, or continue conflict longer than necessary because the intensity or cost of withdrawal or defeat seems too great to bear, even for a short time. Trading duration for intensity may prove justified and reasonable under some circumstances, but the decision should be undertaken in a considered manner, for the trade-off of short-term benefit for long-term cost may be a bad bargain in the end. Certainly, many Americans came to that conclusion about the long involvement in Vietnam.

Evolutionary Motives in Emotion

Most of the models and theories of emotion I have presented have merit in explaining the impact of emotion on international politics in general and war in particular. This section suggests that an evolutionary understanding of the role of emotion as a motivating force in conflict and cooperation offers a useful framework from which to examine the formation, maintenance, and dissolution of coalitions; small group identification and unit cohesion; and punitive sanctions for draft evaders and other noncooperators, including those who violate the norms of war by engaging in behaviors like rape or torture that make the larger nation look bad.

Approaching emotion from an evolutionary perspective proves helpful because it can illuminate the functions that emotions serve within the context of repeated challenges faced by our ancestors. In the words of leading evolutionary theorists Leda Cosmides and John Tooby:

> By "human nature" evolutionary psychologists mean the evolved, reliably developing, species-typical computational and neural architecture of the human mind and brain. According to this view, the functional components of this architecture were designed by natural selection to solve adaptive problems faced by our hunter-gatherer ancestors, and to regulate behavior so that these adaptive problems were successfully addressed. (2000, 91)

Since war has represented an endemic challenge throughout the course of human history, it seems likely that, within such a context, humans developed cognitive and affective strategies designed to provide a fitness or survival advantage. To be clear, an evolutionary approach does not require or posit that these strategies and mechanisms remain adaptive under current circumstances. Rather, the mechanisms that exist evolved and flourished because, relative to the other strategies, they provided across many generations a comparative advantage to those who possessed them. Note that these advantages may have been small, but nonetheless made strategies that offered them superior to the available alternatives. Since evolution progresses through a combination of chance and selection, with benefits from the many millions of iterations possible across people over time, selection prefers the most optimal strategies from random mutations. Further, strategies that worked in the past may not prove adaptive under current conditions; this does not negate their continuing impact on human behavior. Evolutionary processes refer backward, but also outward to context, and progress certainly moves more slowly than modern technological innovations.

According to an evolutionary perspective, emotions developed as specific domain-specialized functions to respond to repeated challenges, such as sexual attraction, fidelity, family relations, cooperation, aggression, predator avoidance, vision, and other problems posed by the need for survival (for a comprehensive review, see Cosmides and Tooby 2000). In other words, an emotion runs like a software program in the architectural hardware of the human mind and body. Just as a person might open different computer programs for different purposes, such as Quicken to do finances and Word to write a letter, individuals engage particular, *specific* mental programs based on the particular challenges they confront. These psychological programs are differentiated by the functions they serve; the strategies that prove best for mate choice are unlikely to prove ideal in avoiding predators, for example. In order to avoid internal conflicts in such programming, the mind evolved superordinate programs, like an operating system, that activate, inhibit, or coordinate particular emotions at the appropriate time, as defined and identified by the environmental circumstances confronted. In many cases, these superordinate strategies involve particular component elements, such as physiological responses, that may subserve other conflicting programs in different contexts; for example, heart rate rises in the case of both sexual arousal and predator avoidance, but for different reasons, and thus with diametrically opposed approach-avoidance responses. This point remains critical in understanding the way in which engaging particular programs entrain a wide variety of discrete responses. For example, fear causes shifts in perception and attention, such that vision, particularly at night, improves, as does hearing.

Emotions can be understood as precisely this kind of superordinate psychological program, defining and determining the appropriate responses to a particular challenge. Specific emotions coordinate a variety of responses, including perceptual, informational, communicative, and behavioral ones, allowing a person to act so as to maximize the likelihood of survival.[1] This point illustrates the artificial divide between cognition and affect, because such mental programs engage a wide variety of responses based on the functional requirements of the situation. Cosmides and Tooby provide the clearest and most comprehensive explanation of this process:

> An emotion is not reducible to any one category of effects, such as effects on physiology, behavioral inclinations, cognitive appraisals, or feeling states, because it involved evolved instructions for all of them together, as well as other mechanisms distributed throughout the human mental and physical architecture. . . . Emotion programs, for example, have a front end that is designed to detect evolutionarily reliable cues that a situation exists (whether or not these cues reliably signal the presence of that situation in the modern world). When triggered, they entrain a specific set of subprograms: those that natural selection "chose" as most useful for solving the problems that situation posed in ancestral environments. (Cosmides and Tooby 2000, 93)

Note, however, that such an approach does not demand a universal response to particular challenges. The intensity and expression of emotion may well vary, as Crawford suggests, depending on the specific environments in which they evolved and the particular cues that triggered them.

How does this approach inform our understanding of the impact of emotion on war? To put it simply, war represents one of the quintessential repeated adaptive problems humans have confronted throughout history. Since emotions evolved in response to such challenges, at least some of human psychological architecture evolved to help people deal with challenges posed by predation, the need for cooperation in defense, the necessity to separate friend from foe quickly, efficiently, and accurately, and the requirement to respond to threat, challenge, theft, or murder with appropriate strategies to prevent or minimize such actions in the future. In this way, specific emotions signal and motivate particular sets of responses based on the cues in the environment that indicate threats of conflict or opportunities for cooperation. From this perspective, emotional programs can serve causes of war *or* peace, depending on the circumstances. It should also be clear that from this perspective war does not necessarily represent a negative outcome, because it is likely that victory in battle brought tremendous survival advantage to ancestral warriors, whose fighting mostly took place in small bands. In many circumstances, fighting feels better than capitulating, because capitulation was not likely to maximize fitness in the smaller conflicts prevalent in the past.

Because specific emotional programs are triggered by reliable, repeated cues in the environment that allow people to detect and respond appropriately to a particular challenge, certain circumstances relevant to fighting and peacekeeping warrant particular attention. Note that one does not have to accept the evolutionary perspective wholesale in order to appreciate that such a view highlights and renders coherent particular challenges, patterns, and responses in new ways that allow insight into processes that might otherwise appear confusing and contradictory. The following sections discuss three of the dynamic processes that emotion helps detect and construct: coalitions, small group identification, and altruistic punishment.

Coalitions

The formation, maintenance, and dissolution of coalitions has been a central issue in international relations for a long time, although most of this discussion has concerned alliances among countries, not among smaller groupings. But in hunter-gatherer societies, political and military coalitions developed in bands much smaller than those that arise in today's nation-states. Thus, human mental architecture evolved in the context of cues provided by these smaller groupings; individuals react with similar strategies to the cues given by the larger groups in current circumstances, whether or not such application is warranted or appropriate.

Earlier scholars in international relations discussed the importance of coalitions in situations of conflict. Allan Mazur (1968), for one, argued that most theories of conflict depended on notions of rationality at variance with the emotional incentives that often characterize them. He suggested that theories of conflict might profitably shift from rational models to more nonrational, or emotional, models of conflict and coalition based on social psychological models of behavior. Indeed, he applied his model to the kind of system he considered representative of "tribal segmentary-lineage political systems." He argued for the integration of ideas involving conflict, support, and emotion in theories of coalitions. However, most models of conflict in international relations still pursue a more rational model of analysis. Such a rational approach to coalitions is perhaps best represented by the seminal work on alliance structures conducted by James Morrow (1991a, 1993). This work, while extremely valuable, excludes the impact of emotion in motivating the formation and maintenance of coalitions. This absence remains unfortunate, since emotions can motivate the choice of partners, the level of trust between them, and the duration of the alliance, as well as the comfort participants derive from such structures.

Robert Kurzban, John Tooby, and Leda Cosmides (2001) have undertaken an evolutionarily oriented analysis of the relationship between coalitions and social categorization, examining the extent to which race-based categorization is automatic. The authors argue that people encode the race of others as a reversible by-product of the cognitive superstructure designed to tell friend from foe in a quick, efficient, and accurate manner. While they showed that individuals do indeed encode coalitional affiliations ("friend" or "foe" or "us" versus "them") as an intrinsic and automatic part of perception, they note that when such cues no longer correlate reliably with race, individuals reduce their reliance on racial categories. In their experiment, less than four minutes of exposure to such an alternative universe proved sufficient to overcome a lifetime of racial categorization, at least in this experimental setting.

The aspect of this study that remains significant here regards the critical importance of detecting coalitions and alliances in human perceptual processing. In ancestral hunter-gatherer societies, such groups often came in conflict with one another (Keeley 1996; Manson and Wrangham 1991), and coalitions and alliance existed to protect and defend one's own community, resources, and territory.

Further, such alliance patterns are not limited to humans; most related primates demonstrate similar patterns of bonding and alliance (Smuts et al. 1987). In fact, Wrangham (1999) reports systematic evidence of coalitionary killing in chimpanzees and wolves. In his imbalance-of-power hypothesis, Wrangham argues for the species distribution of intergroup coalition killing by noting that such lethal raiding appears to be characterized by conditions of preexisting hostility between neighboring groups, and by an imbalance of power that allows one group to kill the other with impunity. Thus, selection can favor the murder of rivals because its costs can remain low. If this analysis is correct, successful hunting, raiding, and killing depend on the formation and maintenance of coalitions because only through them can warriors count on an imbalance of power sufficient to make their actions successful. On the reverse side, failing to obtain coalitionary partners renders one vulnerable to attack at the hands of more numerous enemies.

Importantly, alliance structures can shift and change frequently and quickly, thus requiring actors to develop flexible and adaptive psychological mechanisms that can reliably keep track of transformations. As Kurzban, Tooby, and Cosmides (2001) indicate, such cognitive architecture needs to remain sensitive both to patterns of coordination, cooperation, competition, and conflict among others, and to cues that indicate and predict political allegiance (Tooby and Cosmides 2002; Sidanius and Pratto 1999). Because many alliances are impermanent, as opposed to kin allegiance, which remains more enduring, such cues may not be easy to uncover in a reliable and trustworthy manner. As a result, people develop strategies to correlate transitory or obscure cues with more permanent and visually efficient mechanisms for categorization, of which race is one of the easiest and most obvious because it remains stable over time. But symbols such as flags, uniforms, signals, or badges serve this purpose as well. In this way, any trivial indicator of allegiance can acquire social significance if it reliably indicates categories relevant for securing cooperation under threat. All these mechanisms developed to serve the similar and critical purpose of tracking allegiances, so that a person did not trust or aid an enemy or hurt an ally. Recall that the goal in this environment is to provide quick, efficient, and stable indicators of social categories, the most important of which, in this circumstance, is political allegiance. The most urgent and basic question those under attack must confront relates to the successful and immediate identification of friends and foes: are you with me or against me? Note that under a different emotional program, one not triggered by, say, anger or fear, but by love and empathy, such cues would not indicate relevant social categories. Under emotions provoked by mate selection drives, for instance, race would not matter so much as strength, youth, and health. Under these circumstances, the aesthetics of beauty evolved to prize such characteristics above all others.

What remains significant about the Kurzban, Tooby, and Cosmides (2001) study is not the relative ease with which they eliminated race-

based social categorization but the enduring nature of alliance categorization. Individuals evolved to remain exquisitely sensitive to the manipulation of the coalitions that surround them; such awareness provided
critical advantage for survival. Note how human perceptual sensitivity to
change supports processes necessary for the rapid identification of shifting alliance structures. Because the categorization of race can be quickly
muted under the right circumstances, the evidence suggests that people
remain attuned to the transitory nature of shifting alliance structures, and
continually update the cues associated with them. From this perspective,
it should not be surprising the countries can become close allies with
those against whom they have previously fought brutal wars (as the
United States and Great Britain, Germany, and Japan) as the local and
global circumstances change. Similarly, new enemies can be quickly
identified and old ones reevaluated in the face of new threats. For example, after the 9/11 attack on the World Trade Center, the *New York Times*
reported less prejudice against blacks, less distrust of white police
officers, and increased hate crimes against individuals such as Sikhs
whose turbans indicated to the uninformed an association with Middle
Eastern extremist terrorist groups such as Al Queda.[2]

For current purposes, the important consideration is that individuals
pay attention to the signs and symbols that they have learned to associate
with particular political or social allegiances that indicate friend or foe.
Once such categorizations are provoked, often by an emotional response
such as fear or anger, a set of responses becomes entrained that affects all
subsequent activity and processing, from memory and inference to physiological processes and behavioral responses. Once engaged, such
processes proceed down a path-dependent avenue affecting inferential
and other processes relevant to the interpretation of the given situation.
While such processes can be arrested by the recognition of change in the
environment, some strategies developed to maximize safety will present
thresholds to reduce vigilance higher than would occur under more re-
laxed conditions. Individuals remain keenly aware of the transitory and
shifting nature of these allegiances, but still find it important to be able to
quickly and efficiently recognize and reorient these perceptions in order
to distinguish someone with whom they can cooperate from someone
they should fight. While often wrong in our understandings and assessments when evaluating others, such strategies evolved because the costs
of a mistake were often asymmetrical, in that seeing a foe as friend had
worse consequences, and overall produced lower rates of survival, than

seeing a friend as foe. Thus, in the face of threat, more false identification of a friend as foe will be allowed than under conditions of cooperation. So while prejudice and discrimination produce detestable outcomes, they likely emerged as by-products of naturally occurring processes of social categorization that allowed our ancestors to quickly and efficiently distinguish friend from foe in the face of threat, even at a cost of some accuracy in recognizing friends.

Small Group Identification

One of the powerful ways in which emotion can impact war and peace is through small group identification, or what is often referred to in the military as unit cohesion. There are at least two separate but important aspects of this phenomenon. First, findings from social identity theory show that people naturally demonstrate preferences for in-group members, and often manifest out-group discrimination. Second, questions involving military effectiveness, performance and morale often relate to issues involving small group cohesion. Each of these issues will be addressed in turn.

First, a great deal of research in social psychology reports reliable findings concerning small group behavior. When people are divided into groups, and this division can take place on the basis of the most minimal factors, individuals tend to show profound in-group favoritism and out-group discrimination (Sherif et al. 1961; Tajfel 1978). Prejudice toward out-groups appears especially pronounced when they appear to threaten values held dear by in-group members (Solomon, Greenberg, and Pyszczynski 2000). This discrimination has been demonstrated in the areas of resource allocation and in attributing bad behavior to out-group members. Such discrimination occurs even when individuals are assigned to groups anonymously for short periods of time, and when they know that such group assignment rests on the basis of transitory or arbitrary factors. Moreover, individuals tend to discriminate against out-groups even when they do not personally benefit from this system of allocation, and even when doing so proves personally disadvantageous, a phenomenon often referred to as altruistic punishment (Turner, Brown, and Tajfel 1979). People appear to allocate resources in this way not simply to provide an advantage for the in-group, but to create an explicit relative advantage for the in-group over the out-group (Tajfel et al. 1971). Often in-group members who persecute out-group members see themselves as performing a valuable and useful service to the community by punishing those who might harm the valued group (Bandura 1999). This makes sense evolutionarily, of course, if the relative allocation of resources to groups provided a fitness advantage for one's own group, especially in an environment of scarce resources.

Often it is a short hop from discrimination to aggression or even violence. Social psychology provides a great deal of evidence to suggest that, in the right circumstances, individual proclivities can be overcome, rendering almost anyone susceptible to engaging in violence against another (Haney and Zimbardo 1977). Factors such as heat, stress, or provocation can exacerbate other situational factors and expand feelings of prejudice and discrimination toward out-groups into aggressive and violent action.

Among the most powerful factors that exaggerate discrimination against out-group members are emotions such as disgust and contempt (Dovodio et al. 1996). Recent findings from neuroimaging studies indicate that these emotional responses appear almost instantaneously when individuals consider out-group members. Specifically, when an individual categorizes others into out-group status, the emotional center of the brain, the amygdala, demonstrates a response indicating vigilance and alarm (Hart et al. 2000; Phelps et al. 2000, using racial differences to signify out-group membership). Further, the insula responds in a way consistent with disgust or arousal, depending on the situation. These results do not seem to hold when these same people are evaluated as individuals and not as group members (Wheeler and Fiske 2005). Susan Fiske and her colleagues (Fiske, Harris, and Cuddy 2004) provide intriguing survey data supporting these findings. They asked subjects to evaluate "low status opponents," meaning out-group members who are contemptible or disgusting in some way. They found that such subjects react with a combination of active and passive forms of attack, including fighting and excluding or demeaning out-group members.

The second area in which small group identification can influence violence lies in the area of military effectiveness, through dynamics of unit cohesion (for an excellent review of this literature, from which the following discussion draws, see Kier 1998). Since the seminal studies of the German and American military following World War II, many scholars have argued that small group cohesion at the unit level significantly improves and enhances military performance and morale (Shils and Janowitz 1948; Stouffer et al. 1949). The central idea in these studies is that soldiers in combat fight for each other, if not for specific leaders, nations, or ideologies. Since these early studies, group cohesion has been widely under-stood as an essential element in an effective combat force. Kier (1998) and others (Macoun, Kier, and Belkin 2005) have called into question the va-lidity of this notion, citing the fact that cohesion is only one of many fac-tors that can determine military effectiveness, and also pointing out the important distinction between task and social cohesion, arguing for the primacy of the former over the latter in determining effectiveness. Nonetheless, there appears to be no question that certain structural and situational factors do in fact aid in social cohesion, which tends to de-velop quickly and easily under combat conditions. These elements in-clude factors such as the frequency and duration of contact, shared expe-rience, success in combat, and the presence of a threat to the group. In addition, shared values and background can increase a sense of social co-hesion. Interestingly from an evolutionary perspective, the size of the group also affects social cohesion, with tighter bonds forming among smaller groups.

Whether or not social cohesion improves military performance in any given conflict, such bonds provide comfort and companionship to those who share them, allowing individuals to weather traumatic situations more successfully than they might otherwise manage. Such cooperation serves as the basis for small group identification and bonding, and rests on the advantages that such alliances provided in the past. The following description provided by military psychologists illuminates the way in which cooperation overcomes individual differences in the presence of threat:

> Friendships are easily made by those who might never had been compatible at home, and are cemented under fire. So sweeping is this trend that the usual prejudices and divergences of background and outlook, which produce social distinction and dissension in civil life, have little meaning to the group in combat. Religious, racial, class, schooling, or sectional differences lose their power to divide the men . . . Such powerful forces as anti-Semitism, anti-Catholi-cism, or differences between Northerners and Southerners are not likely to disturb interpersonal relationships in a combat crew . . . The emotional attitudes the fliers take toward each other have less to do with accidents of their individual personalities than with the circum-stances of their association. (Grinker and Spiegel 1945, 21–24, as cited in Kier 1998, 22)

Recall that this description reinforces the Kurzban, Tooby, and Cosmides (2001) study demonstrating that racial cues can be overcome when they no longer provide a reliable signal for political allegiance and cooperation. When under threat, the only categorization that remains salient is that distinguishing friend from enemy, cooperator from competitor.

Altruistic Punishment

One of the issues that the Kier (1998) article addressed directly regards the question of whether and how homosexuals might be integrated into the United States military. Aside from the passionate emotions that the issue raises in and of itself, the larger topic directly addresses the social issue of inclusion. Groups that have sought, and achieved, integration into the military in the past include African-Americans and women. Such a right and privilege is not only valuable as a sign of status within society, but also as an indicator of social in-group acceptance. Yet studies in social identity theory have shown that out-group discrimination remains pervasive. If enemies exist both within and outside of a society, identifying and sanctioning the noncooperators becomes a critical factor in encouraging, supporting, and acknowledging in-group sacrifice.

An historical analogy may prove instructive. In the early days of psychology and psychoanalysis, Freud posited a strong sex drive in all humans, which he saw as the energetic instinct driving most behavior. He believed civilization existed in large part to temper and control this drive (Freud 1961). Strongly influenced by the industrial revolution and the machine age, Freud's notion of Eros provided the fuel for the engine of human behavior and neurosis. Yet at the outbreak of World War I, Freud's theories were challenged by all the young men who went to their deaths by throwing themselves into machine gun fire when ordered to do so at places like the Somme and Gallipoli. This impulse puzzled him, and to explain it he developed an opposing instinct, called Thanatos, or the death drive, to resolve the conflict he witnessed between Eros and a willing sacrifice of one's life in battle. In other words, however positive and life affirming the sex drive might be, it worked in opposition to a powerful internal death instinct. While Freud's notion of Thanatos was not nearly as well received as the idea of Eros, this internal division provides a useful metaphor for the parallel motives of encouraging social cooperation while punishing noncooperators. Of course such actions, while not individually rational, may make more sense from an evolutionary perspective, which shows why any given individual might sacrifice his own life for the survival of kin, who carry the person's own genetic traits.

Much work on cooperation and the sanctioning of noncooperators has been conducted in the area of behavioral economics, notably by Ernst Fehr and his colleagues, who studied processes in the brain connected to punishment:

> Many people voluntarily incur costs to punish violations of social norms. Evolutionary models and empirical evidence indicate that such altruistic punishment has been a decisive force in the evolution of human cooperation. We used . . . tomography to examine the neural basis for altruistic punishment of defectors in an economic exchange. Subjects could punish defection either symbolically or effectively. Symbolic punishment did not reduce the defector's economic payoff, whereas effective punishment did reduce the payoff. We scanned the subjects' brains while they learned about the defector's abuse of trust and determined the punishment. Effective punishment, as compared with symbolic punishment, activated the dorsal striatum, which has been implicated in the processing of rewards that accrue as a result of goal-directed actions. Moreover, subjects with stronger activations in the dorsal striatum were willing to incur greater costs in order to punish. Our findings support the hypothesis that people derive satisfaction from punishing norm violations and that the activation in the dorsal striatum reflects the anticipated satisfaction from punishing defectors. (de Quervain et al. 2004, 1254)

This work indicates that individuals often prove willing to accept costs to themselves in order to punish noncooperators. Michael Price and colleagues (Price, Cosmides, and Tooby 2002) demonstrated that punitive sanctioning can serve as a device for punishing free-riders in collective action problems as well. Specifically, these authors posited that punishing noncooperators restricts any fitness advantage such defectors might enjoy by benefiting from the work of others. Their findings also indicate that other proreward motivational emotional strategies may help with the related but distinct problem of labor recruitment in collective action problems.

The issue of punishing or sanctioning noncooperators plays out most obviously in the military sphere in the punishment of draft evaders or deserters. Recall the earlier discussion of visual cues designed to inform observers and witnesses of the political allegiances of participants. In World War I in Britain, people commonly gave or fitted white feathers to men of combat age in public settings to brand them as cowards, deserters, or, worse, traitors.[3] This public disapprobation may have been designed to humiliate those who refused to fight, but also served as a visual cue that they deserved sanctions and punishment.

Interestingly, altruistic punishment can also be inflicted by followers on leaders who are perceived as serving their own interests and neglecting the collective body (Boehm 1999). Such arrogant leaders may have their heads chopped off—either literally or figuratively. French kings went to the guillotine when they exploited their public beyond tolerance, just as contemporary leaders lose their jobs when they are discovered taking bribes or engaging in criminal activity. But such sanctioning can also take place on the battlefield when men turn their weapons on an incompetent or corrupt leader, as illustrated in the film *Platoon*.

Fear and War

The foregoing discussion has provided a relatively general discussion of emotion and its impact on conflict and cooperation. Two points remain essential. First, emotions differ in their actions in the human body and mind. Particular emotions evolved for specific functional purposes. Second, while there may be an infinite number of emotional shades and states, psychologists find evidence for seven emotions that have essentially universal facial recognition: happiness, sadness, fear, anger, surprise, disgust, and contempt (Ekman and Friesen 1975). Note that many of these appear roughly analogous to the traditional seven deadly sins. Other emotions emerge as shades and combinations of these basic states. Each of these emotions may have an impact on particular processes of war and peace when activated by appropriate environmental cues. Anger or fear may encourage a person to lash out at a perceived threat, while happiness may encourage peacekeeping processes.

For purposes of illustration, it may prove useful to examine the potential impact of one basic emotion on conflict, aggression, and war. Fear is an ideal choice not only because it has been the most widely studied emotion, but also because it is central to realist models of international relations. Recall that in the classic realist model, Morgenthau (1948) posed a more central role for the basic psychological relationship between leaders and followers than did later structuralist renditions endorsed by scholars such as Waltz (1979). Indeed, Morgenthau believed that politics was governed by laws rooted in human nature. Moreover, he argued that political power represented a psychological relationship between leaders and followers that found at least one of its sources in subjects' fear of the disadvantages of disobedience, as well as the love they might feel for leaders or institutions.

Continuing from the proposition that fear, once cued, motivates a series of psychological activities, we should note the specific shifts that take place once an individual feels afraid. Fear may be cued whenever a person senses a threat; such a feeling need not be grounded in present-day objective indicators, since such feelings evolved in a different environment. Once a person becomes frightened, certain responses inevitably follow (see Cosmides and Tooby 2000, upon which the following draws, for a more extended discussion).

First, perception and attention improve. People hear and see farther and more accurately, especially concerning features in the feared person or object. (Incidentally, recent evidence suggests that women's perceptions intensify more than men's, probably because of the extended need to protect children.) Other physiological changes include a rise in blood pressure, movement of blood to the periphery to prepare for action, and the twitching of muscles. As a result of these responses, the person may experience a sensation of cold.

Goals and priorities narrow as safety becomes more important and the individual becomes more willing to bear higher costs to maximize security. Time perception changes, and the shadow of the future shortens. Other needs, however basic, including hunger, thirst, or sex, become suppressed. Even apparent analgesia can be induced, as a person's subjective experience of pain diminishes, most likely to allow a continuation of running or fighting to allow for survival.

Information gathering and processing comes to focus on the immediate threat and searches focus on finding places of safety and trusted sources of cooperation from in-group members. Concepts change as notions of safety and security influence evaluations of physical space in particular, highlighting places to hide or identifying potential weapons. Memory processes concentrate and focus on relevant past events, including where safety was found and secured the last time a similar threat was encountered, or recalling similar challenges confronted in the past. Communication strategies change. Depending on the circumstance, a person may cry out for help, or remain paralyzed and unable to speak so as not to give away her position. Specialized inference strategies and learning programs are activated to determine the most appropriate action: should one flee, fight, freeze, or, particularly if one is female, befriend the threat?

Finally, behavioral changes occur to respond best to the particular threat. Importantly, if a trauma does occur, as the case of a rape or combat-related trauma, the amygdala may sear the experience into memory in a way that may last for the rest of the person's life, such that particular associated triggers (gunfire, helicopter noises, etc.) involuntarily recall the traumatic event as immediately occurring, as often happens in cases of post-traumatic stress disorder (Pittman and Orr 1995).

Clearly many of these strategies may prove functional for survival under conditions of direct and immediate threat of bodily harm. In fact, some research indicates that many of these responses may inhibit attacks by certain kinds of predators, such as rapists (Suarez and Gallup 1979). However, modern perceived threats are often not so obvious or immediate in nature. Fear of ill-defined or amorphous threats, with no means to take immediate or direct action against them, as in the current war on terror, leads to stress-related problems, including health impairments, as people prove unable to turn off internal chemicals such as cortisol that are generated under conditions of fear and stress. Sounding the alarm against threats may have been well suited in the past, and may work well in the face of particular current threats, especially for individuals in combat, but may not serve noncombatants well for extended or distant threats.

Conclusions

Emotion is a complex and multidimensional topic. Emotions can be understood as superordinate psychological programs that evolved to solve recurrent problems faced by our ancestors, of which a noteworthy one was war and conflict over territory, mates, and resources. Emotions entrain a wide variety of cognitive, perceptual, and physiological activities designed to activate some responses, inhibit others, and coordinate still more. Thus, emotions motivate particular processes under certain circumstances that cue such responses.

Specific emotions can contribute to processes that generate war or peace. Fear and anger can encourage conflict, while happiness and empathy can generate peacebuilding. At least evolutionarily speaking, war is not always a bad outcome. Thus, emotions should not be understood as processes that only stand in the way of efficient and effective action. Rather, emotions allow functional responses in many circumstances. Without such processes, people would have less ability to instigate or inhibit processes that remain essential to the human condition. Without emotion, how would individuals know whom to kiss and whom to kill? In particular, emotional processes motivate formation, maintenance, and dissolution of coalitions; small group identification and cohesion; and altruistic punishment of noncooperators, among other events. Future research might examine the specific ways in which particular basic emotions shift perceptions and inferences in the context of international relations.

NOTES

1. It is important to note here that survival does not mean literal physical survival of the individual, for every human life is finite. But genes are potentially immortal, and survival refers to maximizing the reproductive potential of any given genetic code. We all exist because our ancestors lived long enough to pass along to their offspring lessons of survival, in the form of genetic code.

2. "Sept. 11 Attack Narrows Racial Divide," *New York Times,* October 10, 2001.

3. For a wonderful fictional treatment of this pattern, see Pat Barker, *Regeneration* (1991).

PART II

The Onset and Termination of Civil Wars

The Evolution of Theory on Civil War and Revolution

T. DAVID MASON

Introduction: Forms and Frequency of Civil War

The last half of the twentieth century was characterized by some as an age of revolutions (Goodwin 2001a; see also Snyder 1999), and rightly so. Well over 100 major civil wars occurred during this period, resulting in tens of millions of casualties among both civilians and combatants (see Lacina and Gleditsch 2005). The destructive effects of civil wars—on human beings and on the economies of nations—linger on for years after armed combat has ceased. Death rates from diseases and malnutrition are higher in a nation that experiences civil wars than they would be had the nation not experienced a civil war, and this effect lasts for some years after the cessation of hostilities (Ghobarah, Huth, and Russett 2003). Civil wars lower national income through the destruction of assets and infrastructure, the disruption of commerce, the diversion of resources from the civilian economy to war, and the depletion of natural resources (Collier 1999). Civil war depresses growth in income per capita not only in the nation that experiences the war but in its neighbors as well (Murdoch and Sandler 2004, 147). Moreover, the longer a civil war lasts, the more severe is its negative impact on economic growth (Kang and Meernik 2005).

In this chapter, I will begin by reviewing the patterns of civil war occurrence in the post–World War II era: how many conflicts have occurred, what forms have those conflicts taken, and what regions of the world have been especially susceptible to civil war? I will then trace the evolution of social science theory on the causes and dynamics of civil war. Theory on where, when, and why civil wars occur has evolved through the development of several distinct schools, each of which grew out of a different behavioral paradigm and each of which focuses on a different core aspect of the puzzle of why ordinary people join together to take up arms against their government. Following that I will examine recent empirical research on the predictors of civil war onset (other chapters in this volume examine research on civil war duration and outcomes) in an effort to assess the extent to which this emerging body of empirical research provides support for the theoretical frameworks developed earlier or, alternatively, compels us to rethink the conceptual architecture of the frameworks we use to explain why people revolt.

Frequency and Destructiveness of Civil Wars

It is now widely recognized that since the end of World War II, wars *within* nations—civil wars—have replaced wars *between* nations—interstate wars—as the most frequent and destructive form of armed conflict in the nation-state system. This represents one dimension of a major shift in the patterns of armed conflict that has occurred over the last half century. For three centuries prior to 1945, the most frequent form of conflict in the international system had been interstate war, usually involving one or more members of the major power system (which included Europe, the United States, China, and Japan). The Correlates of War project lists only 23 interstate wars occurring between 1945 and 1997, resulting in 3.3 million battle deaths. By contrast, more than four times as many civil wars (108) occurred during this same time period, resulting in almost four times as many casualties (11.4 million; Sarkees 2000). The Armed Conflict Dataset (ACD) produced by the International Peace Research Institute of Oslo identifies 225 major armed conflicts between 1946 and 2002, of which 163 were internal conflicts, 21 were "extrastate" conflicts (mostly anticolonial wars), and only 42 were interstate conflicts (Gleditsch et al. 2002, 620).

The second major shift in patterns of conflict is that almost all of the civil wars of the last 60 years have occurred in the third world nations of Asia, Africa, and Latin America. As noted earlier, this contrasts with the pre-1945 patterns of conflict, in which the overwhelming majority of conflicts were interstate wars fought on the territory of one or more major powers (predominantly in Europe). It was not until the collapse of Leninist regimes in Eastern Europe in 1989 and the disintegration of the Soviet Union and Yugoslavia into their constituent republics in 1991 that civil conflicts of any magnitude took place in Europe. Indeed, John Gaddis (1987) went so far as to label the post–World War II era in major power politics as "the long peace": the longest time span in the post-Westphalian order without a war between the major powers of Europe.

The "long peace" in Europe finally did end with the revolutions of 1989 that led to the collapse of Soviet-backed Leninist regimes in the member nations of the Warsaw Treaty Organization (Poland, Hungary, Czechoslovakia, Bulgaria, Romania, and the German Democratic Republic). With the exception of Romania, none of these "velvet revolutions" involved much violence. When faced with peaceful mass uprisings—and with the Soviet Union no longer willing to come to their rescue with troops—those regimes simply stepped aside rather than fight. Only in Romania did the overthrow of the incumbent regime involve armed violence, and that lasted only a matter of days. Two years later, the Soviet Union disintegrated relatively peacefully, when the newly elected leaders of the 15 republics of the Soviet federal system declined to renew the treaty establishing the Soviet federal system. Once the Soviet Union dissolved, several of the now-independent republics experienced armed uprisings of their own. Among these were Georgia, Azerbaijan, Moldova, Tajikistan, and Russia itself. The disintegration of Yugoslavia into its constituent republics involved a series of armed secessionist revolts (in Croatia, Bosnia, and the Kosovo region of Serbia) that required NATO intervention to end the violence. Clearly, the long peace had ended.

Of course, the long peace was confined largely to the European continent and North America. The major powers themselves were certainly involved in armed conflicts during this period. However, the conflicts in which they did become involved took place almost exclusively in the third world. First, beginning in the 1950s and lasting through the mid-1970s, there was a wave of anticolonial revolts against European powers, all of which were fought on the territory of their colonies. The French faced armed revolts in Vietnam, Tunisia, Morocco, Cameroon, and Algeria. Portugal faced revolts in Angola, Guinea Bissau, and Mozambique. And the British faced rebellions in Kenya and elsewhere. Several civil wars in the third world attracted direct military intervention by one or more of the major powers or their proxies. The United States intervened directly in South Vietnam and the Dominican Republic and provided material sup-

port to governments faced with insurgent challenges (Guatemala, El Salvador, among others) and insurgents challenging regimes that were hostile to the United States (Nicaragua, Angola, and Afghanistan, among others). The Soviet Union did much the same, dispatching Cuban troops to
Angola, intervening directly in Afghanistan, and supporting insurgencies
against regimes allied with the United States. Less direct forms of intervention were employed by one or more major powers in a majority of the
civil wars that occurred in the third world during the Cold War era (see
Regan 2000). The "long peace," then, implied that the territory of Europe
was largely free of armed conflict; the member nations of Europe did their
fighting elsewhere.

A third trend in the patterns of civil wars over the last half century is
that nations that experience one civil war are very likely to experience another. In other words, for a small subset of nations, civil war appears to be
a chronic condition. The 108 civil wars in the Correlates of War data set
occurred in only 54 nations. Only 26 of those nations experienced one
and only one civil war. Ten nations had two civil wars, 12 had three, four
had four, and two nations experienced five civil wars. The 124 civil wars
listed in Doyle and Sambanis (2000) data set occurred in just 69 nations.
Only 36 of those nations had one and only one civil war, while 18 had two
separate conflicts, nine nations had three, five nations had four, and one
nation had five.

A fourth, more encouraging trend in the patterns of armed conflict is
that since the end of the Cold War (about 1987), the number of conflicts
ongoing in any given year has begun to decline. Based on the ACD data,
Gleditsch and his colleagues (Gleditsch et al. 2002, 620) report that the
number of conflicts rose steadily throughout the Cold War, peaking in
1992 with 55 ongoing civil wars. Immediately thereafter, the number of
conflicts dropped considerably and has remained relatively constant
since 1995. Fearon and Laitin (2003, 77–78) reports similar trends, with
the number of wars peaking around 1994 and declining thereafter. The
decline in the number of ongoing wars is largely a function of the international community, through the United Nations and other international
organizations, taking a more proactive role in brokering peace agreements between warring parties. Thus, the recent decline in the number of
conflicts ongoing in the international system at any given time is more a
function of existing wars being brought to an end than of any significant
decline in the rate at which new wars begin.

Finally, on a less encouraging note, civil wars last on average about four times as long as interstate wars: the 108 civil wars in the Correlates of War project lasted an average of 1,665 days, whereas the 23 interstate wars lasted only 480 days on average. This feature of contemporary civil wars is important for several reasons. First, the protracted nature of many civil wars is a major reason for the increase in the number of ongoing conflicts in the world from 1945 until about 1994. Fearon and Laitin (2003, 77) note that throughout this period, the average number of new civil wars starting in a given year remained relatively constant (about 2.31), but the duration of those wars increased, so that the annual rate at which civil wars ended (about 1.85) was lower than the rate at which new wars began. Thus, the steady increase in the number of wars under way was not a matter of increases in the number of new wars, but the consequence of the accumulation of ongoing conflicts, a trend that did not diminish until several years after the Cold War ended. Second, the duration of civil wars has been implicated in their destructiveness as well. On average, casualties in civil wars occur at a much lower rate than in interstate wars. However, because civil wars last so much longer, their cumulative death toll substantially exceeds that of interstate wars. Third, duration has been implicated in the manner in which civil wars end. Mason and Fett (1996) found that the duration of a civil war was the strongest single predictor of whether it would end in a negotiated settlement or a decisive victory for one side or the other: the longer a war lasts, the less likely it is to end in victory for either side (see also Mason, Weingarten, and Fett 1999). After about 10 years, decisive victory by either side is rare, and the conflict is likely to settle into what Zartman (1993) has termed a "mutually hurting stalemate." Fearon concludes that "civil wars last a long time when neither side can disarm the other, causing a military stalemate. They are relatively quick when conditions favor a decisive victory" (2004, 276; emphasis removed).

Forms of Civil War

Before reviewing the schools that have emerged to explain the outbreak of civil war, it is prudent to begin by defining with some precision what range of phenomena those theories seek to explain. Most definitions of civil war employed in social science research include a set of empirical criteria that a conflict must satisfy to be included in the civil war data set.[1] Civil wars are, first, armed conflicts that take place within a nation that is a recognized member of the nation-state system. This requirement distinguishes civil wars from interstate wars, which involve armed conflict *between* two or more nation-states. Civil wars involve armed conflict between the government of a nation and an organized domestic opposition movement that recruits its members predominantly from the population of that nation. The requirement of organized armed conflict distinguishes civil war from spontaneous, unorganized violence such as riots or land invasions or communal conflict (i.e., conflicts between groups in society as opposed to conflict between groups and the state). Most definitions also include a threshold for the level of violence required for the conflict to qualify as a civil war. Typically, this threshold is calibrated in terms of deaths from violence. A critical qualification on this threshold is that each side in the conflict—government and rebels—must inflict some level of casualties on the other. This requirement is intended to distinguish civil wars from genocides or politicides, in which the minimum number of deaths may well be reached (and usually exceeded) but all of the destruction is perpetrated by one side, usually the government.[2] The Rwanda genocide of 1994 resulted in the death of 800,000 to one million citizens in a matter of a few weeks. Almost all of the killing was by government forces or their proxies. Ethnic Tutsi were targeted on the basis of their ethnic identity. Politicides follow a similar gruesome pattern, but targeting is not based on ethnicity. After seizing power through revolution in 1975, Cambodia's Khmer Rouge embarked on a program of killing with targeting officially based on class criteria: landlords, intellectuals, employees of the previous government, business owners, and others who were not clearly workers or peasants were targeted. Approximately one million people were killed in this politicide.

Once we have defined civil wars, it is important to distinguish among types of civil war. Generally, they can be categorized according to the goals of the rebels and the issues that motivate the rebellion. First, most studies draw a distinction between *ethnic* and *ideological* conflict. Second, they draw a distinction between *revolutionary* and *secessionist* conflicts. In a revolutionary civil war, the goal of the rebels is to overthrow the incumbent government and establish themselves as the new government of an existing nation-state. For example, the Sandinista rebellion in Nicaragua overthrew the Somoza regime in 1979 and established the Sandinistas in charge of a completely new regime. By 1981 the Sandinistas faced a new civil war, led by the U.S.-backed Contra rebels. In Cambodia, Khmer Rouge rebels overthrew the government of Lon Nol in 1975 and established themselves at the head of the new Democratic People's Republic of Kampuchea.

In a secessionist revolt, the rebels seek not to replace the incumbent regime but to secede from it and create a new sovereign nation-state out of a portion of the territory of the existing one. The Eritrean civil war in Ethiopia (1974–91) resulted in the establishment of the new sovereign nation of Eritrea in 1991 out of a portion of the territory of Ethiopia. In 1971 East Pakistan seceded from Pakistan to form the new nation of Bangladesh. The Biafran civil war in Nigeria (1967–70) was an attempt by the Ibo ethnic minority to secede from Nigeria and establish their homeland in the southeast of that nation as the new nation-state of Biafra. That rebellion failed after more than three years of fighting and a million deaths, most of them civilians.

The distinction between ideological and ethnic civil wars revolves around the issues that motivate the rebellion and the identity basis of the rebel movement. In an ideological civil war, the issues that divide rebels from government usually concern matters of governance and extreme inequality in the distribution of land, wealth, income, or political power. Many third world conflicts of this sort are peasant based and revolve around issues of access to land. Peasant-based insurgencies escalated to civil war in El Salvador, Nicaragua, Guatemala, Peru, Cambodia, Philippines, and Nepal, to name but a few. Popular support for the revolutionary movement is mobilized around shared class identity and community ties among landless and land-poor peasants.

Ethnic revolutions have a similar dynamic, and the goal is the same as ideological revolutions: to overthrow the existing regime and replace it with a new one. However, what distinguishes ethnic revolutions is the role of ethnicity as a source of identity for the rebels. Often, ethnicity and class coincide in ethnic revolutions. One ethnic group dominates the government and monopolizes high-status positions in the economy, while other ethnic groups are relegated to subordinate status in the economy and the political arena. Under these circumstances rebel leaders can mobilize support for an armed challenge by framing grievances as not just a matter of deprivation but of ethnic discrimination. To summarize, revolutionary conflicts may be ethnically based or class based. Almost all (if not all) of the secessionist conflicts of the last half century have been ethnically based.

Evolution of Social Science Theory on Civil War and Revolution

Until recently, social science theory on civil war and revolution has focused predominantly on the issue of onset: what conditions make the outbreak of civil war more likely? Theory development on this question has followed an identifiable evolutionary path, defined by three central issues. First, what motivates people to engage in political violence? The initial set of behavioral theories to emerge were derived from social psychology and focused on the motives of those revolting: what grievances would motivate an individual to participate in the highly risky endeavor of an armed insurrection against an established government? This puzzle gave rise to *deprived actor* (DA) models of revolution, based on the premise that the greater the deprivation suffered by citizens (conceived of in terms of economic well-being or political rights or both), the more likely civil war is to occur.

Rational actor (RA) models emerged in part as a reaction to deprived actor models' inattention to the collective action problem spelled out by Mancur Olson (1965). The benefits that a successful revolution promises to produce (such as a new political order, a more abundant and equitable economic order, and a more egalitarian social order) are public goods: everyone will be able to enjoy those benefits regardless of whether or not they participated in the collective action—civil war—that produced them. Given that, the rational individual has a strong incentive to free ride by refraining from fighting in the civil war while hoping that enough others do take up arms so that the rebellion succeeds and the public goods of rebel victory become available. But if everyone free rides, there is no revolution. Thus, according to RA theories, unless aspiring revolutionaries can solve the collective action problem, civil war will not occur, no matter how widespread and severe the deprivations suffered by society. RA models focus on how revolutionary leaders solve this collective action problem.

Resource mobilization or *social movement* (SM) theories represent a reaction to the shortcomings of both RA and DA models. With respect to DA theories, Charles Tilly (1974, 302) famously contends that "fluctuations in grievances account for the outbreak of collective protest as poorly as fluctuations in the oxygen content of air explain the incidence of fires." With respect to RA models, social movement theories argued that people do not choose between participation and free riding as isolated, atomized individuals. Their lives are embedded in already established networks of social interaction that exist in part for the purpose of solving collective action problems in everyday life. Thus, the challenge of explaining revolution is accounting for the emergence of revolutionary organizations that are capable of exploiting existing social institutions and networks to mobilize people for dissident collective action, including revolutionary violence.

Finally, *state-centric* theories of revolution emerged as a reaction to the tendency of deprived actor, rational actor, and resource mobilization theories to focus almost exclusively on conditions in society that would make civil war more or less likely to occur. The state—the prize over which civil wars are fought—was conspicuously absent from these earlier conceptual frameworks. Theda Skocpol "brought the state back in" by arguing explicitly that the state has interests of its own, and the pursuit of those interests often generates the crises that contribute to the outbreak of civil war.

Deprived Actor Models

One intuitively appealing way to conceptualize deprivation as a causal antecedent of civil war is in terms of any of several dimensions of economic inequality. In his pioneering study on inequality in land ownership in Vietnam, Bruce Russett (1964, 443) quotes Tocqueville on the salience of inequality as a source of revolution: "Remove the secondary causes that have produced the great convulsions of the world and you will almost always find the principle of inequality at the bottom." Samuel Huntington (1968, 375) linked inequality in land ownership to the outbreak of peasant-based insurgencies in the third world: "Where conditions of landownership are equitable and provide a viable living for the peasant, revolution is unlikely. Where they are inequitable and where the peasant lives in poverty and suffering, revolution is likely, if not inevitable. . . . No group is more conservative than a landowning peasantry and none is more revolutionary than a peasantry that owns too little land or pays too high a rental."

Thus, a set of studies emerged that tested the relationship between outbreaks of political violence and inequality in income (Muller 1985), land tenure (Russett 1964; Midlarsky 1988; Midlarsky and Roberts 1985; Seligson 1996), or both (Muller and Seligson 1987). Unfortunately, the findings on the inequality–civil war link have been less than conclusive. Mark Lichbach (1989) surveyed over 40 studies that test the relationship between inequality and political violence and concluded that there is a decided absence of findings that are robust across studies, and this is not simply a function of differences in measurement, research design, or the sample of countries and time frames employed in the different studies.

Manus Midlarsky (1988, 442) reached a similar conclusion: "rarely is there a robust relationship discovered between the two variables. Equally rarely does the relationship plunge into the black hole of nonsignificance."

Why would this be the case? First, inequality in income, land ownership, wealth or other economic factors changes only at a glacial pace in most nations, whereas the levels of political violence can and do vary substantially over much shorter time frames. Thus, from one year to the next, or one month to the next, the level of inequality in a nation is almost constant, whereas the outbreak of civil war usually represents a sudden quantum leap in the level of political violence at a specific point in time (Moore, Lindström, and O'Regan 1996, 337–38). Most of the findings that indicate a relationship between inequality and political violence are cross-sectional correlations: nations with higher levels of inequality may be more susceptible to civil war than those characterized by lower levels of inequality. However, within a nation, the degree of inequality is unlikely to be a very powerful predictor of *when* civil war breaks out because, as noted earlier, the level of inequality typically varies only marginally over time within a given country. While inequality may make the outbreak of civil war more likely, other factors are required to explain why civil war erupts when it does in a given nation.

An alternative to the inequality-political violence link that emerged is James Davies' relative deprivation (RD) theory. Ted Gurr elaborated this framework in his seminal work *Why Men Rebel* (1970). Davies (1962) begins with the hypothesis that "revolutions are more likely to occur when a prolonged period of objective economic and social development is followed by a short period of sharp reversal." The prolonged period of development produces not only higher levels of what Davies terms "need achievement" but also higher levels of *"expected* need achievement." As long as the gap between expectations and achievement is relatively small, stability prevails. However, the sudden sharp reversal in economic development produces a decline in achievement (the "J-curve") without, according to Davies, a commensurate decline in expectations. As a result an intolerable gap between expectations and achievement emerges, producing a sense of relative deprivation. When the resulting frustration becomes sufficiently widespread, an outburst of revolutionary violence becomes likely.

RD theory contained a number of insights that went beyond the logic of the presumed link between inequality and political violence. First, RD theory suggests that civil war is *not* most likely to occur in the most severely deprived societies. Davies and Gurr argue that the extremes of absolute deprivation corrode the social fabric that is necessary for *collective* violence to emerge. Where severe deprivation prevails, people are too preoccupied with the rigors of mere survival to engage in any collective endeavor. Instead, revolt is more likely to occur where people who have experienced some improvement in their standard of living but are confronted with a short-term crisis that severely reduces their level of well-being. Unlike their counterparts in the most severely deprived societies, they have both the motive and the means to revolt.

As with the inequality–political violence thesis, critiques of RD theory focused on the notion that it overpredicts revolution (Lichbach 1995): instances of the J-curve dynamic of prolonged development followed by a sudden sharp decline in achievement are far more common in human history than are revolutions. One rather obvious case frequently cited is the Great Depression in the United States: a prolonged period of economic and social development in the United States was followed by an extremely sharp decline in economic well-being, yet no civil war erupted in the United States or, for that matter, in any other established industrial democracy during the Depression. In part, the tendency of RD theory to overpredict revolution arises from its silence on the question of why people, when faced with a sharp decline in their standard of living, would not adjust their expectations downward. The assumption of continued rising expectations in the face of a severe decline in achievement is counterintuitive. Yet it is this psychological dynamic that drives RD theory's explanation of political violence. In addition, RD theory, like other deprived actor models, does not address the collective action problem. Even people who share a set of grievances that they attribute to the government will not automatically or spontaneously engage in the sort of coordinated behavior that civil war requires. This concern motivated rational actor models of civil war.

Rational Actor Models

Civil war is a form of collective action that, if successful, produces benefits that are public goods. That is, the benefits are nonexcludable and nonrival. Nonexcludable means that once the benefits of a rebel victory are available to the rebels, they cannot be denied to those who did not participate. Nonrival means that one person's "consumption" of the benefits of rebel victory does not diminish the ability of others in society to consume those benefits as well. These characteristics of the public goods of rebel victory produce what Mark Lichbach (1995) has termed the "rebel's dilemma": why would people participate in a rebellion if they will get to enjoy the benefits of rebel victory regardless of whether or not they contributed to the success of the rebellion?

Lichbach depicts the rebel's dilemma as a prisoner's dilemma game (see fig. 1). Each citizen is faced with the choice of participating or staying home, and the choice is conditioned in part by what the person believes "everyone else" will do. If no one else participates, then to take up arms against the government would be a supremely quixotic act of foolishness. Therefore, if "everyone else" stays home, our typical citizen stays home as well, and the status quo is preserved. If "everyone else" participates in the rebellion, then presumably the rebellion will succeed, and our typical citizen will reap the benefits of a rebel victory. However, that will happen regardless of whether or not he or she participates. Moreover, whether or not the rebellion succeeds is unaffected by the participation of any one individual. Thus, if she stays at home while everyone else rebels, our model citizen reaps the added benefit of avoiding the risks and the opportunity costs of participation. The conclusion, then, is that regardless of what everyone else does, the rational course of action for any one individual is to free ride by staying at home. The dilemma, of course, is that if everyone behaved in this manner, there would be no rebellions.

The temptations to free ride are especially strong in the case of violent collective action such as civil war. First, the benefits of rebel victory, besides being public goods, are unknown and uncertain. They are uncertain in the sense that rebellions often fail. They are unknown in the sense that one cannot be sure that victorious rebels will establish a new order that is any more abundant, peaceful, or ripe with opportunity than the one they seek to overthrow. Indeed, victorious rebels quite often impose a new order that is at least as harsh and repressive as the old regime. The Khmer Rouge in Cambodia overthrew the Lon Nol regime in 1975, but the new order they established was so repressive that an estimated one million Cambodians (out of a total population of about six million) died at the hands of the Khmer Rouge before that regime was deposed by Vietnam in 1978. Second, participation has opportunity costs. Time spent participating in rebel activities is time not spent earning income or enjoying the fruits of one's labors. Participation has risks as well. Unlike most other forms of collective action, participation in armed rebellion carries the very real possibility of capture, injury, or even death.

	Everyone Else's Choices	
	Join the Rebels	*Don't Join the Rebels*
Join the Rebels	*Benefits:* Rebel Victory	*Benefits:* None (no Rebellion occurs)
Rebel's Choices	*Costs:* Time, Resources spent in Rebellion, Risk of sanctions by government	*Costs:* Time, Resources spent in Rebellion, Risk of sanctions by government
Don't Join the Rebels	*Benefits:* Rebel Victory	*Benefits:* None (no Rebellion occurs)
	Costs: None	*Costs:* None

Fig. 1. The Rebel's Dilemma. (Based on Lichbach 1995, 5.)

Olson's solution to the collective action problem is selective incentives, defined as private benefits that are available only to those who participate in the collective action. However, this solution by itself is not sufficient to explain revolutionary collective action. First, the selective incentive solution contains within it its own collective action problem: who would be willing to supply the movement with the resources necessary to provide selective incentives to participants when the benefits of successful rebellion would accrue to those benefactors even if they did not underwrite the costs of selective incentives (Oliver 1993, 273)? The selective incentive solution assumes the existence of a rebel organization capable of raising and dispensing selective incentives, but the genesis of that organization poses a prior collective action problem that cannot be explained by selective incentives alone.

Doug Van Belle (1996) offers the concept of "leadership goods" as an explanation for the emergence of a rebel organization. Leadership goods are those private benefits that will accrue to the rebel leadership, should they succeed in overthrowing the government. They include the perquisites of office as well as the political power that goes with office once the rebels have established the new regime. As such, leadership goods can explain the emergence of revolutionary organizations from scratch and the participation of early joiners, when the risks are greatest, the prospects of victory are lowest, and the rebels lack the means to offer selective incentives to recruits.

Second, while selective incentives are useful for inducing people to contribute to nonviolent collective action, the risks involved in participating in revolutionary violence are so great that there is reason to doubt that any rebel organization will have the capacity to provide enough selective incentives to offset such extreme risks. Other factors must make the risks of not participating great enough that the offer of some sort of side payment, however modest, would be sufficient to induce an individual to join the rebels.

One selective incentive that has been highlighted as a source of rebel recruits is state repression. When a state responds to dissident challenge with repressive violence, that can create an incentive for nonelites who otherwise would prefer to remain uninvolved to join the rebels in the hope of gaining protection against the repressive arm of the state. When state repression becomes so indiscriminate in the selection of targets that a person's chances of becoming a victim are largely unrelated to whether or not he provides tangible support to the rebels, then that person may turn to the rebels for protection (Mason and Krane 1989; Mason 2004). Given this pattern, rebels often employ tactics designed to elicit harsh repression by the state, in the hope that such action will drive nonelites to their side.

Third, one implication of the selective incentive solution is that participation is largely a mercenary consideration, divorced from any consideration of whether the participant shares the rebels' goals or beliefs. As DeNardo (1985, 56) suggests, this "implies that socialists will gladly participate in fascist demonstrations, and vice versa, if the organizers simply provide enough coffee and doughnuts to the marchers." If participants can be counted on to support the rebellion only so long as selective incentives are forthcoming, then the movement is likely to fail because supporters are likely to desert at the first setback that degrades the ability of the rebel organization to pay them.

The selective incentives argument is the basis of Collier and Hoeffler's (2004) "greed" hypothesis that civil wars are most likely to occur where rebel organizations have access to "lootable" goods such as drugs or gemstones. If the rebels can capture the flow of these commodities, they can establish a flow of revenues that allows them to pay, arm, and equip recruits. As for the genesis of the rebel organization, not only do the founders have the prospect of leadership goods as an incentive to form their organization, but the proceeds from lootable goods also allow them to "do well from war" while the conflict is ongoing. I will discuss the empirical findings from this research program later. For now it is worth noting that the greed hypothesis would seem to be of more value in explaining the duration of the conflict than its initial onset. The revenue flows certainly enable rebels to sustain their efforts longer than they would be able to do in the absence of earnings from lootable goods. And, certainly, the prospects of immediate earnings from lootable goods should make it more likely that a rebel organization would succeed in starting from scratch. However, an inspection of the conflicts that fit the greed hypothesis leads one to wonder whether greed-based movements might suffer from the problem DeNardo highlighted (quoted earlier). Rebels recruited exclusively on the basis of selective incentives are likely to desert if the payments are not forthcoming or if the risks of participation increase. This would suggest that greed-based movements are not likely to have a high success rate; they may sustain the conflict for years, but rarely if ever do they win, as has been the case with Sendero Luminoso in Peru and the FARC movement in Colombia (both of which solicit protection payments from coca growers), the UNITA rebels in Angola, or rebel movements in Sierra Leone and Liberia (all of which profited from trafficking in gemstones). Indeed, the groups that rely on lootable goods have a tendency to degenerate into organizations that are more criminal than revolutionary, and, organizationally, they often come to resemble the rebel equivalent of a neopatrimonial state.

Just as deprived actor models tend to overpredict civil wars, rational actor logic underpredicts civil war. By the logic of collective action, it is difficult to see how anyone could be induced to participate in a revolutionary movement. Yet civil wars do occur, even if they are rare in time and space. How, then, do we explain the arrival of such movements?

Resource Mobilization and Social Movements

With the anomalies of both deprived actor and rational actor models of political violence as a starting point, sociologists such as Charles Tilly (1978), Sidney Tarrow (1994), and Doug McAdam (1982) developed a new theoretical framework, initially referred to as *resource mobilization* and later as social movement theory (see also McAdam, Tarrow, and Tilly 2001). Resource mobilization theory begins with the collective action problem and presents a theoretical framework for how dissident leaders go about overcoming it to build a revolutionary movement capable of challenging the incumbent regime.

For Tilly a revolutionary situation arises "when the government previously under the control of a single sovereign polity becomes the object of effective, competing, and mutually exclusive claims on the part of two or more distinct polities" (1978, 191). This is the condition of *multiple sovereignty*. The state no longer exercises a monopoly over the legitimate use of power within the territorial boundaries of the nation because a counter-elite has arisen to challenge the state. Challengers become revolutionary when they develop the organizational capacity to mobilize the support of a significant segment of the population, to the point that, for that segment of the population, the revolutionary organizations is the de facto government in their lives. Civil war, then, is a struggle between the dual sovereigns over which one will prevail as the sole legitimate government. How does the condition of multiple sovereignty arise?

While not rejecting the RA school's assumptions of individual rationality, resource mobilization theories begin with the observation that individuals do not choose between participating and free riding as isolated, atomized individuals. "What [Olson's] view misses is the degree to which individuals are already embedded and ontologically invested in various kinds of social structures and practices" (McAdam, Tarrow, and Tilly 1996, 26). Their lives are embedded in long-standing networks of social relations that exist in part for the purpose of coordinating the behavior of individuals in activities that produce shared benefits. In effect, the wide variety of formal and informal social organizations that make up the fabric of any given society are mechanisms that have evolved for overcoming everyday collective action problems. Those networks and institutions have at their disposal a variety of social incentives to induce members to participate in collective action. Community members are aware of and familiar with these incentives, who allocates them, and by what criteria. Therefore, they can and do anticipate how others in the community will react to a call for action, and they can estimate quite accurately the consequences they will suffer if they do not respond to the appeal in the same manner as their neighbors. Thus, rational actors, as members of communities, can be induced to contribute to public goods and to participate in collective action, even in the absence of selective incentives (see Taylor 1988, 67).

With respect to civil war, the challenge for social movement theorists is to explain how preexisting networks of social institutions can be harnessed by dissident leaders to overcome the special collective action problem involved in mobilizing people to take up arms against their government. Revolutionary movements are not built from scratch, nor are supporters recruited one by one through selective incentives, as most rational actor approaches imply. Instead, dissident leaders take advantage of already existing social networks, community institutions, and other *mobilizing structures* to recruit supporters in groups. Mobilizing structures are those mechanisms communities have developed to mobilize members for cooperative endeavors that produce collective goods for the entire community. Once established, they can be adapted for other, less conventional purposes, including contentious political action. Dissident leaders can harness them as *mobilizing structures* to build a support base for a national social movement. Sidney Tarrow (1994, 22) notes that "the mobilization of preexisting social networks lowers the social transaction costs of mounting demonstrations, and holds participants together even after the enthusiasm of the peak of confrontation is over. In human terms, this is what makes possible the transformation of episodic collective action into social movements."

In order to harness existing social networks for contentious collective action, social movement theories contend, it is easier to persuade members to participate in forms of collective action with which the groups are already familiar and with which they have had some success in the past. Movement leaders tap into existing *repertoires of contention,* which are defined as a "limited numbers of historically-established performances linking claimants to the objects of their claims" (McAdam, Tarrow, and Tilly 1996, 23). They are a set of collective behaviors with which the members of the community have had some experience. As such, they already know how to organize themselves for these forms of collective action, and they have reason to expect that these forms of contentious behavior will succeed in producing the desired collective benefits. Thus, "workers know how to strike because generations of workers struck before them; Parisians build barricades because barricades are inscribed in the history of Parisian contention; peasants seize the land carrying the symbols that their fathers and grandfathers used in the past" (Tarrow 1998, 21). Students in China in 1989 drew on the experience of demonstrations in 1976, 1978, and 1986 to mobilize their members for the Tiananmen Square movement of 1989. They knew how to organize street demonstrations, because they had done so successfully in the recent past. Based on this experience, they also believed they could demonstrate with little risk of violent repression by the state. They clearly miscalculated the state's willingness to use repressive violence (Mason 1994).

To activate local social networks in support of a national movement, dissident leaders employ *framing processes* to persuade the members of local social networks to join a national movement. Framing involves identifying injustices that afflict the community and attributing them to the state or some other entity that is the intended target of the social movement. They frame the issues in such a way as to convince people, first, that their troubles are shared by others beyond the boundaries of their own immediate community. Second, dissident leaders must convince citizens that the conditions that gave rise to their grievances are unjust and by no means inevitable. Third, they must politicize popular discontent by persuading people that the state is either responsible for their grievances or has the capacity to remedy them. Finally, dissident leaders must persuade citizens that only if each member of each community contributes to the success of the movement will they succeed in bringing pressure to bear on the state to undertake reforms or be overthrown. Dissident leaders construct a political reality for the potential participants that makes use of symbols and identities with which their audience is already familiar. However, Tarrow (1998, 110) cautions that "movement entrepreneurs cannot simply adapt frames of meaning from traditional cultural symbols: if they did, they would be nothing more than reflections of their societies' values and would be inhibited from challenging them." Effective framing involves using traditional symbols to attract nonelites to a new set of values and beliefs about the state that will make them more willing to participate in a movement that challenges the state's sovereignty. In so doing, they redefine local groups' collective identity in such a way that members feel a commitment to contribute to the national movement's success.

Social movement theorists highlight the critical role of changes in the dissidents' *political opportunity structure* in determining when and if they will undertake collective action, what form that action will assume (i.e., violent or nonviolent), and what the prospects for successful collective action might be. Even if large segments of the population are aggrieved, and even if dissident leaders and organizations exist to mobilize them for collective action, people are not likely to join such a movement unless they perceive some change to have occurred in the stability of the dominant coalition of elites and classes, and in the capacity and propensity of the state to repress dissident activity. Doug McAdam (1996, 32) contends that "changes in either the institutional features, informal political alignments, or repressive capacity of a given political system . . .

significantly reduce the power disparity between a given challenging group and the state" and thereby affect the chances of dissident collective action succeeding while its participants escape harsh sanctions. Thus, for McAdam (1996, 24), "revolutions owe less to the efforts of insurgents than to the work of systemic crises which render the existing regime weak and vulnerable to challenge from any quarter."

State-centric Models

The theoretical schools discussed so far—deprived actor, rational actor, and social movement theories—focus on forces within society that fuel revolution. The state is treated as little more than the arena in which civil conflicts are fought or the stakes over which they are fought. Theda Skocpol's *States and Social Revolutions* brought the state back into the equation of revolutionary dynamics. Skocpol argued that what catalyzes social revolutions is not conditions or developments in society but a crisis of the state, and these crises are generated in part by the actions of the state itself. She asserts, "the fact is, no successful social revolution has ever been 'made' by mass-mobilizing, avowedly revolutionary movements" (1979, 17). While revolutionary ideology and organization may solidify revolutionary movements during revolutionary moments, in no sense do revolutionary leaders themselves ever create the crises they exploit. Instead, revolutionary situations arise because of politico-military crises of state and class domination.

This central theme of state-centric theories of revolutions echoes the concept of changes in the political opportunity structure that social movement theorists posit as a determinant of *when* revolution erupts. However, Skocpol goes beyond this concept to explore how the structure of the state itself and developmental changes in the both patterns of state-society relations and the state's relationship with its international environment produce the crises that ignite revolutionary outbreaks.

For Skocpol the state is more than just a governing structure composed of a set of administrative, policing, and military organizations headed by an executive authority. It extracts resources from society and deploys them to establish and sustain its coercive and administrative machinery. As such, the state has a set of interests that are distinct from those of the dominant economic class. Through its control of the machinery of the central government, it is at least potentially autonomous from the dominant economic class. It is not simply the instrument of their dominance. Although the state and the dominant economic class share an interest in keeping subordinate classes under control, the state has its own distinct interests vis-à-vis the subordinate classes and pursues these with a logic dictated by its own institutional interests, as opposed to those of the dominant class.

The state's fundamental interests are to maintain sheer physical order and political peace as well as to defend the nation against threats from the international environment. In the pursuit of these interests, it may under certain circumstances make concessions to subordinate classes at the expense of the dominant class because those concessions serve the state's own interest in controlling the population, collecting taxes, or securing enough military recruits and weaponry to defend the nation against external threats. In 1861, Czar Alexander II of Russia liberated Russia's serfs from feudal bondage. This step clearly brought the state into conflict with the landed gentry. But Alexander had determined it to be necessary in order for Russia to industrialize so that it would be capable of defending itself against other European powers that were already developing the industrial capacity to sustain a modern army.

Long-term developmental trends within nations and in the international environment can generate conflicts of interest between the state and dominant economic class. Whether these conflicts produce a crisis of the state that makes revolution possible if not likely is a function, in part, of the degree of state autonomy from that dominant economic class. For Skocpol and for Goldstone (1991), states that lacked sufficient autonomy from the dominant economic classes were more likely to experience revolution. The social revolutions they studied—especially France, Russia, and China—had states they characterized as "agrarian bureaucracies." They were "differentiated, centrally coordinated administrative and military hierarchies functioning under the aegis of an absolute monarchy." However, in contrast to modern strong states, they were only "proto-bureaucratic": some (but not all) offices at higher levels were functionally specialized, some officials and official duties (but not all) were subject to explicit rules and hierarchical supervision. The separation of state offices and duties from private wealth and private interests was only partially institutionalized.

Such states were not fully autonomous from the landed gentry. The gentry retained considerable local and regional authority (Goldstone 1991, 5). They were the local agents of the state, holding formal offices that gave them the authority to collect taxes and fees for the state, exact corvée labor and conscripts for the army, dispense justice locally, and issue and enforce regulations in the name of the state. Though formally subordinate to the monarchy, local elites enjoyed considerable discretion in their exercise of state authority at the local level, in large part because the state lacked the administrative capacity to monitor their performance of official duties. Nor did the state have the means to supplant them with a trained civil service answerable directly to the central state. As such, they were capable of exercising state authority to serve their own interest, sometimes at the expense of the central state's interests.

Under normal circumstances, the imperial state and landed upper classes were simply partners in the control and exploitation of the peasantry. The gentry expected the state to conduct successful military campaigns, maintain domestic order (especially by protecting them from peasant rebellions), regulate coinage, maintain transportation infrastructure, and provide status- or wealth-enhancing opportunities for local elites by restricting access to education, military careers, and civil service positions. Barrington Moore (1978, 20–23) adds that the population in general expected the state to defend the nation against foreign enemies, maintain domestic peace and order (including protection from bandits), and contribute to the material security of the population through public works and direct or indirect support of minimum subsistence guarantees. To perform these tasks, the state required revenues derived from land taxes on privately owned lands and rents on lands owned by the imperial state (Goldstone 1991, 5). In addition to paying taxes, the population was expected to obey the directives of the state and contribute to the national defense when necessary through military service.

The imperial state depended on the landed classes for the revenues required to maintain the apparatus of the state, including its military capacity and conscripts to fight in its wars. These had to be supplied by gentry from among their own peasant labor force. Thus, the state and the landed gentry were competitors for control over the manpower of the peasantry and the surplus generated by the agrarian and commercial economies. The monarch's interest were to appropriate resources from society and channel them into its military or state apparatus, or into centralized, state-controlled economic development. The landed gentry's interest were to minimize state appropriations of economic surplus and peasant labor. Balancing these competing interests posed a challenge. If flow of income to the central state was insufficient, the state would be unable to fulfill its duties. If the flow of income to the central state was too great, local elites would be unable to perform their duties as agents of the imperial state. If the tax burden was shifted to the peasantry, they might be unable to produce the surplus needed to support the state and the agrarian elite.

What raised these conflicts of interests to critical levels was the state being faced with intensified (unprecedented) military challenges from abroad by states that were relatively more powerful due to industrialization. Meeting this challenge required the monarch to extract extraordinary new levels of resources from the gentry. Where the state was more autonomous from the landed gentry—a state with a modern bureaucracy staffed by civil servants who were not members of the landed gentry—the monarch was more able to impose his will upon the gentry and enforce it with an army that was under his direct command. In Prussia, Japan, and Turkey, modernizing elites were able to achieve this "revolution from above" and thereby avoid the sort of social revolution that China, Russia, and France experienced. States that lacked the autonomy to impose modernizing policies on a recalcitrant gentry were either defeated in war with more developed powers or deposed at home by social revolutions.

Skocpol focused on three major social revolutions: Russia, France, China. In all three, externally mediated crises combined with internal structural conditions to erode the capacity of the central state's administrative machinery, generate widespread rebellion by the lower classes (especially the peasantry), and motivate dissident leaders to consolidate local rebellions into a national revolutionary movement. Should the conditions and dynamics that brought down these regimes be substantially different from those that led to civil violence in the post–World War II era? What types of regimes in the contemporary world possess the vulnerabilities that Skocpol attributed to agrarian bureaucracies and, therefore, are most susceptible to revolutionary challenge? Goodwin and Skocpol (1989, 496–500) identify "exclusionary" authoritarian regimes, especially neopatrimonial and sultanistic varieties, as the most likely to experience civil war. Wickham-Crowley (1992, 158–60) concurs, arguing that "patrimonial praetorian" regimes, or "mafiacracies," are the most vulnerable. Examples of this type of regime include the Somoza dynasty in Nicaragua, Mobutu Sese Seku in Zaire, Idi Amin in Uganda, the shah of Iran, the Noriega regime in Panama, Jean-Claude Duvalier in Haiti, Rafael Trujillo in the Dominican Republic, the Batista regime in Cuba, and the Marcos regime in the Philippines.

William Stanley (1996, 5) elaborates this notion in his model of "the protection racket state." In third world nations where export agriculture is the dominant sector of the economy, agro-export elites still need the services of the military to enforce labor-repressive agriculture. They induce the military to act in their interests by allowing the military to exercise control over the machinery of the state in return for repressing labor activism and preserving the economic dominance of the agrarian elite. Under the terms of this bargain, the military can convert the state into what amounts to a protection racket: "the military earn[s] the concession to govern the country (and pillage the state) in exchange for its willingness to use violence against class enemies of the country's relatively small but powerful economic elite" (Stanley 1996, 6–7). The military is allowed to control the machinery of the state and use it to preserve its priority claim on the state's budget, protect its institutional dominance and privileges, and enrich its officer corps. In principle, the landed elite should be willing to acquiesce in this "pillage of the state" or rent seeking behavior, up to the point that the cost to them of repression—the "rent" that they must allow the military to extract from the agro-export economy—equals the cost of acceding to the wage demands of peasants and laborers.

Goodwin (2001b, 45–50; see also Goodwin 1997, 16–21) identifies five state practices or characteristics that make certain types of regimes susceptible to revolution. First, state sponsorship or protection of unpopular economic and social arrangements makes the state itself a source of blame for grievances in the countryside. These arrangements usually include inequitable land tenure arrangements and oppressive labor conditions. This is one element in Stanley's "protection racket" bargain between the military and the state: the military uses repression to preserve the agro-export elites' control over land, and, in return, the military is allowed to use the machinery of the state to preserve its institutional perquisites.

Second, when the state excludes newly mobilized groups from access to state power or state resources, it may leave them with few alternatives beyond a direct challenge to the state's authority. Exclusionary regimes are generally intolerant of grassroots mobilization of any sort. They respond with repression to any hint of a challenge to their power, policies, or prerogatives (Goodwin and Skocpol 1989, 496). Even moderate reformers are confronted with choice of abandoning their cause or resorting to revolutionary violence. Reformers who eschew violence run the risk of becoming marginalized to the extent that their natural constituency comes to see them as hopelessly ineffectual. By default, appeals of revolutionary dissidents begin to attract more popular support (Goodwin 1997, 18).

Third, Goodwin argues that indiscriminate but not overwhelming state violence against opposition leaders tends to radicalize their grass-roots supporters. Just as leaders are radicalized by repression targeted against them, so grassroots supporters are radicalized when repression extends to include the anonymous rank-and-file supporters of opposition social movements (Mason and Krane 1989; see also Mason 2004).

Fourth, "weak policing practices and infrastructural power" of exclusionary regimes allows radicalized groups to establish security zones within the territory of the state from which they can sustain an armed challenge (Goodwin 1997, 19). Eric Wolf (1969, 290) termed this "tactical leverage": If the policing powers of the state are geographically uneven, rebels can establish bases of operations in remote regions that are relatively secure from state repression. From that base, they can attempt to outbid the state for the support of local populations by offering them benefits that the exclusionary state is either unwilling or unable to offer. Secure base areas also allow rebels to offer peasants protection from the repressive arm of the state. Neopatrimonial states are especially ineffective at policing their territory. The military itself is staffed with personnel evaluated not on the basis of their performance but on the basis of their loyalty to the dictator. Corruption and venality are endemic to neopatrimonial military establishments. Divisions within the officer corps not only exist but are often encouraged by the dictator to prevent a unified military from staging a coup (Chehabi and Linz 1998). Corruption and inefficiency are tolerated so long as the military demonstrates its loyalty to the dictator. The result is a "deprofessionalization" of the military that limits its capacity to enforce state authority throughout the nation's territory.

Finally, Goodwin contends that the corrupt and arbitrary rule of sultanistic or neopatrimonial regimes tends to alienate, weaken, or divide elite groups and external supporters who normally would share the state's interest in repressing opposition challenges. Exclusionary regimes often cannot easily defeat revolutionary movements once they come into existence because the coalition of economic elites and military leaders who support the regime under normal circumstances is likely to disintegrate in times of crisis. The turning point for the Somoza regime in Nicaragua was when Anastasio Somoza assumed control of the national reconstruction committee established in the wake of the devastating earthquake of 1972. He engaged in blatant profiteering at the expense of not only the victims of the quake but his middle-class allies as well. The result was the defection of a significant portion of the middle class, which eventually hastened the collapse of his regime (Booth 1985, 88). Neopatrimonial regimes are generally susceptible to sudden collapse due to defections by the military or the middle class at critical junctures in a struggle with an organized opposition. Signs of division within the ruling coalition are readily apparent, and they embolden the opposition to escalate its level of violence. Such divisions can encourage latent supporters of the rebels to jump on the opposition bandwagon because the associated risks are diminished by the appearance of defections among the coalition of elites that controls the state (see Snyder 1992; Bratton and Van de Walle 1994).

Empirical Studies on Civil War

In conjunction with the evolution of the theoretical schools already discussed, a stream of empirical works on civil war has emerged as well. Until recently, however, that research has been impeded to some degree by the lack of appropriate data with which to test the implications of these theories. While a number of scholars have developed data sets on civil conflict over the last 40 years, the pattern has been for individual scholars to develop their own data set customized to the particular puzzles spelled out in their theoretical works or, alternatively, to build large cross-national data sets using whatever data were readily available, which meant macroeconomic and demographic data.[3] This raised some concern with the extent to which the variables included were valid measures of the concepts specified in theories. In short, the fit between data and theory has often been less than robust.

In recent years, a number of scholars have developed new cross-sectional time-series data sets on civil wars.[4] The unit of analysis is the country-year, and most of them begin with 1946 (the first year after World War II ended). They typically include all nations that are recognized sovereign entities and have a population above some minimum threshold. Because they include all nations and not just those that experienced civil wars, these data sets allow researchers to test hypotheses on what characteristics of a nation and its environment make it more or less susceptible to the onset of civil war. Toward this end, these data sets typically include a dichotomous variable indicating whether or not a civil war began during that year. Codes for whether or not civil war was ongoing in a year (whether it began in that year or not) have been employed to model determinants of the duration of civil wars as well. We turn now to the question of the extent to which the findings from recent empirical studies provide support for the implications of each of the theoretical schools summarized earlier. Alternatively, to what extent do the findings from these studies compel us to rethink elements of those theoretical frameworks?

Deprived Actor Models

Cross-sectional time-series data sets have enabled scholars to model the conditions that make a nation more or less susceptible to civil war. Across these studies, the most consistent finding is that economic underdevelopment (measured as GDP per capita, infant mortality rate, or life expectancy) is a significant predictor of civil war onset. This finding provides support for deprived actor models of civil war: the more deprived the population of a nation is, the more likely that nation is to experience civil war. Fearon and Laitin (2003) found this relationship to be robust across various models of civil war onset, though they interpret GDP per capita as a proxy for state strength, not deprivation. They report that "$1,000 less in per capita income is associated with 41% greater annual odds of civil war onset." The poorest 10 percent of nations have an 18 percent chance of civil war breaking out in a given year, whereas the odds for the wealthiest 10 percent of nations are only 1 percent (Fearon and Laitin 2003, 83). Collier and Hoeffler (1998, 568) found similar effects for measures of poverty: the probability of civil war is substantially higher among nations with lower income per capita and with lower proportions of the population having secondary education. They found these effects to be quite robust across different estimations of their model of civil war onset (see also Collier and Hoeffler 2004, 374). They interpret low levels of GDP per capita not as a measure of deprivation but of the opportunity costs of participating in rebellion: where income and education levels are low, the payoffs from participating in political violence approach or exceed what one can expect to earn by devoting one's time to conventional legal economic activity. Noting that findings on civil war onset may be sensitive to differences in data sets, Sambanis (2004) estimated each of several models of civil war onset across multiple data sets and found that GDP per capita and population size were the only two variables that were significantly related to civil war onset across all models and all data sets. The significance levels for these variables do not change much across data sets, despite differences in coding rules across them (Sambanis 2004, 855).

Collier, Hoeffler, and Söderbom (2004, 262) also found that higher income *inequality* has a strong effect on the *duration* of civil wars: the more unequal the distribution of income in a society that experienced a civil war, the longer that war is likely to last. They interpret this in deprived actor terms: rebel recruits are drawn from the poor because the opportunity costs of participating in rebellion are lower for the poor. The higher the degree of inequality in a society, the larger the pool of poor people from which the rebels can recruit and, therefore, the higher the probability that they will succeed in mobilizing a viable rebel movement.

While there is a strong statistical relationship between measures of poverty and the probability of civil war, one could ask whether this finding in and of itself is all that surprising. What this finding amounts to is confirmation that civil war is more likely to occur in poor nations than in rich nations. That, in and of itself, is not surprising. And it is still the case that even among poor nations, most nations in most years do not experience a civil war onset. As Sambanis (2004, 855) notes, because measures of income per capita change only very slowly over time, we cannot rely on them to make accurate predictions of where and when a civil war is likely to erupt. Therefore, the more important question is, among poor nations, what characteristics make them more or less prone to experience civil war?

Rational Actor Models

Rational choice models of civil war suggest that, among poor nations, factors that influence the ability of aspiring rebels to solve the collective action problem should affect the probability of civil war onset. Recalling that Olson's (1965) solution to the collective action problem was the provision of selective incentives, Paul Collier and his colleagues at the World Bank developed the "greed" hypothesis as a counterpoint to the "grievance"-based explanations of deprived actor models. The greed thesis focuses on how rebels can and often do acquire the resources needed to provide the selective incentives necessary to recruit combatants to their movement. They hypothesized that civil wars are more likely to occur where rebels have access to "lootable" primary commodities such as gemstones or drugs. The sorts of commodities that are ideal for this purpose are those that can be produced only in limited geographic regions, both among nations and within a given nation. Gemstones can only be produced where the deposits are, and very few nations in the world—and limited regions within those nations—have exploitable deposits. Similarly, opium poppies and coca plants (from which heroin and cocaine are produced) can be grown only in certain climates, altitudes, and soil types, and this limits their production to only certain regions of a few nations.

Fortunately (for the rebels), the regions where these commodities are produced are often remote rural areas where coercive reach of the central state is often weak. To the extent that rebels can capture the flow of such goods, they can use them to generate revenues to finance their organization, including the purchase of weapons and ammunition and other supplies. These revenues also enable rebel organizations to offer cash payments to those willing to support the movement in any of several ways, including serving as a combatant. Sendero Luminoso guerrillas in Peru and FARC guerrillas in Colombia both financed their insurgency by charging "war taxes" to coca growers and smugglers. In return, they protected the growers and smugglers from police and other state agencies involved in the eradication of drug production.

This highlights another set of influences on the probability of civil war onset that have been explained in rational choice terms: geographic characteristics of a nation that make insurgency possible. These include the extent of mountainous terrain, the share of forested land, and the number of shared borders (Fearon and Laitin 2003; Collier and Hoeffler 2004). All of these factors make civil war more likely by making it possible for rebels to establish secure base camps from which to operate. Their ability to evade the state's counterinsurgency operations reduces the risk of participation and thereby makes it easier for the rebels to recruit supporters and avoid defeat. Fearon and Laitin (2003, 85) found that a nation where half of its territory is mountainous has about twice the probability of a civil war as a nation that is similar on all other predictors but does not have mountainous territory. However, neither Sambanis (2004) nor Collier and Hoeffler (2004) found any support for this effect.

The other side of the recruitment problem in the rebel's dilemma is the supply of potential recruits. For this Collier hypothesizes that the proportion of young males in the population is a proxy for the supply of potential recruits. The propensity of young males to be overly represented among rebels is well established in the literature and is also explained in rational choice terms. Young males have less to risk and more to gain from participation in rebellion. Compared to older males, young males are less likely to have family obligations, an established career, or much property that would be at risk should they be caught and punished for participating in a rebellion. Whatever costs they may suffer will be discounted over a longer remaining life span, and whatever public benefits they gain from participating in a successful revolt will compound over a longer remaining life span as well.[5]

Collier hypothesizes that within this pool of young males the availability of other income-earning opportunities will influence their willingness to join a rebellion. Thus, he argues that the relationship between low levels of GDP per capita and the probability of civil war onset in a nation is less a function of the effect of a weak economy on the level of grievances in society than on the opportunity costs of rebellion for young males: where income-earning opportunities in the legal economy are scarce, the opportunity costs of participating in rebellion are low and, therefore, young males are more likely to join. He refines this argument by proposing that where the average number of years of education among a population is low, rebellion is more likely for the same reasons: the opportunity costs of rebellion are lower the less education one has (Collier and Hoeffler 2004).

By the same token, Collier notes that this logic would also suggest that rebel movements built on "greed" are also subject to desertion for the same reasons. Recruits will stay only so long as the selective incentives are forthcoming and their value (discounted for the risks involved in earning them) exceeds the value of what one can earn in the legal economy. He notes, for instance, that during the Russian civil war (1918–21) both the Red Army of the Bolsheviks and the White army of the czarists suffered high rates of desertion among their largely peasant-based armies, and, not surprisingly, desertion rates were much higher during the summer months, when peasant soldiers had a strong economic incentive to return home for planting and harvesting seasons (Collier 2000a, 94–95).

But even this solution begs the question of how the rebels were able to build an organization capable of capturing the flow of these commodities in the first place, when they did not have any revenue flows to recruit enough combatants to capture the flow of drugs or diamonds. Lootable resources may account for how the nth rebel is induced to join the movement, but it does not account for how the rebel organization came into being to provide the selective incentives. Logically, the availability of lootable resources would seem to be more relevant to explaining the duration of civil wars, rather than their onset. Rebel organizations that have access to revenue flows from lootable resources are more able to sustain their operation than rebel organizations that do not (see Collier, Hoeffler, and Söderbom 2004).

Resource Mobilization Theories

There have been few if any direct tests of resource mobilization theories of civil war, largely because there are no readily available cross-national measures of the key concepts contained in that theory. The one area of empirical research in which scholars have explicitly incorporated direct and indirect measures of mobilization into their research designs is in models of ethnic conflict. The assumption is that shared ethnic identity provides a basis for mobilization. To the extent that a society is fragmented among multiple ethnic groups, conflict becomes more likely because grievances can be framed by dissident leaders in ethnic terms, and deprivation can be equated with ethnic discrimination. In rational choice terms, shared ethnic identity also facilitates mobilization for collective action because members of an ethnically based rebel organization can recruit more efficiently: they target their recruiting efforts only within their own ethnic group. Moreover, when ethnicity is the basis of rebel organization, it is easier to detect and sanction free riders because they can be distinguished from other members of society on the basis of ethnic markers.

The cross-sectional time-series data sets developed by Fearon and Laitin, Sambanis, Regan, Gleditsch and his colleagues, and Collier contain no direct measures of the extent of popular mobilization. Ethnicity, as a proxy for one form of mobilization, does enter their models through the measure of "ethnolinguistic fractionalization" (ELF). ELF is an index that uses the relative size of the various ethnic groups in a society to calculate the probability that two randomly chosen individuals will be from different ethnic groups; the higher a nation's ELF score, the more fragmented it is among ethnic groups.

The findings on the relationship between ethnic fractionalization and civil war are mixed and somewhat less than conclusive. Elbadawi (1999) and Reynal-Querol (2002) found that ethnically polarized societies (a special case of ethnic fragmentation) have a higher risk of suffering civil war. However, neither Fearon and Laitin (2003) nor Collier and Hoeffler (2004) found a significant relationship between the degree of ethnic fractionalization and the probability of civil war. Collier and Hoeffler did find a relationship between "ethnic dominance" and civil war, with ethnic dominance being defined as occurring where the largest ethnic group constitutes between 45 and 90 percent of the population.

Elbadawi and Sambanis (2002) found an "inverted-U" relationship between the amount of civil war and the degree of ethnic fractionalization (see also Sambanis 2001). Civil war is least likely in societies that are ethnically homogeneous (ELF approaches 0) and in those that are fragmented among a relative large number of relatively small groups (ELF approaches 1). Similarly, Collier and Hoeffler (1998) found that more highly fragmented societies are not more prone to civil war than the rest, but the danger of civil war increases with middle levels of ethnolinguistic fractionalization. They argue that coordination between groups for the purpose of rebellion is easier at lower levels of ELF (i.e., fewer ethnic groups), and it becomes more difficult as the degree of ethnic fractionalization increases (Collier and Hoeffler 1998). Implicit in this argument is the notion that shared ethnic identity facilitates coordination—that is, overcoming collective action problems—*within* ethnic groups but exacerbates coordination problems *between* ethnic groups. Rather than rely on the single measure of ethnic fractionalization, Ellingsen (2000) used the number of ethnic groups and their relative size to test this proposition more directly. She found that in societies divided among a relatively small number of relatively large groups, civil war becomes more likely than in nations that have either a large number of relatively small groups or are relatively homogeneous.

With a large number of relatively small groups, it is unlikely that any one group or coalition of groups will enjoy sufficient numerical strength to threaten hegemony over the others. In these circumstances there is little incentive for any one group to devote much of its resources to political activity beyond its own communal borders (Horowitz 1985, 37). The state is more able to accommodate the demands of one group without threatening the interests of the others. Conversely, when the number of ethnic groups is relatively small (say, two to four groups) and each group is relatively large, each ethnic group may be perceived by the other groups as a potential contender for monopoly over the machinery of the central state, either out of hegemonic ambitions of its own or out of a desire to preempt hegemony by a rival ethnic group. In these instances, an ethnic security dilemma can emerge, whereby each group arms out of fear that the others will attempt to seize control of the state through armed rebellion and subordinate them under some institutionalized system of ethnic discrimination. Their arming to prevent this generates the same fears in rival ethnic groups, and a security dilemma emerges that can spiral into civil war (Kaufman 1996; Lake and Rothchild 1996b).

More direct tests of ethnic mobilization have become possible with the data sets produced by Ted Gurr's Minorities at Risk (MAR) project. The MAR data set contains data on 284 politically active "minorities at risk" from 1945 through 2003. The latest version of MAR does contain annual measures of ethnic mobilization by both country and ethnic group. While most models of ethnically based civil wars begin with grievance arguments, empirical studies seem to support the proposition that the extent to which ethnic groups are mobilized for collective action is a stronger predictor of civil war than is the extent and depth of the grievances that motivate them. Gurr and Moore (1997) find that though ethnic rebellion may be motivated by grievances, in the absence of effective mobilization, grievances are not sufficient to bring about armed ethnic conflict. Lindström and Moore (1995) extend the argument by testing the relationship between grievances and mobilization. They find that grievances do not have a direct impact on ethnic conflict behavior. Rather, grievances affect mobilization for conflict. The implication is that if mobilization fails, then conflict may not occur, regardless of the level of grievances among ethnic minorities. Scarritt and McMillan (1995) also find little support for grievances as a predictor of violent ethnic conflict in Africa. Instead mobilization is the critical precondition to the outbreak of violent conflict.

With support for the notion that the extent of mobilization is more critical than the depth of grievances as a predictor of the outbreak of ethnic conflict, the question then becomes what factors affect the ability of ethnic groups to mobilize. Gates (2002) presents a formal model of the impact of both shared ethnic identity and geographic concentration on the ability of rebel organizations to recruit supporters. Those two factors affect the ability of rebels to deter defection and free riding. The extent to which an ethnic group is geographically concentrated has been shown to affect its ability to mobilize its members for collective action generally and for civil war specifically. Saideman and Ayres (2000, 1133) found that geographic concentration was positively related to an ethnic minority's desire for secession. Lindström and Moore (1995, 176) found that geographic concentration was related to both ethnic rebellion and protest. Ethnic groups that are concentrated in their own territorial enclave are less subject to monitoring and repression by rival ethnic groups. Geographic concentration also facilitates the monitoring and sanctioning of members who seek to free ride. Finally, if a group is concentrated in a territorial enclave, it is more able to develop the secure base camps from which to launch and sustain insurgent violence. Thus, empirical models of ethnic conflict do provide some support for the basis premise of resource mobilization theory.

State-centric Models

From Skocpol through Goldstone and Goodwin, state-centric theories of civil war suggest that certain regime types are more prone to civil war than others. As noted earlier, neopatrimonial regimes are predicted to be more prone to civil war than other regime types. The absence of direct measures of types of authoritarian regimes has meant that empirical studies that explicitly or implicitly employ state-centric concepts to inform their research design must rely on proxy measures of regime type.

Fearon and Laitin (2003) present a state-centric theory of which states are most prone to the outbreak of civil war. Echoing Goodwin's (2001b) and Snyder's (1992) characterization of the features of neopatrimonial states that make them more susceptible to civil war, Fearon and Laitin (2003, 75–76) hypothesize that "financially, organizationally, and politically weak central governments render insurgency more feasible and attractive due to weak local policing or inept and corrupt counterinsurgency practices." Echoing Mason and Krane's (1989) arguments about the relationship between repression and support for revolution, they add that "a propensity for brutal and indiscriminate retaliation that helps drive noncombatants into rebel forces" also contributes to the susceptibility of weak states to insurgency. However, the measure of state strength they employ is GDP per capita, which they depict as a measure of "state capacity" in terms of the financial, administrative, police, and military capacity of the state, as well as the extent of infrastructure development that would allow the state to extend its authority throughout the territory and thereby preempt the emergence of insurgent movements. And, as noted earlier, they find a strong relationship between low levels of economic development (GDP per capita) and the probability of civil war in a nation. They also find that the prevalence of mountainous terrain and other physical conditions that favors insurgency create the opportunity for insurgency to emerge, and that these determinants of opportunity have more explanatory power than the extent and depth of grievances in society.

An implication of the proposition that weak authoritarian regimes are more susceptible to civil war is the "domestic democratic peace" proposition: democracies should be relatively immune to civil war. Indeed, Goodwin goes so far as to assert that "no popular revolutionary movement, it bears emphasizing, has ever overthrown a consolidated democratic regime" (Goodwin 2001a, 276; emphasis removed). Several studies have tested this hypothesis employing variations of the Polity democracy-autocracy scale. This scale ranges from –10 (the most autocratic) to 10 (the most democratic), with scores of 7 or more usually treated as full democracies, scores of –7 or less as fully autocratic, and scores between –6 and 6 inclusive constituting a category of "weakly authoritarian" regimes or "anocracies." At one end of the inverted U, democracies should be less likely to experience internal conflict because in a democracy, civil war is not necessary (Krain and Meyers 1997; Hegre et al. 2001; Henderson and Singer 2000). Opposition groups are free to organize for peaceful collective action and to seek redress of their grievances through electoral mechanisms. They are free to organize for collective action to express their preferences without fear of state repression. Elections provide state officials with incentives to accommodate the demands of organized groups through policy reforms. The imperatives of electoral politics also provide them with incentives to eschew repression because repression can be costly at the polls. At the other end of the inverted U, highly autocratic regimes should also be less likely to experience civil war because autocratic states possess the overwhelming coercive capacity to repress opposition groups preemptively and intimidate citizens into political quiescence. In the middle of the inverted U, weak authoritarian regimes or anocracies lack both the democratic institutions to defuse opposition violence and the coercive capacity to repress it preemptively.

Findings on the democracy–civil war link are mixed. Both Fearon and Laitin (2003) and Collier and Hoeffler (2004) found no significant relationship between measures of democracy and the probability of civil war onset. Krain and Myers (1997) and Henderson and Singer (2000) found support for the proposition that democracies are less likely to experience civil war. Hegre and his coauthors (Hegre et al. 2001) found support for the inverted-U relationship: full democracies and autocracies are less likely than anocracies to experience civil war. They carried the analysis one critical step further and examined whether *change* in the level of democracy is implicated in the onset of civil war. The logic behind this proposition is that new, unconsolidated democracies are fragile and unstable and, therefore, may lack the institutional means to contain dissent within conventional channels of participation. They found that, indeed, both full autocracies and full democracies were more likely to survive than "semidemocracies" or weakly authoritarian regimes. The also found that the risk of civil war is increased with regime change: nations that are still undergoing (or more recently underwent) the transition to democracy (or the transition from democracy to a more authoritarian regime) are more likely to experience civil war.

Conclusions

This survey of the major theoretical schools has served as a guide to assess recent empirical findings to determine whether they support elements of each of these schools. The fit between empirical findings and theoretical frameworks is limited to some degree by the availability of data, and that is not a problem easily (or cheaply) addressed, especially for data sets on over 150 nations for 60 years. Given that, what do we know about where and when civil wars occur? Do these findings fit with our theories of why they occur? And do these findings, interpreted through the lenses of the theoretical schools that have evolved, lead us to any insights that might be of interest or use to policymakers?

The most consistent finding is that civil wars are more likely to occur in poor nations: the negative relationship between GDP per capita and the probability of civil war onset is perhaps the most robust single relationship across studies. This provides some support for grievance-based models of civil war onset: where more people suffer from deeper levels of poverty, grievances are likely to be more widespread and more deeply felt, and it is in such environments that civil wars are most likely to occur. As noted earlier, this same finding has been interpreted in rational choice terms as well: increases in income per capita raise the opportunity costs of participation and, therefore, make civil war less likely to occur. Thus, one policy implication of this finding is that economic development should be make nations less susceptible to civil war.

However, even among poor nations, civil war onset is still a rare event. For instance, Fearon and Laitin (2003, 77) report that new civil wars broke out in only 127 out of the total of 6,610 nation-years in their data set. Therefore, we must ask ourselves, among poor nations, what factors make civil war less likely? One other set of hypotheses from state-centric theories is the domestic democratic peace proposition: civil war is less likely to occur in democracies than in nondemocracies. The findings on this hypotheses are decidedly mixed. And it appears that new democracies are vulnerable to failure and to civil war onset for some time after making the transition. Nor, for that matter, is it clear that the transition to democracy is itself a cure for an ongoing civil war: the Philippines, Colombia, Peru, El Salvador, and others all installed nominally democratic institutions while a civil war was under way, and in none of those cases did the initiation of democracy bring about the prompt termination of the civil war. However, there is enough evidence from enough studies to lead us to conclude that even poor nations that adopt democratic institutions become less likely to experience a civil war, and the probability of civil war declines with each year that democracy persists and becomes more consolidated.

Among poor nondemocracies, other indicators of state weakness also find mixed support as predictors of civil war, including physical geography that makes it easier for rebels to establish bases of operation that are relatively secure from the repressive arm of the state, and the availability of lootable resources with which to sustain the rebel organization. One dimension of state weakness that arguably deserves more attention is the tendency of weak states to respond to opposition movements with repression, in part because such states lack the institutional capacity or revenues to respond with policy reforms that address the grievances of organized groups.

Finally, with respect to resource mobilization theory, there is some support for the proposition that ethnic divisions do affect the probability of civil war, although specifying just what configurations of ethnic divisions affect the onset of civil war is still the subject of debate. Ethnicity does serve as a powerful basis for mobilizing people for collective action, and divisions in society that are grounded in ethnic and religious identity are not as easily resolved through negotiations or through the sort of policy compromises for which democracy is supposed to be effective because, as Roy Licklider (1995) put it, the stakes in such disputes are not divisible in the same way that conflicts over the distribution of wealth, income, land, or political office are.

Finally, the further development of the social science of civil war research—and the development of a body of research that is of some use to policymakers—may be enhanced by, first, framing empirical studies more clearly and explicitly in terms of the theoretical schools that have provided us with a rich body of hypotheses. Andrew Mack (2002) wisely counsels that a truly cumulative body of findings will not emerge until researchers come to some agreement on a common data set, at least an agreed-upon set of civil wars with their starting and ending dates. And, he further argues, our findings will not be of use to policymakers unless social scientists make a greater effort to present their findings to the policy community in terms that are comprehensible to them.

NOTES

1. For a discussion of the criteria used in different data sets to determine which conflicts to include and how to determine their starting and ending dates (as well as the merits and demerits of the different criteria employed in different data sets), see Sambanis (2004).

2. On genocides and politicides, see Harff and Gurr (1988, 1998) and Harff (2003).

3. See, for instance, Hibbs (1973), Bwy (1968), Feierabend and Feierabend (1966, 1972), and Gurr (1968).

4. Fearon and Laitin (2003) and Sambanis (2004) have developed their own separate data sets to test models of civil war onset and duration. Regan (2000) uses less stringent inclusion criteria in his and adds variables on external intervention in civil wars. The Armed Conflict Dataset (Gleditsch et al. 2002) also includes conflicts that cause as few as 25 deaths in a year. The Correlates of War does not provide the civil war data set in a cross-sectional time-series format. However, others have built its conflict codes into such data sets. Collier and Hoeffler (1998, 2004) use Correlates of War conflicts in their studies.

5. It should be noted that women have participated in large numbers in several civil wars over the last 30 years, and not just in support roles but as regular combatants. This was especially the case in the Sandinista revolution in Nicaragua, and the Salvadoran revolution. On this subject, see Reif (1986), Mason (1992), and Gonzalez-Perez (2006).

Internal Wars over the State: Rational Choice Institutionalism and Contentious Politics

MARK IRVING LICHBACH

Alexis de Tocqueville's *The Old Régime and the French Revolution* is the classic study of state building and internal war. Over the centuries, Tocqueville shows, French monarchs centralized institutions (administrative structure, feudal apparatus, war-making machine, and ecclesiastical governance) that eventually propelled all of French civil society (clergy, nobility, bourgeoisie, peasants, and sansculottes) to mobilization and organization, violence and revolution. Isser Woloch's *The New Regime: Transformations of the French Civic Order, 1789–1820* is the classic successor to Tocqueville. Woloch shows that the French Revolution produced new frameworks of collective political life—national governments, local communes, tax collectors, elections, political clubs, newspapers, courts, juries, prisons, police, military, militias, national guards, schools, churches, poor relief, and public works—that were sources of the popular revolts of subsequent generations of French. State building thus meets internal war at the interstices of state and society—the practices, values, policies, and institutions of civic order.

Disputes within political society over state building are a critical part of world politics. Democrats, fascists, communists, and Islamists, for example, battle over foreign policies (war and peace, autarky and trade) and fight about domestic policies (regime predation and public welfare, dictatorship and democracy). Contention over paths of development affects interstate relations. Wars between democratic and fascist states and crises between democratic and communist states were in part ideological struggles over modernity. Contention over development also affects transnational relations and the structures of global governance. The growth of multinational corporations and the development of global civil society generate struggles over the direction of the modern world, for example, global protests against war and free trade (Lichbach and DeVries 2007). Since internal wars over grand strategies of state building produce powerful sovereign states in some places and Hobbesian struggles in others, contention influences the types of states that prevail in particular historical eras. In sum, state-building struggles affect intrastate, interstate, and transnational relations.

This chapter probes how such disputes shape intrastate relations. To paraphrase Charles Tilly (1975, 42), internal war made the state and the state made internal war. Contention over development affects domestic actors and their associated interests, ideas, and organizations. Development conflicts create domestic political demands, define collective claim making, constitute domestic dissent, and construct patterns of domestic politics. The results include social movements, protests, strikes, riots, terrorism, coups, guerrilla insurgencies, state repression, genocide, ethnic nationalism, civil war, and revolution. As the French case shows, domestic battles over state building can entail more than disputes about today's decision-making processes and tomorrow's allocation strategies—"who gets what, when, and where" (Laswell 1950). Institutions are long-run patterns of authority over peoples and territories that undergird resource extraction (taxes and conscription) and societal regulation (laws and rules). They create power, or "the ability to get someone to do something they wouldn't otherwise do" (Dahl 1957). Students of comparative politics are thus interested in these structures of domestic governance because they are the objects of power struggles about paths of development. Comparativists thus study violently contentious politics as the perpetual bargaining in a state over the "legitimate monopoly of coercion" (Weber 1968) and "the authoritative allocation of scarce values" (Easton 1953).

From the 1960s onward, social scientific studies of internal war have been based on "event counts" (Gurr and Lichbach 1979; Gurr 1981, 1986). For each country in a data set, conflict events gathered from newspapers and other sources are aggregated by time—by days, weeks, months, or quarters or by 1-, 5-, or 10-year periods. Recent civil war studies, for example, assume that the key "event" is a death and aggregate all conflict events into a body count. If during a single year the number of deaths passes some threshold—1,000, 500, or 25—the strife in the country is called a "civil war." Event-count data are used to test variable-based arguments of the following form: the greater the X in a country/period, the greater the likelihood of conflict in that country/period. Researchers have employed as their dependent variables the extent, intensity, temporal duration, and geographic scope of conflict; they have also used the onset and termination of major conflicts such as a civil war. Independent variables that have appeared include democracy, GNP, state strength, and the character of economic, social, and political cleavages.

Country-level event-count studies narrowly focus on the frequency of compliance with law or on the observation of state breakdown. Tilly (2006a, 122) explains the consequences of overemphasizing the behavioral dimensions of protest and rebellion:

> Some simply lump together all violent encounters—or at least all encounters above a certain scale—into general measures of total damage and death. . . . If we were simply asking where and when the risk of death and destruction rises, that approach would serve us reasonably well. But it would not help us sort out interactions among regimes, repertoires, opportunity structures, and collective violence. It says too little about the what and why of the phenomena we are trying to explain.

In other words, a focus on country-level event counts elides questions of meaningful action and does not take structured contexts and strategic organizations into consideration. Such studies rely on essentially static correlations of variables and, therefore, have paid insufficient attention to the dynamic mechanisms and processes behind institutionalized episodes of peace and conflict. For example, country-level event-count studies have difficulty explaining the phenomenon of zones of peace coexisting with zones of war or of conflict-breeds-conflict institutional equilibria coexisting with peace-breeds-peace equilibria.

The statistical literature on state building and internal wars correspondingly depicts institutions as independent variables and conflicts as dependent variables. Some have explored how various types of democratic institutions—presidential or parliamentary governments, centralized or federal or partitioned nations, majoritarian or consensus systems, and laissez-faire or welfare states—affect contention (Powell 1982). Others have studied how various types of autocratic institutions—colonialism, serfdom, neopatrimonialism, rentier states, monarchies, military regimes, and apartheid—fashion protest and rebellion (Goodwin 2001b; Foran 2005). Still others have wondered how well incoherent, mixed, or hybrid polities perform (Brownlee 2007, 25–26). The purpose here is to find good institutions, that is, the specific kinds or types, properties or aspects of regimes that have favorable consequences. While this research is part of a larger literature that examines how domestic institutions affect grand strategies of domestic and foreign policy, and consequently international peace, economic growth, and domestic tranquility (Bueno de Mesquita et al. 2003), these statistical studies rarely connect to another set of statistical analyses that examines how internal wars produce democratic and autocratic institutions (Przeworski et al. 2000). Researchers, though, have advanced many important causal hypotheses. The GNP-democracy, inequality-democracy, and oil-democracy relationships are three examples. In the statistical literature, in short, institutions are causes or consequences of conflict but usually not both.

Tocqueville and Woloch think about these issues differently. Taking a more dynamic view of state building and contentious politics, they believe that institutions create conflicts and conflicts create institutions. A more theoretical, even philosophical, literature indeed searches for well-functioning and high-performing structures of governance, or the deep institutional features of civic order—the interstice of state building and societal action—that create patterns of conflict and structures of conflict resolution. There is a long tradition of studying the covariance and co-evolution of institutions and conflicts. It extends from Plato and Aristotle to Montesquieu and Machiavelli to Hobbes, Locke, and Rousseau to Marx and Weber to Hamilton, Jay, and Madison to Easton and Almond and Powell to Linz, Eckstein and Gurr, and Huntington to Moore and Skocpol and to Lijphart and Horowitz. Political orders indeed consist of the stability and instability (mobilization and organization, violence and revolution) that characterize the emergence and onset of internal wars, their conduct and termination, and postwar recovery and stabilization.

In recent years, rational choice institutionalism and associated ideas about the bargaining theory of war have developed this richer perspective. Challenging the behavioralist assumptions of country-level event-data studies and of institutions-as-causes theories, prominent rational choice institutionalists, for example those listed in table 1, have turned their attention to internal war. *These rational choice institutionalists study how equilibrium institutions or institutional equilibrium result from the bargaining behavior of governmental and nongovernmental actors and, in turn, how the outcomes of state-society bargaining affect identities, preferences, beliefs, resources, incentives, and strategies.* How is the concept or idea of equilibrium institutions/institutional equilibria used by rational choice institutionalists to study state building and internal war? How does the idea function in practical inquiry? What does it do, what is its purpose, and what is its meaning and significance?

The idea of equilibrium institutions or institutional equilibria permits the development of more structural and strategic theories of state building and internal war. Rebels and states face cooperating, coordinating, and contracting problems. Rebel's dilemmas involve mobilizing several internal, transnational, and foreign constituencies as sympathizers, allies, and patrons. State's dilemmas involve mobilizing bureaucrats, middle-level politicians, and militaries. Rebel-state dilemmas involve both sets of actors bargaining over state building. Since regimes and oppositions have

TABLE 1. Selected Rational Choice Institutionalists and Internal War

Author	Topic
Robert Bates	Global order, states, development, and violence
Daron Acemoglu and James Robinson	Economic origins of dictatorship and democracy
Carles Boix	Economic redistribution and political democracy
Bruce Bueno de Mesquita, Alastair Smith, Randolph M. Siverson, and James D. Morrow	Political coalitions and political instability
James Fearon	Commitment problems and ethnic conflict
Barbara Geddes	Factions within personalistic dictatorships
Avner Greif	Social institutions and peace and prosperity
Mikhail Filippov, Peter C. Ordeshook, and Olga Shvetsova	Ethnic secessionism and self-sustaining federalism
Pauline Jones Luong	Transitional bargaining in post-Soviet Central Asia
Ellen Lust-Okar	Regime's manipulation of opponents in the Middle East
Margaret Levi	Rule and revenue
Beatriz Magaloni	Hegemonic party survival in Mexico
Douglass North	Institutions and economic performance in history
Adam Przeworski	Political and economic reforms
William Riker	Collective choice and the American Civil War
Norman Schofield	Collective choice and social upheavals
Barbara Walter	Credible commitment and civil war
Barry Weingast	Self-enforcing democracy

overlapping and nonoverlapping contracting problems, the result is intra-group conflict and group factions, as well as cross-group alliances and rainbow coalitions. Rational choice institutionalism—and the associated bargaining theory of war—thus explores how states and rebels seek to advance their interests by engaging a variety of actors in long-term group-constituency and state-constituency relationships. Cooperative solutions to contracting problems are contingent on mechanisms becoming embedded in human-made institutions. Markets, communities, contracts, and hierarchies are thus oft-mentioned categories of institutions that affect bargaining within and between state builders and their opponents.

A simple game-tree setup allows rational choice institutionalists to explore contentious politics as state-group bargaining over state building. As indicated in section 1, the game tree follows a state-group dyad through five stages or phases of contention. Time t_0 involves an initial state institution or pattern of state authority. In the first or onset stage, the state chooses whether or not to discipline some portion of its population with a state-building strategy. In the second or dispute phase, the group responds to the state's threat. In the third or escalation stage, the state responds to the group, choosing between accommodative and repressive conflict-management strategies. The group decides on its counterresponses in the final, or negotiation, stage. The outcome of the game is an equilibrium institution or institutional equilibrium.

Since these are bountiful ideas, we need to put some bounds on this chapter. Not all rational choice models of state building and internal wars are directly in the rational choice institutional tradition. Earlier work on the rebel's dilemma, which focused on the dissidents' collective action problems (Lichbach 1995), is not reviewed. I also do not review the work of rationalists who ignore institutions (Enders and Sandler 2006; Wintrobe 2006). Rational choice institutionalists have explored dozens of types of situations, mechanisms, and models: blocking coalitions, tipping points, tit-for-tat, incomplete information, signaling, credible commitments, selective incentives, minimum winning coalitions, prisoner's dilemmas, public goods, Coase bargaining, veto points, moral hazard, adverse selection, shirking, incomplete contracts, transaction costs, principal-agent relations, and monitoring costs. Since these nuts and bolts can be gleaned from textbooks on game theory, they also are not reviewed here. Rational choice institutionalists have used their models to advance many causal propositions. Exploring statistical analyses of the reciprocal relationships between inequality-democracy, development-democracy, and natural resource–autocracy would take us far afield, and hence institutional etiology will also not be explored here. Since joining micro- and mesotheories of bargaining to macrostatistical results is a major gap in the literature—related puzzles plague a union of micro- and macroeconomics—a sister chapter is much needed. Finally, reviewing the works in table 1 seriatim, or comparing and contrasting specific works, would not focus on our central concern—ideas about equilibrium institutions and institutional equilibria. This chapter therefore mines the texts for working insights into our core themes.

Section 2 explains how rational choice institutionalists view cooperative and conflictual interactions. I study the many ideas the approach offers about dyadic peace and conflict processes and about paths of war and peace. The principal concern, however, is rational choice institutionalist arguments about cooperative and conflictual institutions. In section 3 equilibria of the game tree are studied as mechanisms of conflict resolution that undergird political institutionalization and stability: social contracts and political compromises about power, stable balances of power, and good and bad power traps. Section 4 shows how multiple equilibria offer insights into institutional conflict and change that result from shifts in bargaining power, contention over good equilibria, and incongruent institutional spheres of power. In section 5 equilibria are studied from institutional design perspectives: containing power, controlling violence, and institutionalizing conflict-resolution procedures.

Interactions and institutions are studied by other general approaches to peace and conflict processes. Section 6 shows that historical studies by institutionalists, for example, Collier and Collier's work on the inclusion of the Left in Latin American politics, have also drawn on the Tocqueville-Woloch tradition and explored structures of power, patterns of authority, and iron cages of social control. Historical institutionalists remind us that institutions are more than black boxes transmitting popular demands and rebel grievances to politicians. Following Huntington's original insights into mobilization and institutionalization, that is, into popular agitation and state construction, institutions are sites of power and contention. Institutional dynamics—construction, maintenance, adaptation, and breakdown—are thus central to conflict dynamics.

Why have rational choice institutionalists and historical institutionalists converged on so many points? The final section explains that country-level event-count models, which share many of the difficulties of variable-based analyses (Lichbach 2009), do not adequately capture internal war's inherency or its multiple equilibria. The field of conflict studies has moved from behavior to process and finally to institutions—from rebellious repertoires to contentious collectivities and then to structured systems of power. The reciprocal relationship between institutions and conflict will define the work on contentious politics for decades to come. The field will increasingly take on the character of a neoinstitutional theory that produces comparative and historical studies of peaceful and conflictual state building, policy-making, and citizenship rights. By embedding pure theories of protest and repression in historically defined trajectories of political authority, the field will move closer to the mainstream of comparative politics. Such comparative and historical studies, by contrast, will place contentious politics at the center of inquiry. The world-historical context of rebel's dilemmas and state's dilemmas involve the internal wars over the state that have always been the globe's dilemma.

1. State Building and Internal War: The Basic Game Tree

Acemoglu and Robinson (2006) explain why a nondemocratic elite engaged in state building would ever democratize its country. Since a minority elite and a majority of citizens have different material interests, they seek different institutions for allocating political power and ultimately resources. While the elite prefers the allocations under dictatorship, the majority prefers the allocations under democracy. The majority, however, can threaten the elite's dictatorship with protest, rebellion, and revolution. The elite cannot contain instability with short-term policy concessions: because citizens know that the dictatorial elite will withdraw its concessions after the instability subsides, such quick fixes lack credibility. To contain the majority, the elite can employ repression but at a cost to its interests. Democracy thus emerges as a state-building compromise: less costly to elites than repression, democratic institutions offer the majority a credible commitment to redistribution. If elites do not have the incentives to mount a coup against it, democracy can consolidate.

Figure 1 illustrates a general sequence of steps behind Acemoglu and Robinson's rational choice institutionalist approach to equilibrium institutions or institutional equilibria. Contentious politics over state building and internal war, understood as transacting, contracting, and bargaining within and between regimes and oppositions, is divided into five stages.

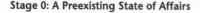
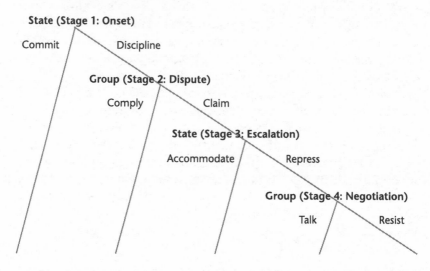

Fig. 1. State building: Stages 0, 1, 2, 3, and 4 of peace and conflict processes

Stage 0: A Preexisting State of Affairs

Rather than beginning with a state of nature or anarchy and assessing how spontaneous order emerges, rationalist thought works best when it grapples with a concrete situation. We thus begin with a regime or authority that imposes rules to which people more or less consent. With respect to the principal areas of state building—war/peace, autarky/trade, predation/welfare, and dictatorship/democracy—some bargain or settlement exists at time t_0. In other words, a certain political equilibrium is operating between state and society.

Stage 1, Onset: State Chooses to Commit or Discipline

Stage 1 depicts the onset or emergence of contention in this political order. While some begin with a group challenging the status quo imposed by the state, here we begin with the state as the agent of state building and hence of political change. We thus think of the first stage as occurring when the state upsets the balance or equilibria at time t_0 and puts the political order at risk. By initiating a new claim on a particular group—

whether citizens, armed militias, religious authorities, bourgeoisie, towns, regions, nobility, peasants, ethnic communities, tribes, social movements, or women—state action or statecraft starts the ball rolling. The state thus chooses between disciplining the group, presumably for some state-building purpose, and remaining committed to the status quo. It thereby initiates the flow of peace and conflict processes.

Commitment is the continuation of the current policy regime or model of state building. The policy can privilege or empower certain groups with a mixture of private and public goods: limited taxes, delegation of administrative control, provision of property rights, or limitations on the acquisition of resources. *Discipline,* by contrast, involves the state's imposition of new demands or claims that threaten the group. More than informal control, the new policy regime regulates, procures, and extracts (material) resources. States choose grand strategies or paths of development that affect many aspects of the welfare of civil society. Specific public policies include

occupying foreign territory (e.g., intervention opposed by nationalists of another state);

opening or closing the country to free trade (e.g., a globalizing regime coalition facing a protectionist one);

discriminating against ethnic or religious groups (e.g., against an Islamic political party);

employing violence against workers and labor unions;

consolidating territory via the imposition of a unitary state opposed by separatists;

disarming civil society (e.g., the state targets armed militias or paramilitary organizations that have been involved in guerrilla wars, civil wars, or lower-level armed conflicts);

seizing power from democratic political parties that won elections; and

installing democracy and thereby threatening nondemocrats opposed to regime change.

The imposition of these new forms of state discipline shocks the current status quo and may have been a result of government response strategies to historical patterns of civil disorder. The government-led changes demonstrate that the state failed to keep the contract established at time t_0. The possibility of shirking or reneging on group privileges recalls Acemoglu and Robinson's concerns about the ex post enforceability of or credible commitment to political concessions.

Stage 2, Dispute: Group Chooses to Comply or Claim

After the state imposes new discipline on a group, the group reacts. Its choices in stage 2 determine the remainder of the game.

The target group could accept the state's new demand or threat and *comply.* Even at the cost of providing the additional resources demanded by the state, the group could consent to the state's new policies and its new model of state building. Acceptance of new controls by the regime, perhaps because the group is unable to mobilize its members, legitimizes a new status quo. Or the target group could reject the new demands or threats imposed by the state, solve its collective action problem, and challenge the state with a collective *claim* about its grievances.

It is useful to distinguish different types and properties of challenging groups.

When insurgents are carrier groups holding alternative visions or programs for state building (e.g., democracy, communism, fascism, political Islam), state-group disputes are the fundamental conflicts providing the contingency—and not teleology—of policies and regimes. When insurgents merely react against state intrusions, state-group disputes are more narrowly focused on group prerogatives.

In the course of either type of state-group dispute, groups develop victimization narratives about suffering from oppression and humiliation. Stories of emancipation from wickedness and inhumanity abound. Groups thus claim that they are disempowered, suppressed, marginalized, and excluded by the state's new policy.

The group could then challenge the state, choosing between the fuzzy boundaries of legal and illegal participation, interest-group politics and social movements, and pluralist politics and extremist politics.

In doing so, the group determines the conduct of its challenge: the extent, intensity, and geographic scope of its tactics; the breadth of its organization; and the radicalness of its goals. The challenge, for example, could involve a particular protest event, short-term episode, or an extended campaign.

Regardless of the nature of its challenge, the group's calculus of response is forward-looking, concerned about the success of its actions. What sorts of new benefits can be expected? Will substantive policies or procedural institutions be altered? Will favorable formal or informal legislative, executive, or judicial outcomes be achieved? Can the group gain, for example, certification as the spokesperson for the group and, as the legitimate representative of a constituency, win a seat alongside the state at the bargaining table?

Aiming to shape the policy pursued by government in the next stage, group collective action takes account of the regime's collective choice mechanisms and political processes. Challenging the state means signaling seriousness, or demonstrating to the structure of political opportunities the breadth and depth of public support for an issue. A challenge conveys information to the regime about the intensity of group preferences and about its potential to mobilize large numbers of people behind a cause. Protest functions like a direct referendum of public opinion.

Social scientists ask theoretical questions about the protest-policy nexus or about the impact of protest on policy. Do movements and protests matter for the outcomes of politics? Are citizen activists, grassroots public advocacy campaigns, and internal wars marginal to the policy process, or do protests and demonstrations and the challenging groups that mobilize them make a difference in public policies? The answers to these quite practical questions come in the next stage.

Stage 3, Escalation: State Chooses to Accommodate or Repress

If the group accepts the new status quo, there is no dispute and the state need not respond. If, however, the group chooses to challenge the state, the dispute enters a pivotal stage of crisis management. At this point, the state acts again, and its responses affect the outcome of the dispute as well as the prospects for postwar recovery and stabilization.

The state's response strategy is often called counterinsurgency, counterterrorism, or riot control. During state building, leaders adopt ruling strategies to sustain the nation, state, regime, or government. While different public-good perspectives on state behavior have been advanced, many now argue that patterns of state building often result from state leaders' efforts to survive in office. Incumbents fend off challenges from internal and external sources—from resistance and war.

What survival strategies are available? Aiming to stay in power so as

to continue to receive the benefits of office, the authorities' most fundamental decision is whether or not to escalate the dispute. The state could
make concessions to the group's grievances, nonviolently address the
group's demands, and hence back down from its threat issued in stage 1.
Accommodating the group's grievances and claims can involve short-
term policy changes. Accommodationist regimes can also commit to
long-run change by co-opting dissidents and facilitating the mobilization of groups. Following Acemoglu and Robinson, we can think of this
sort of accommodation as a structural movement toward more democratic rule. Competitive elections, political parties, and interest groups
are part of an institutional complex that allows groups and movements
to solve their collective action problems and thereby accommodate their
issue concerns. Alternatively, the state could escalate the dispute with a
military response. It could use force and fight the group with *repression*,
attempting to suppress the challenge to state authority violently. Many
strategies that suppress or demobilize dissidents are available. In criminology, for example, fixing broken windows is often seen as a deterrent
to major crimes.

Stage 4, Negotiation: Group Chooses to Resist or Talk

If the state's second choice involves the use of force, the group faces a
more repressive regime and must make its second choice. Its decisions affect the outcome of the game.

The group could decide to *talk* with the state in order to settle the matter. There are a variety of domestic, transnational, and international
peace processes that could be invoked, including direct negotiations and
indirectly brokered talks. Some bargaining between the state and the dissidents, for example, will be formal. Specific negotiations to end conflicts
occurred, for example, in Birmingham, Alabama, in the United States, as
well as in Nicaragua, El Salvador, and Vietnam. Direct negotiations between the state and the dissidents have also occurred during such political crises as a hostage-taking or a siege. Some terrorists wish to negotiate
on issues and eventually compromise with authorities.

While talking is one possibility, the group could decide instead to *resist* the state. Fighting involves an escalation of the menu of choices discussed in stage 2. Protest, for example, can turn into terrorism, or riots
can become armed insurgency.

Repetition of the Stages

Whether a group negotiates or fights, the outcome is a new situation, a new time t_0. The state then again faces its choice at time t_1: commit to the status quo reached at the end of the game or impose a new status quo consisting of a new disciplinary policy regime. For example, negotiations might lead to a new status quo—a pattern of accommodation that brings the group into the state's decision-making apparatus. Alternatively, fighting could ultimately lead the state to impose additional demands on the group or to make new threats to its existence. States and groups, regimes and oppositions, are forever negotiating and fighting over the government's patterns of accommodating and repressing collective claims against state building.

In short, after the stages have occurred, we think of the game tree as repeating itself. Sequences of regulate-retaliate-repress-resist or confiscate-challenge-coerce-compromise constitute the crises and struggles, collapses and reconstructions, of state building and internal war.

2. Interpreting the Basic Game Tree: Peace and Conflict Mechanisms

By parsing the vortex of contentious events, this highly stylized game tree can yield rich interpretations and applications. For example, if different state actors choose at stages 1 and 3, and if different group actors choose at stages 2 and 4, the framework encompasses the collective action problems of regime and opposition or the rebel's dilemma and the state's dilemma (Lichbach 1995). In a related example, Lust-Okar (2005) develops the idea that political conflict in the Arab world is a result of the "structure of contention," or institutional rules regulating oppositions. Whether an authoritarian regime allows all groups to participate legally (a unified structure) or allows some to participate while excluding others (a divided structure) influences incumbent strategies, opposition strategies, incumbent-opposition dynamics, and ultimately regime change or liberalization. More generally, the rational choice institutional approach to equilibrium institutions and institutional equilibria tells us about dyadic peace and conflict processes and about the paths to war and peace. What we find is very different from what we find when we couple event-count studies to studies of institutions as independent variables.

Dyadic Peace and Conflict Processes

We begin by discussing conflict dyads and campaigns, then turn to the multiple, evolving, and interacting repertoires of the state and the group, and finally explore multiple dyads.

Conflict dyad: specific groups and targets. To those who count events, contention is systemic and therefore measured as the total amount of national-level instability, violence, or disorder in a country. Alternatively, contention involves regime versus opposition activities and is measured as the total level of government violence (repression) and the total level of dissident violence (protest and rebellion).

The collective action approach is critical of this type of evidence and its associated ideas. In *Rebel's Dilemma,* I argued that the total amount of contention in a country-period is "unstable and unpredictable," and I highlighted our "inability to predict aggregate levels and particular outbreaks of collective dissent" (Lichbach 1995, 289). Researchers should not aggregate all protest and rebellion in a country and ask "why *all* people rebel" or "why *all* dissident groups mobilize" into, say, a civil war.

The rational choice institutionalist approach to state building also focuses on specific challengers and targets or specific governments and opposition groups. In other words, it studies the group and explores its dynamic interactions with the state: "Which of the many plausible rival solutions to the [collective action] problem actually did the work of mobilizing or demobilizing a *particular* set of dissidents?" (Lichbach 1995, 293). Rationalists thus link conflict events to specific groups and states in a conflict dyad and study which strategies and tactics, including solutions to the collective action problem, are adopted. With this information in hand, they investigate peace and conflict processes, for example, negotiation and escalation.

In sum, rational choice institutionalists replace the event-count perspective with the idea that particular actors interact and thereby produce trajectories of mobilization and countermobilization that manifest themselves in various forms of contention. The concern then becomes dissident activity by group 1, by group 2, and so on.

Campaigns: enduring regime-opposition group rivalries. By focusing on event counts, researchers may fail to see the larger pattern of conflict, for example, interrelated terrorist attacks by the same or aligned groups. Repeated terrorist attacks that coalesce around broader terrorist campaigns are the threats that really concern regimes. Thinking of contention in terms of extended opposition-group campaigns focuses attention on interactions over time: which conditions enable terrorist groups to sustain their operations, and which conditions force them to abandon their campaigns? While groups engage in repeated events linked to ongoing campaigns, states also choose particular response strategies that are part of long-term policy regimes. For example, they engage in campaigns of repression and long-term strategies of accommodation.

Conflict dyads are thus involved in more than one-shot interactions. State-group dyads involve protracted processes of negotiation and escalation. The interactions of dissident campaigns and regime responses produce the peace and conflict trajectories that structure state-group relations. When researchers think in terms of a conflict dyad of group X and state Y, their explanatory variables capture peace and conflict processes within that dyad.

Repertoires: multiple strategies. Researchers who work in the event-count tradition typically aggregate all conflict, say terrorism, in a country and ask, "Why terrorism?" However, our dependent variables should involve more than a group's on/off choice of one particular strategy. Since groups have repertoires of actions, terrorism is but one observable tactic employed against state adversaries. To understand the etiology of terrorism, researchers therefore must study the variety of nonterrorist strategies. To do so, they should compare terrorist groups with base or reference nonterrorist groups.

States also make choices. Researchers therefore want to know the broad range of responses—both political and military—of governments to terrorists attacks. Counterterrorism strategies, to continue the example, show considerable variety in accommodative and repressive approaches. This variance must be explained as well.

An old joke asks, "Who discovered water?" The reply is, "I don't know, but it wasn't a fish." Researchers concerned with one particular form of dissent, for example, terrorism, should collect data on the full range of actions taken by both parties in a conflict dyad.

Repertoires: evolving strategies. In traditional event-count studies, the escalation of conflict is of great importance. Indeed, the concern follows mechanically from such studies: since X leads to conflict, as X increases from time t to time $t + 1$, conflict increases from time t to time $t + 1$. A change in X thus produces conflict escalation or de-escalation. Traditional event-count studies, moreover, focus on the static interrelationship of such forms of conflict as social movements, terrorism, genocide, civil war, and regime change. There is also much work correlating the extent and intensity of protest and rebellion—conceived as continuous variables that aggregate events over some period of time in a geographic locale, for example, a country-year.

Strangely, these two concerns have not been linked. Traditional event-count studies of internal wars have not explored the escalation or de-escalation of conflict into and out of various forms of contention. We would like to know, for example, how

> political parties and interest groups → social movements
> peaceful protest → civil violence
> ethnic activism → political rebellion
> rioting → insurgency
> terrorism → civil war
> guerrilla war → civil war
> purge → coup
> internal war → state breakdown
> governance crises and political instability → revolution

Such questions of dynamic repertoire change have not sufficiently engaged the event counters.

The issue arises quite naturally, however, from the rational choice institutional approach to state building and internal war. For example, the basic game tree reminds us that most terrorism does not grow out of zero terrorism, but rather develops when claims arising from state-imposed grievances lead to the interaction of lower-level strategies of claim making and government response strategies. Three stages of terrorist campaigns thus should be investigated: the emergence/onset of terrorism; the conduct and termination of terrorism, in particular its escalation to greater levels of enduring violence; and postterrorism recovery and stability, in particular the transformation of terrorism via negotiation or defeat into another part of a dissident repertoire (for example, democratic party politics, peaceful protest, armed guerrilla insurgency).

Repertoires: interacting strategies—signaling and bargaining. Dissident strategies evolve in response to government responses. For example, counterterrorism aims to deter groups from resorting to terrorism. States also try to convince groups initiating terrorism to discontinue their terrorist campaigns. Once a group has adopted terrorism as part of its strategic profile, the state tries to alter its decisions.

More generally, state-group dyads are involved in strategic interactions. Decision meets decision. When choosing policy options, groups take the state's anticipated response into account. Both states and groups avoid courses of action that hold undesirable short- and long-term consequences.

If strategic choices involve sequential interactions, moves and countermoves, response and counterresponse, first movers can signal second movers. Such signals can communicate resolve and interest—the resolve to use force and the interest in an acceptable settlement. Since states and groups have incentives to misrepresent their resolve and interest, they often take costly actions that make their threats and promises credible.

Multiple dyads. Though the game tree focuses on a single state-group dyad, of course countries contain several conflict dyads. One state-challenger dyad might involve terrorism; a second, a social movement; and a third, guerrilla insurgency. These other dyads can affect the primary dyad of concern. Actors external to a dyad can serve as coalition participants, patrons, bystanders, and opponents. Researchers thus need to know when and where nonterrorist organizations form alliances and coalitions with terrorist organizations and hence why and how terrorists turn nonterrorist organizations toward terrorism. Dyads outside the country also matter. In the Cold War and post–Cold War periods, foreign states, transnational nonstate actors, and intergovernmental organizations were involved in internal wars.

Observations of conflict dyads are thus dependent in two senses. First, externalities can happen within a game, as a rivalry heats up, remains dormant for a period, and then once again intensifies. Second, spillovers that occur between games affect the development of a state-group rivalry. Contentious actors are thus not billiard balls: between-group dynamics affect within-group dynamics, and vice versa.

Stages, Phases, Paths, and Sequences: Onset-Dispute-Escalation-Negotiation

The sudden onset of terrorism occurs less frequently than do domestic struggles that involve several steps toward the emergence of terrorism. The strategic dynamics of a conflict dyad involve the interaction of paths of diplomacy with paths of violent confrontation, interactions that occur over time. Processes of peace and conflict thus evolve through stages and phases. There is a beginning, a middle, and an end to a crisis—a very old point. When Barrington Moore (1966) wrote about paths of development toward the modern world, he emphasized historical sequences of change. Researchers, he argued, should distinguish between those who start a revolution, those who carry out a revolution, and those who benefit from a revolution. As the story about France was once told, for example, the nobility initiated the revolution, the peasants and the Parisians became the foot soldiers, and the bourgeoisie ultimately claimed power.

The evolution of an enduring authority-dissident rivalry can be disaggregated into the series of phases or causal pathways already discussed. Recall that a dispute is initiated by a group's claim or grievance against the state's alteration of the status quo. Following Huth (1998, 2004) and Huth and Allee (2002), each time period in an enduring or protracted state-group rivalry can be categorized as follows: (1) inactivity, periods of "doing nothing" in which there is no new state challenge to the status quo; (2) political negotiations over the state's claim, with varying levels of concessions offered by both parties possibly turning a stalemate into a settlement; (3) threats of force, with varying types of deterrent threats made by both parties; and (4) use of violence or force, with varying levels of military escalation/de-escalation taken by both parties.

Dissidents and authorities make repeated choices about inaction, talks, threats, and force, and the four stages continually repeat themselves. In a particular enduring rivalry, we thus can proceed operationally, again following Huth, as follows: For each time period in a data set, we classify "action" into

1. a policy concession variable (e.g., agreement) for the state/challenger, say on a three-point limited/major scale, and another policy concession variable (e.g., accede, offer) for the target/group, also, say, on a three-point limited/major scale;
2. a threat/counterthreat variable (e.g., extort) for the state, say, on a three-point verbal threat scale, and a threat/counterthreat variable for the group (e.g., harass), also, say, on a three-point verbal threat scale; and
3. a violent action variable (e.g., boycott, assault) for the group, say, on a three-point military escalation/de-escalation scale, and a violent action variable (e.g., arrest, disrupt) for the state, also, say, on a three-point military escalation/de-escalation scale.

If a particular time period in an enduring conflict has no event, we call that a status quo and include the time period in the data set.

With data subsetted into disputes and recorded this way, we have a record of the inactions, violent actions, policy concessions, and threats made by the challengers/states and targets/groups locked into an enduring rivalry. The four phases need not occur during every time period: inaction precludes the other three; in any time period, threats, concessions, and violence may occur alone or in combination with the other categories. In other words, single or multiple events can occur in any one period. If an enduring dispute manifests a structural change—the actors fragment, a negotiated agreement fails, a new set of issues arises—a new episode has occurred in a longtime rivalry.

Modeling the episodes of an enduring state-group rivalry by dividing them into phases can help explain the dynamic evolution of several variables. Challenger and target can (1) maintain the status quo in the dispute; (2) offer concessions during talks; (3) make verbal warnings or threats; and (4) aggressively employ force. We can then explain maintenance, compromise, threat, and force. When does an enduring state-group dispute escalate to force? Under what conditions is it settled? Why do challengers and targets shift between hard-line and accommodative policy stances? When will a deterrent threat be seen as credible? How is a state's responses to one dispute affected by other disputes in which it is engaged? Is a response path dependent or a function of the information revealed in previous encounters? How do the internal, group-level issues confronting challengers and dissidents affect their external responses to the regime? Given this bargaining framework, many middle-range theories can be probed. For example, one can explore theories of deterrence: to what extent is successful deterrence of terrorism attributable to the size or organization of the terrorist group?

In sum, rational choice institutionalists do not study how institutions cause the extent and intensity of protest and rebellion, operationalized as aggregated country-year data. The basic game tree leads to an exploration of why dissidents fight (why men rebel), how they fight (the rebel's dilemma), and how regime-opposition compromise arises (the bargaining theory of war). Walter (2002) thus divides the problem of settling a civil war into three stages: initiating negotiations, reaching a bargain, and implementing a peace plan. Onset-dispute-escalation-negotiation phases of state-group interactions structure inquiry, a key insight of rational-choice institutionalists.

The sequential stages of state-group interactions produce various outcomes—war and peace, escalation and negotiation, settlement and relegitimation. Rather than a single result, contention involves alternative paths to several possible conflictual and cooperative outcomes. Tilly (2006b, 417) thus makes an important point about the development of the state: No single macropath or sequence of political development exists. There is no invariant "standard and roughly sequential series of crises, challenges, and problems" by which states arrive at a predictable (Western-style) fully effective political system. In other words, states do not experience the processes of state building and nation building, or political, economic, and social crises, in roughly the same order. Neither do crises occur gradually over time, as a slow process of trial and error or as a pattern of compromise and consolidation that prevents the societal stress and social conflict that precedes state breakdown and disintegration. While rational choice institutionalists offer a common game-theory framework for studying state building, they also explore how the processes of peace and conflict combine in various ways to produce different types of outcomes.

3. Political Regimes as the Institutionalization of an Underlying Game of Power

Boix (2003, 3) connects regimes and regime change to economic conflict between the wealthy and the poor. Concerned with "the organizational and technical resources available to each agent to fight the opposite group" (44), he is ultimately interested in the intergroup balance of power, including alliances and coalitions. The stability of authoritarian regimes becomes a function of the distribution of economic and ultimately political power: "If the lower classes are demobilized or the ruling elite has strong repressive capabilities, there is a peaceful and durable authoritarian regime. However, if the organizational capacity of the poor rises, the likelihood of revolutionary explosions and civil wars escalates. If the poor win, they proceed to expropriate the assets of the wealthy and establish a left-wing dictatorship."

Rational choice institutionalists thus elucidate cooperative and conflictual interactions between regimes and oppositions, for example, between the wealthy and the poor, that stabilize as social contracts and political compromises, equilibrium balances of power, and good or bad power traps. As in Boix's work, equilibria that emerge from the game tree can therefore be viewed as political institutions and governing regimes that structure power and bargaining to produce peace and conflict. These interpretations are much richer than those found in the earlier literature on institutions as causes of conflict.

Institutional Equilibria as Social Contracts and Political Compromises about Power

Many historians, political scientists, and sociologists have observed that conflictual and cooperative interactions among groups often evolve into social contracts and political compromises.

Agrarian political orders. Barrington Moore (1966) writes about state/group governing coalitions involving either the ruler plus the middle class versus the landed elite, or the ruler plus the aristocracy versus the peasants. Anderson (1974, 337) analyzes the compact between nobility and monarch in Russia. A common pattern in revolution is when an opposition elite tries to gain power, the governing elite tries to hold power, and both try to mobilize or at least organize a previously quiescent peasant base.

Church and state. Weber (1968, 1161–62) writes about the compromise between religious and secular powers, sometimes through a concordat:

> Thus the spheres of control were mutually guaranteed, and each power was permitted to exert certain influences in the other's realm in order to minimize collisions of interest; the secular authorities, for example, participated in the appointment of certain clerical officials, and the priests influenced the educational institutions of the state ... [Another example is] the secular ruler makes available to the priests the external means of enforcement for the maintenance of their power or at least for the collection of church taxes and other contributions. In return, the priests offer their religious sanctions in support of the ruler's legitimacy and for the domestication of the subjects.

Feudalism. Feudalism, patrimonialism, and serfdom were bilateral agreements between lord and vassal about mutual obligations and reciprocal rights. In return for military and administrative service, lords grant fiefs and benefices, both rent-producing complexes of rights, to lesser lords. The fief may be defined as "any grant of rights, especially of land use or of political territorial rights, in exchange for military or administrative service" (1071). Vassals "are obliged to undergo military training and to be at the lord's arbitrary or limited disposal for military or administrative purposes"

(1071). The many varieties of feudalism (Weber 1968, 1072) involve many different types of obligations (mostly administrative and military) of the vassal to lord and many different types of rights (mostly rent producing) of the vassal. Since they involved a separation of powers and a division of authority, these agreements were an early form of constitutionalism in which labor services were exchanged for the public good of protection (North and Thomas 1973).

Class compromise. Przeworski (1985) points out that early Marxists feared class compromise: workers might exchange employment for industrial peace, or labor unions could exchange moderate wage demands for full employment.

Corporatism. Katzenstein (1985) writes about corporatism, or about interest-group compacts, in European states. A business-labor alignment can buttress a powerful corporatist state.

Consociationalism. Lijphart (1975) explores consociationalism, or compacts among religious and ethnic minorities. Intergroup conflict, he suggests, can beget the intergroup cooperation that reduces intergroup contention.

Peace agreement. States and groups can enter into peace accords. During cease-fire negotiations, constitutional conventions can broker long-term agreements that create various types of regimes.

War agreement. Coordination can occur between the state and its opponents locked in an internal war. Tacit, unwritten, and informal norms about the conduct of their conflict, aimed at eliminating tit-for-tat spirals of violence, allow contention to continue at lower levels. Some potentially effective tactics, for example, assassinating each other's leaders, killing losers, fighting during holidays, and using poison gas, may by mutual agreement be prevented from being chosen.

Political inclusion. One possible conflict outcome is a forum for state-opposition negotiations. Riots by London's weavers resulted in a body in which "both masters and men presented their cases before the justices" and which periodically determined piecework rates (Rudé 1964, 77). Another example is the enfranchisement of the working class in the West: protest groups often became political parties that forced a realignment of the party system.

Postrevolutionary stabilization. After the revolution key political actors attempt to reconstruct the state and consolidate a new regime. This often occurs when contending groups form new governing coalitions and alliances.

A variety of different types of collectivities and social forces, interacting under many different circumstances, have thus forged long-term, institutionalized political relationships. The possible applications are endless. Lust-Okar (2005) explores regimes and oppositions in Middle Eastern autocracies; Luong (2002), central and regional leaders in post-Soviet Central Asia; Przeworski (1991), liberalizers and hard-liners in Eastern Europe and Latin America; and Schofield (2006), the North and the South before and after the U.S. Civil War.

Institutional Equilibria as Stable Balances of Power

Greif (2005, 747) connects the balance of power among interacting groups to the equilibrium institutions that constrain group power. Coercive-constraining institutions "rely on balancing one's coercive power with either the coercive power of others or their ability to inflict economic sanctions on one who abuses rights. [These institutions] deter abuse of rights by creating the shared beliefs that attempt to do so will lead to a costly retaliation." Similarly, Levi (1988, 17–23) argues that the foundation of a state's revenue system is the relative bargaining power of rulers and ruled, and Walter (2002, 56–57) suggests that the balance of power underlies civil war settlements.

More generally, interacting groups attempting to forge social contracts and political compromises turn their balance of power into the institutional equilibria of our game tree. Equilibria in game theory are indeed best understood as institutions and regimes that contain conflictual interactions and encourage cooperative ones. Perhaps the earliest statement of this important idea, Schotter and Schwödiauer (1980, 482–83) indicate that Von Neuman–Morgenstern game theory is

in sum, the theory of the emergence of stable institutional arrangements or "standards of behavior" in a given physical situation or game. In other words, the theory tries to predict what stable institutional form will emerge from a given economic background and what the resulting value relationships will be. As a result, the theory does not assume that any particular institutional arrangement exists at the outset, as does the neoclassical theory, but starts out by describing the states and technologies of the agents in an institutional "state of nature" from which it predicts what stable institutional arrangements or standards will evolve. . . . Social institutions can be seen as the equilibrium outcome of games of strategy whose descriptions are given by the physical capabilities of the agents of the game—the "empirical background." They are an outcome of the game, rather than an input into it.

Given that different stable institutions correspond to different endogenous equilibria created by the players, game theorists ask where a particular equilibrium of agent interactions came from, what sustains it, and where it can head.

Nowadays, an equilibrium means that actors or agents with interdependent beliefs, resources, and strategies follow Nash behavioral norms: the rules of the game (nature), which remain constant and unalterable, create opportunities and constraints for the players; exogenous variables—both observable and unobservable—then determine a Nash (self-enforcing) equilibrium of strategic interactions. In other words, given an equilibrium outcome or institution, everyone is acting optimally. The equilibrium thus limits every actor's ability to change strategies unilaterally. All are prevented from altering course, because everyone has already chosen the optimal response to the situation. All are deterred from changing strategies, because everyone fears retaliation. From an individual's point of view, an equilibrium is a natural and stable point of cooperation, a point at which no one has an incentive to change strategies. From the collectivities' perspective, an equilibrium is a natural and stable point of coordination, a point where there is a tacit understanding on which actors focus. An equilibrium has authority and legitimacy in the sense that people value it as a norm, believe in it as an outcome, and defend it by pursuing their self-interest.

Institutional Equilibria as Good and Bad Power Traps

It is all too easy to equate an equilibrium balance of power, where no one has an incentive to change, with a good compromise and contract, outcome and institution. While there are political-like Coase theorems about costless bargaining that lead to Pareto-optimal collective action or public goods (for example, property rights, peace), the nonzero transaction costs of exchange and contracting mean that less satisfactory outcomes are

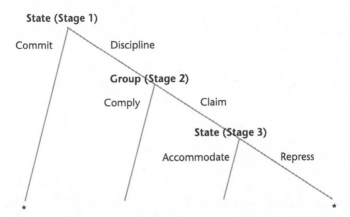

Fig. 2. Stages 1, 2, and 3 of state building. (* = Nash equilibrium)

also possible. Law and government might be efficient or inefficient, just or unjust.

Figure 2 shows two equilibria. In one, the state commits to the status quo and the game ends. In the other, state discipline begets group challenge that begets state force. Leaving aside for the moment the issues of its sustainability by *potential* state violence and the distribution of benefits in the status quo, the first equilibrium appears to be a good trap of joint cooperation. It is a mutually beneficial zone of peace, a virtuous circle of domestic tranquility. The second equilibrium seems to be a bad trap of joint conflict. It is a mutually destructive vicious cycle of internal war.

In some states at some times, contention has indeed been mostly co-operative, with the result being peace, prosperity, and stability. In other states or at other times, contention has been mostly conflictual, and the results have been dependence, authoritarianism, patron-clientelism, and ultimately war, poverty, chaos, and stagnation. Though interconnected or globalized, parts of the world appear identifiably separate. We see some states inhabiting a zone of peace and prosperity, and of democracy and world order. We see other states existing in a zone of war and poverty, and of dictatorship and turmoil. The uneven development of greater and lesser powers is thus manifested in two pure types of equilibrium institutions: a sovereign state, where peace generates peace and where contentious politics consists of peaceful protest; and a state plagued by

Hobbesian internal dilemmas, where conflict generates conflict and where contentious politics consists of violent rebellion.

The two equilibria correspond to the oft-cited quotation from Dickens about the best of times and the worst of times. The two also correspond to Putnam's (1993) stories about good and bad institutions in, respectively, northern and southern Italy. The game tree thus demonstrates that conflict and cooperation can be encompassed by a single theory.

4. Institutions and Regimes as Conflict and Change in an Underlying Game of Power

Social and political forces turn their relative bargaining power into stable compromises that become good and bad traps. In other words, institutional equilibria or equilibrium institutions are mutually reinforcing sites of rationality (behavioral patterns), culture (beliefs), and structure (rules of the game). But if fixed actors, preferences, beliefs, and so on produce fixed institutions, where does evolutionary or revolutionary change come from? Bueno de Mesquita and his colleagues (Bueno de Mesquita et al. 2003, 402) remind us, "Whatever the political arrangements in a society, some individual or group has an interest in changing the institutions of governance." For example, "When the government is not already autocratic, incumbent leaders have an interest in making the system more autocratic. They want to strengthen loyalty to them. This is achieved by reducing the size of the winning coalition and expanding the size of the selectorate."

While institutional equilibria and equilibrium institutions inform us about stable compromises, balances, and traps, they can also help us understand processes of political conflict and regime change. We consider how state building and internal wars result from shifts in bargaining power, good—but not good enough—equilibria, and institutional conflicts over power.

Institutional Equilibrium as Conflict and Change Induced by Shifts in Bargaining Power

Bates (2001) discusses the successes and failures of global paths of development. In early developers, great-power rivalries produced wars, war-making states needed revenue, and states granted representative institutions to those who could help finance state building. Late developers, on the other hand, emerged in the context of Cold War rivalries. Since developing states extracted revenue from the great powers, they could pursue less liberal politics and economics. Authoritarian patron-client ties were thus forged with the help of protectionism and import-substitution industrialization. After states withdrew their foreign patronage, dependent states went through debt crises and economic contraction. The result in the post–Cold War era was either democracy or violent state collapse.

Embedded in its global context, a developmental path can thus perform poorly everywhere and for nearly everyone, except perhaps for a very small group of beneficiaries. A path, such as the creation of a predatory, nondevelopmental state, could produce little economic growth, wasteful and inefficient allocation of resources, crime, violence, and corruption (black markets and bribery). Developmental strategies can also produce misdevelopment, uneven development, or exploitative development. The British approach to colonial development in India, for example, involved a divide-and-rule strategy that generated distortions: the construction of interests, identities, and institutions that favored Britain over India. More generally, development experiments can fail and result in either stagnant or collapsed states. While some regimes are by definition interim, transitional, and provisional, there are dead-end developmental paths that did not look so dead-end at the time they were adopted. The dustbin of history is littered with colonial administrations, world empires, principalities, city-states, territorially amorphous tribal areas, bureaucratic authoritarianisms, feudalisms, slave states, apartheid systems, and fascist and communist regimes.

Poor economic performance in failed and misshapen development experiments produce challenges. State-group disputes over development paths generate uncertainty, disruptions, and social tensions that manifest themselves as civil disorder and political anarchy, leadership and succession crises, and popular illegitimacy and alienation. Developmental models are thus constantly being rethought. For example, until 1990 countries throughout the world sought to emulate the Japanese "miracle." After it sank into a prolonged recession, Japan had to listen to Western advice about reforming its economy. The result of such new thinking can be an evolutionary or revolutionary change of domestic interests, identities, and institutions so as to pursue new strategies of development.

Failed developmental paths can thus be altered by revolutionary change from above. National elites can coalesce into a new regime to resist the global order. For example, to allow middle developers to compete with early developers, the German and Japanese revolutions from above remade social classes, built national identities, and created militant and strong states. Similarly, after the Cultural Revolution, Chinese leaders rethought their development strategy.

Of equal importance, failed development paths are sometimes changed by revolution from below, often after failed attempts at revolution from above. Thus, for example, economic and political liberalization under Gorbachev created new interests, identities, and institutions that brought about the collapse of the Soviet Union. More generally, it appears that certain developmental paths and the coalitions behind them run their course wherever and whenever they are tried and therefore contain the seeds of their own revolutionary demise. Not long ago, many academics and policymakers believed that late-developing countries needed strong states to mobilize resources for industrialization, assure territorial integrity, collect taxes, and staff bureaucracies. As resistance movements began to think otherwise and started to topple many such states, global thought shifted. It now widely argued that strong populist authoritarian regimes, military/bureaucratic absolutisms, patrimonial states that concentrate power in rulers and their families, and corporatist and state-led industrialization generate development problems: bloated public sectors, mismanagement, corruption, waste, and inefficiency result in such economic imbalances as inflation, currency overvaluation, and balance-of-payments crises. The neoliberal regimes, based on expanded free markets, have their own problems. Some now believe that shock-therapy policies of rapid marketization, advocated for many states by the World Bank and International Monetary Fund, can also produce instability and the possibility of revolution. Different types of developmental regimes therefore contain different types of flaws that eventually lead to the appearance of different types of resistance movements. Political struggles associated with the general failure of a development path are responsible for evolutionary and revolutionary changes of developmental regimes.

The world has thus seen grassroots challenges to the development coalitions that run failed or failing states. Resistance movements have opposed governing development coalitions and their connections to global interests, identities, and institutions. They have sought to topple ruling coalitions and to implement new grand strategies of development. States, in turn, have adopted grand strategies with the twin goals of external security and political survival. Some of these strategies have involved foreign wars and imperialism to appease domestic coalitions and divert popular opinion: victories abroad can make up for failures at home. Other strategies have involved protectionism and closed borders. Choices of development regimes and paths of state building, which are contingent on resistance movements, have thus affected the levels and kinds of conflict and cooperation in the global order. For example, according to the advocates of the democratic peace, it matters whether resistance to authoritarian paths of development helped produce a global order of democracies. Similarly, according to advocates of liberal internationalism, it matters whether resistance to import-substituting industrialization helped produce a global order of neoliberal economies. It surely mattered for global peace that resistance to the worldwide depression of the 1930s produced fascist regimes. And it surely mattered for international conflict and cooperation during the Cold War that competing resistances helped produce a global order consisting of a mixed cluster of democratic and communist states.

Suppose, therefore, that there are alternative paths to state building. One historical path leads to war and poverty, another to peace and prosperity. How do states and groups find their way to a particular path? Even more importantly, how can they shift between paths?

Let us rephrase these questions in terms of our game tree. The existence of multiple equilibria raises the issue of moving between them. Multiple equilibria, some good and some bad, are thus the keys to regime change. Can a state-group dyad evolve toward a more efficient equilibrium? How does a country move from an unproductive to a productive outcome? Can a state evolve slowly from a poor zone to a better zone, or can it switch abruptly and make a course change? Is a punctuated equilibrium possible, that is, repeated movements between equilibria in which states try to find best practices?

If institutions derive from the bargaining strengths of the players in a game, "only when it is in the interest of those with sufficient bargaining strength to alter the formal rules will there be major changes in the formal institutional framework" (North 1990, 68). In fact, "changes in bargaining power lead to efforts to restructure contracts, political as well as economic" (84). In other words, "the process of institutional change can be described as follows. A change in relative prices leads one or both parties to an exchange, whether it is political or economic, to perceive that either or both could do better with an altered agreement or contract. An attempt will be made to renegotiate the contract" (86).

There are two scenarios: everyone loses and someone loses. A particular developmental policy backed by a specific regime coalition may or may not be successful. Based on the rule of thumb, "If it ain't broke, don't fix it," one would expect that when development is working well for everyone in a country, regimes would attempt to consolidate their development path. Alternatively, there might be losers who try to become winners by changing the institutions. Riker thus focuses on politics as the use of institutions to manipulate outcomes, and Laitin (1992, x–xi) agrees that "society is often in disequilibrium and that the play of politics is usually about people, unhappy with the status quo, seeking to undermine apparent equilibria." Since the winners will oppose the losers' efforts, a struggle over rules ensues. Politics is thus doubly unstable and unpredictable: institutions produce policy outcomes, but policies often change; institutions are about power, but power arrangements need not endure.

In sum, multiple equilibria characterize paths of state building. A variety of possible combinations of democracy and market exist, as do a variety of possible transition paths. Local resistance, in a feedback loop, influences the origin, consolidation, and transformation of developmental coalitions. By influencing development regimes and paths of state building, domestic struggles affect the global order and world politics.

Institutional Equilibrium as Conflict and Change over Good Equilibria

It would seem that the dynamics of politics, and particularly the dynamics of state building and regime change, are all about moving from bad to good equilibria. Good equilibria, however, are never really good enough, and this provides another dynamic behind regime change.

Why can't we all get along? is the foundational question of an idealistic form of rational choice theory—the bargaining theory of war—that explores cooperation between states and groups. In Fearon's (1995, 1998a; also see Weingast 2002, 683–85) influential bargaining model of ethnic politics, the parties must divide some resource, but fighting over its distribution can impose quite large costs on the minority (c) and the majority (C). Given the potential gains from cooperation, the parties ask: why can't we all get along? If the minority and the majority could commence negotiations, reach a settlement, and assure themselves that their agreement was self-enforcing, they could share the resource and save the $c + C$ costs of ethnic warfare. Avoiding a fight would leave everyone better off.

Fearon's model also locates a potential pitfall: once the minority agrees to negotiate rather than to fight, the majority can take advantage of it. In other words, the majority cannot credibly commit to satisfying a demobilized and disarmed minority. Left to pursue their own interests, majorities behave opportunistically toward minorities, callously taking advantage of them. Since the minority cannot believe in the credibility of the majority's claim to treat it well forever, the minority prefers to fight initially rather than negotiate. Of course, most ethnic groups in most places at most times get along. The central empirical problem of the bargaining theory of ethnic politics is therefore to locate the institutions and environments that allow majorities to make credible commitments to minorities.

Fearon's (1995) general approach, which has quickly become a central theory of interstate conflict, has been extended to civil wars, ethnic conflicts, and terrorism (Lake 2003; Reiter 2003; Cetinyan 2002; Powell 2002a, 2002b; Walter 2002). Since the welfare losses from internal war—human death and economic destruction—seem needless, "the central puzzle about war, and also the main reason we study it, is that wars are costly but nonetheless wars recur" (Fearon 1995, 379). War is an inefficient, Pareto-suboptimal outcome because the eventual loser could concede and the ultimate winner could receive the spoils of war without either having to pay the costs and bear the risks of conflict. In other words, "the *ex post* inefficiency of war opens up an *ex ante* bargaining range," and thus "under very broad conditions, [peaceful] bargains [over time and across issues] will exist that genuinely rational states would prefer to a risky and costly fight" (Fearon 1995, 390, 382).

Fearon's approach thus sees institutions as potentially promoting mutually beneficial advantages through voluntary agreements. The good story, or functional view, is therefore that of institutions efficiently resolving collective action and collective choice problems. Actors devise institutions as solutions to the problems of rule making, rule application, rule interpretation, and rule enforcement. This leads to good equilibria: cooperation, trust, reciprocity, civic engagement, and collective well-being. Efficiency seeking leads to institutions that provide the common knowledge and the common values that lead to coordination at various sites of strategic interaction.

While states and groups share a common interest in finding negotiated settlements that resolve their disputes short of war, they often cannot achieve their shared preferences for a bargained solution and hence often resort to costly violence. The central research question then becomes one of explaining those prewar bargaining failures that prevented contestants from reaching a hypothetical ex ante settlement that could have avoided a costly war that ended up producing the same solution ex post.

While Posen's earlier work (1993) on the security dilemma suggested that the root cause of ethnic conflict is anarchy, the bargaining theory of war maintains that a root cause of any war is incomplete information, mutual uncertainty, and erroneous expectations. As Lichbach (1995, 88) argues, "if information were complete, there would be no need for conflict, no need for the parties to test one another; the winning side would present the losing side with its demands, and the conflict would be over." Fearon (1995) thus suggests that a key mechanism driving bargaining failures is uncertainty about relative power, opportunities, and resources, on the one hand, and about relative will, goals, and intentions, on the other. As Reed (2003, 633) puts it, "Uncertainty about the balance of power can cause the challenger to demand too much from the defender. Likewise, uncertainty about the distribution of power can cause the defender to underestimate the challenger's willingness to fight." He continues:

> When states are uncertain about their opponent's capabilities, they may either overestimate or underestimate their own bargaining leverage. Such miscalculation may enhance the probability of a militarized clash by shrinking the range of acceptable nonviolent agreements. Conversely, if both states are fully informed and militarized conflict is costly, the probability of conflict is zero. The challenger knows what the defender is willing to concede (i.e., the disagreement point or reservation value), and likewise the defender knows precisely how much it must give to appease the challenger and thereby avoid the costs of a militarized clash. In such a scenario, the challenger makes a demand exactly equal to the maximum concession the defender is willing to make. The bargain is made by the defender accepting the challenger's initial offer. However, when information asymmetries arise about relative capabilities, the challenger may overestimate its bargaining leverage and demand more than the defender is willing to concede. This may lead the defender to reject the challenger's offer, thereby making militarized conflict more likely. Asymmetric information may also lead the challenger to overestimate the defender's capabilities and thus make an inadequate opening offer, resulting in the defender's acceptance of the initial offer. (2003, 634)

In sum, states and groups might possess private information and have in-centives to misrepresent or exaggerate their capabilities and resolve.

Fearon emphasizes another mechanism driving bargaining failures: the enforceability of the bargains struck. Since states and groups might be unable to make credible commitments to stick to the bargains they reach, they never actually come to agreement.

North (1990, 52) also argues that equilibrium institutions are not nec-essarily efficient. Inefficient property rights "exist because rulers would not antagonize powerful constituents by enacting efficient rules that were opposed to their interests or because the costs of monitoring, metering, and collecting taxes might very well lead to a situation in which less efficient property rights yielded more tax revenue than efficient property rights." He continues: "If political transaction costs are low and the polit-ical actors have accurate models to guide them, then efficient property rights will result. But the high transaction costs of political markets and subjective perceptions of the actors more often have resulted in property rights that do not induce economic growth, and the consequent organi-zations may have no incentive to create more productive economic rules."

Incomplete information and incredible commitments thus produce transaction costs that trap states and groups in inefficient conflictual equilibria. With full information and complete trust, cooperative out-comes—albeit reinforced by the threat of reversion to the conflict equi-librium—are possible. Whether peaceful policy bargains about produc-tive institutions can be struck depends on the ability of states and groups to extract relevant information. Unobservable private information pro-motes conflict, and public information promotes cooperation. Histories, policies, and institutions that increase transparency and minimize se-crets allow actors to coordinate expectations, thereby reducing the false expectations—the underestimated and overestimated power resources—that are responsible for war. Whether policy agreements can be struck also depends on whether states and groups trust one another. Contend-ing parties must be able to make credible commitments to enforceable bargains that bring peace. In short, internal war is a mistake. More than that, this first question expresses the normative or utopian view that per-haps all of politics is mistaken.

Why not mobilize my resources? This second question the protagonists in a state-group rivalry can ask is the foundation of a realistic form of ra-tional choice theory, the rebel's dilemma theory of dissent (Lichbach

1995). It centers on the perpetual conflict between regimes and dissidents. Lake (2002, 18 n. 13) thus criticizes the application of the bargaining theory of war to terrorism as follows: "Treating any terrorist organization or target as a unitary actor is, of course, an analytic simplification. Some distinguish between concentric rings of social-movement radicals (who share goals), sympathizers (who provide active support, such as apartments), and actual terrorists (who carry out the violence). Moderates would lie outside these groups, and the process of radicalization is understood as a shift of the population from one ring into another (that is, moderates into social-movement radicals, radicals into sympathizers, sympathizers into terrorists)." Lake (2002, 20) then suggests a mechanism for terrorist mobilization: "By provoking the target into massive retaliation, the terrorists hope to radicalize their own moderates and drive them into their arms. If successful, the terrorists enlarge their group of supporters, increase the number of soldiers willing to fight for the cause, expand the financial and others resources upon which they can draw, and augment their overall power." As he explains, the terrorists' strategy aims to overcome the currently feasible bargaining outcomes: "The strategy adopted by extremist terrorists follows from their preferences and, more important, from their political weakness relative to their goals. Their strategy is to shift the balance of power in their favor and, over time, to shift the bargaining range closer to their ideals . . . the object is not to bargain what is acceptable today, but to change the range of what is acceptable tomorrow." Moreover, "when this strategy works, the extremists increase their numbers and bargaining power—and those bargains that initially were impossible become possible" (19).

Lake summarizes the argument as follows: "Terrorists resort to violence not because of private information, incredible commitments, or indivisible issues, although these factors may also matter, but because no bargain is acceptable to them under the current distribution of capabilities. The terrorist act itself is designed to shift the balance of power between the parties and to produce a better bargain at some point in the distant future. Bargaining over particular issues now is subordinated to a broader strategy of using violence to change the relative capabilities of the two sides" (2002, 20).

Lake's mechanism of conflict expansion challenges the rationalist bargaining theory of war: "In extant models, the distribution of capabilities, and, thus, the range of acceptable bargains, are exogenous." However, the terrorists' strategy "implies that the balance of capabilities and, thus, the future division of the issue is endogenous, part of the game it-self." Lake thus suggests that "the 'silence' in the rationalist approach to war arises from the assumption of fixed or, at most, exogenously chang-ing capabilities. The distribution of power, even if evolving over time, provides the basic structure within which the parties negotiate. The phe-nomenon of extremist terrorism demonstrates that changing the distri-bution of capabilities can be an action available to actors and thus needs to be incorporated into the strategic setting. In this way, terrorism forces us to rethink how we model and, in turn, understand violent conflict" (2002, 21).

While Lake criticizes the application of the bargaining theory of war to terrorism, his insights apply to all internal wars over state building. For example, whether a minority ethnic group adopts violent strategies and tactics depends on whether histories, policies, and institutions encourage the mobilization of existing and new resources that can shift the relative power of the protagonists. If dissidents believe that they can maintain or even increase their power in the future, today's information and credible commitments can mean little. There are indeed revolutionary groups who want to win everything and counterrevolutionary groups who will not countenance opposing interests. Politics often involves groups that will not incorporate opponents into the political system, will not admit that others have legitimate rights, do not agree to work out conflicting material and ideal interests by nonviolent means, and oppose any system of political exchange that does not guarantee them overwhelming power.

States and groups may thus fight internal wars over state building be-cause they are dissatisfied with the supposedly mutually beneficial— peaceful and cooperative—status quo. Hoping to improve their relative capabilities, contenders want to shift the bargaining range of possible set-tlements and hence to produce an outcome more to their liking. In short, regimes and opposition groups aim to expand their numbers of support-ers, to obtain allies, and to gain the additional resources needed to achieve their preferred result. Moreover, Lake limits terrorist strategies to provok-ing repression, though dissidents pursue a variety of strategies to mobilize resources and to solve their collective action problems. Other solutions to the rebel's dilemma, including selective incentives, tit-for-tat agreements, bandwagons of dissent, and organizational innovations, figure promi-nently in accounts of contention (Lichbach 1995). Collective action theory thus offers a natural way to endogenize efforts to grow capabilities.

In sum, dissatisfaction with today's good equilibrium invites resource-building challenges. But how can cooperative, Pareto-efficient institutions be seen in the long run as second best, and how can they deconstruct so easily under resource-building ambitions? Are equilibria really so short term and so shallow?

Consider the efficient equilibrium in figure 2. North (1990, 86) suggests that institutional equilibrium would be a situation where, given the bargaining strength of the players and the set of contractual bargains that made up total economic exchange, none of the players would find it advantageous to devote resources to restructuring the agreements. Note that such a situation does not imply that everyone is happy with the existing rules and contracts, but only that the relative costs and benefits of altering the game among the contracting parties does not make it worthwhile to do so. The existing institutional contracts defined and created the equilibrium. The good equilibrium in figure 2 is thus the result of the interests and the bargaining power of the parties operating under the status quo rules of the game.

We must thus start with the real circumstances of politics: a set of ambitious people with different and conflicting self-interests and identities. They will use political power strategically to further their own purposes, including subordinating others to their aspirations in a tyrannical way. To extract resources efficiently, dominant political elites, ruling classes, clans, managers, dictators, or feudal lords try to create structures of domination and norms of legitimacy. At critical moments in history, key actors or dominant players forge institutions to serve their interests. Rather than impediments to conflict designed by protagonists, institutions are thus the legacies of conflicts shaped by yesterday's winners. While these regime-formation coalitions emerge and temporarily prevail—and we call them institutional equilibria or equilibrium institutions—agency in politics ultimately means that political actors will seek to alter their bargaining power and do better in the future. Political contestation and struggle over equilibrium institutions result.

Here is the point. Since even good traps involve some force and coercion, some power and predation, everyone asks, why not mobilize my resources? The hopes and expectations of today's winners (and not just, as Riker says, today's losers) create institutional dynamics and developments: regime formation, maintenance, and change. Underlying this resource-building story is of course a highly distributional view of state building. As Schofield puts it: "*contestation,* rather than *compromise,* is the fundamental characteristic of politics" (2006, 273). Or, as Hall and

Taylor write, "conflict among rival groups for scarce resources lies at the heart of politics" (1996, 937). Lake's power-seeking terrorists are just one part of this story of good equilibria that are never quite good enough, even for the winners.

Institutional Equilibria as Conflict and Change over Spheres of Power

Bueno de Mesquita and colleagues (Bueno de Mesquita et al. 2003, 372) make an interesting argument about state-military dyads: "In small winning coalition systems, the military must be part of the selectorate to protect the system against revolutionary threats. Consequently, the military cannot be separated from politics in such systems. In large winning coalitions, though, the military is not needed to protect the system against revolutionary threats, and so can be professionalized and removed from politics." In other words, civil-military relations affect state-citizen relations and vice versa. A third source of persistence and change of institutional equilibria is the state's and the group's engagement in multiple dyads played in multiple games. Different actor configurations create different institutional equilibria that serve different purposes that can be out of sync.

Speaking generally, under certain conditions and at certain times and places, institutional dyads can create positive externalities for one another. Positive consilience occurs when the system imposes its logic on its subsystems. Burnham writes, "Real-world systemic identity (or major systemic change processes) in society may be thought of as a syndrome of interrelated and specifiable characteristics, which can be analytically subdivided into interrelated but discrete segments (or, pursuing the biomedical metaphor further, into 'symptoms'). It follows that, assuming that a system operates as system, opportunities for an effective pursuit of a 'strategy of coordinating disparate results from multifarious sources' should be rather plentiful" (1994, 61). Institutional complementarities can then be expected.

Negative consilience among dyad-driven institutions is also a possibility. For example, agreements struck in a state-class dyad might conflict with institutions built in a state-religion dyad. There is a potential contradiction between decentralized federalism (resulting from a state-ethnic dyad) and the increasing nationalism of the economy (resulting from a state-class dyad). There is a possible conflict between hierarchical family relations (resulting from a state-gender dyad) and the voluntary organization of civil society (resulting from a state-citizen dyad).

Conflicts among the institutions in different dyadic games are our final motor of political change. The separate institutions in a state could have separate logics and dynamics that result from different origins, different interests and beliefs in regimes, and different rules for operating. Institutions that are dissonant, asymmetrical, and incongruent can be colliding and interfering. The diverse and divergent institutions in a state could thus be in perpetual conflict with one another. Orren and Skowronek (1994) call incompatibilities among multiple institutions and authority structures "intercurrence" and suggest that disjointed institutions create the tensions, contradictions, and schisms that challenge the overall order or systemic equilibrium and hence are responsible for change:

> [A]t any given time, institutions, both individually and collectively, juxtapose different logics of political order, each with their own temporal underpinnings . . . [leading to] the incongruities that political institutions routinely produce. Against the background of institutional frictions that drive and shape political change, pictures of ordered space in bounded time fade away, and with them the boundary that has separated order from change. What is revealed instead is neither chaos nor a seamless flow of events, but rather the institutional construction of temporality that occurs as one institutional ordering impinges on another. (Orren and Skowronek 1994, 320–21)

In other words, dyadically bargained institutions are not necessarily synchronized in their operations and not necessarily coherent in the effects. The independent movements of institutional orderings impinge upon one other, influencing both outcomes. A change in institution 1 at time 1 might have the unintended consequence of changing institution 2 at time 2. The complex interfaces among institutions thus create the "patterned disorder" (Orren and Skowronek 1994, 330) one observes as incoherent, mixed, and hybrid regimes.

5. Institutions and Regimes as Equilibria Designs

This analysis of institutions and regimes began with questions about institutionalization and stability and moved to questions about conflict and change. Equilibrium institutions and regimes turned out to be all about power: balances, traps, compromises, changes, and conflicts. For centuries political theorists have explored strategies for dealing with power: for creating and attacking it, establishing and undermining it, executing and conquering it, using and exposing it, and constructing and criticizing it. Machiavelli studied princes and cities; Hobbes, violent civil war; Marx, radical social polarization; and Nietzsche, the will to power. By focusing on equilibria design, rational choice institutionalists directly confront issues of realpolitik.

Luong (2002, 11) describes the transitional bargaining game that produced electoral institutions in post-Soviet Central Asia: "Elites interact strategically to design institutions such that they attain as large a share of the distribution of goods and/or benefits as possible, given their perceived change in power relative to the other relevant actors—both established and emergent. In short, those who believe that their relative power is increasing with the transition will seek to alter or create institutions such that they receive additional goods and/or benefits, while those who believe that their relative power is decreasing with the transition will seek to retain as much of the distributional advantage accorded to them by previous institutions as possible." If the institution-design game is really a power game, as Luong suggests, Riker's instability problem arises: how can the power-maximizing actors who forge institutions be constrained so that their subsequent use of coercive power will not overturn their handiwork? Filippov, Ordeshook, and Shvetsova (2004, 33) touch on the problem of how institutions persist in the long run: "Because the ongoing processes of negotiation and renegotiation in a federation pose an ever present danger to federal stability and effectiveness . . . the primary purpose of federal design must be to keep those processes in check." Successful equilibrium designs for federalism thus lead power-seeking actors to create stable or self-enforcing institutions: "The motives it engenders among the individual decision makers empowered to change or otherwise subvert its rules and procedures leave them with an interest in maintaining the institutional status quo" (2004, 15). More generally, the Riker problem suggests that proper institutional design is required to contain the power, control the violence, and manage the conflict that often overturn institutions.

Institutional Equilibria as Designs to Contain Power

Arendt (1973, vii) observes that there are "those who believe in human omnipotence (who think that everything is possible, if one knew how to organize masses for it) and those for whom powerlessness has become the major experience of their lives." Underlying the idea of human omnipotence is the enlightenment belief that nothing is impossible and that everything is permitted. The state thus has the unlimited power to remake reality and create utopias. This Leibnitzian optimism—we can have the best of all possible worlds—is often mocked as chasing after windmills or building castles in the air.

But power can also produce evil. In the last century demagogues and tyrants established totalitarianism regimes and operated police states. The fear of power is therefore the fear of the fanaticism of unbounded, unlimited, and unconstrained regimes. There can be a tyranny of the majority or a tyranny of the minority, tyranny of the government or tyranny of the people through government. Majority and minority, governing and nongoverning, factions seek power and produce evil.

We thus observe state rulers who aim to entrench and consolidate their power and advantages by enhancing the state's extractive capacities and building state hegemony. Their goal is to turn the state into a predatory leviathan. Turning to governing majorities or minorities, we observe that these are not necessarily coalitions of the whole. Subsets of citizens can impose their will on the superset of citizens. Those included in the regime, or those insiders who sit at the bargaining table, determine policies and arrangements for those excluded outsiders. When winning coalitions can coerce or impose outcomes on losers, the results are rent seeking, predation, force, and violence.

How can a collectivity manage to discipline and domesticate power? The trick is to place limits on government, including the people who govern. Governments and citizens must limit their will to power and constrain their exercise of rule; they cannot pursue their own self-interest as they please, whatever and whenever and wherever they desire. Since government without limits leads to poverty and violence, rules must be in place to contain state power. Placing limits on the majority—to popular sovereignty—prevents arbitrary and abusive populist governance. Constitutionalists thus aim to control government by assuring the rights of the people and the consent of the governed against governing majorities. They hope to constrain self-interest via the rule of law, a rights regime, the separation of powers, political representation, divided government, and the multiplication of interests. By dispersing power, institutional designers hope to implement political rationality.

Institutions can also limit minority factionalism. Politics is always threatened by activist interest groups, social movements, and protest groups that can stir up disorder and chaos, either through anarchy and instability or through gridlock and paralysis. Hyperactive interest groups and unconstrained group bargaining lead to the free play of preferences and passions, to rent seeking and patronage, and to distributive coalitions that attempt to draw on government largesse. This too results in poverty and violence. Institutional devices and mechanisms can prevent and control veto groups. By carefully concentrating power, institutional designers again aim at political rationality.

A state strong enough to protect property rights from the coercive elements of civil society is also strong enough to abuse civil society (Weingast 1995). The institutional design question is thus how to concentrate power to serve the public good, yet constrain it to prevent abuse. While designers need powerful groups—factions, divisions, oppositions—as barriers against the state, they also needs the state to contain factionalism, division, and opposition. Those who design institutions must therefore achieve a balance between liberty and authority. Violence is economically productive when it is used to protect property rights from, on the one hand, the ravages of civil war and military raids by groups and, on the other, abuse and expropriation by the state. While too much strength on one side produces chaos and disorder, too much strength on the other leads to authoritarianism and dictatorship. Greif (2005) thus argues that markets and social order are based on coercive-constraining institutions that constrain powerful actors from abusing property rights. By giving asset holders some decision-making authority, the rulers' power can be limited.

How do institutional designers construct a state that does both jobs? Can rules constitute and contain power? While utopians believe that interests and actions are disconnected or that selfishness is not the major design problem, the rationalist approach to government is as a self-enforcing and hence self-limiting equilibrium that harnesses self-interest. To discipline private and public power, one must subject power to principle but also to the principle of self-interest. The design question is thus how to achieve mutual advantage, or the public good, by tapping the reality of private goods and self-interest. If people are part of the problem (because of opportunism), they can be part of the solution (with incentives).

In sum, rational choice institutionalists try to design virtuous equilibria circles of self-interest and to prevent vicious equilibria traps of self-interest. Attempting to create limited or constitutional government by coupling the exercise of power to constraints on power, they have grappled with two challenges—violence and conflict—to the persistence of the institutions they create.

Institutional Equilibria as Designs to Control Violence

We usually think of violence as outside the political process. For example, the fact of political violence is taken as proof of the illegitimacy of a regime. Violence is indeed a crucial part of many historical revolutions that overturned political and economic forms of domination, control, and power. Because violence is responsible for change in political opportunity structures and political processes, it is often not seen as part of a stable political order.

McAdam, Tarrow, and Tilly (2001) reject many of the conventional distinctions, found in table 2, between routine and nonroutine politics. In democratic and autocratic states, now and as far back as the nineteenth century, the boundaries between these two forms of popular mobilization are fluid and permeable. The same actors and the same organizations engage simultaneously in routine and nonroutine politics. Adopting complex repertoires of action, conventional and nonconventional activities are complements and not substitutes. Political parties, interest groups, and social movements are mutually dependent, that is, simultaneously cause and effect. And protest politics and conventional politics are consequences of forms of political access and opportunity structures.

TABLE 2. Transgressive and Contained Politics

Transgressive Politics	Contained Politics
Abnormal	Normal
Violent	Nonviolent
Unstable	Stable
Illegitimate	Legitimate
Irregular	Regular
Challengers	Polity members
Outsider, out-group	Inside, in-group
Excluded opponent	Included participant
Marginalized actor	Establishment player
Protest politics	Conventional politics
Extrainstitutional	Courts, legislatures, executives
Social movements	Interest groups, political parties

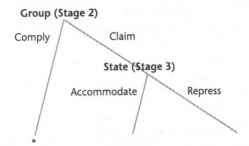

Fig. 3. Stages 2 and 3 of peace and conflict processes. (* = Nash equilibrium)

Meyer and Tarrow (1998) refer to these commingled and overlapping connections as the social movement society.

Now consider figure 3, which abstracts stages 2 and 3 from the larger game. Assume a strong state—one that in stage 3 will not back down from the group's challenge and will certainly use force. A strong state induces the group in stage 2 to accept the state's imposition of grievances and therefore not challenge its authority. This scenario is pregnant with ideas that resonate with McAdam, Tarrow, and Tilly's challenge to the conventional distinctions between peace and conflict.

A strong or powerful state is not challenged and hence need not use force. This is because an equilibrium strategy combination equals off-the-path play plus on-the-path play. We observe on-the-path play, or outcomes that are part of an equilibrium. We do not observe off-the-path play, or outcomes that are never reached but nevertheless are also part of the equilibrium. Although unobserved potential actions that are not taken are off the path, they nevertheless influence observed actions that are taken on the path.

While state force is off the equilibrium path—the equilibrium outcome is that the group accepts the new status quo and does not challenge the state—state violence is still part of that equilibrium. Through a state's credible threat or promise to use force, violence is made endogenous to contention; that is, potential state coercion is not exogenous to or antithetical to a realm of peaceful social order. Violence does not intrude on a separate domain of peace as much as it is constitutive of a peace/war order. Violence is part of the equilibrium of governance institutions, authority patterns, and regime types. It helps construct choices along paths of development and strategies of state building. Just as there is great order in violent disorder, violent disorder is part of a greater order.

While what we find on the path of play is stability and order, and while what we find off the path of play is violence and chaos, state-group relations are simultaneously violent and nonviolent. The dyad contains manifest cooperation and unobservable conflict, and both are components of the same sequential bargaining process. As the sides learn about each other's willingness to absorb costs, peace occurs in the shadow of conflict or under the threat of war; and as the sides learn, conflict takes place in the shadow of peace or under the recognition that every war has to end.

What we observe as peaceful cooperation is thus really an institutional equilibrium or equilibrium institution supported by violence-averse groups and strong states. This structured, stable, and patterned outcome is part of a self-enforcing political order. State violence is thus part of the equilibrium institutions of state building: taxes, property rights, democracy, interethnic bargains, neopatrimonialism, colonialism, class compromise, corporatism, and consociationalism.

State force is therefore a normal part of political life. As a basic component of state-group interactions, state violence lurks just beneath a surface peace, always ready to emerge. All states have rules that permit and punish forms of political transactions, particular words and deeds that challenge the accepted regularity of political behavior. Rules for the legitimate and legal forms of political claim-making define the who, what, where, when, how, and why of participation and inclusion. There are rules, for example, governing how police treat protesters.

Group quiescence is also a normal part of political life. We can thereby explain inertia and nonaction, the nonevent of the absence of protest, a puzzle noted by John Gaventa (1980). Unobservable power mechanisms—the threat of force by the state—create the power relationships that maintain quiescence in civil society. These mechanisms neutralize opposition groups and prevent subordinate actors from acting on their perceived interests and identities. Those who hold power contain their rivals and pursue their preferences by wielding the threat to use force and violence.

Social order is therefore based on both consent and coercion. Weber thus stresses that the state has the legitimate monopoly of violence. Every country is founded on force and fraud, as well as on legitimacy and authority. Rational choice institutionalists can thus appreciate McAdam,

Tarrow, and Tilly's approach to contentious politics as contained *and* transgressive politics.

Institutional Equilibria as Designs to Manage Conflict

Different interests and identities can be a basis of political cooperation. The division of labor and mutual exchange of goods and services can harmonize different material interests. Legitimacy and nationalism can coordinate different identities into a single nation-state. Social alignments and political coalitions can reinforce these solidarities.

The social, economic, and cultural division of labor, however, produces scarcity. Stratification systems come to define conflicts of interests and identities and hence provide the basis for the formation of constellations of social groups, group alliances, or political forces. Stratification systems also generate group resources and hence provide the basis for the power and domination of one group over another. Privileges, exploitation, and oppression result and ultimately generate political discontents and grievances. The struggle over scarce resources during state building thus produces a struggle for power among competing groups. Whoever wins captures the state, which might then operate as a system of political domination. The winners, that is, develop institutions that reproduce the very inequality, power, domination, and control from which they benefit. Who wins the fight over political power is a function of group organization, which, in turn, is a function of group mobilization, which, in turn, is a function of group resources. Resource mobilization and counterresource mobilization—the struggle for power, between dominant and dominated strata—thus define group conflict over governing institutions.

Under these circumstances, as Cohen observes, liberals who stress the market mechanism fail to recognize how coercive hierarchical institutions create social order:

> It assumes that men adjust to the conduct of one another with almost perfect freedom, their choices being limited only by nature and by the need to take note of one another's conduct. No consideration is given to the power which some men have to determine or influence the manner in which others will take account of their own wishes: in short, the theory so stresses the unintended consequences of actions that it overlooks the degree to which *some* intentions are more significant

than others, even when the outcome is not what was intended by any one or more parties. (1968, 27)

Eisenstadt (1978, 20) offers a pointed statement of this position.

In short, different interests and identities can also be a basis of political fragmentation, rather than of political cohesion. While human beings need each other, they do not always work together in perfect harmony. Contradictions and hence conflicts among interests and identities are inevitable. Everyone and every group could pursue its interests and identities through any means possible, including force and fraud, to expand their resources and power. Society is thus always at risk for polarization and conflict—mutually destructive violence, anarchy, and breakdown in a Hobbesian struggle of all interests and identities against all other interests and identities. Following Weber, Laswell, Easton, and Dahl, politics is the struggle over naked power and symbolic authority that results in who gets what, when, and where. It involves conflict, competition, and cooperation over the consumption, exchange, and production of goods and services.

A system of totally unregulated conflict, a free-for-all in which conflict gets out of hand, is intolerable to human beings. Hobbes thus feared a war of all against all, and Madison feared factions. How can conflicts be contained? How can a collectivity secure the advantages of mutual cooperation? How can a social order regulate its conflicts so that cooperation and community are possible?

The answer is institutions. Market institutions resolve conflicts of interest by encouraging the mutual exchange of goods and services. Communal institutions resolve conflicts of identity by encouraging identification with a larger political unit. When these more private institutions fail, more public institutions are needed—a little hierarchy and power, a leviathan or a government.

In the modern world the state is the arena in which conflicts of interests and identities are often resolved. Development strategies in part result from these conflicts. Public policies, in turn, define superordinates and subordinates, or winners and losers. Government then uses coercion to enforce the results. Having become a focal point of conflict, government thus manages that conflict by creating mechanisms of conflict resolution. Having helped create interests and identities, governing institutions mediate preferences and beliefs and hence help avoid Hobbesian war. States thus help eliminate conflict by privatizing issues of distribution and redistribution, through property rights, thereby creating tolerance out of diversity; by repressing conflict, through homogenizing people, thereby creating a melting pot out of pluralism; by refereeing conflict, through creating rules of social order, thereby assuring the compliance with law that controls aggression; and by adjudicating conflict, through arbitration and bargaining, thereby moderating its effects.

By facilitating cooperation, state institutions can generate order, integration, stability, and coherence. Greif (2006) thus refers to coercive conflict-management institutions that constrain actors from employing force and fraud. Institutions of public order control latent social conflicts over differences and inequalities.

Peace negotiations can thus result in institutionalized procedures for conflict resolution, or formal and informal venues for bargaining between regimes and dissidents. States and oppositions may thus reach a settlement, and new political institutions may emerge from the struggle. In this sense, less intensive and less violent conflicts need not be the route to polarization, instability, and revolution but rather may promote solidarity, integration, and orderly social change.

6. Summary and Affinity with Historical Institutional Approaches

Authoritarian equilibria, the survival of authoritarian regimes, and democratization concern Beatriz Magaloni (2006). Deftly combining statistical regressions, causal mechanisms, and an analytical narrative, her study of hegemonic party rule in Mexico illustrates many of the themes we have discussed, as summarized in figure 4.

Magaloni's story begins with the *world-historical conditions* faced by Mexico. As a late developer bordering the United States, Mexico could choose among several models of economic and political development. By the 1930s Mexican elites had designed *state institutions* as a one-party hegemony (Partido Revolucionario Institucional, PRI). With *social contracts and political compromises about power* assuring *a stable balance of power,* the developmental state could pursue import substitution development. *Policy performance* was, in broad comparative perspective, efficient and equitable. Mexico's fairly *good power trap* demonstrated a certain institutional logic of *peace and conflict processes.* Interactions between the PRI, counterelites, and the masses produced first the persistence and then the change of the regime. PRI leaders maintained power

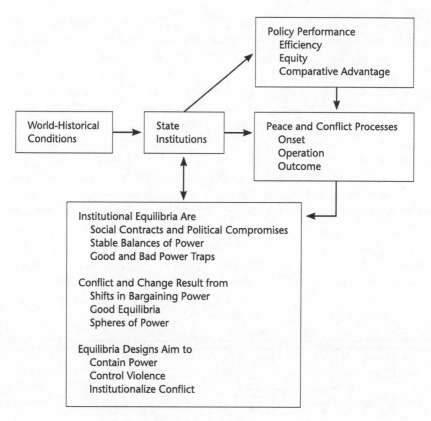

Fig. 4. Institutional logics and internal wars

and domination through an oversized winning coalition. The supermajority party sought to deflect challengers from within its ruling coalition by creating barriers to entering the electoral market—co-opting rival elites, factionalizing opponents, employing divide-and-rule strategies against possible challengers, and generally increasing dissidents' collective action and coordination problems. The governing PRI also sought to institutionalize mass political support by creating a loyal base of dependent voters. Targeting benefits to its key constituencies, the party used government transfers (patronage and pork) to sustain a clientelist network that monopolized the market for votes. The flip side of popular inclusion in the regime was a punishment regime that excluded opponents from the spoils system. Counterelites of course responded but were mostly unsuccessful in their pursuit of a winning opposition voting coalition. The masses were involved in the system mainly as voters and sometimes as protesters. Evidence from election surveys indicates that voters understood the political games being played. Radical social movements (for example, Zapatistas) knew that by threatening postelection violence and insurgency, they could destabilize the system. Since its supramajority status allowed the PRI to redesign the constitution, the party could maintain a generally credible commitment to counterelites and masses. In other words, by controlling the constitutional amendment process, the PRI turned its one-party hegemony into a stable endogenous institution. The result was some electoral repression and voter fraud but never rigged and meaningless elections.

The system worked for decades. The PRI regime managed social tensions between the poor, the middle strata, and the rich; among ethnic groups; between agriculture and industry; and between protectionist and globalizing economic forces. Its hegemonic institutions were in fact designed to *contain power, control violence, and institutionalize conflict.* In spite of regular multiparty elections, the PRI thus maintained popular order and the survival of the entrenched ruling coalition.

However, the system was premised on producing certain macroeconomic outcomes. As economic growth increased, prosperity provided the PRI with the necessary resources to fuel its patronage system and thus increased the chances that the hegemonic spoils-based party could survive. Magaloni also introduced environmental shocks to the status quo into her model and traced their impact. Changes in exogenous conditions—the debt crisis and the peso crisis—led to changes in equilibrium institutions and yielded neoliberalism, the breakdown of the hegemonic PRI, and gradual democratization. The mechanisms behind institutional conflict and change included *shifts in bargaining power, contention over good equilibria, and spheres of power.* For example, economic and political changes were cumulative: trade liberalization, privatization, and market reforms destroyed the hegemonic party's monopoly on economic rewards, weakened the party apparatus, and decreased the chances of regime survival.

In sum, Magaloni demonstrates how institutions are equilibria. The origins, persistence, and change of equilibrium institutions are her central problems, and the renegotiation, realignment, and reconfiguration of institutions are the key historical processes of her investigation. Peace and conflict processes are central to the analysis. This chapter unearthed many points of contact between Magaloni's rational choice institutionalism and other approaches to state building and internal war. We pointed out, for example, that such classic political economists as Marx (1964, 28) and Weber (1968, 1058) recognized the contractual basis of political and economic development. The most striking convergence nowadays occurs between rational choice institutionalism and historical institutionalism (Katznelson and Weingast 2005).

Robert Bates (2001, 77) writes that "in an effort to finance their wars, European monarchs had sought to extract higher levels of resources from their domestic economies. Both to tax and to borrow, they found it necessary to restructure their relationships with those whom they asked to bear the costs of government. The economic imperative—the need for resources and the necessity of raising them domestically—became a political imperative, shaping their institutions of government." States thus "bargain with their citizens to secure public revenue" (82) and "the creation of liberal political institutions was thus a by-product of the impact of military insecurity upon the need for government revenues" (82–83). Turning these historical observations into a general argument about limited government, Weingast (1995, 1) writes that "the fundamental political dilemma of an economic system" is that "a government strong enough to protect property rights . . . is also strong enough to confiscate the wealth of its citizens."

Bates and Weingast, however, are echoing a seminal historical sociologist, Charles Tilly: "When faced with resistance, dispersed or massive, what did rulers do? They bargained. . . . The core of what we now call 'citizenship,' indeed, consists of multiple bargains hammered out by rulers and ruled in the course of their struggles over the means of state action, especially the making of war" (1990, 101–2). Tilly (2006b, 423) also observes that the subordination of citizens to the state follows a common pattern:

Across a wide range of state transformation, for example, a robust process recurrently shapes state-citizen relations: the extraction-resistance-settlement cycle. In that process:

- Some authority tries to extract resources (e.g., military manpower) to support its own activities from populations living under its jurisdiction.
- Those resources (e.g., young men's labor) are already committed to competing activities that matter to the subordinate population's survival.

- Local people resist agents of the authority (e.g., press gangs) who arrive to seize the demanded resources.
- Struggle ensues.
- A settlement ends the struggle.

He continues:

> In all cases the settlement casts a significant shadow toward the next encounter between citizens and authorities. The settlement mechanism alters relations between citizens and authorities, locking those relations into place for a time. Over several centuries of European state transformation, authorities commonly won the battle for conscripts, taxes, food, and means of transportation. Yet the settlement of the local struggle implicitly or explicitly sealed a bargain concerning the terms under which the next round of extraction could begin.

While there are differences between rational choice institutionalism and historical institutionalism (Pierson and Skocpol 2002, esp. 705–7), rational choice institutionalists have approached questions of contentious politics in much the same way as historical institutionalists have done. Both approach state building and internal war with a similar set of concerns. Most importantly, both sets of scholars recognize that an institution that is politically workable—that is, is in equilibrium—constructs agents, fashions the interests and identities that become preferences, defines opportunities, allows choices and alternatives, embodies constraints and resource limitations, creates costs, assigns incentives, manufactures beliefs, and supports norms and values. Equilibrium institutions are therefore structures with causal powers. A variety of capabilities and capacities give institutions the strength to provide incentives at reasonable costs so as to direct the behaviors of citizens and political authorities. Work on contentious politics still focuses on how the mechanisms and processes behind political opportunities, mobilizing structures, and cultural frames cause and constitute contentious politics—or how the institutions enable, shape, constrain, influence, guide, direct, magnify, and inhibit (McAdam, Tarrow, and Tilly 2001).

If institutions are "equilibrium ways of doing things" (Shepsle 2006a; 2006b, 26), several state-society or historical-institutionalist questions arise. What holds such equilibria together? What static coordination mechanisms are involved? Which dynamic processes of reproduction produce lock-in, increasing returns, and positive feedback? When historical legacies are self-reinforcing, how do patterns ultimately freeze and survive over time? What allows crystallized institutions to become robust and persist against the available alternatives? Mechanisms of equilibrium selection, persistence, and change can be examined from institutionalist perspectives.

7. Prospects for Future Inquiry

In the first volume of the *Journal of Conflict Resolution* published in 1957, Mack and Snyder wrote an article entitled "The Analysis of Social Conflict: Toward an Overview and Synthesis." We have been overviewing and synthesizing the field for the past half century. The last 50 years have seen numerous calls to build something called studies of peace and conflict, contentious politics, internal war, political violence, and protest and rebellion. Over 100 review essays, appearing as articles and in books strewn across several disciplines, aimed to create such an interdisciplinary domain of inquiry.

In spite of our continuing efforts, specialization and division of labor—not to mention downright myopia and stubbornness—have meant that the field of conflict studies looks more like separate dining rooms than separate tables (Almond 1988). Nevertheless, another exhortation is not out of place: we need greater exchange between the different communities investigating contention. At present, the internal war literatures are isolated from one another; political economists and international relations specialists studying civil war have not interacted with sociologists, historians, and comparative politics specialists studying domestic contention. Studies of genocide are similarly ghettoized (Midlarsky 2005b). The only way to understand the internal wars of state building is to found a field of contentious politics that includes all of its members. Without collaborative efforts, we ignore the insights of the past and reinvent wheels. With such efforts, we may come to understand why states and citizens engage in mutual destruction.

When I started this chapter, I aimed to update one of my reviews of conflict studies called "nobody cites nobody else" (Lichbach 1992). I quickly discovered that nowadays almost everyone is studying transnational social movements, riots, civil wars, ethnic strife, religious fundamentalism, genocide, democratization, state breakdown, guerrilla wars, terrorism, and of course peacekeeping. There are now so many people not citing so many others that it was nearly impossible to produce an inventory of rational choice studies or of cross-country statistical analyses. I therefore decided that this chapter should offer a specific vision of the future: the emerging confluence of rationalist thought, located mainly in international relations, and historical institutionalism, located in comparative politics. The common concern is an institutionalist perspective on conflict. The chapter thus defined, described, and interpreted the idea of equilibrium institutions and institutional equilibrium.

A theory of state-opposition conflict must be a theory of institutions. Patterns of rule need to be connected to patterns of resistance to rule: regimes create repertoires, but repertoires then become constitutive of regimes. One cannot think of regimes separately from movements: different regimes, different movements, different regime-repertoire equilibria. Social movements, for example, define the equilibrium structure of American democracy today in a way that is different from the way they defined American democracy 100 years ago. Protest and rebellion are thus integral parts of the structures of power and authority. Resistance is not a corrective applied externally to rulers' abuses of power; rather, resistance is constitutive of tyrannical authority and the corruption of politics.

Institutions are thus the sites of authority and conflict, of state building and internal war. Differences in interests and identities, preferences and beliefs, and ideas and values are compounded by inequalities in power, resources, and capabilities. Differences and inequalities result from and are subsequently filtered through institutions. Politics involves the expression and aggregation of preferences and beliefs—publicly expressed claims and collectively organized demands on the state. Politics also involves the choices of strategies and behaviors that produce policy outcomes. Cooperation and mutual benefits, or conflict and mutual costs, result. Over time, these patterns cause the establishment and disestablishment of hierarchies, producing institutional persistence and change.

Studies of contentious politics can be joined to rational choice institutionalism and the bargaining theory of war to create a field in international relations and comparative politics that explores the Hobbesian side of state building: political survival strategies used by incumbent governments, models of accommodation and repression adopted by political elites, authoritative structures of domination and control pursued by regimes, grand strategies of development advanced by governing coalitions, and paths of state- and nation-building followed by political leaders. By moving away from event counts and from institutions as exogenous causes of internal wars, such a theory holds the promise of structuring a genuine domain of inquiry. Equilibria of the game tree can be studied as compromise and contract, balance of power, and good and bad traps. Equilibria can also be studied as conflict and change resulting from shifts in bargaining power, good (but not good enough) equilibria, and institutional conflicts over power. Finally, equilibria can be studied from institutional design perspectives: containing power, controlling violence, and managing conflict. Historical institutionalists and constructivists (who in the interests of space have not been discussed) have much to say about these mechanisms and processes.

Fifty years after Mack and Snyder wrote, it seems that rationalist and historical insights into institutions offer the most promising heuristics for understanding and explaining the last century's internal wars over state building. Indeed, progress has occurred as the field of conflict studies has moved from rebellion, to repertoires, to groups, to contention, and finally to institutions. If we could get the principals talking principles, much more could be accomplished. Such conversations could fulfill the visions of Machiavelli, Hobbes, and Madison, Weber, Laswell, Easton, and Dahl, as well as Moore, Lipset, Eckstein, and Huntington, all of whom placed studies of institutionalized power and social conflict at the center of political inquiry.

NOTE

An earlier version of this chapter was prepared for delivery at the panel "On the Political Economy of Collective Action" at the Annual Meeting of the American Political Science Association, Chicago, August 30–September 2, 2007. Christian Davenport, Paul Huth, Manus Midlarsky, Joe Oppenheimer, Sid Tarrow, Chuck Tilly, and Chalinda Weerasinghe provided valuable feedback on an earlier draft.

Democracy and Civil War

NILS PETTER GLEDITSCH, HÅVARD HEGRE,
AND HÅVARD STRAND

In this chapter, we investigate the question of democratic civil peace—
that is, democratic peace at the intrastate level. We use interchangeably
the terms *civil war* and *intrastate violence* for events where organized violence is used for political goals, although conventionally the term *war* is
often reserved for conflicts where the annual number of battle deaths exceeds 1,000. We study the determinants of the onset of civil war as well as
the incidence, duration, and severity of violent events.

Recent research on civil war uses arguments regarding the opportunity and motivation for rebellion as a theoretical point of departure. We
discuss how democratic institutions may affect both the opportunity and
the willingness to use violence for political purposes. Democratic institutions display great variations, however, in terms of inclusiveness, effectiveness, and stability. The opportunity and motivation framework allows
us to derive expectations concerning when and under what conditions
democratic institutions may succeed in reducing the risk, incidence, duration, and severity of civil war.

The general hypothesis emerging from this discussion is that democratic governance is beneficial for the reduction of civil war and that
specific forms of democracy are likely to reduce violence more than others. Specifically, we investigate these propositions: Democracy is nega-

tively related to the onset and severity of civil war and positively to duration. Democracy relates to civil war through an inverted U-curve: semidemocracies are most prone to violence. Political instability is positively
related to civil war. The curvilinear effect of democracy on civil war persists even when controlling for political instability. Civil war occurs more
frequently in conjunction with elections. The effect of democracy on civil
war is more pronounced for government conflicts than for territorial
conflicts. The effect of democracy on civil war is stronger for developed
countries. A politically different neighborhood is positively related to civil
war. The negative effect of democracy on civil war is more pronounced
for inclusive types of democracy. These relationships are generally
strengthened after the end of the Cold War. We test these hypotheses on
the Uppsala/PRIO conflict data, and investigate the robustness of our results. We use two measures of democracy, the democracy index from the
Polity project and the new SIP index, with some robustness tests using
two additional measures, Vanhanen's Polyarchy index and the Freedom
House Political Rights measure. Overall, we find democracy to be strongly
related to civil war, with the results for severity being the most robust.

Theoretical Framework

Actors

All organized violence is by definition a dyadic phenomenon, where
someone acts violently upon someone else. For the violence to qualify as a
civil war, two actors are required, both organized parties, one of which is a
government of an independent country.[1] Our main interest lies in the
characteristics of the government side. Additional actors may also be involved, including other governments, but here we assume that they are allies of one or the other of the primary actors. In the analyses reported in
this chapter, we use no data about the opposition side, except that it is organized.[2] This is not necessarily a serious limitation, since our interest is in
exploring the effects of the system of governance on civil war. However, in
future extensions it might be of interest to look at the political ideology and
aspirations of the opposition side for a more truly dyadic analysis, comparable to the analysis of the dyadic democratic peace at the interstate level.

Much scholarly debate has revolved around what type of actor a typical rebel group is: Is it the military organization of a broad social movement that seeks to address government injustice or promote democratization (e.g., Lichbach 1995), or the armed branch of a minority group that

requires some sort of cultural autonomy relative to the government or the country's majority (Sambanis 2001), or is it just a military organization designed to forward the private political and economic interests of its leaders (Collier 2000b)? Actors may also be a combination of these types, and transform from one to another in the course of the conflict. Examples of all these types may be found among the world's rebel organizations, but the empirical study of civil war is affected by how common each of these are. Rebel groups are not homogenous either, and the leaders' motivations may be very different from those of ordinary soldiers.

Motivation and Opportunity

We conceptualize civil war as a product of motive and opportunity. On the rebel side, a motive can be negative—a grievance against the existing state of affairs, or positive—a desire to get rich, sometimes called greed in the civil war literature. Researchers that focus on grievance typically discuss broad social movements, whereas greed tends to be associated with narrow groups or elites within such movements. A prominent example of the first category is the decision by the African National Congress to take up arms against the apartheid regime, while the latter category is often illustrated with Charles Taylor's rise (and fall) in Liberia.

Potential rebels must also have a realistic opportunity to achieve their goal. The realization of their desires may be blocked by a powerful, well-organized government army, by geographical factors (if the rebels are thinly spread out or are unable to establish defensible headquarters), by the lack of financial means (if they are very poor), or by the inability to build an effective military organization (Collier 2000a; Lichbach 1995).

Both opportunity and motivation affect the length of conflict. The rebels need motivation to keep on fighting. They also have to meet their financial needs. Group cohesion is necessary to minimize deterrence and the risk that the group splits into two or more competing rebel groups or becomes severely weakened by defection. Conditions that facilitate cohesion may therefore provide another set of opportunities for rebellion.

Various models of conflict are related to this two-factor model of rebellion. Collier and Hoeffler (1998, 2004) formulated their model around the concepts of greed and grievance (see also Berdal and Malone 2000). In other writings, Collier and Hoeffler stress the opportunity for rebellion. To some extent, they focus on economic opportunity, which is akin to greed as a motive, but they also study the geographical opportunity for rebels, notably rough terrain (forest cover and mountains). Collier and

Hoeffler recognize that both opportunity and motivation are necessary for the outbreak of civil war. They argue, however, that a justice-seeking rebellion has to overcome challenges that a rebellion based on greed does not have to address as long as it has the opportunity to organize (Collier 2000a; Collier and Hoeffler 2004, 587–88). They support this argument with an empirical analysis that does not find civil wars primarily in countries where there are many grievances, but rather in countries where there are large opportunities for challenging the government militarily. An analysis of the opportunities and motivation for rebellion is also central in the World Bank project on civil war (Collier et al. 2003).

Similarly, in the study of interstate war, Most and Starr (1989, 23) posit that decisions to go to war require opportunity and willingness. Willingness refers to "the choice (and process of choice) that is related to the selection of some behavioral option from a range of alternatives," while opportunity is a shorthand term for "the possibilities that are available within any environment." In essence this is the model that we use to study civil war.

The two conditions of civil war can also be applied to the government side: The government's motive can be a narrowly self-interested wish to remain in power or a more altruistic desire to keep the nation together and protect the existing structure of governance. The government's opportunities are influenced by the available instruments of repression (including preponderance of, if not a monopoly on, armed force) but also by the minimization of the geographical factors that create opportunities for the rebels.

Both motivation and opportunity is required for armed conflict to occur. The argument we have reviewed implies an interactive effect of the two theoretical concepts: To the extent that we can quantify the extent of motivation and of opportunities for organized violence for a group, the risk of armed conflict is an increasing function of the product of these two quantities:

$$\text{risk of civil war} = f(M \cdot O)$$

Identity

Several authors (e.g., Gurr 1970) see identity as a third factor in rebellion on a par with motivation and opportunity. Ellingsen (2000, 229) identifies the same three factors but labels them frustration, opportunity, and identity.

Whether or not a group of individuals shares a common identity affects both their opportunities and motivations for rebellion or—in the case of individuals loyal to the government—for successful anti-insurgent warfare. A common identity is essential for group formation. Regardless of the motives of the rebels, they will not act together unless they see themselves as being in the same boat. A perception of injustice perpetrated against someone is most likely to be a motivation for an armed conflict if the injustice affects an identifiable group rather than isolated individuals.

A common identity also affects opportunity, however: A rebel group that recruits its members from a social group with a long history of interaction may more easily solve the collective action and coordination challenges that organization of an effective army poses (Gates 2002; Collier 2000a). A government also needs a certain amount of coherence to fight a civil war. Lacking this, it may collapse at the first rebel challenge.

Risk of Onset, Incidence, Duration, and Severity

An analysis of motivation and opportunity is fruitful for the study of onset (when civil war breaks out), for incidence (the proportion of country-years that have an ongoing civil war), and for duration (how long the violence lasts). The incidence of conflict is a function of the risk of onset and of duration—incidence is high in countries where the risk of onset is large, or when conflicts tend to be long. Incidence is highest where conflicts are both very probable and likely to last for a long time. Moreover, motivation and opportunity affect how severe a war becomes. To the extent that actors have motivation and opportunity for initiating violent conflict, they will also tend to have incentives to prolong and escalate the fighting.

There are differences, however. If only a narrow group has the opportunity and motivation to initiate and sustain an armed insurgency, the conflict may be long but not particularly severe. The Basque and Northern Ireland conflicts are examples of such enduring but relatively low-scale conflicts.

Motivations may also shift during conflict. Collier (2000b) argues that rebel group leaders are forced to rely on private incentives even when the initial motivation is to address injustices. This may cause the insurgency to shift its motivation from "justice-seeking" to "loot-seeking," and the factors that help explain a conflict's initiation may be less relevant for explaining its continuation.

Democracy and the Conditions of Violence

Democratic governance in itself can be seen as a conflict management system where different interests meet and are resolved peacefully. Democracy is related to civil war through motivation as well as opportunity.

Motivation

For broadly based opposition groups that organize to change a government's policy regarding redistribution or cultural issues, effective, inclusive, and responsive democratic institutions reduce the motivation for armed resistance. Legitimate demands have a good chance of being met through such institutions. Democratic countries are in general less repressive than nondemocracies (Zanger 2000). The absence of repression and the assurance of some political rights remove some of the motivation for rebellion in and of itself (Muller and Weede 1990).

However, democracy cannot remove motivations for rebellion for all potential rebel groups. The IRA rebelled against the British government over the right to secede, and in Chile a military coup in 1973 removed not only the elected government but the whole democratic system. The majority may perceive the political demands of narrow opposition groups as too extreme, such as a demand for secession or an alternative form of political system. In many circumstances these demands are not compatible with the democratic system present, or the system may not be sufficiently inclusive to handle the demand. Such groups may have a motivation for armed resistance even in democracies.

However, the narrower the group, the smaller the chance that it will succeed through a military strategy. A group that is narrow enough to be excluded from politics will therefore be deterred by bleak expectations. But very narrow groups that primarily seek private gains will not be less motivated to use force in democracies.

Opportunity

Democracy may also offer an opportunity for the rebels to organize an insurrection, given the greater openness and more liberal practices of democratic regimes. These liberal practices not only allow individuals more space and time, but also allow organization of political interests in a way that is unknown under autocratic regimes. This openness is most often used in liberal ways, such as trade and commerce, but under some circumstances it can be detrimental to civil peace.

Because they allow political organizations, in democracies the potential for rebellion is always present, but it is intensified if there is a change in the political regime that limits organizational freedom. In Algeria a very violent conflict was spawned from a failed liberalization process. The aim of that process was to create a modern-style democracy, but in the face of a likely fundamentalist victory a crackdown severely limited political freedoms.

On the other hand, democratic governance severely limits the opportunity of democratic leaders. Through mechanisms often referred to as checks and balances, democracy is as much about limiting executive power as selecting the executive officer. After losing an election, a democratic politician has a choice between adhering to the result and opting for another chance at the next election or mounting a rebellion against the electoral outcome. A consolidated democracy is often defined as a system where the latter alternative always is the worst option.

Summing up how democracy affects civil war through motivation and opportunity, we assume that the motive can be modeled as $(1 - D)$, where the degree of democracy is measured on a scale from 0 to 1. But democracy may also offer an opportunity for the rebels to organize an insurrection, given the greater openness and more liberal practices of democratic regimes. Thus, we may model the opportunity for rebellion simply as D on the same scale of democracy. Ignoring other motives as well as geographic and economic opportunity factors, our simple model of the risk of civil war becomes

risk of civil war $= f(D(1 - D))$,

which yields an inverted U-curve between democracy and the risk of civil war.

Identity

The political norms that keep democracies stable can be seen as a form of identity—a democratic identity. This identity is not created overnight, but is shaped through positive experiences of democratic governance. In contrast, the formal democratization of a country through the setup of electoral institutions can happen much faster. This creates a potentially dangerous situation where identities other than the democratic identity play important roles. Snyder (2000) has shown how nationalism in fragmented societies can lead a process of democratization into civil war, as it did in post-Tito Yugoslavia.

We assume that the identity of a coherent polity is stronger than an incoherent one. However, we believe that a regime with a high level of democracy is more coherent than one with a high level of autocracy. In the former, political challengers will aim to take over the government, but not to change the political system. The incumbent will yield to the response of the electorate and will step aside in an orderly transition. In autocracies, regime changes are rarely that orderly. The regime is more likely to change along with the power-holders, and violence is more likely. To the extent that identity is seen as a separate factor, it should reinforce the inverted U-shaped relationship.

Hypotheses

Level of Democracy

These considerations regarding how democratic institutions affect motivation and opportunity give rise to a set of hypotheses. The most general expectation is that democracy reduces the motivation for conflict. At the same time, however, democracy increases the opportunity of conflict. We argued previously that the risk of civil war is proportional to the product of motivation and opportunities for a country's potential rebels. Democratization in a nondemocracy has therefore two counteracting effects, and the combination of motive and opportunity produces an inverted U-shaped relationship between democracy and rebellion. In other words, in strictly authoritarian states, the probability of rebellion is low, since the opportunity is close to zero. In near-perfect democracies, the motive for rebellion is close to zero, so the probability of rebellion is low. In the in-between area of semidemocracy (or semiautocracy), the probability of rebellion is the highest. Applying the same model to the government side yields the same result. Coherent polities, whether autocratic or democratic, have a strong motivation for maintaining the regime, whether for egotistical or altruistic reasons. Incoherent (or inconsistent) polities in the middle have a much weaker sense of purpose. They are also likely to be weaker in both normative and repressive power. Thus, the likely reaction of the government side reinforces the inverted U-shape posited for the probability of rebellion.

Another implication of the two counteracting effects is that if a group is sufficiently motivated and dedicated to start a rebellion against a democratic regime, we should expect this conflict to be more durable than under other regimes. Not only are groups that use armed force against democratic regimes particularly motivated, but their democratic opponents are less capable adversaries, as they are unable to use the wide range of counterinsurgency methods available to autocrats, such as mass killings and collective punishment. The expectation that democracies will use relatively mild counterinsurgency measures makes us expect that conflicts in democracies will be less severe but also more durable.

H1: Democracy is negatively related to the onset and severity of civil war, but positively related to duration. Democracy has an indeterminate effect on incidence.

H2: Democracy relates to the onset, incidence, duration, and severity of civil war through an inverted U-curve: semidemocracies are most prone to violence.

Change in Institutions

We also relate change in political institutions to civil war. Autocratic countries do not become mature consolidated democracies overnight but usually go through a rough transition. The transition process opens up opportunities for potential rebels. Tocqueville, writing on the French Revolution (1955 [1856], 182) points out that "revolutions do not always come when things are going from bad to worse. . . . Usually the most dangerous time for a bad government is when it attempts to reform itself." The same observation holds true for the Russian Revolution and subsequent civil war.

Even when the change is in the direction of democracy, it may not be sufficient to reduce all relevant groups' motivation for war. Autocrats are likely to release their grip on society only when they find the status quo to be unsustainable, and will not reform more than they find necessary. Przeworski (1991) argues that a partial liberalization will be received as too little in the eyes of civil society, which will give the autocrats a choice between caving in to the demands present and retreating into an excessively repressive regime. Democratization may also motivate former elites to instigate coups or other armed attempts at reinstating the former status quo. If the direction of change is toward autocracy, the deconsolidation of political institutions also implies increasing repression (Zanger 2000, 225–26). In turn, such repression is likely to promote civil war (Lichbach 1987, 1995; Moore 1998).

Huntington (1991, 192ff.) also finds political violence to be coupled with democratization. Autocratic incumbents are unlikely to yield power without some resistance, which could result in serious conflict. Communal groups in liberalizing autocracies have substantial opportunities for mobilization, but such states usually lack the institutional resources to reach the accommodation typical of established democracy (Gurr 1993b, 165). When authoritarianism collapses and is followed by ineffectual efforts to establish democracy, the interim period of relative anarchy is ripe for ethnonational or ideological leaders who want to organize rebellion, as several postcommunist states have experienced.

The initial high level of uncertainty and unrest caused by democratization will gradually diminish as protesters abandon their aspirations or find ways to obtain part of what they want within the new regime. In the case of democratization, new and more open institutions take root and promote a peaceful resolution of domestic conflict. As time passes, these become more entrenched, and the likelihood of regime failure decreases. The pattern works similarly for autocratization. As repressive institutions strengthen, the effect of the regime change is less destabilizing and therefore less likely to generate political violence.

Semidemocracies are politically less stable than either autocracies or democracies (Hegre et al. 2001, table 1, p. 38; Gates et al. 2006). The hypothesis that low political stability predicts civil war is therefore consistent with an inverted U-shaped relationship between civil war and the level of democracy. We hypothesize, however, that a curvilinear effect of democracy on civil war persists even when controlling for political instability.

> H3: Political instability is positively related to the onset, incidence, duration, and severity of civil war, but most clearly correlates with onset.
> H4: The curvilinear effect of democracy on the onset, incidence, duration, and severity of civil war persists even when controlling for political instability.

Elections

In democracies, elections provide the main focal points for political change. The difference between winning and losing an election is larger in some societies and smaller in others. In consolidated democracies losing an election simply means that one has to wait an election period and try again. In other societies, this option is less certain, since an incumbent may cancel or rig a subsequent election. We posit that losing an election can provide strong motivation for rebellion if the loss is accompanied with a high distrust of the winner. This leads us to predict that holding all other political factors constant, violence will be more likely right after an election—or just before, in a preemptive strike by a likely loser. However, as more and more elections are held within a political regime, the less reasonable it seems to doubt the likelihood of another election. We therefore posit a more precise expectation. When the government of a new regime faces an election, the uncertainty regarding democratic procedures is likely to be the highest. We single out this first contest as the point most likely for experiencing armed conflict.

> H5: The risk of civil war is higher in conjunction with elections, and particularly so for the first contested election in a new political regime. Elections also tend to be accompanied by a lower risk of conflict termination and increases in severity.

Territorial versus Governmental Conflict

Several scholars have argued that different kinds of civil war can have different explanations. A violent coup differs dramatically from a secessionist conflict. Fearon and Laitin (2003), for example, perform separate analyses of ethnic civil conflicts. Starting from the distinction between territorial and government conflicts in the Uppsala/PRIO conflict data, Buhaug (2006) argues that the nature of the opportunity determines the direction of the conflict. Large countries are more likely to experience conflicts in peripheral areas where rebels will fight for secession. Capturing the central government is hard and may not even be necessary to redress the rebels' grievances. In such cases, opportunity and motivation are present for territorial conflicts, but not for governmental ones.

Smaller countries are generally less suitable for separatist insurgency, but in such countries, capturing the government is also a more realistic option. Ethnic diversity and rough terrain also offer good grounds for secession, whereas institutional consistency is particularly effective at preventing conflicts over state apparatus. We therefore hypothesize that the relationships discussed above between the level of democracy and onset, incidence, duration, and severity of civil war will be more pronounced for governmental conflicts.

> H6: The effect of democracy on the onset, incidence, duration, and severity of civil war is more pronounced for government conflicts than for territorial conflicts.

Efficiency of Institutions

Democratic institutions primarily reduce the risk of armed conflict by addressing grievances—by allocating government funds to widely useful public goods, by ensuring equitable redistribution, or by granting individuals freedom of choice in religious and cultural issues.

Democracies vary in how successful they are in delivering these policy outcomes, however. A well-functioning parliament that produces optimal decisions may not avert violence if an inefficient and corrupt bureaucracy fails to implement decisions, or if the government has only a limited presence in the home region of potential insurgents. Some students of the democratic peace at the interstate level have argued that the effect is likely to be stronger for highly developed societies, while for low-development countries it will be weak or even totally absent (Hegre 2000; Mousseau 2000; Mousseau, Hegre, and Oneal 2003). A similar argument can be made for civil war (Hegre 2003, 2005): The motivation and opportunity for rebellion are not determined only by the value of a territory, or a group's financial and organizational strength, but also by the usefulness of armed force in obtaining control over the valuables. The mobility of capital in highly developed democracies may reduce the incentives for (territorial) conflict—it may be profitable to use armed force to gain control over a diamond mine or a rich agricultural province, but not to gain control over Silicon Valley. This affects potential rebel groups as much as governments. On the other hand, a highly developed nondemocracy is likely to experience conflicts over the political system itself—a well-educated citizenry has both motivation and opportunity to fight for democratization.

Moreover, an educated and informed citizenry is essential to making democratic institutions fully effective in constraining the political leadership, so that it carries out the policies that the voters prefer. Good systems of education and the free flow of information may in turn be dependent on economic development. In addition, high-income democracies are much more stable than low-income democracies (Lipset 1959; Przeworski et al. 2000; Gates et al. 2006). Confidence in the ability of democratic institutions to provide just and equitable distribution of resources is likely to decrease "grievance." It is clear that this confidence should be larger the more stable the institutions are, and hence greater in high-income democracies. In terms of our opportunity and motivation framework, the citizens of highly developed democracies have greater opportunities for rebellion, but this is offset by less powerful motives to do so. In addition, the opportunities for the government to use armed force at the expense of its own citizens are more limited in highly developed countries. We therefore hypothesize that the relationships between civil war and the level of democracy will be stronger the higher the level of development.

H7: The effect of democracy on the onset, incidence, duration, and severity of civil war is stronger for developed countries.

Democratic Neighborhood

Most civil wars have transnational dimensions. Murdoch and Sandler (2002) and others have found economic spillovers from civil wars to proximate countries, and there are many instances where political instability in one country destabilizes neighboring countries. For example, the 1997 conflict in the Democratic Republic of Congo was influenced by the civil war in Rwanda. One of the possible mechanisms behind the spatial diffusion stems from the character of the political system in neighboring countries. Democratic government is likely to have an effect on neighboring states by setting an example and sometimes by coercion. Rebels in autocratic countries are likely to be motivated by democratic rights won in neighboring countries. Democratic governments may seen neighboring autocracies as a threat and may decide to support rebel movements overtly or covertly in order to weaken or overturn the regime. Gleditsch (2007, 298) hypothesizes that the less democratic the political institutions of neighboring countries, the higher the risk that a country will experience a civil war.

Here, we take a slightly different starting point, inspired by research on the interstate democratic peace, which indicates that mixed political dyads have the highest risk of war (Gleditsch and Hegre 1997). Rather than attacking its neighbor directly, a government can fuel a rebellion, and thereby fight through a proxy. The Indonesian involvement in the Malayan civil war in the 1960s is a clear case. This leads us to expect that civil war is less likely in democracies when neighboring countries are also democracies, but more likely in autocracies and semidemocracies.

> H8: A democratic neighborhood is negatively related to the onset, inci-
> dence, duration, and severity of civil war in a democracy and positively
> related to civil war in a semidemocracy and an autocracy.

Inclusiveness of Democratic Institutions

Democracy can take different forms. Reynal-Querol (2002) finds that more inclusive forms of governance are less likely to experience violence. She defines inclusiveness as the maximum distance between the preferences of any population group and the aggregated preference produced by the political system. Her finding is based both on comparisons of different electoral systems and on the presence of so-called veto players—institutional constraints on the executive branch. The logic behind this argument rests on Downs's (1957) economic theory of conflict and asserts that while a majoritarian system overall produces the most efficient policies, this efficiency might damage a minority to the extent that it chooses to rebel against those policies. A more inclusive system, such as those based on proportional representation, will be more representative and therefore build larger compromises, reducing the motivation for rebellion.

This view, however, is not unopposed. Not all political systems are best described by the model presented by Downs. If a society is split along a single issue, such as identity, ideology, or religion, all political parties must communicate a clear and unambiguous stance on this issue. A proportional representation system will include more parties and most likely increase the level of competition. Writing on Indian politics, Wilkinson (2004) shows that intense political competition over issue salience drives these parties to violent means in order to focus the political agenda on the ethnical cleavages. Extremist tactics polarize these societies further. This might benefit the extreme parties, but for the political system as a whole it results in a dangerous political outcome far from the median voter's preference.

While the two views differ with regard to which set of institutions should be more likely to experience conflict in the first place, they agree that conflicts in more inclusive systems should be shorter as well as less severe. In addition to testing the effect of proportional representation, as does Reynal-Querol, we want to look at federalism and parliamentarism (as opposed to presidentialism). We assume that these more inclusive forms of democracy are likely to have a greater dampening effect on civil war. We hypothesize that this is true for the onset, incidence, duration, and severity of civil war.

> H9: The effect of democracy on the onset, incidence, duration, and severity of civil war is more pronounced for inclusive types of democracy.

The Impact of the Cold War

Finally, we assume that the various relationships between democracy and civil war are generally strengthened after the end of the Cold War. The reason for this is the polarization during the Cold War, which led Western democratic powers to support autocratic, noncommunist regimes as the lesser evil. This external support reduced the opportunities for insurgency against otherwise weak governments. The East and West supplied proxy wars in Angola, Central America, and elsewhere, and most of these conflicts ended when the outside support dried up. After the Cold War, rebel groups have been forced to a much larger extent to rely on the opportunities that are determined by domestic conditions, such as the availability of lootable resources (Collier and Hoeffler 2004) and weak governments (Hegre et al. 2001; Fearon and Laitin 2003).

Such polarization has occurred in other world-encompassing conflicts, too. During the fight against Nazism, Western democracies tolerated (or even supported) Communist regimes and insurgencies as a lesser evil than Nazism. In the present "war on terror," autocratic regimes in the Middle East are more palatable than radical and anti-Western Islamic regimes. Yet most of the period after 1989 has been less polarized than the Cold War years. We might expect to find the world reverting to greater polarization after 2001, but this period is too short to allow testing of a hypothesis.

H10: The relationships specified in the previous hypotheses are generally
strengthened after the end of the Cold War.

Previous Empirical Studies

A number of studies have addressed these issues. Collier and Hoeffler
(2004) dismissed democracy as an influence on the onset of civil war, but
their research design with five-year periods is not well suited to study the
impact of political factors. Fearon and Laitin (2003) and others also fail to
find a linear relationship between democracy and civil war. Carey (2007),
however, found that countries with different forms of executive election
had (in varying degrees) lower risks of large-scale violent dissent (using data
from Banks 2000) than countries with no elections. Several studies have also
concluded that there is no relationship between democracy and the duration of civil war (Collier, Hoeffler, and Söderbom 2004; De Rouen and Sobek
2004; Fearon 2004). However, Elbadawi and Sambanis (2000b) found
democracy to be negatively related to the incidence of civil war in Africa,
and Elbadawi and Sambanis (2002) found the same for a global study.

The inverted U-curve between the level of democracy and civil war
was reported by Muller and Weede (1990) and Ellingsen and Gleditsch
(1997). In a model with an extensive set of control variables, Hegre and
colleagues (Hegre et al. 2001) found the inverted U for the onset of civil
war for the entire Correlates of War period (1816–1992) as well as for the
post–World War II period (1946–92). They also found a minor and non-
significant negative linear effect of democracy on civil war and a positive
and significant effect of political instability, as measured by the proximity
of the most recent regime change. The inverted U-curve has also been
found in global studies by Sambanis (2001), de Soysa (2002), Reynal-
Querol (2002), Bates et al. (2003), Smith (2004), Urdal (2005), and Bussmann and Schneider (2007), but not in Hegre, Gissinger, and Gleditsch
(2003). A similar finding is reported by Auvinen (1997). Fearon and Laitin
(2003) found that a dummy variable for anocracy (semidemocracy) had a
positive influence on civil war, consistent with the inverted-U hypothesis.
Krause and Suzuki (2005) report an inverted U-curve for Asia as well as for
sub-Saharan Africa, as do Henderson and Singer (2000) for the postcolo-
nial states of Africa, Asia, and the Middle East. Bussmann, Schneider, and
Wiesehomeier (2005) report an inverted U-curve for sub-Saharan Africa,
but with such a high turning-point that most of the countries are on the
upward slope of the curve.

The inverted-U finding relies mostly on the coding of the Polity democracy index. Treier and Jackman (2008) argue that measurement errors in the index, especially at the two ends of the scale, necessitate the use of correction methods. This problem is particularly acute when using a nonlinear specification of the variable. In a reanalysis by Hegre and colleagues (Hegre et al. 2001), they conclude that there is no significant relationship between democracy squared and civil war onset. However, unlike Treier and Jackman, we think that the measurement error is greatest in the middle rather than at the end points of the scale. Pure and consistent regimes are easily identified, while the exact nature of a mixed regime is hard to assess. Thus, we question whether measurement error biases the result in the way that they claim.

A more serious problem with the Polity index is pointed out by Hegre and colleagues (2001), Vreeland (2008), and Strand (2006, chap. 5). If there is "factionalism" in a country with democratic institutions, for example, intense intergroup conflicts that may or may not be violent, the Polity index will code the country as an imperfect democracy. Hence, the finding that imperfect democracies have more civil war may have a tautological element. Vreeland and Strand also reanalyze Hegre et al. (2001), and find the evidence for the inverted U to be much weaker when removing the two components of Polity that contain this coding. In an extensive analysis, Hegre and Sambanis (2006) also find robust evidence for the inverted U-shaped relationship when using the Polity variables. They do not find any relationship when replacing these with variables that remove the "factionalism" component. We return to this issue in the empirical analysis.

There are few studies of the relationship between elections and subsequent violence. Bates and colleagues (2003) find that in particular the second election is a critical turning point in partial democracies. Strand (2006, chap. 8) corroborates this finding, and finds a conditional relationship between proximity to an election and a heightened risk of conflict onset.

Hegre (2003) found strong evidence that democracy is correlated with civil peace only for developed countries and for countries with high levels of literacy. Conversely, he found that the risk of civil war decreases with development only for democratic countries. Buhaug (2006) introduced the distinction between civil wars over territory and government and found the inverted U-curve for the latter but not for the former. Gleditsch (2002a, 106; 2007) found that the degree of democracy in neighboring countries had a significant effect on the risk of civil war, in fact greater than the country-specific effect of democracy.

As noted, Reynal-Querol (2002) found empirical support for the conflict-dampening effect of more inclusive types of democracy, as did Schneider and Wiesehomeier (2008). Carey (2007) found that countries with executives elected through multiparty elections have lower risk of insurgency than countries without elections. But so do countries with single-candidate elections. Hartzell and Hoddie (2003) found that power sharing among former combatants specified in a peace agreement increased the likelihood that peace will endure after a civil war. They suggest that this occurs because of the unique capacity of power-sharing institutions to foster a sense of security among former enemies and encourage conditions conducive to a self-enforcing peace. Binningsbø (2006) also found that power sharing—and particularly the formation of a grand coalition—increased the duration of peace after the end of a conflict. However, Hegre and Sambanis (2006, 526) found that presidentialism was associated with a lower risk of civil war onset.

Using a new data set on battle deaths (Lacina and Gleditsch 2005), Lacina (2006) found the determinants of conflict severity to be quite different from those for conflict onset. Democracy, rather than economic development or state military strength, is most strongly correlated with fewer deaths.

Data

Since the content of democracy itself is a highly contested subject, it is not surprising that a large number of different operationalizations are found in the academic literature. Despite some criticism (e.g., Gleditsch and Ward 1997), the empirical literature in international relations and peace research has overwhelmingly chosen to use the data from the Polity project (Jaggers and Gurr 1995; Marshall and Jaggers 2003).[3] The empirical confirmation of the inverted U is largely based on Polity. We start our analysis using this data set, but most of our analyses use the SIP index from the MIRPS[4] data set (Gates et al. 2006), which differs from Polity in that the participation dimension is based on reported election turnout as given in Vanhanen (2000).

The civil war data all come from the Uppsala/PRIO conflict data set. We rely on onset data from Strand (2006, chap. 4); incidence data from Gleditsch et al. (2002), most recently updated in Harbom, Högbladh, and Wallensteen (2006); duration data from Gates and Strand (2006); and data on severity (battle deaths) from Lacina and Gleditsch (2005). We include all the conflicts in the Uppsala/PRIO data set, which has a lower level for inclusion at 25 battle deaths in a given year.[5]

Proximity to regime change is based on the SIP measure, where a change is defined as either a halving or doubling of participation; a change in the institutional recruitment of the executive (i.e., whether the executive is elected or not); or a change in Polity's executive constraints dimension of more than one unit. Political difference is defined as difference between the democracy level as measured by the SIP index of a given country and the average of all nontransitional regime values within a distance of 100 kilometers that meet the Gleditsch and Ward (1999) system membership criterion. The variable is continuous and ranges from −1 (neighbors are democratic while the country itself is nondemocratic) to 1 (the country is democratic while the neighbors are nondemocratic). We include this variable and its square in the analyses to follow. The square term ranges from 0 to 1 and reflects the difference between the level of democracy in the country and among its neighbors.

Data on election dates are from Strand (2006, chap. 8). Our expectation, in line with the finding of Bates and colleagues (2003), is that violence is most likely in connection with the first election in a new political regime where the incumbent government is at risk of losing office. We will therefore include two election measures. One variable measures the proximity to the election that provides the first test of the new regime, and the other variable measures proximity to any other election. Data on presidentialism, proportional representation, and federalism are scored according to Schneider and Wiesehomeier (2008), partially based on data from Golder (2005). For economic development and population we use data from Penn World Tables, but in order to reduce missing data problems, we use the expanded data from Gleditsch (2002b). Both of these indicators are lagged one year and log-transformed. The data on ethnolinguistic fractionalization were collected by Roeder (2001). For the oil dependency variable, we use data from Fearon and Laitin (2003).

Analysis

We start by a bivariate analysis of the relationship between the various democracy variables and four measures of armed conflict: onset, incidence, duration, and severity (table 1). All figures are in ratio form and roughly comparable. These ratios tell us how many times better or worse democracies perform in comparison to other regimes. The column labeled "Onset" provides estimates of the relative risk of onset of armed conflict—the estimated probability of onset of conflict when the explanatory variable is at a value $X_1 = X_0 + 1$ divided by the estimated probability when the variable is at X_0. For variables that range from 0 to 1, this is the same as the risk when the variable is at its maximum divided by when it is at its minimum. The column labeled "Incidence" gives estimated ratios of the odds of a country being involved in a conflict in a given year. The column labeled "Duration" gives an estimate of relative durability of a conflict given that it has started. The column labeled "Severity" reports the estimated ratio of the number of *annual* battle deaths during the war when the explanatory variable is at its maximum divided by the number of deaths when it is at its minimum.[6] For the incidence, duration, and severity analyses, variables are measured independently for every on-going year of conflict.

TABLE 1. Democracy and Four Measures of Civil War, 1950–2000

	Onset	Incidence	Duration	Severity
Polity IV democracy-autocracy index	0.59**	0.95	3.61***	0.37***
Polity IV democracy-autocracy index squared	0.24***	0.30***	1.40	0.37***
SIP democracy index	0.56***	0.90	2.80**	0.41***
SIP democracy index squared	0.40***	0.70***	3.66**	0.44***
Vanhanen index of democracy	0.23***	0.49 ***	4.06	0.21***
Vanhanen index of democracy squared	0.003***	0.072***	1.81	0.059***
Freedom House index	0.35***	0.38***	2.06	0.28***
Freedom House index squared	0.45***	0.51***	0.64	1.19
Proximity of regime change	2.39***	2.17***	0.76	2.02***
Proximity of election	2.29**	0.88	1.70	0.75**
Difference from political system in neighborhood	0.79	1.29**	3.78***	0.52***
Difference squared	2.40**	2.77***	1.22	0.17***
Presidentialism	0.96	1.44***	0.54	1.79***
Proportional representation	0.32***	0.70***	2.26	0.76*
Federalism	2.56***	0.69**	1.17	1.08

Note: The figures for the onset and incidence columns are relative risk ratios, the figures for duration are time ratios, and the figures for severity are casualty ratios. The estimates are based on a data set with 159 countries and 204 civil wars (corresponding to 5,848 country-years). Within each column, all analyses are based on the same set of countries and conflicts. The exceptions are in the final three columns, which are restricted to 49 wars in 93 democracies (2,366 country-years). For all analyses, we removed observations with missing information for the control variables to make the results immediately comparable to those reported in table 4.

Here and in the subsequent tables we report two-sided tests of the hypothesis that the exponent of the coefficient is not equal to 1. See the end-of-chapter appendix with the replication data for the details and also Strand (2007).

$*p < .1$ $**p < .05$ $***p < .01$

The bivariate results are very favorable regarding the effects of democratic governance. The first row shows the ratios for countries with maximum Polity IV score as compared to countries with minimum Polity score. The .59 estimate in the "Onset" column shows that democracies are 40 percent less likely to experience a civil war onset than autocracies. The .95 estimate in the "Incidence" column reflects that they are 5 percent less likely to be in a state of civil war at a given point in time. However, once a conflict has erupted in a democracy, it tends to persist. In fact, democracies experience conflicts that are almost four times longer than those experienced by autocracies. On the other hand, the "Severity" column shows that conflicts in democracies are less intense—in each year of the conflict, they claim only one-third the number of victims of similar conflicts in nondemocracies. Overall, armed conflicts in democracies would seem to claim about as many lives as conflicts in nondemocracies, but they are spread out over a much longer period. This observation does not imply that as many people have been killed in democracies as in nondemocracies. Keeping in mind that armed conflicts are much less common in democracies than other regimes, we can still conclude that inhabitants in democracies are generally safer. Indeed when we look at the period 1946–2002, we find that fatalities in nondemocracies exceed those in democracies by three to one. All ratios are significantly different from 1.

The second row in table 1 shows similar results for the square of the Polity IV index. The index was squared and rescaled such that the squared index ranges from 0 (for the midpoint) to 1 (for the endpoints of the Polity scale). The ratios presented therefore compare the endpoints of the Polity scale to the mean. We see that the inverted U-curve is strong and robust in a bivariate model, both for onset and for incidence: Consistent democracies and autocracies are 77 percent less likely to have conflict onset and 70 percent less likely to be at war at any given time. Consistent autocracies and democracies also have longer wars than the inconsistent regime types, but this result is not statistically significant. Finally, inconsistent regimes have three times more lethal wars than pure autocracies and democracies.

Rows 3 and 4 present the same set of results using the SIP democracy index from the MIRPS project. The SIP index avoids the endogeneity problem in Polity by replacing the participation component of Polity with the corresponding element of Vanhanen's Polyarchy index. Hence, this index is not affected by the "factionalism" problem in Polity. The results for the SIP index (row 3) are roughly the same as for the Polity index. The results for the SIP democracy index squared, however (row 4) are clearly weaker than the corresponding results for the Polity index. The exception is the duration analysis, where we find consistent regimes to have almost four times longer wars than inconsistent ones. Overall, in a bivariate analysis, there seems to be significant support for an inverted U-shaped relationship.

Both Polity and MIRPS combine information on how political power is gathered and how it can be used. Vanhanen's Polyarchy data set focuses exclusively on how power is won, through observing election outcomes. The Polyarchy Index of Democracy is the product of electoral participation and competition. Using this indicator of democracy, we find a very strong support for both a linear and curvilinear relationship between democracy and onset, incidence, and severity, but weaker results for duration. When we use the Freedom House indicator, whose particular strength is to measure how political power is used, we find fairly similar results. The one clear difference is that there is no curvilinear relationship between democracy and severity. The Freedom House scores are partly based on freedom from "acts of violence or terror due to civil conflict or war," which makes this data set, too, biased in favor of our hypothesis (Freedom House 2006).

Table 1 shows that the bivariate relationship between level of democracy and onset of conflict is very robust across different definitions of democracy: Democracies experience fewer conflict onsets than other regimes. Once conflicts occur, they are less brutal in democracies than in other regimes. Figure 1 shows the bivariate relationship between regime type and civil war, with the size of the circles indicating the severity of the conflict, plotted on a background of a tripartite division of regime type. Many of these conflicts have gone on for a long time, but most of them have claimed relatively few lives.[7] Using Polity and MIRPS, we find that autocracies experience the longest conflicts, but these findings are not supported by Polyarchy or Freedom House. There are aspects of the latter two data sets that weaken our confidence in them. First, Vanhanen's data set does not take into consideration how much power the executive has once it is won. This limits its ability to discriminate between liberal and illiberal democracies, and it is this distinction in particular that, according to our theory, makes democracies less capable of fighting rebellions. The Freedom House data set is only available from 1973, while the other data sets span the whole period 1950–2000. This creates a particular problem

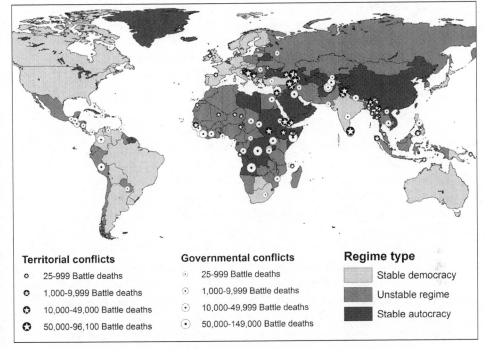

Territorial conflicts

- ○ 25-999 Battle deaths
- ◎ 1,000-9,999 Battle deaths
- ◉ 10,000-49,000 Battle deaths
- ✪ 50,000-96,100 Battle deaths

Governmental conflicts

- ⊙ 25-999 Battle deaths
- ⊙ 1,000-9,999 Battle deaths
- ⊙ 10,000-49,999 Battle deaths
- ⊙ 50,000-149,000 Battle deaths

Regime type

- Stable democracy
- Unstable regime
- Stable autocracy

Fig. 1. Regime type and the severity of civil war, 1989–2004. (*Note:* Conflict data from the Uppsala/PRIO conflict data [Gleditsch et al. 2002], battle deaths from Lacina and Gleditsch [2005], and regime type data from Gates et al. [2006] with some additions for countries with missing scores in their data sets. Countries coded as democracies and autocracies have had stable regime types (democracy = SIP index > 0.80; autocracy = SIP < 0.25). All others—including politically unstable countries and countries stably located in the middle of the scale—are coded as semidemocracies. For the distinction between conflicts over government and territory, see Buhaug [2006]. The dots and asterisks are placed at the center of the conflict zone [Buhaug and Gates 2002]. The larger the dot or asterisk, the greater the cumulative number of battle deaths over this 16-year period. Only conflicts active during this period have been included. For practical reasons, the definitions and time span used in this figure differ marginally from those used in the analysis.)

for duration analysis, since the most durable conflicts, which started early in the period, are excluded. Thus, the conflicts analyzed with the Freedom House data are a sample of shorter conflicts and therefore not representative. These problems, and the fact that regime changes are not dated in these data sets,[8] make Polyarchy and Freedom House less suited for our purpose. We will not use these indicators in our multivariate analyses.

Proximity to regime change is measured using a decay function. This function assumes that the negative impact of a regime change is at its peak immediately after the change takes place, after which it diminishes at a constant rate over time. The decay function is therefore always 1 when time since last regime change is 0 (i.e., the day before), and the decay takes the value 0 when the time since last regime change is infinitely long. The attenuation rate is determined by the half-life parameter, which in this analysis we have set to 4 years. Thus, four years after a regime change, the risk of conflict is 50 percent of the original risk stemming from the regime change. After 8 years, it is 25 percent, after 12 years 12.5 percent, and so on. Whereas regime change does seem unrelated to the chances that a conflict ends, it is clearly related to the risk of its onset. Regimes that recently have experienced a regime change are 2.5 times more likely to see a conflict than regimes that have remained unchanged for several years. Regime changes also lead to a doubling in the violence levels. The incidence of conflict is also increased, but given the insignificant effect on duration, this effect seemingly stems from the increased risk of experiencing a new conflict rather than the prolongation of present conflicts.

The nature of the political systems in the immediate neighborhood is clearly also important. We do not find a particularly high risk of war onset in countries that have political systems that are different from the systems in the immediate neighborhood.[9] Just as we find an effect of level of democracy on duration, however, we find that if a country is considerably more democratic than its neighborhood, the duration of armed conflict increases by a factor of four. We also find that the incidence of conflict is 29 percent higher for countries in heterogeneous neighborhoods than for those in homogenous ones. On the other hand, wars are less intense than wars in homogenous neighborhoods if the country is more democratic than its neighbors. Countries that are politically different from their neighborhood also have less lethal wars. This result cannot be explained by the level of democracy in the country itself, however, since the square of the political difference is also significantly less than 1. Wars that take place in a country with a political system different from its neighborhood lead to only one-sixth of the annual fatalities compared to wars in politically similar neighborhoods. This applies regardless of whether the country in question is very democratic or autocratic.

Among democracies, parliamentary systems experience more severe wars than both presidential and mixed systems. Proportional representation systems have a lower risk of war onset and may be less lethal, but there are indications that they last longer than majoritarian systems. Finally, countries with federal systems have a higher risk of war onset than centralized systems.

Our earlier research has shown that inconsistent regimes are considerably less stable than consistent regimes. Therefore, we need to assess whether or not the inverted U holds up when we control for proximity of regime change. In table 2, the first row repeats the bivariate results for conflict onset from table 1. The second row shows the bivariate relative risk when controlling for "proximity of regime change." Controlling for political stability does not eradicate the effect of democracy on conflict onset, contrary to the results in Vreeland (2008), but the effect for the inverted U is somewhat weaker. A politically different neighborhood now increases the risk of civil war onset. Since democratization is contagious

TABLE 2. The Inverted U, Controlling for Four Single Control Variables, Onset of Civil War, 1950–2000

	Democracy	Democracy Squared	Squared Difference from Political System in Neighborhood	Proximity to Elections
Bivariate results (159/204)	0.56***	0.40***	0.79	2.29**
Control for political stability	0.59***	0.52**	2.42**	1.67
High level of development	0.30**	0.08***	4.54	4.51
Low level of development	0.92	0.76	1.99*	1.91
Governmental conflict	0.41***	0.30***	0.74	2.09
Territorial conflict	0.85	0.58	8.40***	2.56
Cold War	0.79	0.60	1.57	2.66*
Post–Cold War	0.34***	0.24***	5.30***	1.94

Note: All results except the first row (which is copied from Table 1) are based on trivariate models of onset. All figures are relative risk ratios estimated using calendar-time Cox regression. The estimates are based on a data set with 159 countries and 204 civil wars. Within each column, all analyses are based on the same set of countries and conflicts. In the analyses in the last six rows this data set is divided into three pairs of subsamples. The high-development subset has 25 wars in 80 countries The governmental subset has 119 wars in 159 countries. The Cold War subset has 122 wars in 138 countries. Democracy is measured by the SIP index.

*$p < .1$ **$p < .05$ ***$p < .01$

(Gleditsch and Ward 2006), this effect may imply that the most stubborn political regimes are toppled violently. An example of this is the transition to democracy in Rumania in 1989, which occurred after the transitions in the neighboring countries and became quite violent.

The next two rows in table 2 investigate the hypothesis in Hegre (2003) that the effect of democracy is dependent on the level of development by estimating the relative risk of onset of conflict separately for high-income and low-income countries (defined as having an average income of less than $5,500 per year in real 1995 U.S. dollars). Row 3 shows that the relationship between democracy and democracy squared is very strong for developed countries. The relationship is much weaker and not significant in low-income countries. The neighborhood and election variables have strong but insignificant coefficients in the high-development sample, which means that the trivariate model is not very precise. The coefficients are smaller for the low-development sample, where there is some evidence of a neighborhood effect but no effect from proximity to elections.

Buhaug (2006) and Buhaug and Rød (2006) report that conflicts over government have different causes than territorial conflicts. In rows 5 and 6, we reproduce their finding by estimating the bivariate relationship separately for the two types of conflicts. Whereas the danger of governmental conflicts clearly depends on the level of democracy of the regime, there are no connections between the two democracy indicators and territorial conflict. The difference in the political neighborhood, on the other hand, strongly increases the likelihood of a territorial conflict, but not governmental conflict.

Finally, the argument that the absence of democratic institutions has become a more important predictor of conflict after the Cold War, receives support in rows 7 and 8. For the post–Cold War period, the bivariate relationships between our democracy variables and conflict are very strong. Moreover, difference from the political system in the neighborhood increases the risk of war onset strongly after the Cold War. The results for the Cold War period are weaker and not as significant, except for proximity to elections. Here we are probably capturing an effect of political instability in former colonies.

In the analysis reported in table 3, we add several control variables that might explain both levels and stability of democracy. In the table, we only report the estimated coefficients for the democracy variables—these should be interpreted as risk or severity ratios *contingent* on the control variables. (Tables 4 and 5 report the full set of results for some of the onset and severity models.)

The results in table 1 indicated that there are strong bivariate effects between democracy and armed conflict. The contingent relationships in table 3 are generally considerably weaker. In fact, only the squared democracy variables are significantly associated with the risk of civil war onset, and none of the indicators are related to duration. From this we can claim weak support for the hypothesis that semidemocracies have a higher risk of conflict and that regional differences also play a role in increasing this risk. The contingent relationships with war severity, on the other hand, are strong and generally in the predicted direction. Both proximity variables (regime change and election) are reported to have some effect on the risk of conflict, but these findings are not significant. Both of these factors are related to political instability, and it is premature to use the lack of significance as an argument against their importance. We will return to this point later.

As is evident in table 4, low economic development is a strong predictor of armed conflict. We also know from other studies that economic development is strongly associated with stable democratic governance (e.g., Gates et al. 2006). Highly developed countries tend to be democracies and

TABLE 3. Democracy and Civil War, with Control Variables, 1950–2000

	Onset	Incidence	Duration	Severity
With Polity				
Democracy	0.90	0.82	2.06	0.40***
Democracy squared	0.42***	0.53***	0.98	0.52***
With SIP				
Democracy	0.80	0.73	1.23	0.55***
Democracy squared	0.58*	0.79	2.29	0.95
Proximity of regime change	1.35	1.06	1.09	1.63***
Proximity of election	1.58	1.13	1.95	0.88
Difference from political				
system in neighborhood	1.26	1.49	1.93	1.41
Difference squared	2.38*	2.60**	0.12	0.29***
Presidentialism	0.57	0.62	0.48	2.40***
Proportional representation	1.002	2.39**	10.55**	0.48***
Federalism	0.57	0.32**	0.25	2.67**

Note: The figures in the onset and incidence columns are relative risk ratios, the figures for duration are time ratios, and the figures for severity are casualty ratios. The full set of control variables (results not reported in the table) is found in table 4 and described in more detail in Strand (2007). The estimates are based on a data set with 159 countries and 204 civil wars (corresponding to 5,848 country-years). Within each column, all analyses are based on the same set of countries and conflicts. The exceptions are in the final three columns, which are restricted to 49 wars in 93 democracies (2,366 country-years).

$*p < .1$ $**p < .05$ $***p < .01$

peaceful. This explains why there is no relationship between democracy and onset or incidence in table 3: The peaceful quality of democracies may be due to their status as highly developed rather than as democracies. We saw in table 2 that the effect of political regimes is much stronger in developed countries. Hegre (2003) finds this to be true, even when controlling for other variables.

The results in table 3 give us two different versions of the inverted U-curve between conflict and democracy. Using the Polity IV data set, we find evidence of an inverted U-curve regarding *onset* of conflict. The contingent relative risk of conflict in very democratic or very autocratic countries is .42 or 58 percent lower than in a comparable semidemocracy. As noted, this relationship is partly explained by the coding of "factionalism" in Polity. The same effect, using the SIP data set, is 42 percent. The difference between these two findings is due to the endogenous component of the Polity data set. We find no evidence supporting the hypothesis that democracies are less at risk than other regimes, nor does the analysis support a claim that their wars are longer.

For both democracy measures, the results are weaker when we look at incidence than at onset; that is, the coefficient for the squared term for democracy is closer to one. As noted, incidence includes aspects of both onset and duration. Semidemocracies experience fewer conflicts, but their conflicts are more durable when they occur. These two effects pull in opposite directions, and the net effect is indeterminate.

We saw in table 1 that democracies are associated with less intense conflicts, confirming the results in Lacina (2006). In table 3, the annual level of battle-related fatalities is 45–60 percent lower *per year* for conflicts in democracies than in autocracies, even when we take into account population size. In the multivariate analysis, there is only weak evidence that democracies or inconsistent regimes have longer wars than nondemocracies. The analysis clearly shows that the average democratic conflict is less violent than the average conflict in a nondemocratic country.

The effect of the political difference with the neighborhood is greatly reduced when we take into account the control variables, including the level of democracy in the country in question. The "political difference squared" is estimated to increase the incidence of conflict but, as noted in the bivariate analysis, it tends to strongly reduce its severity.

Comparing different democratic regimes, we find no real differences between onset ratios, but the duration and severity analyses seem to echo the initial comparison of democracies and autocracies. Presidential regimes have more violent conflicts. In countries with proportional representation, the conflicts tend to last longer, but they are less violent per year than conflicts in majoritarian systems. Since the conflicts are longer, the incidence of conflict is higher in parliamentary systems. The findings for federalism disappear when we add control variables (country size is particularly important here). Wars in federal democracies seem to be shorter than in centralized systems, and this tendency is strong enough to be reflected in a significant estimate in the incidence analysis.

Summarizing the results from table 3, we conclude that most of the bivariate effects reported in table 1 do not hold up when introducing control variables. However, given that a conflict has erupted, there seems to be strong and persistent effect from political regimes on the severity of the conflict. Democracies tend to experience more protracted conflicts, but this finding is not significant. On the other hand, democracies have less violent wars. We discuss this finding in more detail below.

Several studies of the causes of conflict (Fearon and Laitin 2003; Hegre et al. 2001) report an effect from political instability, which seems to contradict the findings reported in table 3. Table 4 presents a more nuanced result, indicating strong support for the hypothesis that political instability is related to conflict but agnostic on the correct operationalization of this concept. The figures reported are the results from a full, multivariate analysis of onset of armed conflict.

The figures in table 3 are based on Model 1, where we see that the inverted U-curve receives a fair measure of support, while neither regime change nor election proximity is significant. However, a third measure of political instability, proximity to independence, is strong and significant. Proximity to regime change and proximity to independence share the same causal logic. It is the unconsolidated nature of the political regime that is the key factor explaining the onset of conflict. A final proxy for political instability is the institutional difference from the neighborhood. Gates and colleagues (2006) provide evidence for a strong destabilizing effect from such political isolation. As argued earlier, this can be a consequence of the spatial clustering of regime changes. As a proxy for political instability, it differs somewhat from the other measures, as it captures the potential for regime change as much as change that has already taken place. Squared difference from political neighborhood has a quite strong and robust effect on the relative risk of conflict.

In Model 2 we remove the competing operationalizations of political instability, resulting in a stronger and significant effect from proximity to

TABLE 4. The Correlates of Internal Armed Conflict Onset, Hazard Ratios: Multivariate Results with Control Variables, 1950–2000

	Model 1	Model 2	Model 3	Model 4
SIP	0.802	1.115	1.207	0.719
	(−0.581)	(0.415)	(0.454)	(−0.619)
SIP squared	0.576*	0.642	0.520**	0.509*
	(−1.880)	(−1.551)	(−2.026)	(−1.784)
Proximity to regime change	1.351	1.590*	1.730*	1.699
	(1.039)	(1.696)	(1.695)	(1.614)
Proximity to independence	2.792**		2.909**	1.419
	(2.312)		(2.087)	(0.533)
Proximity to first real election	1.577		1.157	3.035**
	(1.077)		(0.302)	(2.391)
Proximity to other elections	0.925		0.983	1.119
	(−0.230)		(−0.042)	(0.224)
Democratic difference	1.262		1.030	1.046
	(0.636)		(0.067)	(0.098)
Democratic difference squared	2.377*		2.060	1.676
	(1.711)		(1.115)	(0.693)
Average income (ln)	0.664***	0.637***	0.622***	0.686**
	(−3.488)	(−3.948)	(−3.675)	(−2.564)
Population (ln)	1.340***	1.325***	1.287***	1.232***
	(4.898)	(4.586)	(3.510)	(3.267)
Proximity to conflict	3.678***	3.465***	1.752***	7.163***
	(6.308)	(5.948)	(2.287)	(7.579)
Ethnolinguistic fractionalization	2.220**	2.327**	2.087*	1.734
	(2.466)	(2.558)	(1.856)	(1.458)
Ethnolinguistic fractionalization squared	0.046**	0.044**	0.099*	0.031**
	(−2.435)	(−2.493)	(−1.676)	(−2.126)
Oil exporter	1.665**	1.706**	1.770**	1.800*
	(2.005)	(2.089)	(2.131)	(1.761)
Log likelihood	−875.98	−881.07	−695.17	−501.46
Log likelihood null model	−983.92	−983.92	−754.29	−579.66
N	25,972	25,972	19,537	14,801
Number of countries	159	159	159	159
Number of civil wars	204	204	157	121

Note: Model 3 excludes intermittent conflicts. Model 4 includes only conflicts with more than 1,000 battle deaths. The figures reported are relative risk ratios, with z-scores in parentheses. The term N refers to the number of snapshots analyzed. At each of the 204 onsets, all countries independent at that moment are observed. Since a number of the 159 countries included in our study gained their independence after 1945, our N is lower than 32,436 (204 × 159).

*$p < .1$ **$p < .05$ ***$p < .01$

regime change. This effect provides good support for our hypothesis of a relationship between political instability and conflict, and it is supportive of the argument made above. Political instability has an effect, but it is unclear through which variables this manifests itself.

To investigate this claim further, we use the robustness checks introduced in Strand (2006, chap. 4). In the analysis reported so far, we have coded a new onset whenever the conflict was inactive for more than two whole calendar years. Inevitably, this includes a number of onsets that are commonly interpreted as a continuation and direct consequence of the previous conflict period. In Model 3, we reanalyze our data with a stricter requirement: new onsets are recorded only after eight years of inactivity. In Model 4, we include only those conflicts that exceed a total 1,000 battle-related deaths.

These robustness checks provide clear support for the instability hypothesis. With the stricter onset requirement (Model 3), we find that proximity to both independence and succeeding regime changes are significant contributors to risk of conflict. The inverted U-curve is present as well. However, neither elections nor difference from neighborhood are significantly associated with increase of risk in this model, although the coefficient for difference from neighborhood is almost as strong as in Model 1.

When we focus on conflicts that exceed 1,000 battle-related deaths (Model 4), proximity to regime change has almost exactly the same effect as in Model 3, but the uncertainty increases to just above the limit of significance. The substantive effect remains the same. On the other hand, proximity to independence is reduced from being very influential to an insignificant factor. Proximity to election is a very potent predictor in Model 4, in contrast to the other models. As expected, it is the first election in a political regime under the initial government that significantly increases the risk of conflict. Since this election very often comes in the initial period of a new political regime, this variable and proximity to regime change can be seen as measuring almost the same thing. The election variable is more sensitive to time, and the effect of an election is quickly reduced, whereas the proximity to regime change variable is much more persistent. Both are decay functions, but have half-life values of six months and 2.9 years respectively. However, they are both measures of political stability, and Model 4 further strengthens our hypothesis.

Table 5 shows correspondingly detailed results for models with severity as the dependent variable. The unit of analysis is a conflict-year, and the dependent variable is the natural logarithm of the estimated number of battle deaths in that conflict-year. We include the lagged dependent variable in the model. If the year before the year of observation was a peace year, we set ln(battle deaths) to 0. The interpretation of the estimates therefore indicates the change in battle deaths from the previous year. The estimates are exponentiated to be comparable to the risk and odds ratios presented earlier. The estimate for the SIP democracy index signifies that given last year's severity and the values for the other control

TABLE 5. Correlates of the Severity of Internal Armed Conflict, Ratios: Multivariate Results with Control Variables, 1950–2000

	Model 1	Model 2
Lagged dependent variable (ln)	1.38***	1.39***
	(19.22)	(19.46)
Polity IV	0.40***	
	(–3.53)	
Polity IV squared	0.52***	
	(–3.34)	
SIP democracy index		0.55**
		(–2.29)
SIP democracy index squared		0.95
		(–0.22)
Difference from political system in neighborhood	1.76**	1.41
	(2.41)	(1.37)
Difference squared	0.39***	0.29***
	(–2.69)	(–3.39)
Proximity to regime change	1.33*	1.63***
	(1.85)	(3.16)
Average income (ln)	0.85***	0.84***
	(–3.30)	(–3.29)
Population (ln)	1.04	1.03
	(0.87)	(0.67)
Election year	0.88	0.88
	(–1.02)	(0.97)
Ethnolinguistic fractionalization	1.17	1.34
	(0.68)	(1.28)
Ethnolinguistic fractionalization squared	0.033***	0.042***
	(–4.15)	(–3.76)
Oil exporter (>1/3 of total exports)	1.35**	1.40**
	(2.09)	(2.30)
Log likelihood	–1,547.39	–1,595.93
Log likelihood null model	–1,771.30	–1,817.57
Number of country-years	877	897

Note: The figures reported are exponentiated coefficients, to be interpreted as ratios relative to the baseline, with *t*-scores in parentheses.

$*p < .1$ $**p < .05$ $***p < .01$

variables, a war in a democracy on average has 55 percent of the fatalities of a war in an average autocracy.

In Model 1 we use Polity, while in Model 2 we use the SIP index. We find a strong conflict-dampening effect of democracy for both measures. Since the main term is smaller than 1 in both models, there is no inverted U-relationship here. The estimated relationship is stronger for the Polity index than for the SIP index, however.

The effects of the control variables are remarkably similar to those found in the onset analysis. The same factors that increase the risk of a war onset contribute to making the war more severe. A regime change during a war increases the expected number of fatalities by 33–63 percent in the first year. As before, this effect is assumed to decrease thereafter at a constant rate with a half-life of one year. Wars that occur in politically different neighborhoods are less lethal than wars in similar neighborhoods, but this does not apply if the difference is positive; that is, for democracies in nondemocratic neighborhoods. Ethnolinguistic fractionalization reduces the severity of wars, possibly because coordination problems in both armies reduce their efficiency and scope. Wars in high-income countries are less intense than in low-income countries, and oil exporters have more violent wars than countries with comparable incomes derived from other sources. The population variable is not significant. This difference from the onset analysis is probably because population has a smaller variance in the war sample than in the full sample, and because much of the population effect is taken up by the lagged dependent variable.

Conclusion

The overall question asked in this chapter is whether democracies experience less conflict than other regimes. "Less conflict" may refer not only to fewer conflicts, but also shorter and less violent conflicts. We formulated 10 hypotheses to test the relationship between democracy and civil war in detail. In general, we obtain well-defined results for our analysis of the severity of war, and somewhat less conclusive ones for the study of the risk of onset. As in earlier statistical studies of civil war, our results for the duration of civil war tend to be the least conclusive. When the onset and duration analyses indicate that variables predict both frequent and long civil wars, corresponding analyses also show a high incidence of war.

Democracies experience fewer conflicts than other regimes (Hypothesis 1), but this effect seems to be caused by the fact that democracies also tend to enjoy other pacifying qualities. In particular, most democracies are high-income countries with stable institutions. Controlling for other factors, we find no linear relationship between democracy and the risk of conflict onset. We find some support for a curvilinear effect indicating that semidemocracies are more at risk of experiencing conflict, but it is not entirely robust to our choice of democracy indicator (Hypothesis 2). When democracies have wars, however, they are clearly less violent than wars in comparable nondemocracies. This relationship appears to be monotonic—inconsistent democracies may have a higher risk of civil wars, but they are on average not as violent as those in nondemocracies.

We find solid evidence for a general relationship between political instability and conflict, but we find no single, robust operationalization of political instability. We do not find evidence supporting the hypothesis that the inverted U-curve relationship is exclusively due to the inherent instability of semidemocratic regimes (Hypotheses 3 and 4). On the contrary, the inverted U-curve is robust when we control for political instability. However, when we control for other factors that are also related to political instability, the inverted U-curve is somewhat more fragile than the effect of instability in onset studies.

We do not find support for a bivariate relationship between elections and civil war but when controlling for other factors, the first "real" election in a new political regime appears to have a partial effect (Hypothesis 5). The effect of proximity to elections seems to be part of the political instability-conflict nexus.

We find evidence that the effect of democracy is much stronger when we look at governmental conflicts compared with secessionist conflicts (Hypothesis 6), and that the bivariate pacifying effect of democracy does not hold for low-development countries (Hypothesis 7). We also study in detail the importance of the political institutions in the neighborhood. When controlling for other factors, there does not seem to be a robust association between neighborhood and the onset, incidence, and duration of wars. We do find clear evidence that civil wars in nondemocracies that are located in democratic neighborhoods are considerably less violent than in other nondemocracies. This is due to the level of democracy among the neighbors rather than the political difference in itself, since we do not find a corresponding effect of difference for democracies located in nondemocratic neighborhoods (Hypothesis 8).

We have also explored differences between different democratic institutions. Again, the results are much more conclusive for the severity analysis than for the other aspects of war. As expected, presidential systems seem more violent than parliamentary ones, and majoritarian systems more violent than those with proportional representation—but the latter may have longer wars.

Finally, we find that the effect of democracy has become much more important after the Cold War (Hypothesis 10).

Overall, we confirm that democracy is strongly related to various aspects of civil war. Both level and stability of democracy contribute to the risk of conflict, but once conflict has erupted, political institutions do not explain the duration of conflict. We find strong effects from democracy on the severity of conflict. Our results, except for severity, are much weaker when we include control variables. Factors that are known to contribute to democracy and democratic stability also robustly contribute to peace, indicating that part of the relationship is spurious. Better theory is needed to sort out the multivariate relationships and the role played by the system of governance. Future research should explore how democracy, democratic stability, and peace interact and strengthen each other.

APPENDIX: DEMOCRACIES WITH
INTERNAL ARMED CONFLICT, 1950–2000

In this chapter, we use the Uppsala/PRIO data set to test the hypotheses about civil war and democracy. This data set is updated annually and published in *Journal of Peace Research* (vol. 5), and posted on www.prio .no/cscw/armedconflict. In this chapter we use the conflict data for the period 1950–2000. For the severity of conflict, we use the Lacina battle deaths data set, posted on www.prio.no/cscw/cross/battledeaths. Cf. Lacina and Gleditsch (2005).

During the period 1950–2000 there were 199 internal armed conflicts. This figure assumes that when a conflict has been inactive (i.e., has had fewer than 25 battle deaths) for more than 10 years or is conducted by new actors, it is a new conflict.

In the following table, we list the 52 internal armed conflicts during this period that partly or completely occurred in a democracy. The conflicts are labeled with the name of the country and in the case of territorial conflicts with the name of the territory. The information provided is their start and end dates; the duration (measured in days); the percentage of these days fought under a democratic form of governance; the regime

Country	Incompatibility	Start	End	Duration (in Days)	% or Duration Democratic	Regime Type at Onset	Severity (abs. no.)
Argentina	Government	01 Mar 73	31 Dec 77	1,767	62.8	Aut	1,361
Bangladesh	Territory: Chittagong Hill Tracts	15 Aug 75	02 Dec 97	8,146	27.7	Semidem	175
Burma	Government	28 Mar 48	31 Dec 94	15,959	13.4	Semidem	1,284
Burma	Territory: Arakan	04 Jan 48	31 Dec 94	15,968	13.4	Semidem	146
Burma	Territory: Kachin	31 Dec 61	31 Dec 92	11,324	0.5	Dem	1,164
Burma	Territory: Karen	31 Jan 49	31 Dec 00	18,018	11.9	Semidem	1,284
Burma	Territory: Karenni	01 Jan 57	31 Dec 57	365	100.0	Dem	290
Burma	Territory: Mon	04 Jan 48	15 Nov 63	5,795	36.9	Semidem	321
Burma	Territory: Shan	30 Nov 59	31 Dec 00	11,617	7.1	Dem	241
Colombia	Government	16 Aug 66	31 Dec 00	12,557	76.8	Semidem	19,779
Congo	Government	03 Nov 93	16 Nov 99	985	22.5	Dem	5,660
El Salvador	Government	01 Oct 79	31 Dec 91	4,475	61.9	Semidem	24,392
Gambia	Government	30 Jul 81	06 Aug 81	8	100.0	Dem	650
Guatemala	Government	01 Oct 66	31 Dec 00	12,511	14.6	Semidem	125
India	Government	25 May 67	19 Jul 72	1,883	100.0	Dem	300
India	Government	10 Oct 90	31 Dec 00	3,736	100.0	Dem	1,658
India	Territory: Assam	29 May 90	31 Dec 00	3,125	100.0	Dem	1,905
India	Territory: Bodoland	16 Mar 89	31 Dec 00	3,578	100.0	Dem	250
India	Territory: Kashmir	11 Dec 89	31 Dec 00	4,039	100.0	Dem	18,360
India	Territory: Manipur	31 Jul 82	31 Dec 00	5,634	100.0	Dem	925
India	Territory: Mizoram	01 Sep 66	31 Oct 68	792	100.0	Dem	1,500
India	Territory: Nagaland	01 Jan 56	30 Jun 68	4,565	100.0	Dem	2,078
India	Territory: Nagaland	31 Jul 92	31 Dec 00	2,184	100.0	Dem	245
India	Territory: Punjab/Khalistan	20 Aug 83	12 Sep 93	3,677	100.0	Dem	18,875
India	Territory: Tripura	01 Jan 78	31 Dec 00	6,880	100.0	Dem	1,097
Indonesia	Territory: Aceh	08 Sep 90	31 Dec 00	1,027	42.6	Aut	349

Country	Conflict party	Start date	End date		%	Regime	
Israel	Territory: Palestine	01 Jan 49	31 Dec 00	18,993	99.9	Semidem	13,175
Lesotho	Government	23 Sep 98	14 Oct 98	22	100.0	Dem	107
Malaysia	Government	01 Jan 58	31 Jul 60	943	36.9	Semidem	22
Malaysia	Territory: North Borneo	01 Jan 63	11 Aug 66	1,319	100.0	Dem	400
Niger	Territory: Air and Azawad	01 Oct 92	27 Nov 97	910	80.8	Transitional	59
Pakistan	Government	01 Jun 90	31 Mar 96	670	100.0	Dem	2,525
Pakistan	Territory: Baluchistan	01 Jan 74	05 Jul 77	1,282	100.0	Dem	8,332
Papua New Guinea	Territory: Bougainville	01 Dec 89	31 Dec 96	2,588	100.0	Dem	375
Peru	Government	01 Oct 65	31 Jan 66	123	100.0	Dem	138
Peru	Government	22 Aug 82	31 Dec 99	6,341	55.4	Dem	23,433
Philippines	Government	04 Jul 46	17 May 54	2,875	49.3	Semidem	4,504
Philippines	Government	21 Sep 72	31 Dec 00	10,329	49.2	Semidem	7,619
Philippines	Territory: Mindanao	20 Aug 70	31 Dec 00	9,996	39.9	Semidem	5,814
Senegal	Territory: Casamance	01 Jun 90	31 Dec 00	3,867	7.4	Semidem	39
Spain	Territory: Basque	01 Jan 80	31 Dec 92	1,827	100.0	Dem	245
Sri Lanka	Government	30 Apr 71	09 Jun 71	41	100.0	Dem	1,630
Sri Lanka	Government	01 Feb 89	28 Feb 90	393	100.0	Dem	5,025
Sri Lanka	Territory: Eelam	01 Jul 83	31 Dec 00	6,394	100.0	Dem	53,975
Sudan	Government	01 Jan 63	31 Jan 72	3,318	11.7	Aut	2,395
Sudan	Government	16 May 83	31 Dec 00	6,440	18.4	Aut	12,975
Trinidad and Tobago	Government	27 Jul 90	01 Aug 90	6	100.0	Dem	30
Turkey	Government	13 Jul 91	31 Oct 92	477	100.0	Dem	50
Turkey	Territory: Kurdistan	15 Aug 84	31 Dec 00	5,983	68.0	Semidem	33,080
United Kingdom	Territory: Northern Ireland	01 Jan 98	15 Aug 98	7,671	100.0	Dem	3,149
Venezuela	Government	02 Jun 62	03 Jun 62	2	100.0	Dem	400
Venezuela	Government	04 Feb 92	29 Nov 92	300	100.0	Dem	183

type at the onset of the conflict (autocratic, semidemocratic, or democratic); and finally the best estimate for the total number of battle-related
fatalities that occurred during a democratic form of governance.

NOTES

1. In the Uppsala/PRIO terminology (see Gleditsch et al. 2002; Strand et al.
2005), which we generally follow, conflicts where no government is involved
(sometimes labeled communal conflicts) are termed nonstate conflicts. Conflicts
where the nonstate actor is unorganized (variously genocide, politicide, or democide) are labeled one-sided conflicts. See Mack (2006) for a presentation of data on
nonstate conflicts 2002–5 and Eck and Hultman (2007) for a presentation of data
on one-sided conflicts 1989–2004.

2. For dyadic analyses of civil war with more data on the opposition side, see
Cunningham, Gleditsch, and Salehyan (2007) and Raleigh and Hegre (2005).

3. Many economists prefer to use the data on political rights from Freedom
House, and a few scholars use the Polyarchy data developed by Vanhanen (2000).
For a survey of nine measures of democracy, see Munck and Verkuilen (2002).

4. SIP = Scalar Index of Polities, MIRPS = Multidimensional Institutional Representation of Political Systems (Gates et al. 2006).

5. Most of the analyses have also been tested on the more restrictive measure of
1,000 or more battle deaths in a year (which is defined as "war" in this data set as
well as in the Correlates of War data). Generally, the results are very similar, so we
do not comment in detail on the alternative analyses.

6. The relative risk of onset estimates were obtained using bivariate Cox regression with calendar time as the time variable (see Raknerud and Hegre 1997 and
Hegre et al. 2001 for a complete description). The odds of incidence ratios were estimated using logistic regression on a country-year data set. The estimated relative
risk of conflict termination was obtained using Weibull regression on a conflict
duration data set, using duration time as time variable. The estimated battle
deaths ratios were obtained by estimating an OLS (ordinary least squares) model
with log battle deaths as the dependent variable, and taking the antilog of the estimated coefficient. Full documentation of the design of the statistical tests is given
in an appendix released with the replication data (Strand 2007).

7. Major exceptions being Sri Lanka and Turkey. For details, see the appendix.

8. See the unpublished appendix posted with the replication data (Strand 2007)
for an explanation of why this is problematic.

9. In an analysis not reported in detail here, we find that a country—irrespective
of its domestic system—in an all-democratic neighborhood has a 62 percent lower
risk of conflict onset than a country in an all-autocratic environment. Indeed, the
effect of living in a democratic neighborhood seems stronger than the effect of being a democratic country.

Civil War Outcomes

ROY LICKLIDER

At one level it seems impossible that civil wars can end. The strongest theoretical argument that civil wars are different from other forms of political violence is that the stakes are different. In interstate wars the victor is likely to eventually go away, especially because modern nationalism and sectarianism make the cost of continued occupation very high, as seen in Afghanistan and Iraq. But, except for the relatively few cases of partition, civil war termination means that people who have been killing one another with considerable skill and enthusiasm will somehow agree to live in the same country under the same government without further large-scale violence. Typically they do this in a country whose social, political, and economic structures have been torn apart and traditional animosities have been greatly heightened by the killing, much of which has been aimed at civilians. This sounds like a recipe for starting a civil war rather than ending it.

And yet we know that it happens all the time. Western Europeans no longer kill one another over different varieties of Christianity. England is no longer crisscrossed by warring armies representing York and Lancaster or king and Parliament. The French no longer kill one another over the divine right of kings. Americans seem to have agreed on independence from English rule, that the South should not secede, and that slavery will not be allowed. Argentines seem reconciled to living in a single state rather than several. The ideologies of the Spanish Civil War now seem irrelevant, and even the separatist issues there are not being resolved by mass violence. India doesn't seem interested in regaining the secessionist state of Pakistan, and Pakistan seems to have accepted the secession of Bangladesh. Nigeria experienced one of the most brutal civil wars of our time, but the major divisions within the country are now different. Other countries that have experienced a civil war since 1945 but where resumption seems unlikely include Bolivia, Cambodia, Chad, Costa Rica, Cyprus, Dominican Republic, El Salvador, Greece, Jordan, Laos, Malaysia, Morocco, Mozambique, Paraguay, South Africa, and Syria.

Presumably the process works differently in different countries, but it seems likely that there are common elements we can use to make predictions about future outcomes and prescriptions to shape them. Some years ago it made sense to say that the literature on civil wars, like that on interstate wars, focused on how they began rather than how they ended (Licklider 1993, 7–8), despite a few exceptions (Iklé 1971, 95; Gurr 1988). This seemed odd, since civil wars usually became a foreign policy problem only after they had begun, and the question of how they ended was precisely the point for most outsiders. Thankfully in the intervening decade this imbalance has been repaired as a new generation of young scholars has tackled the issue with a wonderful combination of skills and enthusiasm. Important work has been done in a variety of academic disciplines as well as governmental and nongovernmental organizations in countries around the world, appearing in many different publications and sources; indeed it is practically impossible for any single individual to keep track of the literature of this burgeoning and very exciting field of study. This necessarily terse summary will try to structure this work around a few central questions and briefly describe some of its ongoing controversies.

The central focus of much of this work has been to better understand why civil wars begin, evolve, and end as they do. The concern, then, is not the classic historian's problem of what has happened in any given civil war and why it has occurred, but to try to establish the plausibility of generalizations that will apply to other such episodes, including those that have not yet occurred. There are two parts to this activity, developing general theories or explanations and testing these theories against a large number of cases to see if they correspond to reality. One hallmark of the best recent work in the field is that it is multimethod. Nonetheless, much of this work has necessarily been quantitative, analyzing a large number of wars and looking for patterns, often using the one or two hundred episodes since 1945 that different criteria have identified as civil wars. These analyses are not without their drawbacks (Kalyvas 2004; Ward and Bakke 2005), but the process forces scholars to pay particular attention to problems of definition, although, as we will see, it has not led to consensus on these issues.

It seems useful to organize this chapter around three questions, all of which remain under debate. (1) What do we mean by civil wars? (2) How do we know when they end? (3) What can outsiders do to end them? I also distinguish between normative and empirical issues, what should be done and what will happen if certain things are done. As we will see, the concerns are often closely related in particular issues, but they require different modes of analysis. It is particularly important to raise and debate ethical issues because work in this field is not simply an academic exercise; it is directed at influencing policymakers. Policy issues combine both ethical and empirical issues, and one of the obligations of outsider commentators is precisely to tease out these different questions so they can be confronted directly rather than simply assumed.

What Is a Civil War?

At one level, this seems a simple question. If interstate wars are wars between states, then civil wars are wars between combatants within states. But in fact things are more complex. The American Civil War is a civil war, but what about the Indian wars in the United States? How about colonial wars such as the French in Algeria or the British in Kenya? What if there isn't a state at all, as in Somalia? Should genocides and terrorist actions be included? What about coups d'état? Is the West Bank part of the State of Israel, and, if not, how should we classify political violence there? Is communal conflict in India or violence by drug rings in Colombia a civil war?

When we are talking about a particular conflict, the problem of definition is usually not serious. But if we want to do systematic comparisons, it becomes essential to develop operational definitions, those that are so clear that anyone else, given the same set of facts, would classify them in the same way. Thus the problem of defining terms has been quite severe for analysts who use statistical techniques to look for patterns among civil wars. In a seminal article that I have used extensively for this analysis, Nicholas Sambanis (2004) demonstrated that different definitions of the same terms in different data sets in fact sometimes produce substantially different results (see also Fearon 2004).

One way to approach the question is to break it down into two separate issues: what is a war and what is a state? Analysis of this sort starts with the Correlates of War project (COW), the monumental data project developed by J. David Singer over the past few decades that has shaped the quantitative study of war in political science. Civil war was defined as military action within a state, with the government as a combatant (so communal conflicts don't count), at least 1,000 battle deaths per year, and effective resistance by both sides (no genocide) (Small and Singer 1982, 210). States were defined as any government recognized by France and Great Britain before 1945 and a member of the United Nations after that. The project created a database of civil wars from 1815; these definitions and data have been the basis for most of the quantitative work in the field (Sambanis 2004).

This definition is certainly helpful, but, as Sambanis and others have noted, it leaves some interesting questions unanswered. Like most operational definitions, it is arbitrary to some extent. The 1,000 deaths has probably gotten the most attention. Obviously the figure is arbitrary. COW itself seems to have vacillated between 1,000 per year and 1,000 for the total war (Sambanis 2004, 817). Fearon and Laitin (2003, 76) use a criteria of 1,000 deaths for the total war with at least 100 in each year. Sambanis (2004, 820–21) suggests using a range of 500 to 1,000 in combination with other defining qualities of a civil war. Moreover, violence on this scale will have very different effects in countries with different populations; India, for example, is often classified as having several civil wars in progress at the same time, but since they are small and on the periphery they have practically no impact on the country as a whole. The violence in Northern Ireland, on the other hand, has obviously convulsed that area but has never crossed the 1,000 deaths per year threshold. Perhaps a per capita figure would be more appropriate, although no less arbitrary; Sambanis (2004, 821) suggests .001. The recent PRIO/Uppsala data set (N. Gleditsch et al. 2002) includes violent conflicts that have casualties as low as 25 in a year, which may allow us to determine the utility of the 1,000 death figure (a first pass at this is Sambanis 2004, 847).

In addition, it isn't clear whether civilian deaths should be counted, a particularly important point in current civil wars where such deaths may be as much as 90 percent of the total. What about genocide or massacres that occur during a civil war, or the death of political prisoners, or indirect casualties such as those from starvation or disease (for estimates of the latter, see Ghobarah, Huth, and Russett 2003)? And this, of course, ignores the fact that any figures on deaths during civil wars are likely to be incomplete, unreliable, and disputed, regardless of the definition used.

A second problem is how to define the combatants. Small and Singer (1982) say that at least one government must be involved for the violence to be a civil war; thus communal rioting would presumably be excluded. But what is a government? Their definition is any group either (before 1945) recognized by both France and Britain or (after 1945) a member of the United Nations. Leaving aside some issues of the first criterion, the second is something of a problem as well. The People's Republic of China was not a member of the United Nations until 1971. Does this mean that the violence between Tibetan rebels and the Peoples Liberation Army in the 1950s was not a civil war, since the Republic of China or Taiwan was not involved? Fortunately there has been no similar violence in Switzerland, another nonmember, avoiding the problem there (an interesting history of an earlier civil war there is Remak 1993).

The Korean War is another difficult case. North Korea and South Korea were separate states in 1950, although neither was a member of the United Nations; should the North Korean invasion of South Korea be classified as a civil war or an interstate war? Of course this was the central issue of the war—North Korea argued that it was trying to reunify Korea (that it was a civil war) while South Korea, while also committed to reunification, contended that the invasion was a violation of its status as a sovereign state. Intuitively, given that the division was only five years old and that the two sides shared a common history, language, and commitment to reunification, it seems more plausible to call it a civil war, but it is a pretty rough fit to the usual definitions. When Saddam Hussein invaded Kuwait, he argued that he was simply regaining control of the nineteenth province of Iraq that had been stolen by the British during colonial times; the amount of time makes this considerably more of a stretch, but it is not completely ridiculous. One attempt to avoid some of these problems is to say that a civil war is one in which one or more of the contestants is seriously concerned about the consequences of living in the same state as the other (Licklider 1993, 9). This would include wars of conquest such as Kuwait as well; James Fearon (2004, 279n) solves this problem by including only cases where violence follows the conquest. However, developing operational coding rules for "serious concern" and similar terms would be challenging.

Most definitions assume a political component to the conflict; a battle between a government and a drug cartel, for example, would usually not be considered a civil war unless the cartel wanted to replace the government. Similarly a riot between ethnic groups in a country would probably also not be included. Actions by a group like Al Qaeda should probably be included since its leadership has articulated political goals.

This in turn raises the issue of "outsiders." The attacks of September 11 would probably not be included because the attackers were foreigners, but if they had been Americans it might have been seen as part of a civil war. (Presumably the critical point is the nationality of the individuals rather than the location of the combat.) But in fact many civil wars involve outsiders as well. Was the Vietnam War a civil war or an interstate war? Does the classification change over time as the French leave and the Americans arrive and depart? I would prefer to classify it both as a civil war, since locals on both sides seem to have been killing one another sufficiently to meet the definition, and as an interstate war as well. Depending on what you are studying, it would then be either a civil war with a lot of outside involvement or an interstate war with the Viet Cong possibly being considered an independent nonstate actor for some period of time. Again there is no real agreement on how to handle this problem.

Nor can we assume that there is only one civil war going on in one country at one time. India has often been coded as undergoing several at the same time; this classification is fairly straightforward since there isn't much coordination between the opponents. But Burma, Bosnia, and Ethiopia are more complex, with a number of different sides interacting with one another in changing patterns over an extended period of time; different analysts classify them as one or many civil wars (Sambanis 2004, 819).

To put it simply, there is no consensus on how to answer any of these individual questions, much less how these answers should be amalgamated to produce a single definition of civil war. This itself isn't a problem; similar problems can be found in defining most important concepts in political science, such as democracy or justice. Indeed it can be seen as a research opportunity; if different definitions produce different answers to the same question (and we will see that they do), this tells us that some of the dimensions we are measuring may be important explanatory variables (Ruggie 1996). However, it is imperative that analysts be careful to specify what definitions they are using, something that has often not been done very well.

How Do We Know a Civil War Has Ended?

When talking about civil war termination, Americans often say that the American Civil War has not ended yet. But there is a fundamental distinction, often obscured, between conflict and war. Conflict is a disagreement, which may or may not result in violence; war involves large-scale killing. Ending a war usually does not end the underlying conflict. If two ethnic groups are suspicious of one another, mass killing is unlikely to increase amity; if a country is poor, a war is unlikely to make it rich. Unfortunately our vocabulary encourages this confusion. We often use the term *conflict* in referring to violence rather than the underlying dispute, and we label efforts to reduce violence *conflict resolution* when *conflict management* is more appropriate.

But if violence is an essential part of war, how do we know when the war starts or ends? In interstate wars there are often events that signal the formal beginning and ending of the violence. These events are less common in civil wars; dating the American Civil War from 1861, for instance, ignores the organized mass violence in Kansas and other areas before that. Similarly Appomattox marked the surrender of the largest Confederate army, not the formal end of the war. Indeed it is not much of a stretch to see the violence of Reconstruction as a continuation of the war, ending only in 1876 in what was essentially a negotiated settlement, with Southern whites abandoning secession and slavery but being allowed to control blacks for almost a century (Stedman 1993a).

If the conflict precedes and often follows the war, presumably war is the time during the conflict when mass violence occurs. Since 1945 the typical pattern has been for violence to occur at a fairly low level and then escalate and decline over time; it is only in retrospect that the earlier violence is seen as the precursor or initiation of civil war. If we accept the threshold of 1,000 battle deaths a year, how do we classify examples where the casualties are below this level for several years, rise to this point for a year or two, drop below for a few years, and then rise again? Presumably, if the participants or the issues change, it is a new civil war. But if not, how much peace must ensue before we say that the first war has ended and a new one has begun? Some use two years (Fearon and Laitin 2003, 76n), others five years (Licklider 1995); not surprisingly this results in different lists of civil wars and differences over their length and intensity.

Moreover, if the definition of civil war termination centers on the resumption of violence, we are back to the question of why civil wars begin in the first place, which has been discussed in an earlier chapter. We can think of civil war resumption as a special case of civil war initiation, among states that have recently experienced civil war. We have evidence that such states (even when we are talking about separate wars either because the first wars ended long enough ago or because the new violence involves new combatants or issues or both) are particularly vulnerable to such wars. In fact, however, there has been so far relatively little quantitative work focusing on postviolence states as a separate category.

Much research distinguishes between civil war termination and state formation after civil war. But if we are concerned about the resumption of civil war, then termination and state formation cannot be separated; a successful example of civil war termination almost inevitably involves either the formation of a new state or the drastic reformation of the old. (For a discussion of this process after the American Civil War, see Benzel 1990.) The classic learning experience of this dogma was Somalia, where the United States intervened with the limited aim of ending the violence and relieving the famine but found its aims widening in an ultimately failed attempt to prevent the renewal of violence after its departure.

To summarize, there are serious problems of definition of civil war, particularly when we attempt to aggregate information about different ones to draw generalizations. As a result we have several civil war data sets that often differ in their definitions and classifications. At this point the major ones are those of Sambanis (2004), Fearon and Laitin (2003), and PRIO/Uppsala (N. Gleditsch et al. 2002). As noted earlier, Sambanis (2004) has shown that these differences matter, that when the same issues are addressed with different data sets, the answers differ in important ways. At this point there is no obvious reason to privilege one data set over the others. A better strategy is probably to use more than one data set in our analyses and look for findings that are robust across them. Moreover, we need to expand our concept of civil war termination to include state formation after the organized violence ends.

How Can Outsiders Help End Civil Wars?

Most of the literature in this field focuses not so much on how civil wars end but on how outsiders can facilitate this process. It is thus implicitly written as policy guidance to such outsiders. Policy choices are particularly difficult both because they usually involve a unique case, while academic work usually focuses on broad patterns, and because they include both ethical and empirical elements that are often conflated in debate and often depend on one another. It is thus particularly important that outside advisors make every effort to clarify the ethical as well as the empirical complexities of the problems in their analysis. Such arguments need to focus on two separate issues, what are the appropriate *goals* and what are the *means* that should be used to achieve them.

In the past few decades, and particularly since the end of the Cold War, we have seen the growth of a new international industry dedicated to discouraging large-scale violence. It includes nongovernmental organizations concerned with humanitarian assistance and conflict management as well as international governmental organizations such as the United Nations that are now sometimes freed to address such issues and occasionally act. It has been supported by a number of governments in significant ways at different times as well. We often refer to this rather inchoate group as the "international community." Its common ideology is that violence is a bad thing that should be avoided or terminated if at all possible. In practice this means that the community usually supports ending civil wars through negotiation resulting in power sharing and democratic governments. It has sought to facilitate such outcomes in a variety of ways and with some success.

As an example, compare the settlements of the civil wars in Colombia in 1957 and El Salvador in 1992. In Colombia no outsiders were involved; the two groups made their own arrangements for negotiations, reached an agreement on their own, and instituted a power-sharing agreement in which the parties rotated in and out of public office for two decades (Hartlyn 1993). In El Salvador a whole variety of outsiders were involved at various stages: the Contadora Group of Central American governments; the Soviet, American, Mexican, Spanish, Colombian, and Venezuelan governments; the International Monetary Fund, the World Bank, and the Food and Agriculture Organization; nonprofit organizations of all sorts; and the United Nations (Call 2002; Orr 2001). I think the major explanation for this difference is simply the times in which they occurred; the El Salvador pattern has become typical in post–Cold War civil wars.

Negotiated Settlements versus Military Victories

In part as a result of all this activity, the percentage of civil wars ending in negotiated settlements has greatly increased since the end of the Cold War (Toft 2009; Hartzell and Hoddie 2007, chap. 1; Fortna 2007). This certainly seems like a good thing; it seems obvious that peace is better than war. But is this really true? Intervention in someone else's civil war raises a set of very difficult moral and ethical questions that have not been well explored. It's not hard to agree that, all other things being equal, it is better to not kill people than to do so. It's much harder to agree on what sort of outcome is desirable or, to put it differently, what outcome is worth killing people to attain. Disagreement on this question is, after all, the reason for the civil war, and the resulting mass killing seems unlikely to have created consensus among the combatants. If outsiders commit significant resources, possibly including the lives of their own citizens, they want some influence over the outcome. However, this is someone else's country, and Western ethics at both the personal and national level (individual freedom and self-determination) imply that the locals should be making this decision by themselves. In traditional peacekeeping missions, this was not a particular problem; if one or the other side asked the outsiders to leave, they did so. However, more recently the international community has felt it appropriate to intervene regardless of the wishes of some of the locals in order to prevent humanitarian tragedies (International Commission on Intervention and State Sovereignty 2001) or for national interest.

This proposition seems to assume that no issues are worth large-scale killing. Phrased this way, this is not a position that would be acceptable to most people in most countries. Perhaps sixty million people died in World War II, but very few would argue it should not have been fought after the Japanese and German wars of conquest had begun. If France and Britain had intervened in the American Civil War in 1862 and offered a compromise peace, guaranteeing the survival of slavery, and saving much of a generation of American men, I hope I would have opposed it (as did the Union Army when its members provided the margin of victory for Abraham Lincoln's election in 1864). More to the point, presumably the combatants on both sides of any current civil war do not agree or there would have not been a war in the first place. We must distinguish between developing strategies that may be useful in ending civil wars (or wars of any kind for that matter) and the assumption that these strategies should always be used. This is particularly true when outsiders are deciding to intervene in someone else's war.

Negotiated Settlements versus Military Victories: Fewer Casualties?

Interventions leading to negotiated settlements are usually justified in terms of the welfare of the people in the target area. In particular the argument is that local casualties will be reduced by negotiating a settlement in two ways—the killing will stop sooner, and the resumption of large-scale violence will be less likely than the alternative of allowing the war to continue until one side wins. The moral argument hinges on these empirical propositions.

Do negotiated settlements really save lives in the long run? These two empirical assumptions are subject to testing. The first seems fairly straightforward; Carolyn Hartzell and Matthew Hoddie found that, between 1945 and 1999, the average number of battle deaths for civil wars ending in military victories was roughly twice the number for those ending in negotiated settlements (2007, chap. 1).

However, if peace from negotiated settlements does not last as long as peace from military victories, negotiated settlements may in fact be associated with higher casualties over time as violence returns. Is there any reason to think this might be true? Negotiated settlements are by definition second-best solutions for everyone (each side would prefer to win) so no one is likely to be very happy with them. Harrison Wagner (1993) has argued that the critical resource in a civil war is organization and that negotiated settlements leave in place the organizations on both sides, making it relatively easy to return to violence. Moreover, a power-sharing government (which is a common result of a negotiated settlement—why else should both sides accept it?) may simply give veto powers to everyone, making it impossible to make major changes in a society that probably badly needs them (Roeder and Rothchild 2005; Talentine 2007).

One recent study of power sharing concludes that it contributes to peace when it is associated with a military victory but that it makes civil war resumption more likely when it is the result of a stalemate, that is, a negotiated settlement (Mukherjee 2006). This directly contradicts the conventional wisdom of using power sharing as part of a negotiated settlement. Hoddie and Hartzell conclude that power sharing is most useful for the few years after the civil war to establish trust and that after that period its drawbacks outweigh its advantages (2007, chap. 7).

On the other hand, there are several plausible reasons that democracy and power sharing (which are not necessarily the same thing since power sharing implies that some groups will keep some positions regardless of election results) might make renewed civil war less likely. All of the major groups have a share of power, presumably limiting the threat that their former enemies will be able to use the power of the state against them and therefore making them feel secure. Leaders of both sides will have paid a substantial price in the disaffection of their subordinates; this demonstrates to the other side that they sincerely desire peace (Sisk 1996; Hoddie and Hartzell 2007). Moreover, even a military victory need not mean the end of violence; even if leaders have been captured or exiled, it is not at all clear when their followers will decide to obey and perhaps even cooperate with their former enemies. Civil war organizations, especially those of the losers, are often quite weak; it is unreasonable to expect that all or most members will automatically obey their leaders, even if told to surrender. Resistance is always possible, especially when you inhabit the same society as your adversary. Thus a negotiated settlement seems a more attractive alternative.

Several different analysts have studied whether negotiated settlements "hold" better than military victories, using different databases; most have concluded that the hypothesis is false (Licklider 1995; Carment and Harvey 2001; Toft 2009), others find no significant difference (Doyle and Sambanis 2006, chap. 3; Hartzell 2004), but to my knowledge no one has confirmed that negotiated settlements actually make the resumption of civil war less likely than military victories. If in fact negotiated settlements do not hold very well, then the most "efficient" way to end the violence and save lives in the long run may be to simply support the stronger side to win the war quickly—to, as Edward Luttwak (1999) puts it, "give war a chance." Of course this would have involved supporting the Serbs in Bosnia and Kosovo, Saddam Hussein in his battles with the Kurds, and several other comparable cases. Clearly this would present a major ethical problem. Empirically it's unclear whether Western democratic leaders would be able to sell this policy to their publics for any length of time.

Recent scholarship has sought to move beyond the simple military victory/negotiated settlement dichotomy. Hartzell and Hoddie (2007, chap. 4) distinguish power-sharing agreements on the basis of the issues involved: political, military, territorial, and economic. They argue that settlements that involve power sharing in more of these areas are more stable than those that include only one or two, both because of the commitment shown by leaders in negotiating them and because groups now have some security even if power sharing in one sector breaks down; a separate analysis suggests that such institutionalized settlements reduce the likelihood of renewed civil war almost as well as military victories (Hartzell 2004).

Philip Roeder and Donald Rothchild (2005, 336–46) contend that the problems of power sharing are so serious that it should be used only to end the violence. They support what they call nation-state stewardship (what others have called trusteeship), whereby outsiders exert long-term control over the state, developing electoral institutions from the local level, limiting the political stakes by moving controversial issues to non-political venues, encouraging new institutions controlled by alternative majorities to reduce the power of factional leaders, and delaying national elections and the formation of national governments for at least a decade. Whether outsiders have the willpower to carry out such a strategy is not clear.

Monica Toft (2009) distinguishes military victories by the identity of the victors. Her analysis finds that military victories by rebels are more stable than either negotiated settlements or military victories by governments. Given that a substantial number of rebel groups these days are Islamist, this suggests some difficult policy prescriptions if our major value is avoiding civil war recurrence, another possible conflict between peace and justice.

Negotiated Settlements versus Military Victories: Democracy?

Another moral argument in favor of negotiated settlements is that they make life better for locals, even if casualties are not reduced, because they are more likely to produce democratic governments than are military victories. (There are actually three separate issues here: do negotiated settlements in fact produce more democracies than military victories, are such regimes better or worse for the locals, and are they are more or less likely to result in resumption of civil violence.) Again, this is an empirical issue and one on which we have relatively little information. There are certainly cases of victories being followed by extreme repression; Spain (Richards 1998; Aguilar 2002) and Greece (Iatrides 1993) are excellent examples, and an early analysis found that military victories were more likely to be followed by genocide than negotiated settlements (Licklider 1995, 686–87). On the other hand, Nigeria is one fascinating example of a military victory followed by a remarkably magnanimous peace; rebel leaders were brought back into politics, some property was restored, and so forth (O'Connell 1993; Anthony 2002).

Research in this area progressed by disaggregating the major concepts. Early work dichotomized civil war terminations into military victories (where one side was judged unable to continue to fight) and negotiated settlements (everything else, on the grounds that if two sides both decided to stop fighting there must have been some negotiation, even if only implicit). Comparisons between these showed that military victories were less likely to break down into renewed civil wars (Licklider 1995). Caroline Hartzell and Matthew Hoddie (2007) separated the original category of negotiated settlements into negotiated truces and negotiated settlements (where the participants agreed on important aspects of the postwar political structure); they found that the more restricted group of negotiated settlements performed about as well as military victories. Monica Toft (2009) separated military victories into those won by the government and those won by the rebels. She found that those won by the rebels were much less likely to break down than negotiated settlements.

Toft also compared the democracy scores of countries before and after civil wars to see the impact of the violence. Five years after the end of the war, countries with negotiated settlements do have higher democracy change scores than those with military victories. However, by ten years after the war the scores are approximately even, and after that the military victory scores hold roughly constant while those for negotiated settlements plummet. These figures are driven by the strong tendency of rebel victories to produce more democratic regimes than government victories. She concludes that negotiated settlements do not produce democracy after the first few years (Toft 2009).

All of these figures need to be taken with some caution. Clearly their conclusions differ substantially. Licklider's data ended in 1993; Hartzell and Hoddie's ended in 1999; Toft's ended in 2000. Frederic Pearson, Marie Olson Lounsbery, and their collaborators took the Hartzell and Hoddie data, changed definitions, and got different results. Toft's figures include negotiated settlements 30 years ago, when such agreements were few and far between and before the end of the Cold War, which radically changed the pattern of civil war termination. On the other hand, they cannot simply be ignored. Indeed, as we will see later, the link between democracy and peace remains controversial. Clearly we cannot simply assume that in fact negotiated settlements will reduce casualties in the long run or will produce more repression and less democracy. It is not certain that military victories will produce "better" outcomes, but it is not impossible. It seems unreasonable to base policy that will affect thousands of people on empirical assumptions that are debatable at best.

Amnesty and Justice in Negotiated Settlements

Morally one of the hardest issues in negotiating settlements to civil wars is the issue of amnesty. During civil wars combatants do terrible things to one another and increasingly to civilians as well, so it seems reasonable to establish some system to judge and punish some of these individuals. However, these are often also people in charge of organizations that have the capacity to undermine any peace settlement.

The conflict management perspective holds that the goal is to end the violence as quickly and with as few casualties as possible, with "justice" if possible, without it if necessary. This means negotiations with people and organizations with blood on their hands, not because we approve of them but because they often have the power to continue the war. Excluding powerful people from negotiations because you don't like them is akin to the drunk who loses his keys in the dark but looks for them under the lamppost because the light is better there. It may be appropriate to accede to their demands (which will certainly include amnesty and may well include future restrictions on human rights) if this is the only way to end the fighting, with the hope that, after the violence ends, progress on these other issues may be made (Baker 2001).

The human rights perspective holds that civil war settlements without human rights provisions are flawed because such settlements will not last and will simply result in delaying rather than ending the violence. Thus combatants should be strongly pressured to include them in the settlement. The extreme position is that agreements without such provisions should be rejected, even at the cost of continued civil war.

Again there is an empirical question here—do settlements that give amnesty to human rights violators last as long as those that do not do so. As far as I know, this proposition has not been tested. On the other hand, we can be fairly sure that settlements without major players will fail, resulting in more short-term casualties. Under the circumstances, it seems to me that outsiders should be prepared to accept settlements with amnesty if the locals generally support them.

Can Settlements Be Negotiated?

Assuming for the moment that negotiated settlements are desirable, how can they be facilitated? It seems likely to be difficult. One of the justifications for studying civil war as a distinctive form of political violence is that the stakes are so high. Interstate war may involve conquest, but recently this is likely to be fairly short-term. Civil war, however, determines the government(s) the protagonists will live with indefinitely and to which they and their families and friends will be subject. In his classic book, *Every War Must End,* Fred Iklé argued that compromise was more difficult to arrange after civil wars than interstate ones.

In conflicts that are predominately civil wars ... outcomes intermediate between victory and defeat are difficult to construct. If partition is not a feasible outcome because the belligerents are not geographically separable, one side has to get all, or nearly so, since there cannot be two governments ruling over one country, and since the passions aroused and the political cleavages opened render a sharing of power unworkable. (1971, 95)

Several quantitative analyses have confirmed that negotiated settlements are much less common in civil wars than in interstate wars (Pillar 1983, 25; Miall 1992, 124; Stedman 1991, 9; Licklider 1995, 684). However, we also know there has been a radical change in this pattern. Before 1990 negotiated settlements were relatively rare, but after the Cold War many more civil wars ended than in previous decades and these endings were divided roughly evenly between negotiated settlements and military victories (Toft 2009; Hartzell and Hoddie 2007, chap. 1).

The classic explanation for negotiated settlements is William Zartman's notion of a mutual hurting stalemate (1985, 1993, and 2001). The argument is that settlement will only be possible when *each* side believes that it will be worse off if the war continues than if it ends and that a single outcome will satisfy each side more than continued war. Settlement is always a second-best solution; each side would prefer to win. Settlement can thus become more likely either if war becomes more costly or if a settlement becomes more attractive or, to be more precise, if both sides believe either of these things to be true at the same time. Thus the notion of mutual hurting stalemate—if only one side believes this, it is most unlikely that any negotiated settlement can be reached since the other side will press for very favorable terms. Hartzell and Hoddie (2007, chap. 3) develop this argument; their statistical analysis concludes that power-sharing agreements are more likely when the war has lasted for a long time (presumably because of stalemate) and has caused relatively few casualties (perhaps reducing the level of animosity), and when outside peacekeepers are available (perhaps by reducing the mutual concern about security that dominates civil war endings).

Since 1945 most civil wars have taken place in poor countries. Government presumably can finance themselves by access to international credits, but a new and intriguing line of research by economists has sprung up about how rebel groups are able to maintain armed forces strong enough to prevent government victories. This research, led by Paul

Collier and his colleagues at the World Bank, concludes that it will be more difficult to end civil wars in countries in which "lootable" resources are available. Examples of such resources would be drugs and alluvial diamonds, the so-called resource curse (Collier and Hoeffler 2004; Berdal and Malone 2000; Ross 2004a, 2004b; Fearon 2005; Humphreys 2005; Collier and Sambanis 2005).

But the "resource curse" only works if outsiders buy the resource. This in turn points up a larger point, that outsiders may be able to decisively shape both the prospects of future war and the attractiveness of an alternative settlement. The end of the Cold War seems to have drastically reduced resources to a number of governments and rebel groups as the Soviet Union went out of business and the United States reduced aid; thus there was an outbreak of peace in a variety of places from Mozambique to El Salvador. Other qualities of the international system may also have been involved, such as the disappearance of an alternative form of government, the decrease in unilateral military interventions (which some scholars have linked to longer wars), and changes in international norms (Hironaka 2005). In addition the United Nations and other international organizations were able to mount efforts such as economic sanctions and, in a few cases, military forces to raise the cost of continued warfare substantially.

Outsiders can do several things to end civil wars and make negotiated settlements more likely. One possibility is to bring pressure to bear on one or both sides, making it more costly to continue the war. A striking example was the support for economic sanctions against South Africa's apartheid regime over decades. At the time there was little evidence that they were making a difference, but after the fact, most South Africans seem to believe that the sanctions were in fact a major factor in bringing about change. Since economic sanctions are widely thought to be ineffective in persuading a government to change important policies (Daoudi and Dajani 1983; Licklider 1988, 6–7, 21–25; Hufbauer, Schott, and Elliott 1990; Pape 1997), this is a counterintuitive conclusion.

A less successful initiative has been to try to control the flow of "light weapons" throughout the world (Boutwell and Klare 1999; Dahinden, Dahlitz, and Fischer 2002; United Nations Institute for Disarmament Research 2003; Kurlantzick 2006). The Kimberley Process campaign against "conflict diamonds" attempts to restrict the resources of rebels in some countries (Goreux 2001; Campbell 2002; Tamm 2004; Grant and Taylor 2004; Smillie 2005; Winer 2005); the idea is innovative and interesting, but it is too soon to judge its success. Moreover, Hegre (2004, 249) notes that this strategy only works when goods are legally traded; it will not be useful against commodities such as illegal drugs. The reverse of this process is to offer concessions and promises to support if the combatants can reach a settlement. Often these promises focus on economic assistance after the war ends. In other cases the incentives can look very close to bribes for particular individuals and groups; in cases such as Mozambique, this may be money well spent (Ottaway 2003, 316).

At another level, it is often difficult to get negotiations started in a civil war. Aside from the usual problems of trust, governments feel with some justification that the act of negotiating concedes the major demand of the rebels. Outsiders can serve as private intermediaries to establish contacts with the other side, provide a venue, and sometimes provide resources of money and expertise to balance the sides. Once the negotiations are under way, they may be able to suggest novel solutions to difficult problems or increase confidence that the opponents are honest. Andrew Kydd (2006) notes that neutrality must mean both a preference for moderate outcomes and a concern about the issue; this should help prevent the exploitation of either side, which is essential for credibility. Prominent examples include the World Council of Churches and the All Africa Conference of Churches in Sudan in 1972 (Rothchild and Hartzell 1993, 76–83), the Community of Sant'Egidio in Mozambique (Bartoli 1999), and the Norwegian Institute for Applied Social Sciences (FAFO) in the Oslo Accords between the Palestinians and Israelis (Crocker, Hampson, and Aall 2004, 45–71). These mediators must be neutral and nonthreatening, and nongovernmental organizations are often better able to do this than governments.

Another approach is "mediation with muscle," something that usually only governments can do. In this case the mediators may well be threatening and not neutral. The key, however, is that the mediators must pressure their own allies to agree to terms that otherwise would not be acceptable; this ability to deliver one's ally is what gets credibility with the other side. Interesting examples include the behavior of the Ethiopian government in the 1972 Sudan agreements (Rothchild and Hartzell 1993, 83–85), the ultimatum from Mozambique to Robert Mugabe to end the war in Rhodesia (Stedman 1993b, 157), and the actions of the United States over the past few decades vis-à-vis Israel.

One of the most intractable problems in reaching a negotiated settlement is trust. Ending a civil war means disarmament by someone, but, even if your adversary has agreed to an acceptable settlement, disarmament means putting yourself and your family and friends at the mercy of your enemies if they cheat. Outsiders can play an important role by verifying disarmament and monitoring other activities that might be seen as threatening. They may also make violations less likely by threatening sanctions against violators; military coups to overturn peace settlements in Latin America, for example, have been defeated in part because of such responses. Barbara Walter (2002) has argued that these external commitments are essential to successful peace settlements.

The most extreme forms of intervention to end civil wars have involved committing military forces, sometimes essentially taking over a country and trying to bring about major changes in a fairly short period of time; prominent cases include Somalia, Cambodia, Bosnia, and Kosovo. (Iraq is an interesting case, but there was no civil war when the United States intervened, although there may be one when it leaves.) The success of these actions has been mixed at best. In Somalia mass starvation was ended and, until for over a decade, there was no resumption of mass violence. However, no government was formed either, and recently violence has flared again. In Cambodia the war ended, but the new government set up by the United Nations and elected by the population was overthrown in a coup; the result has been an unjust peace. In Bosnia and Kosovo the violence has ended and new governments were set up, but it is unclear when external forces will be able to leave without the resumption of violence. One result has been a series of very critical analyses of such efforts (Callahan 1997; Dempsey 2001; Paris 2004). Hartzell and Hoddie (2007, chap. 5) suggest that we should not assume that outside militaries will necessarily be strong enough to control countries in civil war; multinational forces are not usually composed of troops from the major powers, and the problems in Afghanistan and Iraq show the military problems even when such troops are involved. Andrea Talentino (2007) finds that state building by outsiders has helped end the violence but has failed to construct working states that can function independently.

However, it is hard to evaluate the success of these missions without comparing them to similar situations where there was no intervention. There has been an interesting argument about whether the United Nations in particular intervenes in difficult or easy cases; if it only goes to easy ones, this is a bad record, but if the cases are hard, maybe it's not so bad. Some analysts have attempted to control for the "degree of difficulty" of the cases and have concluded that, compared to similar cases, multinational peace forces seem to have been helpful when they are part of larger, multidimensional interventions; more limited interventions, even if international, seem to have less effect (Doyle and Sambanis 2000, 2006; Fortna 2004, 2008; Mullenbach 2006). On the other hand, unilateral intervention has been associated with more violence and longer civil wars (Regan 2000, 2009; Elbadawi and Sambanis 2000a; Balch-Lindsay and Enterline 2000); Afghanistan and Iraq presumably would fall into this category. Nonetheless, given the high costs and apparent difficulty of exit, it seems likely that most civil wars will have to end without the benefit of this large-scale activity.

Partition

An entirely separate issue from negotiated settlement is partition. A substantial number of civil wars are waged by groups that wish to separate from their current government. The international community has generally opposed such actions, which is probably one reason why so few secessionist civil wars have succeeded. Apparently the major reason for this position is the opposition of most governments to secession since they might be vulnerable to similar efforts, although there has been some mention of the casualties of partition particularly in India.

On the other hand, Chaim Kaufmann (1996b, 1998) has argued strongly that in some cases of ethnic violence, particularly when a large enough number of civilians have been killed, the animosity between the groups is so great that they cannot live together without periodically engaging in further large-scale violence. He contends that this is particularly true when the groups are intermingled; each group sees itself as vulnerable and therefore justified in striking first. In such situations Kaufmann argues that the only solution is to physically separate the two groups into different states, allowing each to regain security by being able to defend itself and that, in order to make this occur, the international community should be prepared to move people apart, forcibly if necessary. Since this strategy is contrary to the rhetoric of the international community, it has created quite a stir, with critics contending that partition would simply change civil wars into interstate wars, would encourage similar movements elsewhere, and was essentially ethnic cleansing and therefore unacceptable on moral grounds (Licklider and Bloom 2006). Interestingly, Roeder and Rothchild (2005, 10–12 and 320) argue that partition may be the best alternative when ethnic groups are deeply divided.

Democracy

As noted above, the international community has generally supported the establishment of democratic governments after civil wars. It is reasonable to ask whether this is appropriate, particularly since many of these countries were not democratic before the war. On the other hand, the prewar political system almost certainly helped bring about the civil war, so reconstructing it is probably not a good idea.

Democracy is usually justified as a good way to prevent the resumption of civil war and therefore good for the local population. The evidence often cited is the democratic peace, the assertion that democratic governments do not fight one another, a hypothesis that has been remarkably robust in a number of different statistical tests (Levy 2002). However, while this may explain foreign policy, it's not clear how it applies to renewed civil war. Certainly both sides are not usually democratic. The more precise hypothesis would be that democratic postwar governments are less likely to experience renewed civil war than nondemocratic governments.

The theoretical arguments in favor of this hypothesis are fairly straightforward, as noted earlier; a democratic government should allow all parties to believe they can gain power and, if they do not, be secure nevertheless. Such governments are more likely to support human rights policies that make life easier and more secure for all, thus reducing the tensions that might produce renewed violence.

On the other hand, there is some theoretical reason to think the hypothesis may be false. Winning elections requires mobilizing large numbers of people to participate; particularly after a civil war this may encourage candidates to appeal to their deepest fears, deepening the cleavages and leading to renewed violence, particularly in countries that lack long-term traditions of tolerating political dissent (Lyons 2005). Minorities may see themselves threatened by permanent majorities (whether justly or not) and feel impelled to strike first (Fearon 1993; Posen 1993). Sectarian parties and venial politicians may undercut trust in government, which in any event is likely to be in short supply. Weak democratic governments may be unable to deliver the critical public goods of security and economic progress, encouraging the revival of old tensions.

Do postwar democratic governments last longer than nondemocratic ones? Recent scholarship confirms the intuition that civil war rarely breaks out in established democracies. However, established autocracies seem similarly resistant to civil war. Civil war seems most common among the countries in the middle that are undergoing transition; interestingly it's not clear that it matters much whether the transitions are from democracy to autocracy or the reverse (Mansfield and Snyder 2005; Hegre et al. 2001; Jakobsen 1998; Fearon and Laitin 2003; Fearon 2004; Sambanis 2004, 847). However, our real concern is with a somewhat different set of states, those that have recently emerged from civil war. Attempts to test the hypothesis on these cases have yielded mixed results; some have supported the hypothesis (Dubey 2002); others have not (Toft 2009); still others are indeterminate (Mukherjee 2006). Given this record, it seems inappropriate to simply assume that democratic governments will necessarily prevent the resumption of civil war.

Even if democracy is desirable, is it realistic to try to create it, particularly in countries that do not have many of the conventional preconditions of democracy such as high literacy levels, civil society, and an independent middle class? Building on earlier work by Elisabeth Wood on El Salvador and South Africa (2001), Leonard Wantchekon (2004) presents an intriguing theoretical argument that under certain conditions contending leaders of nondemocratic factions within a country will agree on democracy, that is, allow citizens to make choices, when their economic interests require investments from citizens, popular preferences are not too biased, and an external agency is available to monitor the process. Certainly the example of former rebel leaders as senior politicians in countries like El Salvador, South Africa, and Mozambique suggests that something like this can happen.

However, Marina Ottaway (2003) argues that the model of democratization has escalated substantially over time. It started as a way to leave countries after the war was over and stressed demobilization of the competing forces and the formation of a new army and the establishment of a constitution and an election in two years. However, this model had obvious problems, and over time additional tasks were added: reforming the police and judicial system, building up civil society, strengthening the media, and improving local and regional governments. None of these is a bad thing, but no postwar country has the ability to do all of them at the same time. Moreover, the international community has not been willing to give resources or time to actually make it work. Even in Bosnia, which has gotten a lot of resources over a considerable time period, there has been very little progress, and the major problems in Afghanistan and Iraq show the difficulty of applying the model in practice (Donini, Niland, and

Wermester 2004; Diamond 2005). Thomas Carothers (1999, 351) argues that democracy promoters are learning what does work and what doesn't but that "no dramatic results should be expected from democracy promotion efforts."

Outsiders have traditionally assumed that democracy should be the outcome of negotiated settlements. However, as already mentioned, such settlements often involve power sharing agreements between the participants. These settlements often make democracy more elusive by empowering the groups and leaders who specialize in violence as opposed to more political ones, guaranteeing control of government positions regardless of election, and impeding the development of political organizations that cut across old divisions. A recent study makes a very strong case that powersharing and democracy in a postwar setting are in many ways contradictory and present a series of choices (framed in terms of dilemmas) that need to be directly faced (Jarstad and Sisk 2008).

Security

Widespread violence is a problem in most post-civil war societies; the U.S. case is particularly notable in this regard, both in the South during Reconstruction and in the West, where it became a staple of American myth and entertainment. Usually you have large numbers of former fighters on all sides, often still armed, not well suited to enter a peacetime economy that has its own problems (see later), and not in the habit of obeying authority. Indeed in negotiated settlements two or more armed forces may continue to exist, perhaps covertly. There are thus two separate security problems in such cases: (1) making former warring elites secure to reduce their incentives to restart the war and (2) making civilians secure so they will not feel dependent on their wartime organizations, which would make resumption of civil war easier.

Security for elites is difficult because the disarmament involved in the settlement necessarily leaves them vulnerable to cheating by their opponents. Several analysts, borrowing from international relations, have used the concept of security dilemma to describe this situation; each side is insecure because of disarmament, but building up their own forces frightens the other side into doing the same (Posen 1993; Fearon 1998a; Walter and Snyder 1999; Roe 2006; Kalyvas 2008). Outsiders can help by monitoring (and in many cases developing and executing) a strategy of disarmament, demobilization, and reintegration into society (DDR) that will reduce the competing forces proportionally and transparently. This is often a very demanding and difficult process, but we do know a fair amount about it (Ball 1996; Colletta, Kostner, and Wiederhofer 1996; Knight 2004).

Another strategy, complementary rather than competitive, is a security guarantee by outside powers backed up by troops on the ground, one aspect of peacekeeping as it is now understood. There is some dispute as to the utility of such intervention; Barbara Walter (2002, chaps. 4 and 5) found that third-party guarantees were associated with successful negotiated settlements of civil wars ending between 1940 and 1990; two other studies, looking at 1945–97 and 1815–1992 respectively, found that such guarantees were not especially useful (Hartzell 1999; Werner 1999). Other studies found that they were not very effective by themselves but when used as part of a multipurpose intervention the overall effort was likely to be successful (Doyle and Sambanis 2006; Mullenbach 2006; Fortna 2008; Howard 2008).

Security for civilians has traditionally received somewhat less attention; one study noted that out of 18 negotiated settlements of civil war, only 12 even mentioned the subject, and in most cases there were no details at all (Call and Stanley 2002, 304). Nonetheless it is of fundamental importance.

> In communities tormented by repeated violence . . . safety is the most compelling motive for action. Unstable conditions tend to be exacerbated by the return of community members who fled during earlier bouts of fighting; land disputes, threats, retribution, and intimidation are common. Individuals may be frightened by other individuals or gangs, identity groups as a whole may be afraid of large-scale retribution of attacks based on association, and the community at large may be threatened by other regions, the military, or government persecution. Healing under these conditions can be extremely difficult. Therefore, freedom of movement within the community, absence of personal or group threats or attacks, property security, and access to community resources are necessary first steps on the path to recovery. The principle of safety must apply to all members of the community, regardless of status. (Maynard 1999, 132)

Thus it is not surprising that Stephen Stedman (2002) argues that security should be one of two tasks given priority over all others in postwar peacekeeping and Monica Toft (2009) calls for making security sector reform (SSR) the task that must be undertaken before any others can succeed.

Civil war usually undercuts the legitimacy of the local police and security forces; a negotiated settlement is likely to also reduce their resources and resolve. This is not necessarily a bad thing since they have often been forces of simple repression rather than providers of real security, but without some sort of force in the streets, violence can escalate quickly. Clearly local forces are necessary in the long run, but they often are simply not available immediately after a settlement. Michael Dziedzic (2002) calls this problem the deployment gap.

Call and Stanley (2002, 312–16) suggest four alternatives. The first is a new, quick-start local force, but in practice it is usually impossible for such a group to be effective; they cite one partial success, police cadets in El Salvador, but they were working in a rural area with public support and no organized crime.

The second is to use preexisting forces with international monitoring. Especially if they are drawn from former combat forces, they may be effectively organized, but they are also likely to have relatively little legitimacy and to treat their former opponents harshly. It is also common for governments to transfer soldiers into police units to avoid disarmament. Reforming and retraining the police should be a high priority item, but many international donors have been reluctant to get involved. It looks better to give food to starving children rather than support a justice system that might reduce corruption and allow them to get food on their own. As a holdover from the Vietnam War, the U.S. military is normally not allowed to train police. Some organizations such as the International Criminal Investigative Training Assistance Program, sponsored by the U.S. Department of Justice, have provided training for police, but at best this is a slow process.

A third alternative is the use of international military forces. However, most militaries dislike this task, and their training in using high levels of violence is inappropriate for police tasks. For illustration consider a possibly apocryphal but telling vignette. In an American city troops had been brought in to help suppress rioting. A policeman asked his military colleagues to "cover him" as he entered a building; in his terms this meant being ready to fire if he was fired upon. The soldiers, however, immediately hosed down the building with bullets to prevent any possible resistance.

Kosovo proved an interesting example of national differences on these issues. American soldiers in particular resisted this mission and wanted to turn it over to locals as soon as possible. British forces, perhaps because of extensive experience in Northern Ireland, seemed more comfortable using their military to do it. The Italian Carabinieri and the French Gendarmerie Nationale are examples of forces combining police and military skills; as a result the Italian and French NATO contingents in Kosovo were willing to use these groups to do local policing (Dziedzic and Hawley 2005, 261). Interestingly, however, the same author who has strongly argued that an international gendarmerie force should be created for just such situations also suggests that in Kosovo even the Italian and French military did not really understand their capabilities or know how to best use them (Perito 2004, 181). Any such forces, of course, are likely to face formidable barriers of language and culture in an unfamiliar land.

The fourth strategy is the use of international civilian police personnel. The most prominent supplier has been the United Nations CIVPOL program, which recruits police personnel from around the world and dispatches them to areas of need. However, the inevitable problems of language and culture are accentuated by differences among CIVPOL personnel themselves. Good police are in demand in most countries, so recruitment is difficult, and the quality of the personnel has been questionable. Moreover, in general they have functioned as monitors of the local police rather than as independent forces. Last, the process of recruitment, training, and deployment into country has often been painfully slow.

Obviously all of these strategies for dealing with the deployment gap have their own drawbacks. But Dziedzic (2002) notes that the deployment gap is succeeded by the enforcement gap. The lack of police is only one part of a much larger issue of establishing an efficient and fair justice system. Police require laws to enforce, but often the preexisting laws are totally inappropriate for a new situation and have no legitimacy with much of the population. Without a fully functioning government, it's not clear who should decide how the laws should be changed. In Somalia it was decided to reinstitute a prewar set of laws, and old manuals and books were reprinted to facilitate the process (Hirsch and Oakley 1995, 60–61, 87–95, 103–6). In another case,

> the applicable law in Kosovo became an almost unfathomable combination of old law, international and European human rights conven-

tions, UNMIK [United Nations Mission in Kosovo] regulations, and police directives. (Perito 2004, 207–8)

Moreover, reform of the police forces is often easier than dealing with the judicial system of prosecutors, defense lawyers, judges, and the prisons. After a civil war the number of personnel with even minimal qualifications for these demanding tasks is likely to be small indeed. Judicial reform is not usually a high-priority item in peace settlements, so incumbents are often left in office to obstruct reforms indefinitely. Alternatively, in Kosovo Albanian judges were quickly put in place, but this resulted in unfair treatment of Serbs, and international judges had to be brought in for some time (Hartz, Mercean, and Williamson 2005, 182–83, 186–87).

This in turn leads to Dziedzic's (2002) institutional gap, the ability to build permanent legal institutions that can continue to function well after foreigners leave. The key elements to build in are transparency and accountability (Hartz, Mercean, and Williamson 2005, 165). The lack of outside support for such reform efforts is particularly ironic given the recent concern for "rule of law" as a criterion for these new governments. One intriguing suggested remedy is the Stanley Foundation's call for an International Legal Assistance Consortium, a group of lawyers and judicial specialists who could be mobilized on short notice to help bring about judicial reforms when called upon (Stanley Foundation 2000).

Economic Growth

Peace is usually expensive. Typically the country, probably not very rich to begin with, is economically prostrate and has massive human and organizational needs that it cannot satisfy with its own resources. One cost estimate of yearly needs in the early 1990s suggests $250 million for El Salvador, and $750 million for Mozambique (de Soto and del Castillo 1994); obviously these figures would be much higher today. Outsiders can provide resources and expertise to assist in creating a functioning economy, although the combination of prewar economic problems and wartime damage makes this a formidable task.

The central need is to create employment opportunities, both for those unemployed by the war and for former combatants who are being (or should be) demobilized. One of the first and most expensive tasks is to rebuild infrastructure devastated by the war; such things as schools, roads, bridges, electrical systems, running war, and waste disposal are immediate priorities. In the middle term, the destruction or flight of capital, low level of savings, and displacement of skilled labor become important. Corruption is often a major problem as well. The banking system has usually collapsed or been taken over by criminals. Coping with such problems requires a skilled civil service that often does not exist (Junne and Verkoren 2005).

However, as in the case of supporting democracy, it is not clear that outsiders will provide sufficient resources to actually create an economy strong enough to reduce the likelihood of renewed civil war. Part of the problem is a lack of political will in the developed countries to make such an open-ended commitment to states that often seem fairly insignificant, especially when the number of potential candidates seems to increase over time. Aid promises are often not kept, and aid is often given slowly and in ways that are less than efficient. We also know that aid agencies and NGOs often inadvertently harm the economy by creating inflation by spending large amounts of money and by hiring skilled locals for their own use, making it more difficult for both private and public local organizations to function well. Coordination among the many organizations, each independently funded, is always weak and often nonexistent (Anderson 1999; Jones 2002; Covey 2005).

It is also true that we do not know the proper strategy to create successful economies in poor countries in general (as witness the problems of development programs for the past 50 years), let alone those that have been ravaged by wars. One prominent example is macroeconomic policy. The tax bases of postwar countries have usually been decimated, and their tax collections systems are practically nonexistent, so they have very little domestic revenue and are necessarily dependent on foreign assistance. The International Monetary Fund and other organizations, based on the perfectly reasonable assumption that economic development rests on a strong currency and a solid trade balance, require that governments spend not much more than they take in. But this means that they cannot respond to the desperate needs of their population, making a resumption of large-scale violence more likely. Unfortunately there is no easy solution to this problem unless outsiders are prepared to underwrite the country's economy for some time (Carbonnier 1998; Harris 1999; Woodward 2002; Tabb 2004; Jeong 2005, 123–53; Blair et al. 2005; Collier et al. 2003; Kang 2008).

The situation is not entirely bleak. Studies suggest that postwar states do in fact experience substantial economic growth, albeit less than comparable states with no war, averaging about 6 percent per year, at least for the first five years, although there is some decline afterward. This increase may be due to the weakness of the economies during the war and the decrease in military expenditure. Roughly similar patterns appeared in other development indicators (Chen, Loayza, and Reynal-Querol 2007; Lounsbery and Pearson 2008, 206–11).

Transitional Justice and Memory

Combatants in civil wars often do terrible things to one another and increasingly to civilians as well. Often, indeed, these actions trigger the intervention of outsiders. Actions by the government were probably legal at the time, so its members are presumably immune from normal justice proceedings, even assuming that the court systems are functioning. The term *transitional justice* has been developed to cover policies to deal with human rights violations during the civil war and perhaps earlier.

In practice there have been several different approaches to the problem. (1) An international court can take jurisdiction. Special international tribunals have been set up to deal with cases from Former Yugoslavia and Rwanda. It is expected that the International Criminal Court will eventually take jurisdiction over some cases as well. They are run by international judges applying international law, often outside the country. (2) Special criminal proceedings can be set up within the country, sometimes with international as well as local judges. Examples are in Kosovo (Perriello and Wierda 2006a), Sierra Leone (Perriello and Wierda 2006b), and Timor-Leste (Reiger and Wierda 2006). (3) Truth commissions are another strategy. While they vary widely (Hayner 2001), they generally do not have the power to punish; instead their task is to determine what happened and make the facts public. (4) Another strategy is simply to ignore the issue altogether. Often all sides feel they would be vulnerable to such proceedings and are concerned that they may stir up old enmities just when peace seems to be at hand.

The institutions in the first three categories share a common purpose—to shape a memory of the previous events that will reduce the level of enmity among the combatant groups and make the renewal of mass violence less likely. The arguments in favor of war crimes tribunals and truth commissions are psychological, that the victims (and perhaps the perpetrators) will be more able to accept the past and work together in the future if guilt is acknowledged and compensation of some sort is offered. This is expected to occur because victims will have a sense of justice, reducing grievances and healing psychological trauma (Mendeloff 2006, 4). The theory is not implausible, but it is drawn from ideas that have been applied with somewhat mixed success to individuals in Western cultures. (At least in my family, at holidays some subjects are "forgotten" for the sake of harmony.) And Western psychology usually would not simply ask people in grief to tell their story once in public and then go away, which is what courts and truth commissions usually do; it would recommend a more gradual process, followed by support of various types.

> There has been no study to date of the psychological impact of truth commissions on survivors, but the evidence that is available is enough to raise some serious questions. . . . The assumption that knowing the facts about what happened will always contribute to healing is too simplistic, and is sometimes just not true. (Hayner 2001, 135, 142; cf. Minow 1998, 70–74; Mendeloff 2004, 363–69; and Stover 2005)

Mendeloff (2006, 7–15) reaches a similar conclusion based on a summary of a number of clinical studies from South Africa and Former Yugoslavia.

Do settlements that include provisions for transitional justice last longer than those that do not? To put it simply, there is absolutely no evidence that this is true, since we have basically no historic examples to draw on. (More detailed and sophisticated critiques of the arguments for "truth telling," which have received much less attention than they deserve, are Mendeloff 2004 and 2006.) Such provisions have not been included in negotiated settlements to civil wars (which have themselves been fairly scarce) until the past few years. Interestingly we have somewhat more evidence of a related topic; apology does seem to be useful in interstate relations (Barkan 2000; Feldman 1984; Wolffsohn 1993; Lavy 1996; Lind 2003; Berger 2003), although here it is usually between groups of people who no longer live in close proximity.

Of course we do have some indirect evidence. If transitional justice is necessary for reconciliation, then presumably no prior civil wars has ever ended since "transitional justice" institutions have not been built into their settlements. In fact this is not true; most civil wars do end and are not resumed (Licklider 1995, 683–84). That is not to say that the conflicts that "caused" the war have been solved, but people all over the world for hundreds of years have somehow managed to live together without killing one another in large numbers, not a trivial achievement, without the assistance of transitional justice. "There can be no peace without justice" is a plausible slogan; unfortunately there is no evidence that it is true.

Transitional justice, punishing people guilty of terrible deeds, is undeniably attractive. The uncertainty about its utility would not be so troubling if it did not sometimes come at a high price for conflict management. No leaders are likely to agree to a civil war settlement that would put them and their followers at risk, so their first (and probably nonnegotiable) demand for a settlement is likely to be amnesty. Since the definition of a negotiated settlement is one that either side can reject and continue the war, the choice may be to grant their request or continue the war. Tonya Putnam (2002, 240) lists Angola, Guatemala, Namibia, Sierra Leone, and Bosnia as cases where amnesty has been critical in getting settlements; South Africa might be another candidate. (She also notes that amnesty is recognized in international law as an appropriate response to internal war, citing Dinstein and Tabory 1996, 319.) In practice this has been resolved by two strategies: (*a*) agreeing on truth commissions and similar institutions that will not penalize individuals for their prior actions, even though this in turn may undercut the already tenuous hope that they will aid in reconciliation, and (*b*) giving amnesty and then reneging on the promise when the political system allows it.

The poster child of the first strategy is South Africa's Truth and Reconciliation Commission. It has justly attracted attention and admiration around the world. In a stunning series of public hearings, held all over the country and televised almost nightly for years throughout South Africa, the historical record of human rights violations on both sides under apartheid was written for all to see. Fortunately an extraordinarily sophisticated study is under way to attempt to determine its impact. Presumably the underlying theory of the TRC was that by persuading people of its version of what had actually happened ("truth"), they would become less hostile toward members of other races ("reconciliation"). The study shows quite clearly that whites who have accepted this "truth" are less hostile to blacks than whites who have not done so, confirming the value of the strategy. However, it also shows no relationship whatsoever among the 70 percent of South African blacks who attend church; accepting the "truth" of the TRC is quite unrelated to their attitudes toward whites. (Better predictors turn out to be close contact with whites and religion;

interestingly, age and education are also unrelated [Gibson 2004, 132–35].) There are many reasons to admire the work of the TRC, in particular for creating a record of the apartheid regime, but aiding reconciliation of blacks toward whites does not seem to be among them.

One of the critiques of the TRC has been that it does not have the power to actually punish evildoers. It is not clear that simply revealing the truth about terrible atrocities and then seeing the perpetrators go free will lead to reconciliation. Gibson's work suggests that it has not, at least among South African blacks. We do not know if a different system, in which the malefactors were punished, would have different psychological effects. We do know that we are unlikely to have a more favorable environment than South Africa for a truth commission; if it does not succeed here, the strategy is unlikely to work in less favored locations.

> It remains an open question whether through taking testimony and publishing reports, a truth commission can also help to reconcile groups that have been warring or otherwise engaged in deep animosities. (Minow 1998, 79)

We badly need more research on this topic.

The second strategy is to promise amnesty to get peace and then break the promise when it becomes politically possible. This seems a dubious strategy. It raises several different issues. (*a*) I understand the argument that it is morally acceptable to break promises to people who have done evil deeds in order to end those actions. (*b*) However, within the country this involves violating the terms of a negotiated settlement of a civil war as well as risking triggering similar repudiations on all sides and reigniting the conflict. Still, presumably the local people doing it can make reasonable judgements about this, and so far this hasn't happened. (*c*) However, it's hard to believe that this strategy will not make it more difficult to reach negotiated settlements to other civil wars in the future. Prosecutions by third parties such as the Spanish case against Pinochet raise the same difficulty. If leaders cannot count on amnesty, they have little reason to end the war short of military defeat, which may be very costly, although probably not for the outsiders who recommend the policy. And if war crimes trials are supposed to deter future human rights violations, it's hard to believe that breaking amnesty promises will not deter the same people from accepting settlements based on such promises (Licklider 2008).

Conclusion

We have examined a number of ethical issues about the role of outsiders in ending civil wars. In many of these cases, however, the real issue seems to be empirical. If military victories establish longer-lasting peace and are more likely to produce democracy over time, how strong is the moral case for negotiated settlements? If partition will reduce casualties, what is the moral argument for opposing it? If postwar democracy makes renewed violence more likely, why should it be encouraged? If following conventional macroeconomic theory undermines the ability of postwar governments to survive and makes renewed violence more likely, why should we support it? If transitional justice strategies do not have their desired effect, why should we encourage others to adopt them?

All of these empirical questions remain open to debate. And so, at one level this chapter is about another failure of social science. The task of social science is to establish generalizations buttressed so solidly with replicable evidence that they will be widely accepted, even by people who initially disbelieve them. We don't do this very well for a variety of reasons. This is only one of many issues in which the critical questions are empirical and for which we have no unanimous, persuasive answers.

The moral implications of this failure are substantial. As human rights and conflict management have become more prominent in foreign policy, the research in those fields takes on a new importance. We are not just engaged in academic debates now; we are talking about other people's countries and other people's lives. And we do not know, in such a manner as to persuade others, what is true, what will work, even in general, much less in particular situations that may not follow the general patterns we seek to trace.

And yet, we cannot simply stand aside from the debate. Many years ago, when I was presenting a paper on economic sanctions, someone asked about the food blockade of Germany by the Allies after World War I, and I said truthfully that I didn't know anything about it. A senior scholar jumped up in the audience and demanded that I answer the question, saying that I knew a lot and that if I didn't answer people who knew less and were less careful would answer the question instead. We were both right; that is our dilemma.

I have no magic answer to this problem, although I think (or at least hope) that more research would be helpful. But I do think that, when making recommendations about war and peace in other people's coun-

tries on the basis of empirical assumptions that are not well substantiated, a lot of humility on our part is appropriate. It is particularly troubling that many of the assumptions underlying the generally accepted
policies of how to deal with civil wars cannot be substantiated and may
well be incorrect. Social science, of course, deals with generalizations;
policymakers often deal with individual cases. But policymakers deal with
those specific cases on the basis of generalizations, and if those generalizations are wrong, the policy is not likely to be helpful. At a minimum we
need to be very careful in assuming that we know the likely outcomes of
our policies.

PART III

Ethnic Conflict, International Relations, and Genocide

The Origins of Ethnic Wars: A Historical and Critical Account

MONICA DUFFY TOFT

The volume of research on ethnic wars has grown tremendously in the last decade.[1] While there are a number of useful ways to summarize and compare major contributions to this important field of inquiry, in this chapter I employ a historical review—an intellectual history of inquiry into the causes, dynamics, and consequences of ethnic war as a category of substate violence—in which I divide the literature into three broad time periods: the 1960s to 1989, 1990 to 1999, and 2000 to the present.

I should add that while it is now largely taken for granted that the study of ethnic violence is an important undertaking in its own right, it was not always so. A historical division of the literature allows us to see how key facets of our pursuit of general knowledge have changed with our appreciation of the nature and intensity of the threat. We can also trace changes in the nature of the academic communities engaged in this pursuit over time; beginning with area specialists, anthropologists, comparative political scientists, diplomatic and military historians, and so on in the early literature, to the present-day alliance of these early communities with specialists in terrorism, strategic studies, international politics, international relations theory, and even economics.

I begin this chapter with a discussion of what is meant by "ethnic war." I follow this with a structured historical comparison of three generations of work on subjects on or close to ethnic war. For practicality's sake

I start with the period of the 1960s, by no means the first decade of important research on the origins and nature of ethnic violence, but for our purposes a useful starting point. This first wave of scholarship—tracking as it does with the attempt by European states to reestablish control of their colonies and with the coming of the Cold War—was often driven by increasing concern over the difficulties experienced by the United States in its expanding roles in Asia, Africa, and the Middle East; but concern with ethnic war remained overshadowed by the threat of global thermonuclear war between the United States and the Soviet Union. Ironically, the end of the U.S. war in Vietnam did little to increase the interest of security studies and international politics researchers in substate violence. In the 1980s—far from intensifying their focus on the causes, dynamics, and consequences of substate violence—most academics and policymakers in the United States were instead turning with renewed interest toward the study of large-scale but nonnuclear interstate war. This turn away from substate violence as an important empirical category of war was powerfully abetted by the publication of Kenneth N. Waltz's *Theory of International Politics* (1979), which, in its insistence that progress in understanding interstate violence—in Waltz's view the most important type of violence—demanded commitment to positive theory, tended to further diminish interest in a category of violence most often relegated to the sui generis category (Waltz 1979). Thus, in the 1980s, only a very few researchers of substate violence appreciated the importance of understanding ethnic identity and nationalism as a cause of large-scale substate violence and dissent. It was this group, almost alone, who correctly anticipated the demise of the USSR when those in the state-centric security studies and international politics communities were caught by surprise. Second, I explore and analyze second-wave research into ethnic war, from 1990 to 1999. This literature was driven by a widely perceived rise in ethnic and nationalist violence around 1990, following the end of the Cold War, and by a concomitant decline in the likelihood of interstate war following the first Gulf War. I track the subject of ethnic war's evolution from backwater to mainstream, and the productive new alliance of diverse research communities and methods now employed to help us understand and, ultimately, diminish either the frequency or intensity of ethnic war. Third and finally, I summarize and critique the most recent scholarship on ethnic war, from 2000 to the present. Here the watershed event did not come from the real world, so much as the publication of a controversial series of articles originally supported by the World Bank, which suggested that "ethnic" war was in fact a myth, and that the true cause of substate violence was greed or poverty.

I conclude the chapter with a brief summary, and a discussion of emerging questions of, and approaches to, the study of ethnic war.

What Is "Ethnic" War?

There have been two basic debates in the literature about the origins of identity, including ethnic identity. A primordialist school holds that identity is fixed, and that attachments and sentiments "are the irreducible bedrock on which group material and political interests and claims tend to be based" (Comaroff and Stern 1994, 38).[2] Constructivists, by contrast, view ethnic identity as malleable; seeing it as the product of a particular time, place, and series of events. Just as an identity can be constructed, they argue, it can be reconstructed (Fearon and Laitin 2000). Although the primordialist and constructivist understandings of identity are often treated as exclusive and irreconcilable, in fact their differences are often overstated and hence "misleading" (Comaroff and Stern 1994, 39). Furthermore, although quite a few scholars make a strong case for constructivist understandings of identity, there are very few scholars who adopt a strictly primordialist position, instead working from a sort of hybrid position. As Comaroff and Stern explain, a "more sophisticated hybrid has emerged," and this hybrid "treats ethnic consciousness as a universal potentiality that is realized—objectified, that is, as an active political identity—when a population recognizes common interests, usually when it finds its existence, interests, or integrity under threat" (1994, 39). The most sophisticated treatment using this hybrid approach is Stuart Kaufman's *Modern Hatreds* (2001), in which he argues that emotionally laden symbols and myths that are constructed and can be reconstructed explain why and how ethnic groups struggle for status and security.

But what is an *ethnic* group? According to Anthony Smith, a leading scholar of ethnicity, an ethnic group is a group of individuals who share (1) a common trait such as language, race, or religion; (2) a belief in a common descent and destiny; and (3) an association with a given piece of territory (1986, 22–31). So, for example, "Serbs" see their ethnic brethren as sharing a common language (Serb), common religion (Orthodoxy), and a common homeland in and around contemporary Serbia, Kosovo, and parts of Croatia and Bosnia, while Croats share the common language of Croatia, Catholic faith, and a homeland of Croatia.

While ethnic groups are largely descriptive categories of groups, the concept of nation entails self-recognition (Connor 1978). Each member recognizes his or her own membership in that nation, the membership of fellow co-nationals, and the "nonmembership" of nonnationals (Gellner 1983, 7). There is thus both a subjective and an objective aspect to nations: subjective in the sense that any ethnic group that considers itself to be a nation on the basis of the criteria previously listed is a nation; and objective in that the group shares some common objective characteristic that identifies it as distinct and differentiated from other groups (Hobsbawm 1990, 5–9). Such differentiation may come about in two ways. First, nations may emerge as the result of exclusion that forces groups of individuals to identify themselves in relation to that nonmembership. Roman Szporluk argues, for example, that non-Russians of the Soviet Union took notice of the de-Sovietization of Russia and the reemergence of Russian national identity. Non-Russians responded "by raising analogous demands for the rehabilitation of their respective cultural figures. . . . This movement has been stimulated, and certainly legitimized, by the developments in ethnic Russia" (1990, 15). For these groups to be categorized as nations, however, it is not simply enough for them to share exclusion as their common bond; they must also possess a common, salient trait.

The second way nations may emerge is the result of a classification scheme imposed or structured from outside. States and imperial metropoles, for instance, often rely on objective criteria—such as language, religion, or race—in order to politically structure and regulate their subjects and territories (e.g., Laitin 1986). Here Jews under the German National Socialist regime stand out. While Jews viewed themselves as part of the German nation—"we are Germans"—the regime classified them as outsiders, or non-Germans. It was only later and tragically that Jews came to accept the identity imposed on them by others, and began to view themselves as distinct. Whereas an ethnic group is a latent nation, a nation is a politically active ethnic group that demands greater cultural autonomy or self-determination.

At its root level, ethnic war means groups of people fighting with other groups, where the "other" is usually defined in terms of race, language, or religion, resulting in large-scale, organized violence.[3] In some cases one of the groups may dominate the state and use state institutions and resources to defeat a competing ethnic group. This was the situation in Former Yugoslavia in the early 1990s whereby Serbs were able to harness the power of the Yugoslav National Army in its fights with the Slovenes,

Croats, and Bosnian Muslims. Alternatively, the war might involve two ethnic groups fighting each other, without the provocation of a central state.[4] The conflict between Armenians and Azeris over Nagorno-Karabakh is a prime example of this type of fight. Finally the war may or may not involve territory, that is, communal wars versus wars of secession. However, it is fair to say that territory and its control are often at the heart of ethnic wars.[5]

In the remainder of this chapter I use *ethnic* and *national* interchangeably, and this way of understanding ethnicity and ethnic war gives rise to a number of important questions. Often the nature of the questions researchers ask and ignore depends upon the historical context in which they and their work are embedded. As we will see later, each generation of scholars and policymakers tended to ask different questions about ethnic war. Perhaps the first and most basic question asked of ethnic war, then, is "What causes it?"

First Wave: 1960–90

In the 1960s relatively little was written on the subject of ethnic war, largely because the United States had only recently emerged as the leader in an alliance of victors in the massively destructive World War II. That war appeared to be a great teacher, and the lessons learned by policymakers generally proved inimical to the study of substate violence. Key among these lessons was that the power to overcome one's enemies or, conversely, defend one's state against them resided in the capacity to produce large, technologically sophisticated mechanized militaries. These militaries were most decisive in terrains and climates matching those of the advanced industrial states, namely, North America, Europe, the Soviet Union, and Japan. The "third" or "developing" world was neither capable of producing such militaries nor, as a result, considered worthy of assault by the militaries of advanced industrial powers: there was little cost to ignoring them and little benefit from taking them seriously.

On the other hand, as U.S. allies began to return to "their" colonies following the war, something unanticipated happened: advanced technology and combat experience in the European theater did not result in the inexpensive reestablishment of political control in the colonies. On the contrary, one after another, countries such as Netherlands, France, Britain, Belgium, and Portugal experienced unexpected defeats against "backward" indigenous fighters in Asia, Africa, and the Middle East.

By the 1960s this turn of events had given impetus to a new look at the origins and nature of substate violence, resulting in a rebirth of sophisticated treatment of the subject of substate violence. A number of these works stand out, including those by Rupert Emerson, Harry Eckstein, Karl Deutsch, Walker Connor, and Eric Wolf.

Emerson's book, *From Empire to Nation: The Rise to Self-Assertion of Asian and African Peoples* (1960), is an early excellent entry, especially in its handling of the thorny (for Marxists) issue of the relationship of ethnic identity and nationalism to dissent and revolution. Almost alone among many contemporaries, Emerson hits the nail on the head when asking whether Marxist ideology or national self-determination was the real engine of revolutionary resistance to colonial rule. Here he quotes M. N. Roy:

> Communism in Asia, essentially, is nationalism painted red. . . . The Leninist program was to regard nationalism as an ally; now communism plays the role of nationalism, and appears in its most extreme form, having a corresponding share of all its vices—racism, cultural revivalism, intolerance, jingoism and resistance to Western bourgeois influence. (1960, 373–74)

Emerson devoted a chapter of his book to elaborating the relationship of nationalism to resistance, and concluded that as a cause of the sharp rise of costs in maintaining or reestablishing colonial control in Asia, Africa, or the Middle East, nationalism far outweighed socialist ideology in places where the two overlapped.

Eckstein's contribution was more general and took the form of an edited volume entitled *Internal War: Problems and Approaches*. In it, Eckstein assembles an all-star ensemble of scholars on the problem of substate violence. He introduces the volume with an important note on the relative dearth of good research on substate violence:

> When today's social science has become intellectual history, one question will almost certainly be asked about it: Why did social science, which has produced so many studies of so many subjects, produce so few on violent political disorder—internal war? (1964, 1)

Similarly, in his own contribution, Lucian Pye laments that

the problem of coping with armed insurrection has been largely ignored in the modern literature of both military and political science. One must go back to the Renaissance and the early formation of the Western nation-state system to find writers on statecraft who are primarily concerned with the problem of creating republics in the face of insurrectionary attempts by would-be tyrants. (1964, 158)

Yet none of Eckstein's twelve contributors in a volume on internal war focuses on ethnicity, ethnic groups, or group rivalries. Instead, the focus is on other important causes and contributors to substate violence, such as revolutionary ideology, economic development or lack thereof, and political corruption. Eckstein's volume thus stands as important to the study of ethnic war less for its subject matter than for its insistence that substate violence is important in its own right and worthy of attention by researchers and policymakers who want to understand an important source of organized violence.

Perhaps the most influential scholarship to reach publication in this period is Karl Deutsch's *Nationalism and Social Communication* (1966), in which Deutsch incorrectly predicted the end of particular ethnic loyalties as a consequence of the continued development of the modern nation-state.

Connor's piece, published a mere three years later, goes a considerable way toward correcting the omission of ethnicity as an important variable. In "Ethnology and the Peace of South Asia" (1969), Connor specifically evaluates ethnic group identity as a cause of resistance to the U.S.-supported government of South Vietnam and a cause of continued support for the Democratic Republic of Vietnam.

Connor's piece was visionary in a number of ways, yet few contemporary theorists of interstate violence and fewer policymakers gave it much attention. Then as now, the United States was good at handing out rifles and sacks of rice, but relatively poor at developing the tools and experience necessary to change a person's mind or redirect national identity toward constructive rather than destructive ends. Contemporary analyses of socialist ideology emphasized its critique of the income inequality inherent in capitalism, and thus many in the United States and elsewhere accepted as settled that the task of insulating a people against the blandishments of socialism—and hence to "communist domination"—could be usefully reduced to redistributing material values or providing relatively simple security from unsophisticated "insurgents." This is a point well made by the final entry in this period's major contributions to the study of ethnic violence, Eric Wolf. Wolf's identification of the main pillars of U.S. weakness vis-à-vis substate violence plays as well today as it did over 30 years ago:

> Specially insulated from other continents and their tribulations by virtue of her geographic position and by her extraordinary prosperity, America finds herself ill prepared in the twentieth century to understand the upheavals which are now shaking the poor nations of the world. Yet ignorance courts disaster. Viet Nam has become a graveyard because Americans did not know enough or care enough about a little-known part of Southeast Asia. (1969, ix)

In *Peasant Wars of the Twentieth Century,* Wolf, an anthropologist by training, adapted Karl Polanyi's "double movement" mechanism to explain why so many wars against European colonial authorities were peasant based. The link between Wolf's argument and ethnic violence is difficult to appreciate until one understands that Wolf's explanation, like Polanyi's, focused on the capacity of an economic system—in this case, capitalism—to conceive of "land" and "labor," for example, as objects that could be commodified and then exchanged. Since most ethnic groups identify with a particular piece of territory—a homeland—the stage is set for tension when portions of that homeland are commodified for sale. Thus in Wolf's argument, it is the arrival of the Western merchant and his particular way of reconceptualizing a peasant's reality in particular land, natural resources, and social relations that sets the stage for revolt and leads to the frequency of peasant-based revolutions in the twentieth century.

In the 1970s, interest in ethnic war as a subset of substate violence remained sporadic. In *Why Men Rebel* (1970) Ted Robert Gurr published a study that explored a psychological dimension to resistance to central authority. Gurr argued that repression acted like a spring that stored energy, and that too much of it eventually caused the spring to snap, releasing the energy and putting the state at risk. It proved an important contribution to our understanding of a key cause of substate violence, yet did not differentiate between ethnic, ideological, and resource motivations or abuses per se. When ethnicity *was* engaged definitively, it was usually focused on ethnicity in Africa or Asia (e.g., Bates 1974; Weiner 1978).

In sum, in the 1960s and 1970s, those taking the problem of ethnicity and ethnic violence seriously tended to be marginalized as compared to those whose focus was interstate violence and nuclear warfare. There is some justification for this: the (1) absolute and compressed-in-time destructiveness of world war and especially nuclear war was indisputable as compared to ethnic violence and civil war more generally, and the proximity in time of World War II to researchers of the day made civil wars seem marginally important; (2) the Cold War rivalry of the United States and the Soviet Union, and the eagerness of both superpowers to supply weapons and other supports to combatants engaged in substate violence, made it seem that local, bottom-up issues exercised a marginal effect on violence or peace efforts as compared to the issues that dominated superpower calculations: additive power, ideological legitimacy, and so on; and (3) most of those analyzing ethnicity and nationalism were disinclined by training to look for broad patterns or to seek general explanations. Instead, they accepted the view that most cases they studied were sui generis. Thus, the question "What causes ethnic violence?" was both scarcely asked and only sporadically answered. Little in the way of comprehensive theory on civil war emerged, largely because the focus of inquiry remained causes of revolutions, riots, and societal discontent more generally. In terms of policy implications, most U.S. policymakers appeared to hope the thorny and complex issues raised by the observable rise in substate violence could be ignored.

Ironically, perhaps, the strongest moves toward a general understanding of substate violence came from those in the security studies community who viewed post–World War II ethnic war as part of a larger struggle between the socialist and capitalist blocs. Proponents of this view hypothesized a broad strategy—designed by the USSR and later supported and advanced by the People's Republic of China—to overwhelm the capitalist world by means of a series of "brushfire" wars (LeMay 1968; Blaufarb 1977). This was a type of "protracted war" for which the United States and its allies were unprepared either by design or by temperament. Even though this group went wrong by assuming—as the socialists themselves often did—that socialist ideology mattered more than ethnic and national identity, they opened the way for later scholars of substate violence to generalize across cases and detect patterns that raised interesting questions about the nature of substate violence independent of its potential threat to the security of the advanced industrial states.

In the 1980s, however, interest in substate violence by mainstream scholars of international politics and security studies waned. Far from turning increased attention to the problem of substate violence after an unexpected defeat in Vietnam, U.S. academics and policymakers turned with renewed interest to the conventional balance of forces in Europe and Asia, and toward strategic nuclear issues. The consensus seems to have been that domino theory—the idea that the value of intrinsically unimportant states might aggregate to cause a meaningful shift in the balance of power between the United States and USSR—had been proven wrong. Thus "intrinsic value," a euphemism for "advanced industrial state," would be the guiding cost and benefit consideration for the next generation of U.S. policymakers. If a country had a skilled population and large GNP, it mattered; and if it had neither, it did not.

Two books in particular highlight this turning away from substate violence. The first was Kenneth Waltz's *Theory of International Politics* (1979), as much an argument for the value and necessity of positive theory as a true theory of international politics in itself. Waltz argued that only by means of theory building and systematic testing could we arrive at a useful understanding of interstate politics. He also argued that while many forms of violence mattered—perhaps all forms—the most important was interstate war. After all, South Vietnam had fallen; yet Japan, South Korea, and Taiwan remained independent. Thus it seemed obvious, albeit in hindsight, that the Vietnam War should not have been fought, because its fate one way or another had a marginal impact on U.S. security. And because most scholars of interstate violence accepted as axiomatic the notion that states could be imagined as rational actors while substate actors could not, Waltz's argument implied there was very little utility in exploring substate violence or attempting to generalize from observations of such violence to advance theory.

The second was John Mearsheimer's *Conventional Deterrence* (1983), a book whose appeal to nervous policymakers after Vietnam cannot be overestimated. Mearsheimer suggested that, as Waltz "reminded" us, the type of violence that mattered most was interstate violence. His book presented policymakers and security studies academics with a more comfortable vision of a world in which "force-to-space" ratios and "defense-in-depth" strategies mattered again. This was a world in which security and victory could be bought, in which material power mattered most and the power of ideas—strategy excepted—and identities mattered less. For a wealthy, industrial-technological giant of a state such as the United

States, the world Mearsheimer presented promised to be both more simple and more secure.[6]

Contrast this vision with the reality of an increasing decline in the likelihood of great-power interstate war and we can appreciate both that Mearsheimer was right and that he and his cohort were right for a dwindling proportion of people and states. The view that security could be reduced to material and strategic considerations—complex as these sometimes seemed—was simple as compared to the intellectual tools, training, and experience needed to understand what a majority of the world's people were actually thinking and why foreign languages must be mastered, fieldwork must be undertaken, and so on. In November 1989, the Berlin Wall tumbled. Two years later, the Soviet Union collapsed. None of the experts—the students of Hans Morgenthau, Kenneth Waltz, and others in security studies and international politics—anticipated it. And in fact none of the very excellent state-centric theories of the day could account for it. The two most likely scenarios at the time, consistent with state-of-the-art international relations theory, was either a third world war (less likely) or an indefinite extension of Cold War rivalry (more likely).

But while the academic communities most focused on interstate politics failed to predict the collapse of the USSR, other scholars in the 1970s and 1980s were tracking events in the Soviet Union and reporting a collapse or breakup as likely, resulting from ethnic and national contradictions of the Communist state. These were mostly anthropologists, demographers, sociologists, or comparative political scientists.[7] Three political science works in particular stand out.[8] The first was Hélène Carrère d'Encausse's *Decline of an Empire: The Soviet Socialist Republics in Revolt* (1979),[9] which elaborated the escalating costs to Moscow in holding the USSR together by means short of violence. She paints a picture of costs that cannot be sustained and, in the event, were not sustained. The second was Walker Connor's *The National Question in Marxist-Leninist Theory and Strategy* (1984b), in which, like Emerson before him, Connor highlights the fundamental and legitimacy-challenging contradictions in Marxist-Leninist theory concerning national minorities. The third was Rasma Karklins's *Ethnic Relations in the USSR: The Perspective from Below* (1986), in which Karklins gives us a window into the workings of ethnicity in the USSR—how it affected the distribution of scarce resources ranging from educational opportunities and consumer goods to offices.

All three works sounded dire warnings that fell on deaf ears. Policymakers and security specialists were instead much more focused on things like nuclear submarine propeller cavitation, the capabilities of the latest Soviet MiG fighter, or the security implications of advances in image resolution on satellite intelligence photographs. The Soviet failure in Afghanistan—which highlighted the implications of substate violence for regional and interstate security—was chalked up to the wise decision by the U.S. government to supply Stinger surface-to-air missiles to the mujahideen, rather than to the potent combination of adapted fighting ability, religious conviction, porous borders, and outright stubbornness that created the conditions that enabled the Stinger to be decisive.[10]

Of course, there were specialists not in security studies who missed the end of the Cold War, as well as a few within security studies who got it right. On balance however, the fall of the Berlin Wall came as a shock—as much to the academic communities who specialized in state-to-state security issues as to the policymakers responsible for that security.[11]

Also not to be overlooked in this period was the more general theoretical literature in comparative politics, which advanced arguments about the impact of modernization and development on the likelihood and intensity of ethnic violence. This school was dominated by comparativists who tended to focus on individual countries or regions of the world, most notably, Africa.

Two economics-oriented models of the causes of ethnic violence emerged: (1) level of economic development; and (2) resource distribution. Differential economic development models, for example, focus on the relative development of groups within a state's borders, and claim that as the economy and state structures modernize, individuals will transfer their loyalties from their ethnic group to the state.[12] Ethnic wars that remain are therefore caused by uneven economic development among the groups. Groups with greater economic development will come to resent the transfer of their wealth to lesser developed groups as state subventions, while less-developed groups will come to fear economic domination, or perhaps increasingly resent perceived exploitation, by the advanced groups. Disparate development leads to tensions among the ethnic groups. Equalize economic development, so the argument goes, and these ethnic conflicts will disappear (Hechter 1974; Horowitz 1985, especially chap. 6; Laponce 1987; Tiryakian and Rogowski 1985).

Closely related to differential economic growth arguments are those that implicate resource competition among the groups themselves as a cause of violence, rather than disputes over the distribution of resources from the center. This group of scholars argues that the principal cause of violent ethnic conflict is resource competition and relative deprivation (Olzak 1992, chap. 3). Whereas resource competition relates the simple causal story about ethnic groups fighting over a limited economic and political pie, relative deprivation explanations add the dynamic element of the relative decline or improvement of economic or political condition of different ethnic groups as a source of civil war.[13]

In both explanations what is needed for ethnic violence to emerge are at least two ethnic groups and a sense that the other ethnic group is to blame for a decline or lack of access to economic and political resources.[14] Competition for resources sparks ethnic collective action within groups and conflict between groups over access to declining or increasing goods.

Overall, what emerges from the wealth and resource approach is that the economic well-being of the ethnic groups is what drives ethnic conflict between groups. Disparate economic development leads to the belief, founded or unfounded, that ethnic groups are not able to develop their full potential and that other ethnic groups are responsible. Resentment and fear builds that may result in violence between ethnic groups. A key question is the capacity of the state and its ability and willingness to moderate or mediate the demands and concerns of the different ethnic groups.[15]

Despite providing a source of conflict, this approach tends to underplay ethnic and identity dimensions and consequent intergroup tensions that might also contribute to war (Connor 1984a). Proponents fail to explain why some groups are willing to risk death, internment, or mass deportation; or why they sometimes seek autonomy even when the economic conditions of independence are certain to be more desperate than those they are fighting to leave behind. Rather than exclusively seek to insure their material well-being, ethnic groups may rationally choose violence as a means to insure their cultural and historical livelihood (Agnew 1987). Control over economic development can mean providing for the material needs of the group, as well as securing a part of the identity. In other words, even if we could redistribute wealth from richer to poorer and alleviate economic disparity between the groups, this would not necessarily overcome underlying fears and resentment between them. Finally, this approach provides us no necessary or logical reason why, among all the potential values over which two actors might struggle, material values should matter most. The priority of material values is simply assumed, and this leads to weaknesses in the ability of such approaches to offer a general explanation of violent conflict. Finally, the true dependent variable for this group of scholars was not ethnic war, but conflict that may or may not have escalated to war. Most did not even broach the issue of war on its own terms.

Second Wave: 1990–99

It is in this second period that we see accelerated advancement of theoretical and policy relevant work on *ethnic* substate violence. Let me be blunt: so long as the Cold War lasted, genuine interest in the causes, dynamics, and consequences of substate violence was likely to remain marginal as compared to issues connected with interstate war, in particular nuclear war.

With the end of the Cold War, interest in substate violence came to the fore. Three overlapping factors made an understanding of substate violence more important for policymakers, and more interesting to the security studies and international politics communities. First, the very nature of the demise of the USSR had been clearly nationalist and had come not from without but from within. The real capacity of ethnic identity to bring down a state had been clearly demonstrated. Groups *within* a state had acted in a way that fundamentally—structurally—altered the reality of inter*state* politics. Second, ethnic war was about to come back to continental Europe in a way not seen since World War II. Civil wars may not be as absolutely destructive as world or nuclear wars, but the horrors of Yugoslavia's progressive disintegration were real, public, and proximate. Other civil wars—in Africa and Latin America—had also come to demonstrate an increased capacity to destroy life and infrastructure. Ethnic wars were also more difficult by nature to halt by means of intervention and negotiation, because the object of such wars often seemed to be the physical destruction of an ethnic group either by killing or by forced migration. Material inducements and nod-and-wink security guarantees could no longer be relied upon to stop the violence.[16] Third and finally, transportation and communications technology had made it possible for the first time in history to cause the rapid movement of large numbers of people from the developing to the developed world. Now the costs of disease, poverty, and war in the developing world could no longer be so easily contained south of the equator.[17]

In sum, in the 1990s the advanced industrial countries found themselves in a situation in which they had a rapidly growing demand for knowledge of, and solutions to, problems of substate violence, but a low supply of knowledge capable of identifying effective policy options. Four pieces of scholarship profoundly shaped the next decade of scholarship both empirically and theoretically, and thus our understanding of the origins and consequences of ethnic war.

One of the first works was Roy Licklider's "The Consequences of Negotiated Settlements in Civil Wars, 1945–1993," a mainly empirical account of all civil wars since 1945 (Licklider 1995). In that "research note," as the *American Political Science Review* categorized it, Licklider accomplished two important tasks. First, by publishing in the flagship journal of the political science discipline, he helped bring the study of civil wars into the mainstream. Second, although he presented only a rudimentary data set of civil wars, Licklider divided them into two types, distinguishing between identity-based and non-identity-based.[18] He then presented some preliminary findings about the differences between the two.

Licklider's article proved a watershed in the study of civil wars for two reasons. First, substate violence became more widely accepted as a subject worthy of research in its own right. Second, his separation of civil wars into two types appealed to scholars who were witnessing the outbreak of ethnic violence in places that were supposed to have been immune, and more important, suggested there were useful—even crucial—generalizations that could emerge from a systematic comparison of civil wars across time and space.

A second important contribution in the early 1990s was Barry Posen's article "The Security Dilemma and Ethnic Conflict" (1993). Posen was the first scholar to apply well-established theoretical concepts from the international relations theory tradition to civil wars, applying the principle of anarchy and fear to relations between ethnic groups within states.

A third key entry in this period is Stephen Van Evera's "Hypotheses on Nationalism" piece in *International Security* in 1994. In this article Van Evera lays out the logic of a number of plausible explanations of a perceived rise in the frequency and intensity of nationalist violence following the collapse of the Soviet Union. Note that like Licklider, Van Evera's goal is not really explanation per se, but a laying out of a research agenda for academics interested in pursuing research on substate violence and, in Van Evera's case in particular, for international relations theorists and security studies specialists.

Taken together, Posen's and Van Evera's articles accomplished two important things. First, they increased the acceptability of conceiving of ethnic groups as rational actors, with the clear implication being that existing theories of interstate violence could—with some modification—be usefully applied to problems of substate violence, perhaps resulting in useful policy implications as well. Second, they blazed a trail for later members of the same community to focus increased attention on problems of ethnic war.

One additional work of importance must be mentioned here. It is the Minorities at Risk data set put together by Ted Robert Gurr and his colleagues at the University of Maryland.[19] Gurr, a comparative political scientist who specialized in rebellion, assembled a crucial empirical database with which contemporary and later scholars were able to make important comparative analyses, allowing them to examine and weigh political, economic, cultural, and other factors bound up with the question of ethnic and identity issues in substate violence.

To understand the importance of these four pieces of scholarship in helping to establish a research program, simply consider my own book, which was based on my Ph.D. dissertation at the University of Chicago. I am scholar who was trained in international relations theory and security studies in the 1990s under the tutelage of John Mearsheimer, Stephen Walt, and James Fearon. My first book, *The Geography of Ethnic Violence* (2003), explored the question of why, given apparently similar structural conditions, ethnic civil wars break out at some times but not others. Using the Minorities at Risk data set, and focusing on the Russian Federation and Georgia following the collapse of the USSR in comparative case studies, I show that ethnic groups concentrated in a homeland—as they were, for example, in Chechnya—are much more likely to experience ethnic war. By contrast, even when economic or strategic factors might make a move toward political autonomy rational, national minorities not concentrated in a homeland—as in Tatarstan—or those concentrated in urban areas are dramatically less likely to escalate a dispute to violence. Nor are they likely to level demands of a state sufficient to provoke it to respond with violence, something states most often do out of concern for establishing a secession precedent. The book accomplished two tasks. On the theoretical side, it challenged the prevailing tendency to imagine that state-centric theory à la Posen and Van Evera—however parsimonious and elegant—was sufficient to explain the likelihood of conflict escalation in a substate context. Instead, the book showed that although a state perspective was necessary, a sufficient explanation must also take into account a bottom-up ethnic group actor perspective; a nod to comparative work done by Walker Connor and Ted Gurr. Second, it revealed the power of statistics in helping us to understand the general conditions for when we can expect ethnic conflict to erupt in full-scale civil war, a question I may not have asked were it not for Licklider and Gurr.

Consolidating Approaches: What Causes Ethnic Violence?

Overall, the 1990s witnessed the consolidation of three broad approaches to the study of ethnic civil wars, each focusing on a different cause as key: (1) the security dilemma, (2) elite-driven arguments, and (3) collapse or flawed implementation of political institutions.[20] A fourth approach, already discussed previously as material-based economic development and distribution, remained out of play until the late 1990s; for this approach, see the subsequent discussion.[21]

The Security Dilemma

In the security dilemma approach, the central driving force is fear. When the authority of a multinational state declines, the central regime can no longer protect the interests of ethnic groups. The decline of the central regime creates a vacuum in which ethnic groups compete to establish and control a new regime that will protect their interests. Considering the future composition of a new regime, dominated by opposing groups, and the probable treatment of their own group within such a new regime, ethnic groups fear widespread discrimination and even death. Adopting a worst-case scenario, each group assumes offensive capabilities and hostile intentions of competing groups.[22] The likely result is violence. As I have already noted, Barry Posen was the first scholar to apply this widely known international relations concept to the problem of ethnic violence (Posen 1993).[23]

Although the security dilemma explanation is logically quite powerful, we can find many cases in which fear was not the motivating factor for ethnic violence. Roger Petersen, for instance, has shown that emotions other than fear can come into play. Simple hatred may drive ethnic violence, as might resentment (Petersen 2002). There is no logical or necessary reason to accept fear as the sole emotion that provokes violence. Furthermore, the precondition for violence in the form of the weakening or total dissolution of the state itself may be nonexistent, yet violence never-theless emerges; or this precondition itself needs to be explained. So, for example, Stuart Kaufman's (2001) theory does not presuppose a weak or nonexistent state. Rather, his theory of symbolic politics and mythmaking reveals how predatory politics emerge, undermining the state and ethnic groups relations—in essence creating a security dilemma.

The main difference between security dilemma approaches and ma-terial-based arguments such as that represented in the development and modernization literature already cited is that a security dilemma ap-proach recognizes that individuals as part of groups can be mobilized in order to protect elements of their identity. But this difference is also one of its main limitations: it tends to overemphasize the local or bottom-up aspects, while downplaying or even ignoring a state's concerns as an ac-tor in the international system. Another problem is that logically, these arguments gain a great deal of their credibility by assuming that material values matter most, and then using cases in which actors fought over val-ues of low material worth or did not fight when significant material values were at stake as evidence to support the general claim that ethnic actors are subrational. Yet as I have observed, there is no reason to assume that of the many possible values over which two actors are willing to risk vio-lence, material values should take priority. Moreover, empirically, we see many cases in which ethnic groups do fight over material values. If we ac-cept that the same group can act rationally in one conflict but irrationally in another, then either the assumption will damage our attempt to build a general explanation, or we will need to back up and explain why some groups act rationally sometimes but not others. Moreover, explanations based in security dilemmas provide no logic to account for variation in the intensity of ethnic group solidarity and nationalist feeling. Even if we accept that all ethnic groups want their own states, in other words, we still need to explain why some seek autonomy gradually by nonviolent means, while others more readily resort to arms.

The logic of the security dilemma was originally invoked to explain how actors not interested in aggression might nevertheless end up fight-ing a war. It does not address other motivations such as greed or aggres-siveness.[24] The point is that if one side is not fearful or wants war, then there is no security dilemma. In his efforts to mobilize Serbs to attack Bosnia in 1992, for example, Slobodan Milošević was more likely moti-vated by greed or personal ambition than he was by fear.[25] The collapse of central authority may make some actors fearful, but greed or outright ag-gressiveness cannot be excluded as possible motivations for others.[26]

Elite-Driven Approach

As to elite-driven arguments, these were driven by concerns over the independent causal impact of charismatic political elites such as Franjo Tudjman and Slobodan Milošević, each of whom had played major roles in the fomenting of ethnic violence in the former Yugoslavia.[27] Some elite-driven explanations focus on the material incentives either positive or negative leaders use to rally support, while others cite nonmaterial incentives or appeals, such as a leader's personal charisma, and his or her particular use or construction of history and national identity in the pursuit of national or personal aims. Milošević, for example, invoked both: the history of the Serbian nation as victim of atrocities dating back centuries, as well as fears that the economic well-being of Yugoslavia (read: Serbs) was being threatened by the secessionist republics of Croatia and Slovenia. Serbs needed to rally in order not to fall victim again to the Croats and to save their economic system from collapse.

The popularity of the elite-driven approach in the United States is twofold. First, it flatters a deeply held conviction that people, like children, are generally good, and that as a consequence, bad behavior is best explained by bad leaders, teachers, or parents. Second, it has the advantage of, in its "unitary" aspect, simplicity: what caused World War II? Hitler. What caused war in Yugoslavia? Milošević.

The weakness of the elite-driven approach is that it relies on a necessary gap between national aspirations and the will of the leader. In short, it denies the possibility of representative leaders. Moreover, this approach cannot explain why leaders endowed with similar charisma, and promulgating similar messages, nevertheless experience quite varied levels of popular support: some fail and some succeed beyond even their highest hopes.

Political Institutions

A third strand of argument explains ethnic violence as the failure of political institutions. In essence the claim is that there already exist ideal structural or institutional mechanisms for allowing disparate groups to live and work together in peace and prosperity. There are a number of ways these have come over time to be described and represented, including federalist versus centralist, presidential versus parliamentary systems, and proportional versus majoritarian-based legislative arrangements. Thus, ethnic conflict can be expected to escalate to violence in places where these institutions have come under siege or failed completely.

The popularity of this approach to ethnic war had waned in the 1970s but received a tremendous boost after the death of Tito and subsequent "failure" of Yugoslavia's federal system to contain ethnic war, and after the collapse of the Soviet Union—another federal system—in 1991. As with elite-driven arguments, another source of popularity for the political institutions approach—in the United States at least—is the appeal of "democracy" and "democratization" as proxies for all things good and right. In 1986, Michael Doyle observed that although many different types of states had gone to war over the centuries, we would be hard-pressed to find a case of two liberal democracies doing so. This spawned virtually an entire academic subfield devoted to the question "What is it about liberal democracies that keeps them from going to war with each other?" The connection to a political institutions approach to ethnic war is clear: where mature democratic institutions are in place we can expect to see not only a reduction in interstate violence (Mansfield and Snyder 1995, 2005), but perhaps a reduced likelihood of *intra*state violence as well (Snyder and Ballentine 1996; Snyder 2000).

As an explanation of ethnic violence, the institutionalist approach has a number of important advantages. First, institutions, unlike "identities" and "charisma," appear to be more easily quantifiable and comparable. To the extent this is true, testing and theory building are facilitated. Second, the logic is sound: power-sharing institutions allow affected groups a say in their own government. It makes sense that groups within states that are more democratic should be able to resolve ethnic disputes short of violence (Hegre et al. 2001). Furthermore, to the extent that groups within a federal structure, for example, are insecure, or have concerns about the state's distribution of resources, federalism provides a sound structural solution to two of the most common sources of friction between groups, and between groups and central governments.

On the other hand, debate continues among scholars within this approach about whether federalism, for example, inhibits or fosters ethnic violence and separatism. Arend Lijphart, for example, argues that through the diffusion of power, federalism is useful for managing ethnic conflicts (1977, 1984).[28] Other scholars argue that the diffusion of power causes precisely the opposite effect, allowing groups greater control over institutions and resources and thereby facilitating collective action (Roeder 1991; Kymlicka 1998; Bunce 1999). Thus, the logic, though sound, only gets us so far: federalism diminishes the demand for autonomy even as it increases a group's capacity to obtain it. Moreover, this logical difficulty is perhaps reflected in more recent empirical studies, the results of which have to date been equivocal regarding the causal weight of institutions in ethnic violence. Stephen Saideman and coauthors, for example, report that democratization, federalism, and presidentialism may not be as violence-prone as some have argued (Saideman et al. 2002).[29] They, along with Reynal-Querol (2002), find that proportional representation in a legislature may reduce the likelihood of violence. Yet Brancati finds more nuance: although decentralization might decrease ethnic conflict and the tendency toward secessionism in the short term, decentralization also promotes regional parties, reinforcing ethnic cleavages and separatist tendencies down the road (Brancati 2006; Roeder 1991).

Several problems have emerged from the study of political institutions. The first problem is a basic historical, distributional one: the number of proportional representation and federalist systems is low compared to majoritarian-based legislative and centralist systems. Furthermore, we know from other studies that authoritarian states are also less prone to ethnic violence and that transitional regimes are the most problematic (Leff 1999; Snyder 2000; Hegre et al. 2001). A bigger problem for this approach in terms of coherence and policy relevance, however, has been its tendency to focus on the structure of the institutions themselves, as opposed to the process of how actors within states relate to those institutions. Jack Snyder, for example, in *From Voting to Violence* (2000) demonstrates that the practice of voting is beset by a host of problems that a focus on the structure of the institution itself cannot reveal.

In sum, the last half of the twentieth century saw a rise in demand for policy-relevant knowledge on substate and ethnic violence, but one paradoxically paralleled by an almost total lack of interest by scholars of violence and security who insisted that nuclear and conventional inter*state* war remained the greater problem and hence most deserving of attention. This was true despite the unexpected defeats and high costs of victories sustained by advanced industrial states as they struggled after World War II to maintain control of colonies. Research in substate violence remained the province of anthropologists, sociologists, and comparative political scientists. Domino theory had been the keystone supporting the arch that connected war, disease, and poverty in the developing world to a potential security threat to advanced industrial states. When U.S. and

Soviet defeats in Vietnam and Afghanistan respectively made domino theory appear bankrupt, the way was clear to return to interstate concerns—both within the academic and policy-making communities.

But that respite proved short-lived. The collapse of the Soviet Union from internal pressures—and the briefly open window that allowed those in the West to see just how weak and bankrupt that superpower had been in recent years—pulled the rug from under those who had insisted for a generation that substate and ethnic violence could have only a marginal impact on the interstate system. With the Cold War over, interest in ethnic war virtually exploded, resulting, first, in an attempt, sometimes successful but often not so, to apply state-centric conflict theory to the domain of substate conflict, and, second, in an increasingly sophisticated, useful, and policy-relevant body of knowledge on the causes, dynamics, and consequences of ethnic violence.

Third Wave? 2000 to the Present

The present decade has continued previous trends in the study of ethnic violence. The most notable exception has come from economists who have turned their attention to the problem of civil war. As already noted, a large portion of the literature in the 1980s was devoted to exploring how economic development or the distribution of resources might affect the likelihood of ethnic violence. Yet in the 1990s this approach faded somewhat, as researchers began to accept that ethnic groups were rational, despite the fact that they often acted against their best economic interests. Late in the 1990s, however, a successor to this earlier line of reasoning emerged. "Ethnic" war drops out of the analysis as the focus shifts almost exclusively on prosperity: rich countries are less likely to suffer civil wars than are poor ones.

In testing the relationship between poverty and war, Collier and Hoeffler, for example, claim that origins of civil war are related to the share of primary products in GDP: as the share of primary products in GDP increases, so too does the likelihood of war (Collier and Hoeffler 1998, 2004). In a similar vein, Fearon and Laitin—two well-known political scientists—found a negative, statistically significant correlation between wealth and civil war, using per capita income as the best predictor of the likelihood of civil war (Fearon and Laitin 2003).[30] They claimed that it predicted better than other factors, including political grievance and ethnic diversity.

There seems to be consensus that poor states are more likely to suffer civil war, including ethnic war. Yet this empirical finding gets us only so far, because, as it turns out, different scholars have different—and plausible—explanations to account for it (Humphrys 2003). So, for example, while Fearon and Laitin stress state capabilities (a poor state means a weak state), Collier and Hoeffler stress the opportunity costs of war (a poor state means lots of unemployed males who can readily take up arms). This is a problem because the main reason we are trying to understand the origins of civil wars is to prevent them. If, however, the findings provide little by way of guidance for how lack of wealth proxies for civil war onset, then policies designed to avert civil war may be targeting the wrong area.

The main problem with these empirical studies is that they have been limited to a single index, for example GDP. This leads to two additional problems. First, these are aggregate figures for an entire state. They do not allow for analysis at the substate or regional level, which is the place where most ethnic wars occur. As it turns out, if we control for the distribution of resources *within* a state, resources are unrelated to the likelihood of ethnic war. Ethnic groups that inhabited regions of the state that were well endowed and poorly endowed with natural and man-made resources were equally unlikely to be engaged in civil wars (Toft 2002–3, 2003). Second, these variables are too broad. More recent research has shown that it matters what kinds of wealth and resources are available. So, for example, lootable resources such as diamonds and oil have been shown to be a better predictor of war onset than are wealth and resources more generally (Le Billon 2001; Ross 2004a, 2004b).

In theoretical terms, too, this strand of argument suffers. Because scholars advancing this approach do not accept any meaningful difference between ethnic and nonethnic civil wars, and because their research design does not distinguish between them, lumping ethnic and nonethnic substate violence into one category, they understandably find no meaningful difference in their analyses.[31] Given that in reality it makes little sense to ignore this key difference, one can acknowledge the distinction without at the same time disparaging the importance of economic factors in causing ethnic violence. Scholars advancing this approach will find it difficult to responsibly advise policymakers whose interests lie in preventing or ending ethnic violence.[32]

Empirical and theoretical weaknesses aside, I think it fair to say that this approach has had a dramatic effect on all work on civil wars pub-

lished since 2000, and on policy-making as well.[33] What we have witnessed so far is a return to the 1960s and 1970s, when few studying substate violence gave ethnic war much attention.[34] Here the return has been
led not by a historical shift but by a preference for methods that require
quantifiable data. Quantifiable data, in turn, tend to demand reduction
and simplification; and so we are led by a general and recent preference
for large-N research designs, to a situation in which ethnic war becomes
subsumed by the more lumpy concept of civil war. The gains observed in
elegance and parsimony of hypothesis testing and model manipulation
are counterbalanced by a loss of policy relevance, not to mention a back-
sliding as regards general theory development.[35]

Conclusions

This chapter has introduced an overview of the last 50 years of inquiry
into the causes, dynamics, and consequences of ethnic violence. The bulk
of the chapter is devoted to a historical overview, in which I highlighted
the links between real-world events—mainly war and the threat of war
within and between states—and the nature and quality of research into
ethnic violence. My summary of the literature from the 1990s to the present added a thematic element, in which I argued that the study of ethnic
violence or in some cases substate violence not distinguished by type increasingly coalesced around four approaches: (1) security dilemma, (2)
elite-driven, (3) political institutions, and (4) material factors.

I began my overview by arguing that the increasing costs functionally,
a euphemism for a potential or actual threat to security of engaging indigenous fighters in the developing world in the 1950s and 1960s, did not
spark a research program devoted to the study of substate or ethnic violence—at least not among academic communities most commonly associated with interest in foreign policy, national security, strategy, and international relations. Domino theory—the notion that incremental gains
or losses in countries with little or no intrinsic worth, where "worth" is
defined narrowly as industrial-technological capacity and a skilled population, could tip a balance of power in the Cold War struggle for global
dominance—was convincingly rebutted when South Vietnam fell to
North Vietnam in 1975, and Afghanistan fell to the mujahideen in 1990.
With domino theory in retreat, the way was clear for a return to interstate
concerns and a theory-building project—neorealism—that systematically discounted evidence from the substate conflict domain. The col-

lapse of the USSR then served as the permissive condition for a merging of academic communities, as security studies specialists and international relations theorists finally turned their attention to the problem of ethnic violence.

By the end of the 1990s, four approaches—each emphasizing a different type of cause of ethnic violence—emerged and solidified. I argued that a security studies approach focused on explaining ethnic violence by imputing fear to relevant substate actors and explaining ethnic violence as the consequence of security seeking under threat of destruction. The advantage of this approach is that it seems a good fit with a number of ethnic wars that were preceded by the collapse of central government and with it, regular expectations about physical security. The weakness of this approach, however, is that many ethnic wars are fought by actors who are not motivated by fear, but by greed or revenge. This limits the generality of security dilemma arguments as regards ethnic violence.

I identified elite-driven arguments as a second approach. These hold that "people" are generally good, or have as high a latent potential for nonviolent resolution of conflicts as for violent resolutions. What causes ethnic violence, then, is the action of a nervous or greedy political elite, which activates a latent capacity for violence and then directs it at an "other" with devastating effect. The strengths of this approach are that it is simple, and that it appeals to a popular conception of people as inherently good. It also fits well with a number of recent and destructive conflicts, in which an elite calls for violence and violence ensues. Yet theoretically, this approach suffers from a problem of assuming that people are necessarily peaceful and that leaders are generally apt to seek violent confrontation. It ignores, in other words, both the possibility of a charismatic leader who works to de-escalate calls for violence—one thinks here, for example of Gandhi or Nelson Mandela—and the possibility of a charismatic leader who is advancing a call to violence in response to the genuine wishes of a majority of her constituents.

I identified political institutions as a third approach, and highlighted the links between the existence or development of institutional arrangements—such as federalism, specifically designed to allow "others" to live peacefully within a single state—and the likelihood of ethnic war. In this view, ethnic wars are the result of a lack or failure of such institutions, and if this account is true, the cure would be to promote the establishment of such institutions where they do not exist, or to support their stability where they do. The real weakness of this approach is that it ignores how a given people is most likely to relate to the institutions they have or are given. Moreover, any power-sharing institution can increase the capability of participants to secede from a political community, even while it may reduce the willingness of those participants to seek autonomy. Finally, like the security dilemma and elite-driven approaches, the political institutions approach tends to err by assuming that people are good, so good institutions will facilitate good outcomes. If we consider just the example of democracy, it is just as logical that a people who wanted war, but were prevented from seeking it by a nonrepresentative institutional structure, could finally achieve their goal once democratic institutions came into being.

Finally, I identified wealth and resources as a fourth approach. Two substrands have emerged. The first focuses on differential economic development, and essentially makes the case that when people are poor, or feel they are unjustifiably poorer than their neighbors, they are much more apt to find cause to escalate a dispute to violence. A second substrand focuses on the distribution of valued goods among different groups, arguing that conflict results when one or more groups perceive they are being unjustly deprived of deserved goods. The strength of this approach is that as an empirical matter, we know that economic issues are an important piece of the puzzle in explaining why ethnic groups escalate to violence sometimes but not others. But on the other hand, we see many cases in which rational actors ignore economic costs and benefits when contemplating an escalation to violence. Ethnic groups sometimes fight over territory that has no natural resources, or they seek to secede from a state even knowing that they will be much worse off economically. The only way to respond to this observation and maintain theoretical coherence is to move such groups into the "irrational actor" category, but doing so would sacrifice generality, leaving this approach to explain a very few cases.

Finally, I highlighted the most important and most recent trend in the study of ethnic and civil war: the impact of the argument that substate violence can be explained almost entirely by reference to greed, not ethnicity. Sponsored by the World Bank in the late 1990s, this literature came of age after 2000, when the publication of a series of articles and edited volumes developed and sharpened this theme: "ethnic" conflict is a myth; what's driving the violence is the pursuit of wealth by individuals and groups. The advantage of this approach is twofold. First, it implies that control over access to resources can stop violence. Actors contemplating violence can be bribed into giving it up, and actors relying on diamonds or oil to fund their wars can be forced to the bargaining table by the imposition of controls on exports of the goods exchanged for cash. Second, well-intentioned policymakers need not bother with the difficult practice of grasping the historical, cultural, linguistic, religious, and other issues that drive conflict; the human beings involved can be reduced to "inputs" and "preference functions" and by such means quantified and compared. Policymakers can instead focus on the much simpler task of finding the right bribe or a way to reduce a given actor's access to funds obtained from the sale of valued resources. The downside is twofold as well, however. First, although wealth matters everywhere, as I have already observed, in many cases rational actors acted in a way that made them poorer. In other words, ethnicity and identity still matter. Second, and related, the evidence that supports the theory, such as it is, comes almost entirely from a handful of cases in one region of the world: sub-Saharan Africa. Beyond that zone, the "greed causes substate violence" thesis simply falls apart.

With the exception of this latest trend, there is much room for optimism about our collective understanding of the causes, dynamics, and consequences of ethnic war. We know, for example, that wealth, in the form of both greed and poverty; identity; and fear are all necessary pieces to the puzzle of ethnic war. As a result, we can move toward resolving or preventing such violence with policies that take all three important pieces into account. In addition, the study of ethnic violence has brought together academic communities ranging from anthropologists and psychologists to historians, comparativists, international relations theorists, and security studies specialists.

This theoretical collaboration is not only fortunate in terms of its ability to advance *theory*, but as events in the real world continue to demonstrate, demand for such knowledge to inform policy is likely to remain high for the foreseeable future. Ethnic conflicts are taking place all over the globe, and the few that escalate to war have rivaled or exceeded the destructiveness of many interstate wars. Yugoslavia, for example, no longer exists as a state, and Rwanda is missing several generations of Tutsi.

The most recent research on ethnic war continues to be driven by concern over this destructiveness, and by the apparent merging of ethnic with religious and ideological motivations in ongoing struggles over autonomy or resources. Beyond refining and testing existing theories on the causes of ethnic war, there remain other important theoretical questions to explore, as well as additional empirical work to complete. On the theoretical side, we would like to know a number of things, including what makes ethnic wars so difficult to end; what similarities and differences between ethnic and religious wars, for example, tell us about why they happen, why they take the forms they do, and how to end them;[36] and how a group's composition in terms of size, age, and sex affects the likelihood it will escalate its claims.[37]

On the empirical side, the field of inquiry remains challenged by a dearth of substate data: most of the large-N data available to researchers, even today, are state-level data. What is needed are data that measure and track characteristics of ethnic groups and their environments, political, social, and economic. Although excellent databases such as the Minorities at Risk data set provide some of these data, simple economic data are inadequate, and, paradoxically, even important state-level characteristic data are missing.[38]

In sum, demand for knowledge about ethnic war is high, and the collective efforts of a number of scholars have slowly, over time, risen to the challenge of developing a body of knowledge capable, if well implemented, of altering political outcomes. However, there remains much left to do in advancing this all-too-crucial goal.

NOTES

For helpful comments on earlier drafts, I would like to thank Ivan Arreguín-Toft, Henry Hale, Chaim Kaufmann, Manus Midlarsky, and Steve Saideman.

1. The number of edited volumes published in the 1990s demonstrates the multitude of scholars and practitioners interested in understanding the dynamics of ethnicity, nationalism, and violence since the end of the Cold War (e.g., Brown 1993; McGarry and O'Leary 1993; Tiech and Porter 1993; Kupchan 1995; Brown and Ganguly 1997; Brown et al. 1997; Lake and Rothchild 1998a; Walter and Snyder 1999).

2. Clifford Geertz (1963) is often credited with first articulating the primordialist view. Also see Issacs (1970).

3. For a discussion of the differences between ethnic and ideological wars see Kaufmann (1996a).

4. These types of wars are commonly referred to as communal wars. Although related, communal wars are typically differentiated from ethnic riots; riots are seen as more spontaneous and less organized. The scholarship on ethnic rioting

has been growing recently. See, for example, Brass (1997); Horowitz (2001); Varshney (2002); and Wilkinson (2006).

5. From 1940 to 2000, 98 percent of civil wars fought for territorial control were incited by ethnically based demands, while 73 percent of all ethnically based civil wars involved fights over territory. See Toft (2006a, 44).

6. It is in this context that Mearsheimer's "Back to the Future" essay is best understood. Mearsheimer argues that among the virtues of the Cold War were its simplicity: each side had but one adversary to worry about, and each adversary had armed itself in a similar way. See Mearsheimer (1990a, 1990b).

7. The journalist Bernard Levin is credited for predicting the 1989 demise of the Soviet Union in 1977 in *The Times* of London. A reprint can be found as Levin (1993).

8. For an assessment of scholarship and thinking about the fate of the Soviet Union see Lipset and Bence (1994). Surprisingly, none of the three works included here is included in this article.

9. It was originally published in France under the title *L'Empire éclaté* in 1978. The English version is d'Encausse (1979).

10. For a concise analysis the causes of Soviet defeat in Afghanistan, see Arreguín-Toft (2005).

11. Even as the Berlin Wall was coming down, the relevance of the third world to the security of advanced industrial states was coming under increased—and productive—scrutiny. See, e.g., the healthy debate within the security studies and international relations communities concerning whether the third world "mattered." See David (1989, 1992–93); Desch (1993).

12. This school of thought falls in line with the views of Benedict Anderson, Ernest Gellner, and Eric Hobsbawm. Nationalism served as a mechanism for the homogenization of the masses by states in their efforts to modernize (Anderson 1983; Hobsbawm 1990; Gellner 1983). Also see Hroch (1985).

13. This theory derives from the earlier J-curve theory, which posits that *rising expectations* resulting from *economic growth* lead to violence (Davies 1979; Gurr 1970). A nice review of the theoretical and empirical literature is found in Lichbach (1989). Lichbach found little support for the thesis, concluding that people have a high tolerance for inequality.

14. This scapegoating might involve groups who are or are not relatively better off. In explaining the occurrence of genocide following revolutions, Mershon found that better off-groups were more often the targets for genocide. The Roma of Europe, Turks of Germany, and Arabs/Muslims of France, albeit not victims of genocide, reveal that lesser advantaged groups may be targets for persecution as well. The empirical record thus provides evidence that both relatively better off and worse off groups may end up as scapegoats. See Mershon (1992). Also see Midlarsky (2005a, 2005b).

15. A discussion of different strategies for dealing with ethnic conflict can be

found in Horowitz (1985). Also see Esman (1994); Rothchild (1997); and more recently, Byman (2002).

16. For an analysis of how intense ethnic violence often causes groups to pursue ethnic cleansing and become less interested in other modes of settlement or conflict resolution, see Kaufmann (1996b, 1998).

17. Though it proved premature by about a decade, this thesis made Robert Kaplan something of a celebrity for a time. See Kaplan (1994).

18. Although Singer and Small provided some data on civil wars in their landmark data set, even cursory familiarity with the data and with the period in which it was collected and published makes it clear that civil wars were of marginal importance to the authors or to most researchers. See Small and Singer (1982).

19. Findings from the data set were originally published in Gurr (1993a). A later volume, using a revised version of the data set, appeared under the title *People versus States: Minorities at Risk in the New Century* (2000). The homepage for this extensive research program is http://www.cidcm.umd.edu/inscr/mar/.

20. This chapter includes only domestic-level causes of ethnic war. For a discussion of international causes of ethnic war, see the chapter in this volume by Stephen M. Saideman and Erin K. Jenne.

21. An exception is Susan Woodward (1995), who attempted to explain the demise of Yugoslavia in terms of economic malaise and international interdependence. Her argument was overlooked at the time, because most scholars and policy-makers were focused either on the ethnic dimensions of the conflict or charismatic political elites, such as Franjo Tudjman and Slobodan Milošević. See especially Kaplan (1993). This was one of the first books on the 1990s civil wars in former Yugoslavia. Kaplan advanced a controversial "ancient hatreds argument," which posited that Serbs and the Croats always hated each other, in a sense making violence between them inevitable. Glenny (1992) focused on the elites.

22. These are conditions that Robert Jervis (1978) identified as leading to the most intense security dilemma.

23. A later variant is Fearon (1998a). This approach has produced a vast cottage industry. A comprehensive review can be found in Rose (2000), and an earlier review can be found in David (1997).

24. For recent work see Glaser (1992, 1997).

25. On Milošević's motivations see, Glenny (1992) and Zimmerman (1995).

26. For an analysis that combines elite competition and the security dilemma, see Saideman (1998a).

27. Four of the best works are Brass (1991); Gagnon (1994/95); Hardin (1995); and de Figueiredo and Weingast (1999). An earlier article stressing the role of elites is Gourevitch (1979).

28. A thorough application and empirical investigation can be found in Brancati (2003, 2006).

29. Also see Lustik, Miodownik, and Eidelson (2004).

30. They argue that civil war results from a failure of governance. This argument gained credence as a result of the state failure project, an interdisciplinary task force led by academic experts and funded by the Central Intelligence Agency's Directorate of Intelligence. The task force investigated an array of variables to explain the occurrence of civil war and state failure more generally. The project continues under the name of the "Political Instability Task Force," http://globalpolicy .gmu.edu/pitf/.

31. An exception is Sambanis (2001). He finds that political grievance, as opposed to lack of economic opportunity, explains ethnic violence.

32. Note that Collier and Hoeffler's work resulted in publication of the edited volume *Greed and Grievance* (Berdal and Malone 2000), in which the thesis that the causes of contemporary civil wars could be reduced to economic factors was advanced. Signaling, perhaps, that this approach was recognized as excessively reductionist, the follow-on volume (Ballentine and Sherman 2003) was entitled *The Political Economy of Armed Conflict: Beyond Greed and Grievance.* The tone of the second book is far less strident than that of the first, and accepts that economic factors are necessary but not *generally* sufficient to explain civil wars, even while highlighting the fact that some civil wars, notably an important subset in Africa, can be sufficiently explained by reference to material issues.

33. The release of the World Bank's findings related to economic factors as causes of civil war in June 2000 was widely covered in major newspapers in Europe, the United States, and Asia. It lent legitimacy to development of the "Kimberley process certification scheme," which was an attempt to regulate trade in diamonds implicated in major conflict zones.

34. As a related example, consider John Mueller's argument that "ethnic conflict" is itself a dangerous and distracting myth. Instead, Mueller argues that substate violence attributed to ethnic conflict reduces to criminal activity by "thugs." See Mueller (2000, 2004).

35. The best discussion of the impact of this trend on policy-relevant research on substate violence ethnic and civil war is Mack (2002). See also Kaufmann (2005).

36. On the role of religion in civil war see, Toft (2006a, 2006b, 2007a).

37. Existent work on demographics and ethnic war includes Ellingsen (2000); Besançon (2005); and Toft (2007b).

38. In this light, the International Peace Research Institute in Oslo (PRIO) has started a major program to compile local and regional data.

The International Relations of Ethnic Conflict

STEPHEN M. SAIDEMAN AND ERIN K. JENNE

Long a focus of scholarly interest in the fields of history, sociology and anthropology, ethnic conflict[1] has only recently gained the sustained attention of international relations scholars as a phenomenon with major implications for world politics. In political science, the study of ethnic conflict was generally believed to be the province of regional scholars who focus on the domestic politics of a particular country or comparativists who specialize in examining the political systems of two or more states.[2] Indeed, research on the international relations of ethnic conflict is still in its infancy.[3] Of course, the international features of ethnic conflict are far from new, even if the interest it holds for international relations scholars is.

During the Cold War, the fixation on ideological "proxy wars" between the United States and USSR distracted scholars from other sources of intrastate violence as well as the effects that these conflicts had on the international system. As events unfolded in the Balkans and Africa's Great Lakes Region in the 1990s, scholarly attention focused increasingly on intrastate conflicts and their influence on the stability of the region and the world writ large. It was becoming clear that ethnic conflicts were not isolated events and had ramifications well beyond the locations in which they were fought. Indeed, it is nearly impossible to draw a line between comparative politics and international relations in this area since ethnic conflict often fuses domestic and international processes, as in the cases of secession (the creation of new states from the fragments of old ones) and irredentism (the merging of territories across state boundaries). In light of the complexity of intergroup, interstate, and group-state relations, this chapter seeks to map the international relations of ethnic conflict more generally.

We consider a conflict "ethnic" when its principals are defined according to markers that are perceived to be inherited, such as race, religion, or language. Ethnic conflicts and civil wars are overlapping phenomena in that some ethnic conflicts are civil wars, and many civil wars are ethnic conflicts. Nevertheless, they are distinct categories.[4] Protests, riots, and repression are forms of ethnic conflict, but we would not consider them civil wars. Likewise, civil wars need not be ethnically defined, as can be seen in the war in Vietnam, the U.S. Civil War, and so on. We limit the scope of this chapter to the international relations of *ethnic* conflict, as this still leaves us much ground to cover.

There is no single overarching question in this subfield. This stands in contrast to other research programs such as the causes of the democratic peace. Nevertheless, the work in this area can be broken down into three distinct sets of concerns:

Is ethnic conflict contagious? How do ethnic conflicts in one place affect ethnic politics elsewhere?

How do dispersed ethnic groups or diasporas influence ethnic strife? Do diasporas always exacerbate ethnic conflicts?

What effects do neighboring states, international organizations, and changes in the world system have on ethnic conflict?

Our chapter is organized around these themes. First, we consider the effects that ethnic conflicts have on the larger ethnopolitical landscape. These include *direct* effects, where one conflict triggers another by crossing an internal or international boundary (also known as spillover or contagion), and *indirect* effects, where a conflict in one place inspires a second conflict in another region or state (also known as diffusion or demonstration effects). Second, we investigate the impact of diaspora communities on their homelands and the foreign policies of their host states. Third, we examine how outside actors influence the course of ethnic conflicts at the domestic level. At the end of each section, we assess the questions that have been addressed in each debate and identify issues that require further examination. We conclude the chapter by suggesting directions for future research.

Contagion and Diffusion of Conflict

The simultaneous disintegration of Czechoslovakia, the Soviet Union, and Yugoslavia in the early 1990s suggested to some that ethnic strife spreads like a virus from country to country. Events in and around Rwanda in the mid-1990s seemed to support this hypothesis, challenging the tendency among scholars to treat internal conflicts as sui generis events with causes unique to each case. This expanded focus led to studies questioning whether ethnic conflict is contagious, and if so, how it might be transmitted from one place to the next. Three mechanisms have been identified in the literature. The first two are (1) the direct effects or "spillover" from one country into another; and (2) the indirect effects or "lessons learned" from one conflict to the next (Lake and Rothchild 1998a). These are known as contagion and diffusion, respectively.[5] The third pathway—outside intervention by third parties (also known as escalation or internationalization)—is discussed in further detail later in this chapter.

It is a truism that ethnic strife does not respect international boundaries.[6] It produces refugee flows, spreads disease, triggers an influx of fighters and weapons, and fosters the growth of trafficking and terrorist networks. Most obviously, a conflict in one country can spread to another by pushing refugees across borders, upsetting the ethnic balance in a neighboring state, and creating tensions between the two states. During the 1999 war in Kosovo, for example, NATO officials were concerned that the flow of Kosovar Albanians into Macedonia might destabilize the fragile peace in that country by altering its ethnic composition to the disadvantage of ethnic Macedonians. Although conflict spillover was averted in 1999, former Kosovo Liberation Army (KLA) fighters did succeed in sparking violence in Macedonia in 2001. Similarly, the inmigration of genocidaires from Rwanda in 1994–95 exacerbated ethnic conflict in Congo, leading to a multilateral intervention by Rwanda, Uganda, and several other African countries and culminating in a regional war (Quinn 2004). These examples illustrate the dynamics of dangerous neighborhoods in which one conflict sets off another, adding fuel to the first, and so on in a vicious cycle (Weiner 1996).

The second mechanism of conflict transmission is known as demonstration effects or diffusion. Diffusion occurs when a successful movement in one place encourages copycat movements elsewhere. Demonstration effects—which may be little more than an idea or strategy borrowed by one organization or group from another—are both harder to quantify and more difficult to control than spillover effects. To illustrate, when former KLA fighters began to move into Macedonia, NATO forces were able to extinguish the spiraling conflict by physically blocking the insurgents from making further incursions into the country. However, there is little that NATO, or anyone else, can do to staunch the spread of *ideas* from one place to another. Moreover, diffusion may take unexpected, sometimes even surprising, turns. Martin Luther King Jr., for example, modeled his strategy of nonviolent protest from Gandhi's example in India. King's tactics were adopted in turn by European activists in the summer of 1968 and later by indigenous communities in Central America, Australia, and New Zealand. Stuart Hill and Donald Rothchild (1986, 1992; Hill, Rothchild, and Cameron 1998) have explored the conditions under which the tactics and strategies of dissidents in one place are likely to be applied elsewhere. They argue that diffusion is most likely to occur where activists have information about the outside world through access to communication technologies. In this way, the actions of foreign ethnic activists can "heighten a nation's awareness of its divisions" (Kuran 1998, 48–49).

There are, of course, limits to the diffusion of conflict. Indeed, not all scholars believe that ethnic conflict is as contagious as it might appear. In contrast to conventional wisdom, Fearon (1998a), Bunce (1999), and Saideman (1998b) argue that it was *domestic political processes* that led to the collapse of the three multinational socialist federations. According to Fearon (1998a), ethnic conflict is inherently self-limited because ethnic identities—unlike universal identities—are local by nature and therefore constrained in their mobilizational reach. Saideman (1998b) holds that the effects of diffusion are also indeterminate because many lessons can be derived from any given conflict. Slovenia's abbreviated independence movement might encourage secessionists, while Bosnia's bloody war counsels restraint. Individuals are therefore likely to "learn" the lessons that match their predispositions. Saideman argues that ethnic conflict is most contagious when it leads ethnic groups in a single country to draw the same conclusion about a common opponent—the government.[7] Statistical analysis provides some support for contagion arguments: groups are more likely to be separatist if their ethnic kin are separatist (Ayres and Saideman 2000).

Where is the debate likely to go from here? At present, scholars are trying to identify the precise pathways by which ethnic conflict in one place sparks ethnic or civil war elsewhere. The causal mechanisms need to be fleshed out more systematically. Refugees (Lischer 2005; Salehyan and Gleditsch 2006; Salehyan 2007) appear to be associated with increased violence in the receiving state.[8] For example, Hutu refugees from the 1994 war in Rwanda destabilized the neighboring state of Congo. However, the fact that refugee flows did not destabilize Rwanda's *other* neighbors suggests that more work is needed to determine the conditions under which refugees promote conflict spillover. Was it because the new government in Rwanda pursued the genocidaires into Congo that the conflict was exacerbated? Are particular kinds of identities, like religion, more likely to promote the spread of conflict (Fox 2004)? Not all refugee-producing conflicts generate conflicts in neighboring countries, so we need to understand under what conditions one conflict instigates another.

Other scholars have explored the effects of technological change on the contagion and diffusion of ethnic conflict. With increased access to the Internet, information about the tactics and strategies of insurgencies is now widely available. This provides leverage to otherwise disempowered groups, increasing the overall likelihood of both violent and nonviolent conflict worldwide (Bob 2005; Jenne 2007). One challenge to these arguments, and to those who assert that globalization tends to exacerbate ethnic conflict, is that there is less ethnic conflict (of all kinds) in today's world than there was 10 or even 20 years ago (Gurr 2000).[9] These arguments (Chua 2003) suggest an overall increase in conflict, which is what we saw from 1960 to 1995, but not since then.[10] Why then is globalization no longer exacerbating ethnic conflict, as it once apparently did?

These patterns demonstrate the need for closer analysis of the interactions between apparently discrete conflicts, particularly those that take place in the same geopolitical region. Balch-Lindsay and Enterline (2000) find that civil wars are longer if they border on countries undergoing civil strife. There is clearly something to the negative synergistic effects of bad neighborhoods, but how much conflict is due to bad neighborhoods and how much is a legacy of past conflict needs more sorting out.

Diasporas: Relatives and Homelands

The term *diaspora* refers to "a people with a common origin who reside, more or less on a permanent basis, outside the borders of their ethnic or

religious homeland—whether that homeland is real or symbolic, independent or under foreign control" (Shain and Barth 2003). Salient examples include Jews outside Israel,[11] Cubans and other Latinos in the United
States (Haney and Vanderbush 1999; de la Garza and Pachon 2000),
Croats in North America (Hockenos 2003), Kurds (Lyon and Uçarer 2001),
and Armenians around the world (Shain 2002). The creation of a new Russian diaspora with the collapse of the Soviet Union has also gained attention as of late (Melvin 1995; King and Melvin 1999; Barrington, Herron,
and Silver 2003; Zevelev 2000). The bulk of this scholarship focuses on diaspora politics in the United States (Shain 1994–95, 1995, 1999; Smith
2000).

Several key questions animate the research on diaspora politics:

Why do diasporas tend to be more nationalistic than the population of
their homelands?
What impact do diasporas have on the politics of their homelands?
What effects do diasporas have on their host state's foreign policies—
with regard to their homelands and more generally?
When are diasporas likely to have the greatest impact on policy?

Spatial factors play a key role in diaspora politics (Anderson 1998).
One might expect that time and distance would lead diasporas to become
less nationalistic than those who are directly affected by daily events in
their home countries. Yet the literature suggests that diasporas, or at least
politically mobilized members of diasporas, tend to be more nationalistic
or extreme than their homeland counterparts. Hungarian-Americans, for
example, are far more interested in regaining the territories lost under the
1920 Treaty of Trianon than are those residing in Hungary.[12] Similarly,
Croats in North America gave their support to the ultranationalist Croatian elites in the late 1980s and early 1990s, helping to set the stage for Yugoslavia's violent disintegration (Hockenos 2003; Mandelbaum 2000).

There are several explanations for the nationalistic bent of diasporas.
First, when we speak of diasporas, we are really only referring to the most
mobilized members of the group. As is the case with activists more generally, politically mobilized members of diasporas tend to have preferences
that are more intense or extreme than those of the populations from
which they are drawn. Therefore, those who comprise diasporas are those
who have organized to promote a particular policy—by lobbying members of Congress, for example. There are likely to be many more members

of the diaspora whose relative moderation renders them invisible, biasing our perceptions of the median preferences of the group.

Second, the dispersal of diasporas is rarely random. Those who emigrate from their home countries during political upheaval are often the losers of that conflict who expect to fare poorly under the new regime (Walt 1996). They also have a tendency to take their politics with them to the new country. The Croats who left Yugoslavia at the end of World War II included members and supporters of the fascist Ustashe regime (Hockenos 2003). Generally speaking, they did not discard their nationalist worldviews when they landed in the United States or Canada. This suggests that the preferences of diasporas are largely determined by the circumstances under which they left their homelands. The *process* of dispersion, too, has an important impact on diaspora politics. Those who live in refugee camps, for example, share a similar experience of expulsion or flight and are able to keep these collective memories alive in their day-to-day interactions with other members of the group (e.g., Rwandan Tutsis in Uganda, Palestinians). These interactions help to nurture their grievances, making them more likely to join insurgencies against their homeland governments. This can be seen in the case of Hutu refugees who had fled Burundi in the 1970s, but who kept their grievances alive in refugee camps over the border (Malkki 1995).

Third, the distance of diasporas from their homelands facilitates extremist positions. This is because their distance protects them from paying the costs of nationalistic policies. The costs that they do pay tend to be selective and largely voluntary.[13] A diaspora member can help finance a conflict back home or even volunteer to fight in it. In general, however, it is far easier to advocate nationalistic policies when the costs are paid by others.

Diaspora organizations seek to influence their homeland—or the policies of their adopted country toward their homeland—in a variety of ways. Much of the scholarship in this area focuses on diasporas from developing countries that now reside in wealthy democracies. The economic resources and political access afforded by their adopted countries often gives them disproportionate influence over the politics of their poorer homelands. Diasporas are able to exercise their influence through transnational ties with friends or organizations back home. For example, Croat groups in North America were a major source of funding for the electoral campaigns of Franjo Tuman, leading his nationalist party to victory in the early 1990s (Gagnon 2004; Tanner 2001). The Tamil diaspora in

North America and Europe has long funded the Tamil Tigers in their decades-long military campaign against the Sri Lankan government (Wayland 2004). The role of Irish-Americans in the "troubles" of Northern Ireland is well known. Indeed, a major source of funding for insurgencies around the world is remittances from ethnic kin abroad. Individual members of diasporas can also use the resources and skills they acquired in their adopted countries to launch successful campaigns for political office in their homelands. An infamous example is Gojko Šušak, a Croatian Canadian who assumed the post of Croatia's defense minister after having funneled campaign contributions from the Croatian diaspora to Tudjman.

Diasporas in the United States also seek to influence U.S. foreign policy toward their respective home countries (DeConde 1992; Shain 1994–95, 1995, 2002; Smith 2000). Examples of successful lobbying include the following:

A bid by Greek-Americans to delay U.S. recognition of Macedonia in its dispute with Greece over the name of the new country

Cuban-American efforts to sustain U.S. trade and travel embargoes against Fidel Castro's Cuba

Armenian-American lobbying to limit U.S. engagement with Azerbaijan over the conflict in Nagorno-Karabakh

American Israeli Political Action Committee's influence over arms sales to Israel's adversaries in the Middle East. (Goldberg 1990)

Diasporas enjoy influence in other countries as well. Until recently, Canada was the only Western nation not to include the Tamil Tigers on its list of terrorist organizations. The Canadian government was reluctant to blacklist the organization because of the considerable voting power wielded by the Tamil diaspora in key electoral districts. It may be the case that diaspora communities have greater influence in democratic systems where they can lobby legislators, make campaign contributions, and vote. Diasporas are often small and regionally concentrated, as in the case of Cuban-Americans in Florida. These features help them to overcome problems of collective action in mobilizing politically (Olson 1965; Saideman 2002). The fact that foreign policy toward countries in far-off lands tends to fall under the radar of the average voter further enhances the ability of diasporas to secure the necessary support for a desired policy.

Nevertheless, the influence of any single diaspora is likely to be significantly constrained for several reasons. First, there is often a "competitor" diaspora lobbying for a different, sometimes diametrically opposed, policy. Croatian-American influence over U.S. foreign policy, for example, was partly offset by the lobbying efforts by Serbian-Americans and Muslim Americans. There may also be other actors whose interests conflict with those of an ethnic lobby. To gain access to Caspian Sea oil, for example, the energy lobby in the United States successfully pushed for lifting U.S. sanctions against Azerbaijan. These sanctions were eased over the objections of the Armenian lobby, which was concerned with Azerbaijan's treatment of Armenians in Nagorno-Karabakh. Second, the power of diasporas is importantly limited by the resources they have at their disposal. These include the size of their membership base (large, territorially concentrated groups constitute influential voting blocs); money for campaign donations and political advertising; and connections to state, international, or transnational actors. Finally, the intensity of member preferences has a direct impact on the power of the ethnic lobbies; diasporas whose members are highly motivated, well-organized, and disciplined are more likely to mount successful lobbying campaigns than diasporas whose members are not.

The next generation of scholarship might assess more systematically whether the power of diasporas is greater than in the past, roughly the same, or ebbs and flows in tandem with shifts in globalization.[14] Adamson (2005, 2006) has argued that key aspects of globalization—increased mobility, porous borders, and enhanced communication—have given nonstate political actors a greater role in global security than in the past.

At this point, it may help to refine the central research question: *what are the conditions under which* diasporas are more likely to influence the foreign policy of their adopted countries? Diasporas appear to be more influential in democratic systems of government, although this is based more on informal observation than sustained empirical analysis. The next question is whether diasporas are more influential in the United States (because of its immigrant tradition or political institutions) or whether they are similarly influential across *all* democratic states. Some democracies grant citizenship more easily than others, so it may be that diasporas have more power where they have full access to formal political institutions.[15] Relatedly, do diasporas constitute independent actors, or is their behavior driven by powerful groups or individuals inside their homelands (Lyon and Uçarer 2001)?[16] For instance, is the Tamil diaspora an autonomous actor with respect to the conflict in Sri Lanka, or is it controlled by the Tamil Tigers who use it as a source of funding for local operations?

Much of the work on diasporas assumes uniform group preferences. New lines of research might therefore explore intradiaspora dynamics. Under what conditions are diasporas more or less cohesive? Do the principles of ethnic outbidding (Horowitz 1985; Rabushka and Shepsle 1972) apply to diaspora politics? When will significant internal cleavages develop, and how do these divisions affect the political power of diasporas? It is clear from the literature that ethnic lobbies can have a significant impact on politics in their homeland and in their adopted country. Given that most of this scholarship focuses on diasporas in advanced industrialized counties, it remains to be determined whether diaspora politics work the same way in less developed countries. Finally, comparative studies of successful versus unsuccessful ethnic lobbying may tell us much about why third parties intervene in some ethnic conflicts but not in others.

External Actors and Ethnic Conflict

Ethnic civil wars affect and are affected by the policies of outside actors. Consequently, internal disputes often assume the dimensions of international war. World War I, for example, began as an internal conflict. While this global conflagration was driven by many factors, the violence itself was triggered by a Serb assassin who was working on behalf of a larger movement to expand Serbia's territory. Indeed, the bloodiest wars of the twentieth century had some basis in irredentism—the desire on the part of a homeland state or kin group to reclaim "lost" territories. For these and other reasons, external actors intervene in internal conflicts to alter their outcomes; potential interveners include cross-border kin groups, foreign governments, and multilateral or private institutions.[17]

Beware Thy Neighbors: Irredentism and Meddling Mother Countries

Efforts to unite peoples by altering state borders often lead to violent conflict. State governments rarely cede territory willingly, because of the material value of the land, nationalist sentiments, or fears of creating a precedent for other secessionist regions (Toft 2003). Cases of irredentist conflict include Serbia before World War I and after the Cold War; Germany's expansion into Czechoslovakia and Poland prior to World War II; Hungary's irredentist bids in Slovakia, Romania, and Yugoslavia; Somalia's clashes with its neighbors (particularly Ethiopia in 1977–78); the on-going conflict between Pakistan and India over Kashmir; clashes between Greece and Turkey over Cyprus; the conflict between Russia and Japan over the Kurile Islands; the Armenian-Azerbaijan war over Nagorno-Karabakh; and Croatia's incursion into Bosnia-Herzegovina in the early 1990s. Carment and James (1995, 1997) and Brecher and Wilkenfeld (1997) use quantitative analyses to show that pairs of states with irreden-tist disputes are more likely to engage in both violent conflict and inter-state crises. This provides empirical support for the connection between irredentism and international conflict.

Weiner (1971) was a pioneer in the study of irredentism, theorizing re-lationships between the homeland state, its coethnics abroad, and the host state where the kin resides. Brubaker (1996) held that these relation-ships were intertwined in an interdependent "triadic nexus." Ambrosio (2001) tried to unpack this nexus by arguing that irredentism is the prod-uct of aggressive nationalism at home in addition to a permissive interna-tional environment. Chazan (1991), Carment, James, and Taydas (2006), Gagnon (1994–95, 2004), and Saideman (1998a) build on this logic by identifying the precise *conditions* under which the homeland's domestic politics will lead to an irredentist foreign policy. Gagnon (2004) argues that Franjo Tudjman of Croatia and Slobodan Milošević of Serbia used vi-olence not out of a primordial desire to unite with their ethnic kin, but as a technique for demobilizing popular movements for political reform. Saideman (1998a) avers that, given sufficiently powerful incentives, politicians may pursue an irredentist course regardless of the expected costs to the state or its population.

In the broader scheme of international politics, irredentism is rare. Most "homeland" states do not engage in serious efforts to reclaim their kin abroad, even when they reside in "lost" territories. Indeed, given the prevalence of risk factors in postcommunist Europe, the big surprise in the post-1989 period was the relative *lack* of irredentist aggression. Am-brosio (2001) and Linden (2000) have pointed out that Hungary, Roma-nia, and Russia refrained from territorial expansionism despite the pres-ence of kin outside contested boundaries. According to Ambrosio (2001), this was because their governments faced a much less permissive inter-national environment than in earlier periods. Kornprobst (2007) argues that changes in international norms make it hard for potential irreden-tists to justify their claims, making it easier for countries to resolve terri-torial disputes. However, the "international environment" does not explain why Hungary, Romania, and Russia exercised restraint whereas Armenia, Croatia, and Serbia engaged in aggression. Linden (2000) argues that this pattern can largely be explained by the variable level of democratization and European Union pressures in the region.[18] These silent dogs—violence that did not occur despite widespread expectations to the contrary—stand as crucial tests of theories of irredentist conflict. They also serve as a reminder that there is far more peace in the world than strife. To be useful, our theories need to account for both the occurrence of war *and* the maintenance of peace (Saideman and Ayres 2008).[19]

Other scholars have explored the peacemaking potential of homeland states. Credible commitment theories of secessionism hold that ethnic war may occur when the government of a transitioning state cannot guarantee to protect a minority under the new regime, creating incentives for the minority to secede while it still has the ability to do so (Fearon 1998a). Van Houten (1998) posits that the presence of an active kin state may help solve the government's commitment problem because it is unlikely to violate a minority that enjoys the backing of a strong homeland state. As Laitin (2001) pointed out, van Houten qualifies this prediction by noting that the kin state's peacemaking capacity only holds when it sends *mixed* signals to the minority (as Russia has done with regard to the Russian minorities in the Baltics). In so doing, it creates the requisite uncertainty on both sides to facilitate a compromise solution.

Whether or not they are able to induce ethnic peace, there is no real evidence that national homelands are motivated by the needs of their ethnic kin. Quantitative analysis has shown that homeland states are no more likely to intervene on behalf of their coethnics when they are repressed than when they are not (Cetinyan 2002; Davis and Moore 1997). Indeed, it appears that states intervene primarily to secure their own national interests (or those of the ruling class) rather than to ensure the well-being of their ethnic kin (Saideman and Ayres 2008).

Whatever the intervener's motives, the *expectations* of intervention have important implications for intergroup conflict. Cetinyan (2002) examines the bargaining dynamic between the minority and majority in the presence of a national homeland and concludes that minorities are likely to use the threat of homeland intervention and other sources of leverage to extract a better deal from their governments. Jenne (2004, 2007) concurs that externally leveraged minorities are more likely to use threats to extract concessions from their governments. However, she warns that such threats are *also* likely to exacerbate internal tensions at the substate level. Rather than yielding a better deal for the minority, external interventions may thus encourage a minority to overreach, increasing the overall potential for ethnic conflict and possibly interstate war.

If interventions are driven primarily by the interests of the intervener, then third-party participation is equivalent to adding another player to the conflict. The entrance of an additional actor with its own set of interests is likely to *exacerbate* rather than mitigate such disputes.[20] A recent analysis confirms the overall deleterious impact of homeland or neighbor state interventions on intrastate wars (Balch-Lindsay and Enterline 2000). Nor are homeland interventions so rare. According to Harbom and Wallensteen (2005, 628), the "vast majority (21) of external interventions [into internal wars since World War II] were carried out by neighboring states. This type of intervention dominated . . . the whole 1946–2004 period." Given these patterns, we are likely to see growing scholarly interest in the link between regional and ethnic conflicts, particularly with regard to the dynamics (the causes and consequences) of third-party intervention.

Cross-Border Kin Groups and International Strife

Irredentism is only one way that cross-border ethnic ties complicate international relations. The relationship between neighboring states is also affected by "transnational alliances," where a geographically concentrated kin group is separated by an international boundary. Although Davis and Moore (1997) find that ethnic alliances have only a marginal impact on the likelihood of interstate conflict, Petersen (2004) replicates their efforts with improved data and finds, in contrast, that ethnic alliances are strongly associated with conflict. Woodwell (2004) extends this work by examining the conflict potential of a variety of transnational configurations; he finds that interstate conflict is most likely when a single ethnic group is in the majority in both states.

Trumbore (2003) takes this debate one step further by examining whether conflict at the substate level is likely to lead to *interstate* conflict, and if so, whether states suffering from internal strife tend to be the victims, or the instigators, of interstate war. State governments may be tempted to prey upon states that have been weakened by internal conflict. For instance, India invaded East Pakistan during its secessionist struggle with Pakistan. Countries facing domestic problems may also engage in aggressive foreign policies in order to divert public attention from their other failures (Levy 1989). Another motive might be to deprive a domestic insurgency from outside sources of support. Interestingly, Trumbore finds that states plagued by internal conflict are more likely to act aggressively than they are to be victimized. Caprioli and Trumbore (2003) show that a state is more likely to initiate interstate war both when it faces internal rebellion and when it engages in minority repression. Thus, countries that are engaged in internal conflict also tend to be more dangerous internationally.

Beyond the Neighbors: Intervention and Management

The Westphalian norm of sovereignty holds that states enjoy a monopoly of legitimate use of force within their respective territories. However, the long history of foreign interference into one another's domestic affairs shows that this norm was never particularly robust (Krasner 1999). In secessionist conflict, sovereignty is violated whenever external actors aid a secessionist group in altering the existing boundaries of a state.

Some have argued that the power of this norm is derived from the implicit threat of retaliation. In this view, countries that are vulnerable to separatism refrain from supporting secessionist movements in other states out of fears of retaliation in kind (Jackson and Rosberg 1982; Herbst 1989; Zacher 2001). However, the deterrence value of this norm appears to be greatly exaggerated. Many countries that are susceptible to secessionism have supported secessionist activities elsewhere. Indeed, governments have been known to battle one another for years by supporting secessionists on each other's territory. Somalia and Ethiopia, Pakistan and India, and Iran and Iraq are all examples.

What motivates governments to assist secessionist movements in other states in spite of well-founded fears of retaliation? Heraclides (1990) argues that interventions are driven more by *instrumental* motivations (maximizing one's own utility) than they are by *affective* motives (helping one's ethnic brethren). However, this dichotomy is not without problems. To begin with, too many motives fall into the catchall category of instrumentalism, including providing national security, satisfying constituent interests, promoting economic growth, and securing access to scarce resources. To say that a state has intervened in a conflict for instrumental reasons does not tell us very much. Second, it is clear that affective and instrumental motivations are not mutually exclusive. Saideman (1997, 2001) argues that ethnic ties *do* matter, among other things, for determining which side of an ethnic conflict outside actors will take. In this fairly limited sense, interventions are driven by affective motives. However, the *logic of the intervention itself* is instrumental in that politicians typically adopt foreign policies to satisfy their constituents (who may themselves be affectively motivated). In sum, ethnic ties matter primarily for determining the lines of conflict, at both the domestic and international levels (Carment and Rowlands 1998; Carment, James, and Taydas 2006). While conceding the influence of ethnic ties, Bélanger, Duchesne, and Paquin (2005) use quantitative analysis to show that regime type is a far stronger predictor of intervention. More empirical work is required to adjudicate these conflicting claims.[21]

Other analysts claim that interventions are driven at least in part by their expected probability of success. Regan (1998, 2000) argues that because politicians are rewarded for their policy success, they undertake only those interventions that are likely to succeed—interventions aimed at resolving relatively minor conflicts, for instance. Indeed, Mullenbach (2005) points out that foreign interventions are almost never undertaken on behalf of beleaguered minorities in powerful states. However, this speaks more to the *constraints* on third-party interventions rather than to what motivates them.

Recently, scholars have sparred over whether international organizations can best prevent ethnic conflict through persuasion or coercion.[22] Much of this work has focused on the role of the European Union as a conflict mediator. Kelley (2004a, 2004b) and Vachudova (2005) have argued that the EU accession process[23] was itself a sufficiently large carrot—and the threat of exclusion a big enough stick—to force the laggard transition countries in Europe (Bulgaria, Romania, and Slovakia) to treat their minorities better and improve their relations with their neighbors. Others posit that the norms set forth by international institutions helped socialize the newly democratic countries of eastern Europe to treat their minorities better (Cronin 2002; Linden 2002; Checkel 2005). Thus far, "rationalist" arguments appear to enjoy greater empirical support in this area than "constructivist" arguments, although time will tell whether socialization and identity change (processes that take some time) will lead to changes on the same order of magnitude as inducements and threats.[24] Either way, it seems unlikely that international institutions will be able to replicate the successes achieved by NATO and the EU in regions outside of Europe, where the carrots are smaller and the sticks weaker.

Scholars have also debated whether the *method* of intervention has an impact on ethnic conflict, and if so, what strategies third-party mediators can use to resolve armed conflicts most effectively. Walter (2002) argues that establishing external security guarantees to both sides of a conflict are important for creating a sustainable peace. Fortna (2004) concurs, showing through data analysis that peacekeeping operations tend to enhance the durability of peace settlements. Meanwhile, Regan and Aydin (2006) find that diplomatic interventions work better than other kinds. Another question is whether outsiders should take sides in a conflict (Svensson 2007). Balch-Lindsay and Enterline (2000) show that intervening on behalf of challenger groups tends to prolong conflicts, whereas intervening on behalf of governments helps to shorten them. Krain (2005) contends, in contrast, that interventions can end mass killing if the international community targets the perpetrators and that other forms of intervention are likely to be ineffective or worse.

Several strategies of conflict resolution have received considerable attention, including partition, economic sanctions, and criminal tribunals. Because of space constraints, we cannot deal with any of these methods at length, but will highlight a few of the most salient studies. The liveliest debate has focused on partition. Kaufmann (1996a, 1996b, 1998) famously argued that separating ethnic groups is sometimes the only viable solution for ending severe ethnic conflicts. Further justification for partition as a conflict-mediating device was given by Downes (2004, 2006). Kumar (1997) and Sambanis (2000) disagree, using empirical analyses to show that partition is very difficult, if not impossible, to undertake as Kaufmann has specified. Jenne (forthcoming) reexamines Kosovo and Bosnia as two conflicts that are often cited as candidates for partition, showing that the features of these settlements that most faithfully reflect the principles of partition are most responsible for the continuing violence in both regions. On the other hand, Chapman and Roeder (2007) find that partition tends to produce positive results when applied to situations for which it is designed—conflicts due to competitive nation-building. While the literature on sanctions is vast, Andreas (2005) is particularly germane here, as he focuses on the effects of sanctions on ethnic conflicts in particular, finding that sanctions tend to criminalize the political and economic systems of the target states to the long-term detriment of their populations. Other scholars have argued that international criminal tribunals might deter ethnic violence by serving as a credible threat to prosecute the leaders of ethnic-cleansing campaigns (Barria and Roper 2005; Meernik 2005).[25]

Needless to say, meaningful international collaboration is critical to the success of all of these strategies (Saideman 2002). However, effective cooperation may be the most difficult hurdle for the international community. As suggested by the preceding discussion, governments usually formulate policies toward countries in conflict on the basis of self-interest. As a consequence, there is often substantial disagreement among the major actors over what to do and whom to support. The next generation of research should unite these two streams of scholarship by investigating how international cooperation so essential to effective conflict resolution can be achieved.

Next Steps

We conclude this chapter by suggesting three potentially fruitful lines of research: the factors that affect a minority's relations with external actors; the patterns of outside intervention in different types of ethnic conflict; and the differences between ethnic and nonethnic strife.

Most of the existing scholarship treats ethnic groups as unitary and passive, with outsiders acting upon them. However, the internal dynamics of ethnic organizations play a major role in the outcome of such conflicts; leadership skills as well as the chosen strategies and tactics make a difference in what these movements are able to achieve. Scholars have only recently begun to consider how groups market themselves (Bob 2005) or alter their identities (Saideman, Dougherty, and Jenne 2005) to gain international support for their cause. More work should focus on how internal group politics affect relations with outside actors. Does it matter if a single organization monopolizes representation of the group? Contrasting the Palestinians and the Sri Lanka Tamils may be instructive in this respect, as the long hegemony of the Palestine Liberation Organization has broken down, while the Tamil Tigers have largely maintained their domination of internal group politics. Does this matter for their relations with the rest of the world?

Second, different types of ethnic conflict may be associated with different types (and degrees) of external intervention. Much scholarship has been devoted to the causes of violent ethnic conflict and separatist movements. However, there has been little consideration of whether ethnic regime wars (coups, revolutions) inspire more or less intervention than do ethnic secessionist movements. This may be another way of testing where violations of sovereignty are most likely to occur—in changes to the regime itself or changes to state boundaries.[26]

Third, scholars have questioned the extent to which ethnic conflict differs from civil war. While Kaufmann (1996a) and Sambanis (2001) suggest that there are substantial differences, Collier (2000b), Fearon and Laitin (2003), and Hironaka (2005) argue that there are no qualitative differences between ethnic wars and wars fought along nonethnic lines. However, the work discussed in this chapter showing, for example, that external states tend to side with their ethnic kin and that diasporas and mother countries have a unique impact on ethnic conflicts strongly indicate that ethnic conflicts are indeed distinct from other forms of civil strife, at least in terms of how outsiders relate to them. More worryingly, the ethnic element of these conflicts may exacerbate interstate crises. Nonetheless, the jury is still out, as the civil war and ethnic conflict literatures remain largely segregated. More work is needed to assess the comparative dynamics of international relations in the different kinds of conflicts.[27]

There has been significant progress in this subfield, despite its relative youth. We know a great deal more about the nature of the spread of ethnic conflict, the role of diasporas in ethnic conflict, and the causes and effects of intervention in ethnic wars than we did even 20 years ago. Just as no single question has driven the research in this area, the study of the international relations of ethnic conflict has not been limited to any particular region, methodology, or theoretical perspective. This is all to the good, as the field has benefited from the diversity of questions and approaches.

NOTES

1. We consider a conflict "ethnic" when the divide between one's allies and adversaries is based on ascriptive features such as race, religion, language, or custom. See Horowitz (1985) for a classic definition of ethnicity and ethnic conflict. Importantly, the lines of conflict may change over time as the group's leadership variously adopts and discards different identities to attract external allies and increase internal group cohesion (Saideman, Dougherty, and Jenne 2005).

2. For an explanation of previous omissions and a call for new work in this area, see Stack and Hebron (1999).

3. Suhrke and Noble (1977) were among the first to analyze systematically the external dimensions of ethnic strife.

4. Kaufmann (1996a) may oversell the point, but still, ideological and ethnic conflicts are overlapping but not mutually exclusive categories.

5. Midlarsky, Crenshaw, and Yoshida (1980) distinguish between contagion and

diffusion by focusing on whether the spread of conflict is purposive (contagion) or conditioned (diffusion). We maintain that the primary distinction between contagion and diffusion is that the former is direct while the latter is indirect; this is consistent with much of the existing literature and seems to us more intuitive. For more on the international spread of conflict see Most, Starr, and Siverson (1989); Siverson and Starr (1991); and Vasquez (1992).

6. Gleditsch (2007) makes this point in the context of civil wars, and the new Counter-Insurgency field manual (U.S. Army and Marine Corps 2007) also recognizes the tendencies for civil wars to breach borders.

7. Beissinger (2002) demonstrates how both demonstration and contagion effects spread conflict within the Soviet Union.

8. This was an analysis of civil wars, rather than merely ethnic wars, but their findings are still relevant here. For more on refugees and conflict, see Davenport, Moore, and Poe (2003); Lischer (2003, 2005); Weiner (1996).

9. The Human Security Centre (2005) confirms that all forms of violence are down, not up. It may be the case that we are currently in a down-cycle and that conflict is cyclical, but that still contradicts the idea that globalization fosters strife, since globalization, according to most indicators, has been steadily increasing.

10. Kathleen Gallagher Cunningham pointed out that different kinds of information can travel via globalization, including how governments and other actors might counter challengers more effectively (personal correspondence).

11. The literature on the Jewish diaspora is vast. The impact of America-Israel Political Action Committee (AIPAC) in securing Likud-oriented U.S. foreign policies with respect to Palestine has been much debated in the popular press.

12. Findings from a series of interviews conducted by Saideman in 2003 and 2004 (Saideman and Ayres 2008).

13. However, members of diasporas are sometimes threatened or otherwise coerced into paying remittances to diaspora organizations (Human Rights Watch 2006).

14. DeConde (1992) suggests that it is a mistake to think of past foreign policy in the United States as being nonracial or unethnic; rather, the interests of the majority Anglo-Saxon ethnic group tended to dominate policy.

15. We are grateful to Idean Saleyhan for suggesting this line of inquiry.

16. We thank Arnav Manchanda for raising this question.

17. We omit Huntington's clash of civilizations theory (1993) from this analysis, as it has been thoroughly debunked in numerous studies on the subject (Fox 2001; Gartzke and Gleditsch 2006; Henderson 1997, 2005; Henderson and Tucker 2001; Midlarsky 1998; Roeder 2003). Therefore, we do not replicate this debate here.

18. We focus more directly on the role of the EU and other international organizations later.

19. This illustrates the importance of selecting cases without regard to their

value on the dependent variable, as it risks introducing bias into the results (King, Keohane, and Verba 1993).

20. We address Krain (2005) subsequently, as he suggests conditions under which interventions can end mass killings.

21. Saideman (2007) replicates Bélanger, Duchesne, and Paquin (2005) with some additional data, finding that ethnic ties explain better the patterns of support for secessionists than does regime type.

22. The Carnegie Commission on Preventing Deadly Conflict has devoted considerable resources to the study of preventative diplomacy (Cortwright 1997; Davies and Gurr 1998).

23. Other organizations have also played a role in conflict resolution in Europe, most especially the Organization for Security and Cooperation in Europe (OSCE), the North Atlantic Treaty Organization (NATO), and the Council of Europe (CoE).

24. For a critique of these arguments, see Saideman and Ayres 2007.

25. See the special issue of *Journal of Conflict Resolution* 50, no. 3 (2006).

26. Of course, given our own work, we are skeptical, but still this research agenda might be fruitful.

27. For a recent effort which focuses on ethnic diversity, see Mishali-Ram (2006).

Genocide Studies: Large *N*, Small *N*, and Policy Specificity

MANUS I. MIDLARSKY

With the onset of the Rwandan genocide in 1994 and the more recent genocidal activities in Darfur, the world has once again confronted the unthinkable—the attempted or actual annihilation of a distinct group of people. The exemplar of twentieth-century genocides, the Holocaust, was presumably so horrific as never to be repeated. Yet the systematic mass murders in Srebrenica, those in Africa, and even the contemplation of murderous ethnic cleansing in Poland at the end of World War II after the defeat of the Nazis (Gross 2006), remind us that unmitigated brutality is part of the human condition. Why that is so is the subject of this chapter.

First, I review earlier studies by historians, sociologists, psychologists, and political scientists for their distinctive contributions to understanding the onset and magnitude (severity) of genocides. I compare contributions by large-*N* and small-*N* analyses along with their definitions of genocide. I then develop and apply the theory of loss as a progenitor of genocide to the three most deadly genocides of the twentieth century (including the behavior of German allies during World War II), as well as the more recent genocides of Srebrenica and Darfur, and the genocide of Vietnamese within the Cambodian politicide. I examine Darfur more fully in the section on genocide prevention. I then consider relationships between war and genocide, followed by contributions of this literature to genocide prevention.

Earlier Studies

The preponderance of research in the field of genocide studies has been by professional historians, almost always on a single case of genocide, most frequently the Holocaust. And, until now, this is as it should have been. Even the Holocaust, as by far the most extensive genocide of the twentieth century, had received very little attention from historians until the Eichmann trial in Israel and the virtually simultaneous publication of Raul Hilberg's (1961; 3rd ed., 2003) magisterial study of the Holocaust in the early 1960s. Only then, and with the gradual disappearance of the generation of German perpetrators, as well as the even more recent end of the Cold War, did historians, especially German ones, take a serious interest in the Holocaust. The passing of the survivors also has quickened the pace of Holocaust research, before their oral testimony and the writing of their memoirs will no longer be added to the store of evidence. Even a basic issue such as the timing of Hitler's decision to murder *all* of Europe's Jews, not just those in the Soviet Union presumably infected with the Bolshevik bacillus, has only received a modicum of consensus among historians in the past several years. Interestingly, this issue will arise later in connection with the uses of theory.

Among historians, two basic approaches have been taken to understanding the annihilation of European Jewry, in some ways the most puzzling of genocides because of its magnitude and the absence of identifiable Jewish provocation. The first is the "intentionalist" (Dawidowicz 1986; Jäckel 1981; Fleming 1984), which posits an ultimate intention on the part of Hitler and his henchmen to destroy all of Europe's Jews. The second is the "functionalist" argument (Fraenkel 1941; Neumann 1942; Broszat 1981), which points to the coercive build-up (by the Germans) of Jewish populations in unsanitary ghettos that were not only disease prone but required the material support of the occupying German forces, as the root cause. With so many "unwanted" Jews excluded from the economy and the bickering between bureaucratic agencies of the Third Reich over the ultimate responsibility for their welfare, the decision to liquidate them was made.

Neither of these two explanations, nor others such as Friedländer's (1997, 2007) more recent emphasis on "redemptive anti-Semitism," explains the essentially dynamic circumstance of the increasing propensity to murder Jews as World War II progressed. In other words, some recent research, especially my own, seeks to explore the transition from genocidal behavior—the tendency to massacre *some* people having a particular ethnoreligious identity—to genocide itself, wherein the murder is systematically extended to include *all* people with that identity.

This distinction is not merely a matter of definitional semantics, for the lives of millions of people were forfeited in the transition from the more limited behavior to the far more extensive one. Massacres can be used to terrorize and cow a hated civilian population, as occurred in the large-scale murder of both Polish and Jewish leaders (Communists, high church and army officials, rabbis, professors) after the invasion of 1939. Or consider the massacre of approximately two hundred thousand Armenians by the Ottoman authorities in 1894–96 (Dadrian 1997; Marashlian 1999). This large-scale massacre is qualitatively distinct from that of the genocide of 1915–16 when as many as one million or more Armenians were systematically murdered in the Ottoman Empire. One can make similar distinctions between the episodic massacre of Tutsi by Hutu in Rwanda after 1959 and the genocide of 1994 in which a likely maximum of 800,000 Tutsi were killed (Des Forges 1999; Mamdani 2001).

In addition to historians laboring principally on the Holocaust (Eric Weitz's [2003] comparative study of utopianism in four cases of genocide is an exception), other scholars have also analyzed the phenomenon of genocide. An early systematic study was that of Helen Fein (1979), who used correlational methods to understand the extent of victimization of Jews in various locations within Nazi-occupied Europe. Among other findings, the extent of pre–World War II anti-Semitism distinguished between countries with high levels of Jewish victimization and those with lower levels.

Systematic cross-national studies have now been introduced. Using a set of genocides and politicides (definitions to be given later), Matthew Krain (1997) found that civil war involvement was the most consistent predictor of the onset and severity of genocide. Interstate war and extra-constitutional changes also were associated with severity, as well as onset. Interstate war as a progenitor of genocide will be examined in more detail later.

Interpreted somewhat differently, these findings are consistent with Robert Melson's (1992) emphasis on revolution as an antecedent of genocide in his comparison between the origins of the Holocaust and those of the Armenian genocide. These findings also are indicative of the salience of political upheaval found in Barbara Harff's (2003) cross-national study of genocide and politicide based on data from the U.S. government-sponsored State Failure Project (renamed the Political Instability Task Force).

In that study, democracy also was found to be negatively associated with genocide and politicide, as it was in Rudolph Rummel's (1997, 1998) work, a finding that is consistent with that of the chapter by Nils Petter Gleditsch, Håvard Hegre, and Håvard Strand in this volume. Recall that democracy in that chapter was found to be an inhibitor of civil war severity. Given the positive association between civil war and genocide, these findings are all of a piece.

Democracy here is taken to be that of the country unit at a given point in time. This is as it should be in cross-national research. Indeed, there is little choice in the matter. But what of democracies as bystander countries that could aid threatened populations? Here democracy is found not to be helpful and perhaps even inhibits the impulse to aid human beings in distress, albeit of a different nationality. Failures of the democratic governments of the United States, the United Kingdom, Canada, Australia, and New Zealand to permit more than a small number of Jewish refugees and expellees to find refuge in these democracies are salient cases in point (Wasserstein 1999; London 2000). The U.S. immigration quotas for Germany and Austria were never even close to being filled during most of the period leading up to World War II (Zucker 2001). At the conference on immigration held at Evian-les-Bains in 1938, only the Dominican Republic, a thoroughgoing autocracy under Rafael Trujillo, agreed to accept European Jewish refugees. Without the need to defer to public opinion that might harbor anti-Semitic sentiments as in the Australian case ("as we have no real racial problem, we are not desirous of importing one" [quoted in Wyman 1985, 50]), autocracies could accept Jewish immigrants.

Additionally, democracy as a fully realized political condition should be distinguished from democratization as a process. Michael Mann (2005) suggests that this process increases the likelihood of ethnic cleansing and genocide because of the sudden political importance of formerly marginalized or excluded minorities.

Large *N*, Small *N*, and Definitions of Genocide

As we know, different definitions of political phenomena can yield different results. Most directly, definitions when operationalized give rise to data sets that sometimes are at great variance with each other. Combining genocides as attempts by organized elites or opponents to destroy in whole or in part a communal or ethnic group, on the one hand, with politicides as attempts by the same parties to destroy partially or completely political or politicized groups, on the other (Harff and Gurr 1988), a total of 37 cases between 1955 and 2001 was found by Harff (2003). Only 5 of the total are genocides having no relation to politicide; all of the remaining cases are either politicides (12), or some combination of the two forms (20). Krain (1997, 2005) uses data sets very closely derived from Harff. As a somewhat different approach, by focusing on state-sponsored genocides having the purpose of eradicating an ethnoreligious group from a given territory and entailing victimization rates at least in the 66–70 percent range, I found that three genocides emerged with a minimum of 800,000 dead, as in the case of Rwanda in 1994. We shall now see how definitions and databases are utilized and the outcomes associated with each.

The cross-national large-N studies have been successful in yielding generalizations concerning the origins of genocide and politicide. Political upheavals, extraconstitutional changes, civil and interstate wars, among other factors, have been implicated as antecedents of genocide. (From a different set of studies, Fein [2000] singles out the absence of civil liberties, political exclusion as the result of ethnic hierarchy, conflict over land use, growth of hate movements, and immunity from external restraint.) Similarly, democracy as a regime type within polities has been found to be an inhibitor of genocide. Yet with the exception of findings on external interventions in ongoing genocides, to be discussed more fully in the section on genocide prevention, these results have not generated sufficient specificity to be useful as policy guides. Political upheavals and civil wars, as two cases in point, are past or existing conditions; although they may warn us to be vigilant concerning the possibility of genocide, they do not yield prescriptive schemas. Small-N studies that tend to be more focused comparisons, while lacking the generalizability of large-N methodologies, can generate more policy-relevant outcomes. A critical element, as we shall see, is the presence of testable theory.

Using a definition of genocide as "the state-sponsored systematic mass murder of innocent and helpless men, women, and children denoted by a particular ethnoreligious identity with the purpose of eradicating that group from a given territory" (Midlarsky 2005b, 22) leads to a focus on the highest range of estimated deaths within the targeted country areas, 66–70 percent victimization rate in the twentieth century (Fein 2004). In turn, this emphasis yields three cases: the Holocaust (1941–45), the Armenian genocide (1915–16), and Rwanda (1994). Other cases, those of the genocides of Muslim males in Srebrenica (1995), ethnic Vietnamese within the Cambodian politicide of 1975–79, or the more recent genocidal

activities in Darfur (2003–present) also conform to the theoretical expectations to be introduced shortly.

Genocide here is distinguished from politicide "as the large-scale
killing of designated enemies of the state based on socioeconomic or political criteria" (Midlarsky 2005b, 22). In contrast to genocides, politicides
not only typically leave the majority of the population intact after purging
the economic or political "offenders," but do not necessarily destroy the
cultural infrastructure of the victim. Even if attacked and partially destroyed, enough of the infrastructure survives to build anew, as in the former Communist countries (especially Cambodia) that experienced this
form of state-sponsored mass murder. The same cannot be said of the mi-
nuscule Jewish communities of eastern Europe, the Armenians of Anatolia, or the surviving Tutsi in Rwanda (in contrast to returning Tutsi
refugees). As one would expect, proportions of the victimized populations differ greatly. Whereas the percentages of murdered Armenians,
Jews, and Tutsi within the targeted country areas centered around 66–70
percent, that of Cambodians was approximately 20 percent.

Genocide also is distinguished from ethnic cleansing—the removal of
people from a given territory, including the occasional massacre as in-
ducement to flee, but without exterminatory intent. This distinction is
also made in international law (Schabas 2000, 196).

With the Holocaust occurring over most of Europe, the theory is found
to distinguish between allies of Germany that participated in genocide
and those that did not. Loss, especially territorial loss, is salient both as a
shrinkage of authority space—the distance from a national capital that a
government's authority legitimately extends—and the somewhat larger
concept of socioeconomic space. Loss, an identifiable empirical regula-
tory, is suggested by an extensive analytic framework, and is found to pre-
cede all of the cases considered here (Midlarsky 2005b).

The Domain of Losses and State Insecurity

In each of the cases of genocide, the socioeconomic space was contracted. By socioeconomic space, I mean the context within which groups
live their lives spatially (meaning physical territory), economically, and in
their hierarchical relations with each other. I argue that this shrinkage, especially if it occurs on all three dimensions, is the single most important
long-term progenitor of genocide.

Clearly, not all states experiencing loss are expected to be genocidal.

Vulnerability of a targeted group with a real or purported connection with state security (e.g., ethnic kin in an enemy state) is a necessary condition for the genocide to occur. For example, as a result of the 1846–48 Mexican-American War, Mexico was truncated without genocide occurring. There was no vulnerable ethnic group within the boundaries of the shrunken country that could be reasonably blamed for the disaster.

The shrinkage of empire and the loss of state strength are both situated within the domain of losses and comprise international sources of state insecurity (Midlarsky 2003). In two of the cases of genocide—Germany and the Ottoman Empire—the empires were contracted as the result of defeats in war. Economic catastrophe, as in the disasters of German inflation after World War I, or the extreme indebtedness of the Ottoman state, was an important factor that magnified insecurity. In the third, Rwanda, state insecurity was amplified by ongoing conflict that began with the virtual inception of the modern state, followed by territorial losses to the invading Rwandese Patriotic Front (RPF; see Barnett 2002; Straus 2006) after 1990, and entailed serious economic weakness as well. Further, the recent Hutu political dominance over the Tutsi was threatening to revert to the earlier, more enduring governance of Hutu by Tutsi.

In all of the following analyses of genocide, initial loss is understood quite specifically as territorial loss. It has a concrete specification and strong consequences, not the least of which is the presence of refugees from the lost territories. World War I was to have far more intense consequences in Germany than in any other western European country, despite roughly comparable numbers of battlefield dead in the three principal contestants, England, France, and Germany. Territorial loss was not confined to relatively small colonial areas (relative to the British and French), principally in Africa, or former Polish lands in the East. At the time of the armistice, Germany was still occupying large swaths of territory in Belgium and France, and especially in Russia. At the war's end, it must have seemed to most Germans that an enormous shrinking process had occurred (Evans 2004, 52–53). In the midst of later wars during which genocide occurred in all three cases, loss also can refer to battlefield casualties and civilian deaths.

Territorial loss also can be understood within specific national contexts that, beyond a common susceptibility to increased ethnic conflict, can yield different consequences for different countries. Contrasting Germany's sudden collapse in 1918 with France's *levée en masse* in response to French defeat by the Prussians at Sedan in 1870, Wolfgang Schivelbusch (2003, 196–97) suggests that

The most important difference between the two was that the collapse of 1870 did not leave France in a free fall. France's safety net was its sense of national pride, which had developed over the course of two centuries of European hegemony. The vanquished Germans of 1918 lacked any comparable heritage. The memories of centuries of national inferiority, supposedly relegated to the past by the victory of 1870–71, by the founding of the empire, and by forty years of power politics, now reappeared like an unwelcome guest on Germany's doorstep.

The burden of the past helps explain the response to the news of German defeat. People reacted not with manly composure, as the heroic vision would have it, but with everything from bewilderment to literal paralysis and nervous breakdown.

Facing the uncertainty of the postwar era, Germany would be haunted far more by its disunified and nationally (qua nation-state) undistinguished past relative to its competitors. The same holds true for the Hutu-led government in 1994, which, facing a future replete with uncertainty after territorial loss to the RPF and likely implementation of the Arusha Accords to its detriment, could only hark back to its earlier period of political servility both under the European colonial powers, Belgium and Germany, and still earlier under the Tutsi since the eighteenth century. Or as Christopher Taylor concludes, colonialism "is in the hearts and minds of every . . . Hutu and Twa, who imagines him or herself superior or who feels the need through the force of arms to overcome an imagined inferiority" (1999, 95).

Interestingly, when we examine the Cambodian genocide of its ethnic Vietnamese population within the overall politicide, a similar historical context is found. Perception of the Khmer Rouge that Kampuchea Krom, essentially the Mekong River region of Vietnam, had been lost to the Vietnamese was important. Earlier political subjection of the Khmer to the Vietnamese, and continued subordination even of the Communist Party of Democratic Kampuchea to its Vietnamese counterpart, suggested a past that easily could be invoked in the future (Kiernan 1996; Chandler 2000).

Even more decidedly, the Ottoman Empire experienced a series of losses, even to Balkan states that were formerly part of its empire prior to the start of World War I. In Srebrenica, genocide of the Muslim males took place at the same time that the *krajina*, a region of Croatia that had long been populated by Serbs, was about to be lost to a virtually unstoppable Croatian offensive (Burg and Shoup 1999, 324–25; Judah 2000, 235–36).

At least five analytically distinct perspectives inform the consequences of loss. First, as physical space contracts, the presence of considerable numbers of refugees may lead to an emotional reaction that in turn can result in brutality or even murder. As Sandra Blakeslee (2001, F3) put it, "People who are emotionally wrought by anger or disgust, say over . . . the condition of the downtrodden, may decide that certain brutal actions are morally acceptable." This conclusion is based on findings that decisions having moral import are far more likely to be based on emotional reactions than on reasoned deliberation (Greene et al. 2001). Identification with the downtrodden because of ethnoreligious commonality may lead to brutal actions against those, often of a different ethnicity, who are perceived to be at fault in generating the refugee influx.

Additional evidence is found in studies indicating that anger, in contrast to sadness or a neutral emotion, increases the probability of negative reactions to people of a different ethnicity (Bodenhausen, Sheppard, and Kramer 1994; DeSteno et al. 2004). External threat can stimulate anger, which in turn is most frequently directed against members of a group different from one's own.

Second, the placing of blame for perceived or actual injury to ethnoreligious kin suggests that revenge—a kind of loss compensation—can be exacted. And recent neural findings indicate that the experience of actual or anticipated revenge activates regions of the brain associated with "feeling good" (Knutson 2004; de Quervain et al. 2004). Thus, revenge can be pleasurable.

Third, if those perceived to be at fault also arrive as refugees or are viewed as comfortable and wealthy, then they can be targeted for massacre or ultimately genocide. The intersection of migration, ethnoreligious identity, and social class is combustible. Refugees sharpen an existential contrast with the "other," Jews as the anti-German, Armenians as the anti-Turk, or Tutsi as the anti-Hutu, especially if the victims are, on the whole, wealthier or more visible than the majority. Competing for the same resources in a shrunken environment, refugees and "native" populations can come to see each other as inevitable opponents in a contracting socioeconomic space (Midlarsky 1999).

Introducing the element of social class in the context of refugees competing with the "other," Hitler himself remarked, "our upper classes, who've never bothered about the hundreds of thousands of German emigrants or their poverty, give way to a feeling of compassion regarding the fate of the Jews whom we claim the right to expel" (2000 [April 4, 1942], 397).

Fourth, prospect theory also tells us that losses are valued more highly than gains (Kahnemann and Tversky 1979, 2000; Levy 2000). Experimental evidence has consistently demonstrated the asymmetry between losses and gains, even to the extent that in contrast to gains, losses can generate extreme responses. Losses as the result of a shrinking spatial environment, therefore, may have a magnified role in the public consciousness out of all proportion to the real-world consequences of loss. Again, brutality may be justified in the mind of the observer.

Fifth, the importance of territoriality in its own right should not be minimized, especially if the presence of refugees serves as a continual reminder of the territorial loss. Territory is so fundamental to state security that massive brutalities may be justified in the name of the state. When compared with general foreign policy disputes and those involving contrasting regime types, territorial disputes have a higher probability of escalating to war than either (Senese and Vasquez 2004; Vasquez 2000; Diehl 1999; Huth 1998). This suggests the fundamental importance of territoriality, even in comparison with other issues that are typically thought to be critical in fomenting conflict.

A contributing element to the importance of territoriality stems from the signaling of state weakness associated with territorial loss in time of war. Territory can be used to protect the state, as a buffer zone between the state core and its enemies. When that territory is lost, state weakness can be perceived by both defenders of the state and its external opponents. Under certain conditions, that weakness can lead to elimination of internal "enemies" in order to buttress the newly vulnerable state (Midlarsky 2000b).

There are three possible responses to the perception of a shrinking spatial environment. All three contain within them possibilities for genocide and depend in large measure on the force capability available to the potential perpetrator. First, given sufficient force capability, the perpetrator can embark on expansion to directly counter the recent contraction. The concept of *Lebensraum* that became emblematic of Hitler's drive to the east exemplifies this alternative. Instead of German-speaking refugees pouring westward into Germany after World War I, Slavic and Jewish refugees would either move eastward, or later as it developed in Nazi genocidal policy, be murdered en masse. The newly acquired space would then be safe for the perpetrator. New German settlements gradually began to occupy the eastern spaces vacated by the fleeing or murdered inhabitants.

Second, the contracting state can attempt to insure that remaining territory will remain part of the original state. Without force sufficient to expand territorial boundaries, defense of the remaining territory becomes the major focus. Any real or perceived "alien" threat to dominate that territory, as in a secession by a minority population, can generate a genocidal response. Ottoman fears of the creation of a "new Bulgaria" in eastern Anatolia by the Armenians is a case in point. Muslim refugees would no longer be forced into remaining Ottoman territory by newly independent Christian populations, but Christians (Armenians in this case) would be deported or murdered.

Finally, even if the national state territory can no longer be defended, at least a minority population can be prevented from governing it. In this, the case of minimal force capability, the perpetrators are losing control of national territory to enemy forces. If a kindred enemy population is destroyed, then the capability of the enemy forces to govern the conquered territory is minimal. Eventually, demographics would dictate governance. In Rwanda, after the Tutsi-dominated RPF began conquering Rwandan territory at a more rapid rate, genocide of the Tutsi became the most rapidly (although not the most extensively) executed genocide of the twentieth century.

The domain of losses implies the existence of changes in state security in a negative direction. As security of the state diminishes, the probability of violence, and when violence occurs, its intensity, increases, even against hapless nonparticipant civilians.

State security can be defined as the relative freedom of the state from threats to its existence emanating from either its domestic or its international environment (Midlarsky 2003). The term *relative* is important because state security often is assessed by policymakers relative to some recent period in national history, or in some instances relative to other states. A state that recently has emerged from defeat in a major war also may experience a sense of insecurity. Of course, the ultimate condition of state insecurity is found during major war itself when the state could be torn asunder as the result of defeat, as in fact happened to Nazi Germany at the end of World War II. And it was during wars that boded extremely ill for the state that the Ottoman Empire during World War I, Germany during World War II, and Rwanda in 1994, engaged in the most destructive form of identity conflict, genocide, respectively against the Armenians, Jews, and Tutsi.

A renewed determination and an acceleration of the killing can stem from a perceived threat to state security. Hitler apparently recognized as early as November 1941, as the Germans bogged down in their advance toward Moscow, that the war could not be won. The pattern suggesting impending loss already was established earlier in the Lend-Lease agreement of March 1941 sending 50 American destroyers to Britain, and the Atlantic Charter issued by the two countries in August that saw, among other provisions also anathema to the Nazis, a demand for withdrawal of all conquering forces from formerly sovereign occupied territories. On November 29, 1941, Dr. Fritz Todt, minister for armaments and war production of the Nazi government, after returning to Berlin from the Russian front, reported to Hitler: "Given the arms and industrial supremacy of the Anglo-Saxon powers, we can no longer militarily win this war" (quoted in Gilbert 1989, 265).

Thus, when the Russians launched their successful counteroffensive before Moscow against the Germans on December 5, 1941, and the Pearl Harbor attack brought the United States into the war on December 7, it must have become clear to Hitler that Germany could not win the war against such an array of opponents (Gilbert 1989). The predicted relationship between state insecurity and political violence suggests that shortly after these virtually simultaneous events, the Nazis would escalate the violence. And indeed on December 12, Hitler spoke to high-level Nazi Party officials, very likely informing them of his decision to murder all European Jews (Gerlach 2000).

Territorial Loss and the German Allies

In addition to these principal cases, there exists variation in genocidal behavior by Germany's allies in World War II (Midlarsky 2005a). Without the presence of German troops on their soil (Hungary was occupied by Germany in 1944), and sufficient size to demand internal autonomy (in contrast to the puppet states of Croatia and Slovakia), how would these allies react to German requests for deportation of their Jewish citizens to near-certain death? Three of these allies sooner or later agreed to these requests: Italy, Vichy France, and Romania. Two of the allies, Bulgaria and Finland, did not comply. The unique distinguishing feature between the two groups is territorial loss in the former collaborating group, but territorial gain in the latter.

Italy, though Germany's closest military ally, nevertheless had consistently resisted German requests for deportation of Jews under Italian authority in occupied France and in Croatia (Steinberg 1990). Until mid-1943, Mussolini would waver on these requests, ultimately declining to deport the Jews. Now, in the midst of experiencing the loss of nearly 10 percent of core Italian territory in Sicily as the result of the Allied invasion of July 1943, his position was unequivocal. State weakness, signaled by the loss of Sicily and an expected immediate Allied invasion of the Italian peninsula, ultimately proved decisive. German military support would be required to salvage his regime, and so the Germans had to be propitiated by deporting the foreign Jews. He then approved the deportation of 1,000–2,000 Jews from occupied France; they were saved only because Mussolini was deposed a few days later. Given the extent of Italian state weakness, had Mussolini stayed in office, it is most likely that he would have extended the deportation to Italian Jews as well, especially in light of his agreement with Jewish deportation in his later tenure as leader of the rump northern Italian state under German occupation (Zuccotti 2000, 291–92). Among these Italian Jews was the young Primo Levi, a future Nobel laureate, and a suspected suicide many years after his Auschwitz experience.

Although technically neutral, Vichy France, governing the two-fifths of France not occupied by the Germans, from the start complied with German requests for deportations. When truncated to the borders of the rump Vichy regime, France, the traditional home of continental liberalism, in its own anti-Jewish laws actually *preceded* those imposed by Germany within the occupied zone. The earliest transports contained few French Jews. Later, when the internment camps containing the foreign Jews (built by Vichy) had been emptied and deportation quotas still had to be filled, French Jews were routinely included in the transports to the east (Marrus and Paxton 1995; Levendel 1999).

Romania also confirms the importance of truncation as a key stimulant to domestic anti-Semitism, leading ultimately to the perpetration of mass murder. While Hungary was truncated after World War I and, for the first time since 1867, promulgated anti-Semitic legislation, Romania was expanded at that time and, for the first time, ceased its earlier anti-Jewish campaigns. According to Radu Ioanid (2000, 12), "The period between 1923 and 1938 represented a golden age of human rights in Romania." Later, however, just prior to its entry into World War I, when it too experienced territorial and population losses, the first anti-Semitic legislation of the interwar period was passed. The case of Romania, therefore, is important, because it provides a longitudinal demonstration that territorial gain after World War I was associated with liberal policies toward minorities, while losses in 1940 were associated first with anti-Semitic legislation and then with widespread massacre.

As of 1920, the territory of Romania doubled, absorbing Transylvania, Bessarabia, Bukovina, and Crişana, and in the process, Romania was transformed from a relatively homogenous state to one with 28 percent of its population composed of non-Romanian minorities (Jelavich 1983, 122–24).

No anti-Semitic legislation was proposed until the actual takeover of Romanian territory, first by the Soviet Union (Bessarabia and northern Bukovina, June 1940), then by Hungary (northern Transylvania, August 1940), and finally by Bulgaria (southern Dobrudja, September 1940) (Jelavich 1983, 226). Iaşi was the first of many massacres of Jews that were to take place later in nearby Bessarabia and Bukovina, territories that had been transferred to Soviet control in 1940 but were now, after the German invasion of the Soviet Union, under German and Romanian authority.

Jews were now interned in transit camps throughout Bessarabia. In October, deportations to Ukraine began. During the first months of the war, it is estimated that at least 65,000 Jews from Bessarabia and Bukovina were killed in mass murders, in the transit camps and during deportation (Ioanid 2000, 172–73). If we add the number of Jews deported who died in southwestern Ukraine, the number reaches approximately 130,000. Adding to this the number of native Ukrainian Jews in Odessa and elsewhere killed by the Romanian and German authorities, the number reaches approximately 250,000 murdered under Romanian jurisdiction. According to Hilberg (2003, 809), "No country, besides Germany, was involved in massacres of Jews on such a scale."

Instead of relinquishing territory at the start of World War II, Bulgaria actually gained territory. Indeed, territories lost in 1913 at the end of the Second Balkan War, and at the end of World War I, were mostly recovered. As the result of German intercession on its behalf in 1940, Bulgaria received southern Dobrudja; after Bulgaria's adherence to the Axis in March 1941, one month later the Bulgarians assumed control (but not annexation) of Macedonia and Thrace (Todorov 2001, 4–5). And in contrast to Italy, France, and Romania, virtually the entire Bulgarian Jewish community was saved, although the Jews of Macedonia and Thrace were lost to the deportations. A reason for this outcome is found in the absence of territorial loss and its accompanying refugee influx. Without the large number of refugees of like ethnoreligious identity, sympathy can be extended to others of a different identity, who through no fault of their own are subject to deportation and probable death.

Finland too, saved all of its Jewish citizens while allowing a small number of foreign-born Jews to be deported. As in the case of Bulgaria, Finland gained territory prior to its brush with genocide. At the start of the later Continuation War with the Soviet Union, by December 1941 the Finns had regained all of the territory lost to the Soviets in the Peace of Moscow of March 1940 ending the earlier Winter War (Polvinen 1986, 282). Now, instead of losing one-ninth of their territory as in 1940, the Finns regained it all plus a substantial amount. They were to retain this territory until June 1944, well after the period during which even minor German pressure for deportation had ended (Kirby 1979, 141).

Equally important was the status of refugees. In 1940, 11 percent of the total population was relocated westward on newly created holdings, a process that proved to be a colossal undertaking (Jutikkala and Pirinen 1974, 279). After the territorial advances of 1941, these refugees returned to their old homes. Instead of refugees streaming into the country invoking feelings of anger and identification with their unfortunate ethnic kin as in 1940, the nation could feel satisfied that this earlier wrong had been corrected. We would expect, as in the case of Bulgaria, a sympathetic response to other refugees in Finland, many of them Jewish. Thus, even among the German allies we find territorial loss and gain to be critical in distinguishing between states that agreed to participate in genocide, and those that declined to do so.

Note that the well-worn explanation of a prior history of anti-Semitism, although valid in many instances, is not applicable here. Until World War II and the Vichy collaboration in genocide, France was the home of continental European liberalism, never having promulgated an anti-Semitic law after the time of Napoleon I. Pogroms in France were unknown. Bulgaria, on the other hand, experienced episodic pogroms, including the most famous one in Pazardzhik (1895), as well as Sofia (1884), Vratsa (1890), Lom (1903), and Kyustendil (1904). Most were sparked by rumors of ritual Passover murders by Jews, the infamous blood-libel (Chary 1972, 32). Thus for France the leap to state-supported anti-Semitism and complicity in the deportation of Jews, including many citizens of France, was far greater than that for Bulgaria, and certainly Romania. Although Romania did take that plunge into the abyss, as did Vichy France, Bulgaria ultimately declined.

As it does not differentiate effectively between Vichy France and Bulgaria, an emphasis on a history of anti-Semitism as a potential explanation for genocidal behavior also does not distinguish between Italy and Finland. In both instances, before the 1930s, widespread anti-Semitism was virtually unknown in the modern period, yet the outcomes differed in the two cases.

War, Affinity, and Genocide

All of the studies examined here conclude that both interstate and civil war vastly increase the probability of genocide. These findings also agree with others stemming from somewhat different research traditions (Markusen 1987; Reid 1992; Shaw 2003; Valentino 2004; and Chirot and McCauley 2006). Losses during war, such as those experienced by the Ottoman Empire, Nazi Germany, and Rwanda, are extremely difficult to compensate. First, while the war is ongoing, battlefield position is almost always nonnegotiable. Second, especially during the opening stages of battle, losses generate uncertainty—the fog of war—that leads to magnification of the losses in decision makers' perceptions (Körding and Wolpert 2004) and that may yield genocidal outcomes. Absence of loss compensation at the outset and loss magnification during the war yield very different conceptions and behaviors from those stemming from the give-and-take of ordinary political discourse. Losses in war build on earlier losses experienced in older wars (Nazi Germany) or nationalist uprisings (Ottoman Empire). Loss of power as the result of political subjugation becomes a possibility once again as a consequence of more recent losses in war (Rwanda).

War also inverts the affinity condition—the existence of potential affine ethnic or governmental protectors close to the target that can prevent or at least postpone genocide. While earlier, the east European Jews were protected by the existence of politically powerful Jews in the Soviet Union (a German ally early in the war), when war broke out between the two countries, the Jewish "threat" had to be neutralized. Armenians protected by the February 1914 agreement between the Ottoman Empire and Russia to allow external monitors of the Armenian condition were suddenly transformed by the war into highly threatening Russian handmaidens that needed to be dealt with harshly. And when the United Nations as a local protector decided to withdraw its troops from Rwanda, this was the signal for the genocide to be enacted throughout the country. Ottoman Greeks were saved from extinction not only by the affinity condition of extreme Allied protectiveness toward them (especially by Britain) and the existence of the Greek state itself, but by the emergence of Turkey as victorious in the later Greco-Turkish War that removed it from the domain of losses.

Genocide of the Vietnamese in Cambodia accelerated rapidly as the Khmer Rouge were being decisively defeated in the quickening border war with Vietnam. So too was the genocide of Muslim males at Srebrenica made far more probable by recognition of the impending nearly certain loss of the *krajina* by Bosnian Serbs such as Ratko Mladić, former commander of the Serb garrison at Knin in the *krajina*, and now the officer in charge of the genocide at Srebrenica (Midlarsky 2005b, 133).

Precisely because the affinity condition restricts the decision latitude of the potential victimizer and in that sense magnifies the threat of both the potential victims and their affine protector, when war breaks out, these strictures no longer hold. Genocide then becomes a distinct possibility. This, perhaps, is the paradox of affinity—protection in peacetime, but much greater vulnerability in time of war. Yet the power of the affinity condition in preventing or at least postponing genocide is still evident, if only in the differential treatment accorded Armenians and Ottoman Greeks, even in the midst of a full-scale war in 1915–16.

Genocide Prevention

A criterion for evaluating the utility of a research methodology is its contribution to preventing heinous acts. Along with explanatory power, predictive capability and robustness of findings, this policy-relevant criterion of prevention stands as a measure of theoretical and methodological import. Here interestingly, both large-N cross-national studies and small-N focused comparisons can make contributions. I choose one of each as illustrations. Among the large-N studies, that of Krain (2005) stands out as a major contribution to genocide/politicide prevention. Examining the effectiveness of various kinds of external intervention in genocide—impartial, witness based (international troops present), no intervention, support of the perpetrator, support of the victim, and attack on the perpetrator—only the last of these interventions, those that directly challenge the perpetrator, are effective in diminishing the severity of genocide. A policy prescription is evident.

Why is this study so effective in its policy recommendation in contrast to other cross-national studies that, for example, are successful in disclosing the sources of genocide, but do not suggest specific policies? The reason is self-evident. By choosing to examine a specific military activity, intervention, Krain is explicitly evaluating the consequences of several potential policies. Effectively, this is a research design that is directly amenable to policy prescription. However, most of the studies that use cross-national analysis to discover underlying uniformities among a large number of cases *without* an explicit focus on an array of policy choices, generally do not yield policy relevant outcomes.

Because of concentration on a specific category of behavior, say magnitude of killing over a given threshold (66–70 percent), small-N studies tend to be more focused in disclosing uniformities. The emphasis on loss as an antecedent of genocide emerged from one such set of studies (Midlarsky 2003, 2005a, 2005b). How does this finding translate into policy specificity?

The experience of loss and the importance of loss compensation (a form of revenge) in effecting genocide suggest a potential preventive measure. Instead of loss compensation taking the form of genocide, as it has in the three principal cases (and in the instances of Srebrenica and the ethnic Vietnamese in Cambodia), it can be introduced much earlier in relations between states or communities. For example, Allied recognition of the potential impact of German territorial concessions at Versailles, especially in light of the massive relinquishing of non-German territories occupied by German troops (including territories governed by Prussia since the late eighteenth century), might have led at that time to Allied compensations. Reparations might have been imposed, as they were, but then immediately forgiven, as they were not. Only after the French occupation of the Ruhr in 1923 to guarantee payment had embittered many Germans and energized the Nazi Party were the reparations ultimately forgiven. Clear readmission into the network of European great-power politics also could have yielded compensation in the form of increased international status.

Compensation also can take the form of credible territorial guarantees to compensate countries for major territorial losses. If the Ottoman Turks had been convinced that, despite the war, the whole of Anatolia would remain Ottoman and not be divided into the Turkish, Greek, and Armenian enclaves, then the Armenian genocide and ethnic cleaning of the Greeks would have been less likely to occur. Great-power guarantees of continued Hutu political influence in Rwanda in proportion to their number, not envisioned in the Arusha Accords, could have compensated for Hutu concessions in those accords. For countries experiencing serious losses, even the substantial effort by significant international actors to achieve loss compensation could go far in allaying fears about an extremely uncertain future. This is a form of prudent realpolitik for great powers that replaces the far more prevalent (historically) cynical variety, and can avoid the imprudent, brute force realpolitik of mass political violence (Midlarsky 2005b).

The case of Darfur is instructive, for it graphically illustrates the importance of a likely impending loss. As a result of protocols signed on May 26, 2004, between southern Sudanese leaders of the black, predominantly Christian and animist Sudanese People's Liberation Army (SPLA) and the Khartoum government of the north, a six-year interim period would be specified, after which a referendum would take place allowing for the possibility of independence for the oil-rich south. This outcome would lead to the loss of approximately one-third of Sudanese territory, including its oil. The possible presence of oil in the Darfur region as well makes this territory potentially as valuable economically as the oil-rich south. If Darfur were to be Arabized through the massacre and ethnic cleansing of its black population, then it could serve as compensation for losses in the south, especially in the face of an incipient rebellion by the black Africans in Darfur.

Encouraged by the success of the black southern rebels both on the battlefield and at the conference table, two groups of black Muslims from Darfur rebelled, apparently representing black populations persecuted through raids and other violence by nomadic Arabized tribes. Confronted by another separatist rebellion like that of the SPLA, ethnic cleansing of another black population was unleashed, with a genocidal component of hundreds of thousands dead. One purpose of this effort has been to compensate for the potential losses in the south by ensuring that another potentially valuable territory, Darfur, remains within a Sudan dominated by its Arabized population.

The international community was intensely concerned that a settlement between the Khartoum government and the SPLA be reached. Colin Powell, then the U.S. secretary of state, visited the negotiations between the SPLA, and the Khartoum leaders in October 2003 and Darfur itself in June 2004. The United Nations has also taken an active role. And like Arusha in the Rwandan case, an international agreement implying heavy losses in the future, whether in political power (Rwanda, territory already having been lost to the RPF) or valuable territory (Sudan), may have spurred this effort at loss compensation. As with the Interahamwe in Rwanda, much of the killing and ethnic cleansing has been carried out by a government-supported militia, the Janjaweed, an Arabized military group.

These considerations suggest that even more active intervention is required to stem these massacres and ethnic cleansing. A pairing of the two regions of Sudan, Darfur and the south, should be a focus of international diplomacy, without forsaking one region for the other. Unfortunately, just the opposite appears to have occurred. According to John Prendergast, a former African affairs director at the National Security Council under President Clinton, "When the secretary [Colin Powell] was in Naivasha [location of the negotiations between the Khartoum government and the SPLA], and a major problem was getting worse in Darfur, everyone agreed to deal with the southern problem first and with Darfur later. *That was a monumental diplomatic error*" (quoted in Weisman 2004; emphasis added).

Integration of Sudan into elements of the international economy, including appropriate financial incentives (e.g., firmly guaranteed access to oil in the south in the event of southern independence), might serve at least as a partial loss compensation to offset the loss of one or both regions.

All of this indicates that, as in any medical or social pathology, early and informed intervention is required to avoid a fatal outcome. Hitler in Germany and Vladimir Zhirinovsky in Russia experienced very different historical trajectories in part because of the contrasting reactions of international diplomacy in the two cases. One additional avenue of genocide prevention is the intense analysis and understanding of the origins of political extremism. In this fashion, one may be able to identify individuals and groups who are most likely to commit genocide, and close the political space (Linz 1980) that allows their access to potential future adherents. This recommendation emerges from a detailed analysis of over twenty cases of political extremism and its absence. The most egregious of these cases ended in genocide (Midlarsky, forthcoming).

Conclusion

Genocides are complex events that typically are inspired by an earlier history of unpunished massacre, which emphasizes vulnerability of the victims (Midlarsky 2005b, 43–63). For this reason, among others, including the facilitating condition of widespread warfare, genocides occur less frequently than might be expected, given the fairly common presence of ethnoreligious animosities. Nevertheless, both large-N and small-N studies have disclosed not only uniformities in the origins of this form of mass killing, but possible avenues for genocide prevention. It is to be hoped that this emerging research program will be buttressed by studies that may lead directly to the prevention of genocide in the future. The lives of many human beings could depend on the success of this effort.

Finally, although this chapter has emphasized certain findings in the origins of genocide and its prevention, this clearly is not the whole story. Much remains to be done in these areas. In addition to the large-N and small-N research methodologies, experimental approaches might be helpful. Certainly Stanley Milgram's (1974) work on obedience to authority, based almost entirely on laboratory studies, was useful in understanding the genocidal behavior of the "ordinary men" of the German Reserve Police Battalion 101 in Poland during World War II (Browning 1992). Also helpful has been Philip Zimbardo's laboratory work on authority structures in prisonlike confinements (e.g., Haney, Banks, and Zimbardo 1973; Zimbardo 2008). Multimethod approaches to the study of genocide can suggest additional insights into this phenomenon, as well as providing validation for findings yielded by different methods.

Bibliography

Acemoglu, Daron, and James A. Robinson. 2001. "Inefficient Redistribution." *American Political Science Review* 95:645–61.

Acemoglu, Daron, and James Robinson. 2006. *Economic Origins of Dictatorship and Democracy*. Cambridge: Cambridge University Press.

Adamson, Fiona. 2005. "Globalisation, Transnational Political Mobilisation, and Networks of Violence." *Cambridge Review of International Affairs* 18:31–49.

Adamson, Fiona. 2006. "Crossing Borders: International Migration and National Security." *International Security* 31 (1): 165–99.

Agnew, John. 1987. *Place and Politics: The Geographical Mediation of State and Society*. Boston: Allen and Unwin.

Aguilar, Paloma. 2002. *Memory and Amnesia: The Role of the Spanish Civil War in the Transition to Democracy*. New York: Berghahn Books.

Allison, Graham T. 1972. *The Essence of Decision*. Boston: Little, Brown.

Almond, Gabriel A. 1988. "Separate Tables: Schools and Sects in Political Science." *PS* 21:828–42.

Almond, Gabriel A., and G. Bingham Powell Jr. 1966. *Comparative Politics: A Developmental Approach*. Boston: Little, Brown.

Altfeld, Michael F., and Bruce Bueno de Mesquita. 1979. "Choosing Sides in Wars." *International Studies Quarterly* 23:87–112.

Ambrosio, Thomas. 2001. *Irredentism: Ethnic Conflict and International Politics*. Westport, CT: Praeger.

Anderson, Benedict. 1983. *Imagined Communities*. London: Verso.

Anderson, Benedict. 1998. "Long-Distance Nationalism." In *The Spectre of Comparisons: Nationalism, Southeast Asia, and the World*, ed. Benedict Anderson. London: Verso.

Anderson, Mary. 1999. *Do No Harm: How Aid Can Support Peace—or War*. Boulder: Lynne Rienner.

Anderson, Perry. 1974. *Lineages of the Absolutist State*. London: NLB.

Andreas, Peter. 2005. "Criminalizing Consequences of Sanctions: Embargo Busting and Its Legacy." *International Studies Quarterly* 49:335–60.

Anthony, Douglas A. 2002. *Poison and Medicine: Ethnicity, Power, and Violence in a Nigerian City, 1966 to 1986*. Portsmouth, NH: Heinemann.

Arendt, Hannah. 1973. *The Origins of Totalitarianism.* New ed. San Diego: Harcourt Brace Jovanovich.

Arnsten, Amy. 1998. "The Biology of Being Frazzled." *Science* 280:1711–12.

Arreguín-Toft, Ivan. 2005. *How the Weak Win Wars.* New York: Cambridge University Press.

Atlas, Pierre M., and Roy Licklider. 1999. "Conflict among Former Allies after Civil War Settlement in Sudan, Zimbabwe, Chad, and Lebanon." *Journal of Peace Research* 36:35–54.

Auvinen, Juha. 1997. "Political Conflict in Less Developed Countries, 1981–89." *Journal of Peace Research* 34:177–95.

Axelrod, Robert. 1984. *The Evolution of Cooperation.* New York: Basic Books.

Ayres, R. William, and Stephen Saideman. 2000. "Is Separatism as Contagious as the Common Cold or as Cancer? Testing International and Domestic Explanations." *Nationalism and Ethnic Politics* 6:91–113.

Baker, Pauline H. 2001. "Conflict Resolution versus Democratic Governance: Divergent Paths to Peace?" in *Turbulent Peace: The Challenges of Managing International Conflict,* ed. Chester Crocker, Fen Osler Hampson, and Pamela Aall. Washington, DC: United States Institute of Peace Press.

Balch-Lindsay, Dylan, and Andrew J. Enterline. 2000. "Killing Time: The World Politics of Civil War Duration, 1820–1992." *International Studies Quarterly* 44:615–42.

Ball, Nicole. 1996. "Demobilizing and Reintegrating Soldiers: Lessons from Africa." In *Rebuilding Societies after Civil War: Critical Roles for International Assistance,* ed. Krishna Kumar. Boulder: Lynne Rienner.

Ballentine, Karen, and Jake Sherman. 2003. *The Political Economy of Armed Conflict: Beyond Greed and Grievance.* Boulder: Lynne Rienner.

Bandura, Albert. 1999. "Moral Disengagement in the Perpetration of Inhumanities." In "Perspectives on Evil and Violence." *Personality and Social Psychology Review* 3 (3): 193–209.

Banks, Arthur S. 2000. *Cross-National Time-Series Database.* Machine-readable data file. Cross-National Time-Series Data Archive. www.data banksinternational.com/32.html.

Barber, James David. 1985. *The Presidential Character: Predicting Performance in the White House.* Englewood Cliffs, NJ: Prentice-Hall.

Barkan, Elazar. 2000. *The Guilt of Nations: Restitution and Negotiating Historical Injustices.* Baltimore: Johns Hopkins University Press.

Barker, Pat. 1991. *Regeneration.* New York: Viking.

Barnett, Michael N. 2002. *Eyewitness to Genocide.* Ithaca: Cornell University Press.

Barria, Lilian A., and Steven D. Roper. 2005. "How Effective Are International Criminal Tribunals? An Analysis of the ICTY and the ICTR." *International Journal of Human Rights* 9:349–68.

Barrington, Lowell W., Erik S. Herron, and Brian D. Silver. 2003. "The Motherland Is Calling: Views of Homeland among Russians in the Near Abroad." *World Politics* 55:290–313.

Bartoli, Andrea. 1999. "Mediating Peace in Mozambique: The Role of the Community of Sant'Egidio." In *Herding Cats: The Role of Mediation in Multiparty Crisis,* ed. Pamela Aall, Chester Crocker, and Fen Osler Hampson. Washington, DC: United States Institute of Peace Press.

Bates, Robert H. 1974. "Ethnic Competition and Modernization in Contemporary Africa." *Comparative Political Studies* 6:457–84.

Bates, Robert H. 2001. *Prosperity and Violence: The Political Economy of Development.* New York: Norton.

Bates, Robert H., David L. Epstein, Jack A. Goldstone, Ted Robert Gurr, Barbara Harff, Colin H. Kahl, Kristen Knight, Marc A. Levy, Michael Lustik, Monty G. Marshall, Thomas M. Parris, Jay Ulfelder, and Mark R. Woodward. 2003. *Political Instability Task Force Report: Phase IV Findings.* McLean, VA: Science Applications International Corporation.

Bates, Robert H., Avner Greif, Margaret Levi, Jean-Laurent Rosenthal, and Barry R. Weingast. 1998. *Analytic Narratives.* Princeton: Princeton University Press.

Beissinger, Mark R. 2002. *Nationalist Mobilization and the Collapse of the Soviet State.* Cambridge: Cambridge University Press.

Bélanger, Louis, Érick Duchesne, and Jonathan Paquin. 2005. "Foreign Interventions and Secessionist Movements: The Democratic Factor." *Canadian Journal of Political Science* 38:435–62.

Benzel, Richard Franklin. 1990. *Yankee Leviathan: The Origins of Central State Authority in America, 1859–1877.* New York: Cambridge University Press.

Berdal, Mats, and David M. Malone, eds. 2000. *Greed and Grievance: Economic Agendas in Civil Wars.* Boulder: Lynne Rienner.

Berger, Thomas. 2003. "On the Importance of Being Sorry: The 'History Problem' in Japan's Foreign Relations." Paper presented at the Annual Meeting of the International Studies Association, Portland, OR, March 1.

Besançon, Marie L. 2005. "Relative Resources: Inequality in Ethnic Wars, Revolutions, and Genocides." *Journal of Peace Research* 42:393–415.

Binningsbø, Helga Malmin. 2006. "Power-Sharing and Postconflict Peace Periods." Paper presented at the 47th Annual Convention of the International Studies Association, San Diego, March 22–25, http://64.112.226.77/one/isa/isa06/.

Blainey, Geoffrey. 1988. *The Causes of War.* New York: Free Press.

Blair, Stephanie A., Dana Eyre, Bernard Salomé, and James Wasserstrom. 2005. "Forging a Viable Peace: Developing a Legitimate Political Economy." In *The Quest for Viable Peace: International Intervention and Strategies for Conflict Transformation,* ed. Jock Covey, Michael J. Dziedzic, and

Leonard R. Hawley. Washington, DC: United States Institute of Peace Press; Arlington, VA: Association of the United States Army.

Blakeslee, Sandra. 2001. "Watching How the Brain Works as It Weighs a Moral Dilemma." *New York Times*, September 25, F3.

Blaufarb, Douglas. 1977. *The Counterinsurgency Era: U.S. Doctrine and Performance*. New York: Free Press.

Bob, Clifford. 2005. *The Marketing of Rebellion: Insurgents, Media, and International Activism*. Cambridge: Cambridge University Press.

Bodenhausen, Galen V., Lori A. Sheppard, and Geoffrey P. Kramer. 1994. "Negative Affect and Social Judgment: The Dfferential Impact of Anger and Sadness." *European Journal of Social Psychology* 24 (1): 45–62.

Boehm, Christopher. 1999. *Hierarchy in the Forest: The Evolution of Egalitarian Behavior*. Cambridge: Harvard University Press.

Boix, Carles. 2003. *Democracy and Redistribution*. Cambridge: Cambridge University Press.

Booth, John A. 1985. *The End and the Beginning: The Nicaraguan Revolution*. 2nd ed. Boulder: Westview Press.

Boutwell, Jeffrey, and Michael T. Klare. 1999. *Light Weapons and Civil Conflict: Controlling the Tools of Violence*. Lanham, MD: Rowman and Littlefield.

Boyle, Francis A. 1996. "Negating Human Rights in Peace Negotiations." *Human Rights Quarterly* 18 (3): 515–16.

Brams, Steven J. 1975. *Game Theory and Politics*. New York: Free Press.

Brancati, Dawn. 2003. "Design over Conflict: Managing Ethnic Conflict and Secessionism through Decentralization." Ph.D. diss., Columbia University.

Brancati, Dawn. 2006. "Decentralization: Fueling the Fire or Dampening the Flames of Ethnic Conflict and Secession?" *International Organization* 60:651–85.

Brass, Paul R. 1991. *Ethnicity and Nationalism: Theory and Comparison*. New Delhi: Sage.

Brass, Paul R. 1997. *Theft of an Idol: Text and Context in the Representation of Collective Violence*. Princeton: Princeton University Press.

Bratton, Michael, and Nicolas Van de Walle. 1994. "Neopatrimonial Regimes and Political Transitions in Africa." *World Politics* 46:453–89.

Brecher, Michael, and Jonathan Wilkenfeld. 1997. "The Ethnic Dimension of International Crises." In *Wars in the Midst of Peace: The International Politics of Ethnic Conflict*, ed. David Carment and Patrick James. Pittsburgh: University of Pittsburgh Press.

Broszat, Martin. 1981. *The Hitler State*. London: Longman.

Brown, Michael E., ed. 1993. *Ethnic Conflict and International Security*. Princeton: Princeton University Press.

Brown, Michael E., ed. 1996. *The International Dimensions of Internal Conflict.* Cambridge: MIT Press.

Brown, Michael E., Owen R. Coté Jr., Sean M. Lynn-Jones, and Steven E. Miller, eds. 1997. *Nationalism and Ethnic Conflict.* Cambridge: MIT Press.

Brown, Michael E., and Sumit Ganguly, eds. 1997. *Government Policies and Ethnic Relations in Asia and the Pacific.* Cambridge: MIT Press.

Browning, Christopher R. 1992. *Ordinary Men: Reserve Police Battalion 101 and the Final Solution in Poland.* New York: HarperCollins.

Brownlee, Jason. 2007. *Authoritarianism in an Age of Democratization.* Cambridge: Cambridge University Press.

Brubaker, Rogers. 1996. *Nationalism Reframed: Nationhood and the National Question in the New Europe.* New York: Cambridge University Press.

Bueno de Mesquita, Bruce. 1981. *The War Trap.* New Haven: Yale University Press.

Bueno de Mesquita, Bruce. 2006. *Principles of International Politics: People's Power, Preferences, and Perceptions.* 3rd ed. Washington, DC: CQ Press.

Bueno de Mesquita, Bruce, and George W. Downs. 2006. "Intervention and Democracy." *International Organization* 60:627–49.

Bueno de Mesquita, Bruce, and David Lalman. 1992. *War and Reason: Domestic and International Imperatives.* New Haven: Yale University Press.

Bueno de Mesquita, Bruce, and Rose McDermott. 2004. "Crossing No Man's Land: Cooperation from the Trenches." *Political Psychology* 25 (2): 271–87.

Bueno de Mesquita, Bruce, Rose McDermott, and Emily Cope. 2001. "The Expected Prospects for Peace in Northern Ireland." *International Interactions* 27 (2): 129–67.

Bueno de Mesquita, Bruce, James D. Morrow, Randolph M. Siverson, and Alastair Smith. 1999. "An Institutional Explanation of the Democratic Peace." *American Political Science Review* 93:791–807.

Bueno de Mesquita, Bruce, James D. Morrow, Randolph M. Siverson, and Alastair Smith. 2004. "Testing Novel Implications from the Selectorate Theory of War." *World Politics* 56:363–88.

Bueno de Mesquita, Bruce, and Randolph M. Siverson. 1995. "War and the Survival of Political Leaders: A Comparative Study of Regime Types and Political Accountability." *American Political Science Review* 89:841–55.

Bueno de Mesquita, Bruce, and Alastair Smith. 2009. "Political Survival and Endogenous Institutional Change." *Comparative Political Studies* 42: 167–97.

Bueno de Mesquita, Bruce, Alastair Smith, Randolph M. Siverson, and James D. Morrow. 2003. *The Logic of Political Survival.* Cambridge: MIT Press.

Buhaug, Halvard. 2006. "Relative Capability and Rebel Objective in Civil War." *Journal of Peace Research* 43:691–708.

Buhaug, Halvard, and Scott Gates. 2002. "The Geography of Civil War." *Journal of Peace Research* 39:417–33.

Buhaug, Halvard, and Jan Ketil Rød. 2006. "Local Determinants of African Civil Wars, 1970–2001." *Political Geography* 25:315–35.

Bunce, Valerie. 1999. *Subversive Institutions: The Design and the Destruction of Socialism and the State.* Cambridge: Cambridge University Press.

Burg, Steven L., and Paul S. Shoup. 1999. *The War in Bosnia-Herzegovina: Ethnic Conflict and International Intervention.* New York: M. E. Sharpe.

Burnham, Walter Dean. 1994. "Pattern Recognition and 'Doing' Political History: Art, Science, or Bootless Enterprise?" In *The Dynamics of American Politics: Approaches and Interpretations,* ed. Lawrence C. Dodd and Calvin Jillson. Boulder: Westview Press.

Bussmann, Margit, and Gerald Schneider. 2007. "When Globalization Discontent Turns Violent: Foreign Economic Liberalization and Internal War." *International Studies Quarterly* 51:79–97.

Bussmann, Margit, Gerald Schneider, and Nina Wiesehomeier. 2005. "Foreign Economic Liberalization and Peace: The Case of Sub-Saharan Africa." *European Journal of International Relations* 11:551–79.

Butler, Christopher, Mary J. Bellman, and Oraz Kichiyev. 2006. "Assessing Power in Spatial Bargaining: When Is There Advantage to Being Status-Quo Advantaged?" Working paper, Department of Political Science, University of New Mexico.

Bwy, Douglas. 1968. "Dimensions of Social Conflict in Latin America." *American Behavioral Scientist* 2 (4): 39–50.

Byman, Daniel L. 2002. *Keeping the Peace: Lasting Solutions to Ethnic Conflicts.* Baltimore: Johns Hopkins University Press.

Byman, Daniel, Peter Chalk, Bruce Hoffman, William Rosenau, and David Brannan. 2001. *Trends in Outside Support for Insurgent Movements.* Santa Monica, CA: RAND.

Call, Charles T. 2002. "Assessing El Salvador's Transition from Civil War to Peace." In *Ending Civil Wars: The Implementation of Peace Agreements,* ed. Stephen John Stedman, Donald Rothchild, and Elizabeth M. Cousens. Boulder: Lynne Rienner.

Call, Charles T., and William Stanley. 2002. "Civilian Security." In *Ending Civil Wars: The Implementation of Peace Agreements,* ed. Stephen John Stedman, Donald Rothchild, and Elizabeth M. Cousens. Boulder: Lynne Rienner.

Callahan, David. 1997. *Unwinnable Wars: American Power and Ethnic Conflict.* New York: Hill and Wang.

Calvert, Randall L. 1995a. "Rational Actors, Equilibrium, and Social Institutions." In *Explaining Social Institutions,* ed. Jack Knight and Itai Sened. Ann Arbor: University of Michigan Press.

Calvert, Randall L. 1995b. "The Rational Choice Theory of Social Institutions: Cooperation, Coordination, and Communication." In *Modern Political Economy: Old Topics, New Directions*, ed. Jeffrey S. Banks and Eric A. Hanushek. Cambridge: Cambridge University Press.

Campbell, Angus, Philip Converse, Warren Miller, and Donald Stokes. 1960. *The American Voter*. New York: Wiley and Sons.

Campbell, Greg. 2002. *Blood Diamonds: Tracing the Deadly Path of the World's Most Valuable Stones*. Boulder: Westview Press.

Caprioli, Mary, and Peter F. Trumbore. 2003. "Ethnic Discrimination and Interstate Violence: Testing the International Impact of Domestic Behavior." *Journal of Peace Research* 40:5–23.

Carbonnier, Gilles. 1998. "Conflict, Postwar Rebuilding, and the Economy: A Critical Review of the Literature." War-Torn Societies Project Occasional Paper No. 2. Geneva: United Nations Research Institute for Social Development.

Carey, Sabine C. 2007. "Rebellion in Africa: Disaggregating the Effect of Political Regimes." *Journal of Peace Research* 44:47–64.

Carment, David, and Frank Harvey. 2001. *Using Force to Prevent Ethnic Violence: An Evaluation of Theory and Evidence*. Westport, CT: Praeger.

Carment, David, and Patrick James. 1995. "Internal Constraints and Interstate Ethnic Conflict: Toward a Crisis-Based Assessment of Irredentism." *Journal of Conflict Resolution* 39:82–109.

Carment, David, and Patrick James. 1997. "Secession and Irredenta in World Politics: The Neglected Interstate Dimension." In *Wars in the Midst of Peace: The International Politics of Ethnic Conflict*, ed. David Carment and Patrick James. Pittsburgh: University of Pittsburgh Press.

Carment, David, Patrick James, and Zeynep Taydas. 2006. *Who Intervenes? Ethnic Conflict and Interstate Crisis*. Columbus: Ohio State University Press.

Carment, David, and Dane Rowlands. 1998. "Three's Company: Evaluating Third-Party Intervention in Intrastate Conflict." *Journal of Conflict Resolution* 42:572–600.

Carothers, Thomas. 1999. *Aiding Democracy Abroad: The Learning Curve*. Washington, DC: Carnegie Endowment for International Peace.

Cetinyan, Rupen. 2002. "Ethnic Bargaining in the Shadow of Third-Party Intervention." *International Organization* 56:645–78.

Chandler, David P. 2000. *A History of Cambodia*. 3rd ed. Boulder: Westview Press.

Chapman, Thomas, and Philip G. Roeder. 2007. "Partition as a Solution to Wars of Nationalism: The Importance of Institutions." *American Political Science Review* 101:677–92.

Chary, Frederick B. 1972. *The Bulgarian Jews and the Final Solution, 1940–1944.* Pittsburgh: University of Pittsburgh Press.

Chazan, Naomi, ed. 1991. *Irredentism and International Politics.* Boulder: Lynne Rienner.

Checkel, Jeffrey, ed. 2005. "International Institutions and Socialization in Europe." Special issue of *International Organization* 55 (4).

Chehabi, H. E., and Juan J. Linz. 1998. "A Theory of Sultanism 1: A Type of Nondemocratic Rule." In *Sultanistic Regimes,* ed. H. E. Chehabi and Juan J. Linz. Baltimore: Johns Hopkins University Press.

Chen, Styen, Norman V. Loayza, and Marta Reynal-Querol. 2007. "The Aftermath of Civil Wars." Post-Conflict Transitions Working Papers No. 4. WPS 4190. Washington, DC: World Bank.

Chiozza, Giacomo, and Hein E. Goemans. 2003. "Peace through Insecurity: Tenure and International Conflict." *Journal of Conflict Resolution* 47:443–67.

Chiozza, Giacomo, and Hein E. Goemans. 2004. "International Conflict and the Tenure of Leaders: Is War Still *Ex Post* Inefficient?" *American Journal of Political Science* 48:604–19.

Chirot, Daniel, and Clark McCauley. 2006. *Why Not Kill Them All? The Logic and Prevention of Mass Political Murder.* Princeton: Princeton University Press.

Chua, Amy. 2003. *World on Fire.* New York: Doubleday.

Cohen, Percy. 1968. *Modern Social Theory.* New York: Basic Books.

Colletta, Nat, Marcus Kostner, and Ingo Wiederhofer. 1996. *Case Studies in War-to-Peace Transition: The Demobilization and Reintegration of Ex-combatants in Ethiopia, Namibia, and Uganda.* Washington, DC: The World Bank.

Collier, Paul. 1999. "On the Economic Consequences of Civil War." *Oxford Economic Papers* 51:168–83.

Collier, Paul. 2000a. "Doing Well out of War: An Economic Perspective." In *Greed and Grievance: Economic Agendas in Civil Wars,* ed. Mats Berdal and David M. Malone. Boulder: Lynne Rienner.

Collier, Paul. 2000b. "Rebellion as a Quasi-criminal Activity." *Journal of Conflict Resolution* 44:839–53.

Collier, Paul, Lani Elliot, Håvard Hegre, Anke Hoeffler, Marta Reynal-Querol, and Nicholas Sambanis. 2003. *Breaking the Conflict Trap: Civil War and Development Policy.* Oxford: Oxford University Press and Washington, DC: World Bank. http://econ.worldbank.org/prr/CivilWarPRR/.

Collier, Paul, and Anke Hoeffler. 1998. "On the Economic Causes of Civil War." *Oxford Economic Papers* 50:563–73.

Collier, Paul, and Anke Hoeffler. 2004. "Greed and Grievance in Civil War." *Oxford Economics Papers* 56:563–95.

Collier, Paul, Anke Hoeffler, and Måns Söderbom. 2004. "On the Duration of Civil War." *Journal of Peace Research* 41:253–74.

Collier, Paul, and Nicholas Sambanis. 2005. *Understanding Civil War: Evidence and Analysis.* 2 vols. Washington, DC: World Bank.

Collier, Ruth Berins, and David Collier. 1991. *Shaping the Political Arena: Critical Junctures, the Labor Movement, and Regime Dynamics in Latin America.* Princeton: Princeton University Press.

Comaroff, John L., and Paul C. Stern. 1994. "New Perspectives on Nationalism and War." *Theory and Society* 23 (1): 35–45.

Connor, Walker. 1969. "Ethnology and the Peace of Southeast Asia." *World Politics* 22:52–86.

Connor, Walker. 1978. "A Nation Is a Nation, Is a State, Is an Ethnic Group, Is a . . ." *Ethnic and Racial Studies* 1:377–400.

Connor, Walker. 1984a. "Eco or Ethno-Nationalism?" *Ethnic and Racial Studies* 7:342–59.

Connor, Walker. 1984b. *The National Question in Marxist-Leninist Theory and Strategy.* Princeton: Princeton University Press.

Connor, Walker. 1994. *Ethnonationalism: The Quest for Understanding.* Princeton: Princeton University Press.

Cortwright, David. 1997. *The Price of Peace: Incentives and International Conflict Prevention.* Lanham, MD: Rowman and Littlefield.

Cosmides, Leda, and John Tooby. 2000. "Evolutionary Psychology and the Emotions." In *Handbook of Emotions,* ed. Michael Lewis and Jeanette Haviland-Jones. 2nd ed. New York: Guilford Press.

Covey, Jock. 2005. "The Custodian of the Peace Process." In *The Quest for Viable Peace: International Intervention and Strategies for Conflict Transformation,* ed. Jock Covey, Michael J. Dziedzic, and Leonard R. Hawley. Washington, DC: United States Institute of Peace Press; Arlington, VA: Association of the United States Army.

Crawford, Neta. 2000. "The Passion of World Politics: Propositions on Emotion and Emotional Relationships." *International Security* 24 (4): 116–56.

Crocker, Chester A., Fen Osler Hampson, and Pamela Aall. 2004. *Taming Intractable Conflicts: Mediation in the Hardest Cases.* Washington, DC: United States Institute of Peace Press.

Cronin, Bruce. 2002. "Creating Stability in the New Europe: The OSCE High Commissioner on National Minorities and the Socialization of Risky States." *Security Studies* 12 (1): 132–63.

Cunningham, David, Kristian Skrede Gleditsch, and Idean Salehyan. 2007. "It Takes Two: A Dyadic Analysis of Civil War Duration and Outcome." Revised version of paper presented at the GROW-net Workshop, Oslo, February 10–11, 2006. http://privatewww.essex.ac.uk/~ksg/papers/CGS_dyadic.pdf.

Dadrian, Vahakn N. 1997. *The History of the Armenian Genocide: Ethnic Conflict from the Balkans to Anatolia to the Caucasus.* Providence, RI: Berghahn Books.

Dahinden, Erwin, Julie Dahlitz, and Nadia Fischer. 2002. *Small Arms and Light Weapons: Legal Aspects of National and International Regulations; A Contribution to the United Nations Conference on the Illicit Trade in Small Arms and Light Weapons in All Its Aspects and Its Follow-up Process.* New York: United Nations.

Dahl, Robert. 1957. "The Concept of Power." *Behavioral Science* 2 (3): 201–15.

D'Amasio, Antonio. 1994. *Descartes' Error: Emotion, Reason, and the Human Brain.* New York: Putnam.

Daoudi, M. S., and M. S. Dajani. 1983. *Economic Sanctions: Ideals and Experience.* London: Routledge and Kegan Paul.

Davenport, Christian A., Will H. Moore, and Steven C. Poe. 2003. "Sometimes You Just Have to Leave: Threat and Refugee Movements, 1964–1989." *International Interactions* 29:27–55.

David, Stephen R. 1989. "Why the Third World Matters." *International Security* 14 (1): 50–85.

David, Stephen R. 1992–93. "Why the Third World Still Matters." *International Security* 17 (3): 127–59.

David, Steven R. 1997. "Internal War: Causes and Cures." *World Politics* 49:552–76.

Davies, James C. 1962. "Toward a Theory of Revolution." *American Sociological Review* 27 (1): 5–19.

Davies, James. 1979. "The J-Curve of Rising and Declining Satisfaction as a Cause of Revolution and Rebellion." In *Violence in America: Historical and Comparative Perspectives,* ed. Ted Robert Gurr and Hugh Davis. Beverly Hills, CA: Sage.

Davies, John L., and Ted Robert Gurr, eds. 1998. *Preventative Measures: Building Risk Assessment and Crisis Early Warning Systems.* Lanham, MD: Rowman and Littlefield.

Davis, David R., and Will H. Moore. 1997. "Ethnicity Matters: Transnational Ethnic Alliances and Foreign Behavior." *International Studies Quarterly* 41:171–84.

Dawidowicz, Lucy. 1986. *The War against the Jews, 1933–1945.* New York: Bantam Books.

DeConde, Alexander. 1992. *Ethnicity, Race, and American Foreign Policy: A History.* Boston: Northeastern University Press.

de Figueiredo, Rui J. P., Jr., and Barry R. Weingast. 1999. "The Rationality of Fear: Political Opportunism and Ethnic Conflict." In *Civil Wars, Insecurity, and Intervention,* ed. Barbara F. Walter and Jack Snyders. New York: Columbia University Press.

de la Garza, Roldofo O., and Harry P. Pachon. 2000. *Latinos and U.S. Foreign Policy.* Lanham, MD: Rowman and Littlefield.

d'Encausse, Hélène Carrère. 1979. *Decline of an Empire: The Soviet Socialist Republics in Revolt.* Trans. Martin Sokolinsky and Henry A. LaFarge. New York: Newsweek Books.

Dempsey, Gary. 2001. *Fool's Errands: America's Recent Encounters with Nation Building.* Washington, DC: Cato Institute.

DeNardo, James. 1985. *Power in Numbers: The Political Strategy of Protest and Rebellion.* Princeton: Princeton University Press.

de Quervain, Dominique J.-F., Urs Fischbacher, Valerie Treyer, Melanie Schellhammer, Ulrich Schnyder, Alfred Buck, and Ernst Fehr. 2004. "The Neural Basis of Altruistic Punishment." *Science* 305:1254–58.

DeRouen, Karl R., and David Sobek. 2004. "The Dynamics of Civil War Duration and Outcome." *Journal of Peace Research* 41:303–20.

Desch, Michael. 1993. *When the Third World Matters: Latin America and United States Grand Strategy.* Baltimore: Johns Hopkins University Press.

Des Forges, Alison. 1999. *"Leave None to Tell the Story": Genocide in Rwanda.* New York: Human Rights Watch.

de Soto, Alvaro, and Graciana del Castillo. 1994. "Obstacles to Peacebuilding." *Foreign Policy* 94:69–74.

de Soysa, Indra. 2002. "Paradise Is a Bazaar? Greed, Creed, and Governance in Civil War, 1989–99." *Journal of Peace Research* 39:395–416.

DeSteno, David N., Nilanjana Dasgupta, Monica Y. Bartlett, and Aida Cajdric. 2004. "Prejudice from Thin Air: The Effect of Emotion on Automatic Intergroup Attitudes." *Psychological Science* 15 (5): 319–24.

Deutsch, Karl. 1966. *Nationalism and Social Communication.* 2nd ed. Cambridge: MIT Press.

Deutsch, Karl W., and J. David Singer. 1964. "Multipolar Power Systems and International Stability." *World Politics* 16:390–406.

Diamond, Larry. 2005. *Squandered Victory: The American Occupation and the Bungled Effort to Bring Democracy to Iraq.* New York: Times Books.

Diehl, Paul F., ed. 1999. *The Road Map to War: Territorial Dimensions of International Conflict.* Nashville: Vanderbilt University Press.

Dinstein, Yoram, and Mala Tabory, eds. 1996. *War Crimes in International Law.* The Hague: Martinus Nijhoff.

Dixit, Avinash K. 2004. *Lawlessness and Economics: Alternative Models of Governance.* Princeton: Princeton University Press.

Donini, Antonio, Norah Niland, and Karin Wermester. 2004. *Nation-Building Unraveled? Aid, Peace, and Justice in Afghanistan.* Bloomfield, CT: Kumarian Press.

Dovidio, John, John Brigham, Blair Johnson, and Samuel Gaertner. 1996. "Stereotyping, Prejudice and Discrimation: Another Look." In *Stereotypes and Stereotyping,* ed. Neil Macrae, Charles Stangor, and Miles Hewstone. New York: Guilford.

Downes, Alexander. 2004. "The Problem with Negotiated Settlements to Ethnic Civil Wars." *Security Studies* 13 (4): 230–79.

Downes, Alexander. 2006. "More Borders, Less Conflict: Partition as a Solution to Ethnic Civil War." *SAIS Review* 26:49–61.

Downs, Anthony. 1957. *An Economic Theory of Democracy.* New York: Harper.

Downs, George W., and David M. Rocke. 1990. *Tacit Bargaining, Arms Races, and Arms Control.* Ann Arbor: University of Michigan Press.

Downs, George W., and David M. Rocke. 1994. "Conflict, Agency, and Gambling for Resurrection." *American Journal of Political Science* 38:362–80.

Downs, George W., and David M. Rocke. 1995. *Optimal Imperfection? Domestic Uncertainty and Institutions in International Relations.* Princeton: Princeton University Press.

Doyle, Michael W. 1986. "Liberalism and World Politics." *American Political Science Review* 80:1151–69.

Doyle, Michael W., and Nicholas Sambanis. 2000. "International Peacebuilding: A Theoretical and Quantitative Analysis." *American Political Science Review* 94:779–801.

Doyle, Michael W., and Nicholas Sambanis. 2006. *Making War and Building Peace: United Nations Peace Operations.* Princeton: Princeton University Press.

Drake, H. A. 2000. *Constantine and the Bishops: The Politics of Intolerance.* Baltimore: Johns Hopkins University Press.

Dubey, Amitabh. 2002. "Domestic Institutions and the Duration of Civil War Settlements." Paper presented at the International Studies Association, New Orleans, March.

Dziedzic, Michael J. 2002. Introduction. In *Policing the New World Disorder: Peace Operations and Public Security,* ed. Robert B. Oakley, Michael J. Daiedzic, and Eliot M. Goldberg. Honolulu: University Press of the Pacific.

Dziedzic, Michael J., and Leonard R. Hawley. 2005. "Linkages among the Transformation Strategies." In *The Quest for Viable Peace: International Intervention and Strategies for Conflict Transformation,* ed. Jock Covey, Michael J. Dziedzic, and Leonard R. Hawley. Washington, DC: United States Institute of Peace Press; Arlington, VA: Association of the United States Army.

Easton, David. 1953. *The Political System: An Inquiry into the State of Political Science.* New York: Knopf.

Eck, Kristine, and Lisa Hultman. 2007. "One-Sided Violence against Civilians in War: Insights from New Fatality Data." *Journal of Peace Research* 44:233–46.

Eckstein, Harry, ed. 1964. *Internal War: Problems and Approaches.* New York: Free Press of Glencoe.

Eckstein, Harry. 1980. "Theoretical Approaches to Explaining Collective Political Violence." In *Handbook of Political Conflict: Theory and Research,* ed. Ted Robert Gurr. New York: Free Press.

Eckstein, Harry, and Ted Robert Gurr. 1975. *Patterns of Authority: A Structural Basis for Political Inquiry.* New York: Wiley.

Eisenstadt, S. N. 1978. *Revolution and the Transformation of Societies: A Comparative Study of Civilizations.* New York: Free Press.

Ekman, Paul, and Wallace Friesen. 1975. *Unmasking the Face: A Guide to Recognizing Emotions from Facial Cues.* Oxford: Prentice-Hall.

Elbadawi, Ibrahim A. 1999. "Civil Wars and Poverty: The Role of External Interventions, Political Rights and Economic Growth." Paper presented at the World Bank conference "Civil Conflicts, Crime and Violence," February, Washington, DC.

Elbadawi, Ibrahim A., and Nicholas Sambanis. 2000a. "External Intervention and the Duration of Civil Wars." World Bank Policy Research Working Paper No. 2433.

Elbadawi, Ibrahim A., and Nicholas Sambanis. 2000b. "Why Are There So Many Conflicts in Africa." *Journal of African Economies* 9 (3): 244–69.

Elbadawi, Ibrahim A., and Nicholas Sambanis. 2002. "How Much War Will We See? Explaining the Prevalence of Civil War." *Journal of Conflict Resolution* 46:307–34.

Ellingsen, Tanja. 2000. "Colorful Community or Ethnic Witches' Brew? Multiethnicity and Domestic Conflict during and after the Cold War." *Journal of Conflict Resolution* 44:228–49.

Ellingsen, Tanja, and Nils Petter Gleditsch. 1997. "Democracy and Armed Conflict in the Third World." In *Causes of Conflict in Third World Countries,* ed. Ketil Volden and Dan Smith. Oslo: North-South Coalition and International Peace Research Institute.

Elman, Colin, and Miriam Fendius Elman. 1997. "Lakatos and Neorealism: A Reply to Vasquez." *American Political Science Review* 91:923–26.

Emerson, Rupert. 1960. *From Empire to Nation: The Rise of Self-Assertion of Asian and African Peoples.* Boston: Beacon Press.

Enders, Walter, and Todd Sandler. 2006. *The Political Economy of Terrorism.* Cambridge: Cambridge University Press.

Esman, Milton J. 1994. *Ethnic Politics.* Ithaca: Cornell University Press.

Evans, Richard J. 2004. *The Coming of the Third Reich.* New York: Penguin.

Fearon, James. 1993. "Ethnic War as a Commitment Problem." Paper presented at the Annual Meeting of American Political Science Association, September.

Fearon, James D. 1994a. "Domestic Political Audiences and the Escalation of International Disputes." *American Political Science Review* 88:577–92.

Fearon, James D. 1994b. "Ethnic War as a Commitment Problem." Paper presented at the Annual Meeting of the American Political Science Association, New York, August 30–September 2.

Fearon, James D. 1995. "Rationalist Explanations for War." *International Organization* 49:379–414.

Fearon, James D. 1998a. "Commitment Problems and the Spread of Ethnic Conflict." In *The International Spread of Ethnic Conflict*, ed. David A. Lake and Donald Rothchild. Princeton: Princeton University Press.

Fearon, James D. 1998b. "Domestic Politics, Foreign Policy, and Theories of International Relations." *Annual Review of Political Science* 1:289–313.

Fearon, James D. 2004. "Why Do Some Civil Wars Last So Much Longer Than Others?" *Journal of Peace Research* 41:275–302.

Fearon, James D. 2005. "Primary Commodity Exports and Civil War." *Journal of Conflict Resolution* 49:483–507.

Fearon, James D., and David D. Laitin. 2000. "Violence and Social Construction of Ethnic Identity." *International Organization* 54:845–77.

Fearon, James D., and David D. Laitin. 2003. "Ethnicity, Insurgency, and Civil War." *American Political Science Review* 97:75–90.

Fehr, Ernst, and Simon Gachter. 2000. "Cooperation and Punishment in Public Goods Experiments." *American Economic Review* 90 (4): 980–94.

Feierabend, Ivo, and Rosalind Feierabend. 1966. "Aggressive Behavior within Polities, 1948–1962." *Journal of Conflict Resolution* 10:249–71.

Feierabend, Ivo, and Rosalind Feierabend. 1972. "Systemic Conditions of Political Aggression: An Application of Frustration-Aggression Theory." In *Anger, Violence, and Politics: Theories and Research*, ed. Ivo K. Feierabend, Rosalind L. Feierabend, and Ted Robert Gurr. Englewood Cliffs, NJ: Prentice Hall.

Fein, Helen. 1979. *Accounting for Genocide: National Responses and Jewish Victimization during the Holocaust.* New York: Free Press.

Fein, Helen. 2000. "The Three P's of Genocide Prevention: With Application to a Genocide Foretold—Rwanda." In *Protection Against Genocide: Mission Impossible?* ed. Neal Riemer. Westport, CT: Praeger.

Fein, Helen. 2004. "To Prevent and to Punish Genocide: Rwanda." Paper presented at "Remembering Rwanda: Conference on the Rwanda Genocide Tenth Anniversary," New York, May 8.

Feldman, Lily Gardner. 1984. *The Special Relationship between West Germany and Israel.* Boston: George Allen and Unwin.

Fey, Mark, and Kristopher W. Ramsay. 2007. "Mutual Optimism and War." Working paper, Department of Politics, Princeton University.

Filippov, Mikhail, Peter C. Ordeshook, and Olga Shvetsova. 2004. *Designing*

Federalism: A Theory of Self-Sustaining Political Institutions. Cambridge: Cambridge University Press.

Fiske, Susan, Lasana Harris, and Amy Cuddy. 2004. "Why Ordinary People Torture Enemy Prisoners." *Science* 306:1482–83.

Fleming, Gerald. 1984. *Hitler and the Final Solution.* Berkeley and Los Angeles: University of California Press.

Foran, John. 2005. *Taking Power: On the Origins of Third World Revolutions.* Cambridge: Cambridge University Press.

Fordham, Benjamin. 1998a. "Partisanship, Macroeconomic Policy, and U.S. Uses of Force, 1949–1994." *Journal of Conflict Resolution* 42:418–39.

Fordham, Benjamin. 1998b. "The Politics of Threat Perception and the Use of Force: A Political Economy Model of U.S. Uses of Force, 1949–1994." *International Studies Quarterly* 42:567–90.

Fortna, Virginia Page. 2004. "Does Peacekeeping Keep Peace? International Intervention and the Duration of Peace after Civil War." *International Studies Quarterly* 48:269–92.

Fortna, Virginia Page. 2007. "Where Have All the Victories Gone? War Outcomes in Historical Perspective." Saltzman Institute of War and Peace Studies, Columbia University.

Fortna, Virginia Page. 2008. *Does Peacekeeping Work? Shaping Belligerents' Choices after Civil War.* Princeton: Princeton University Press.

Fox, Jonathan. 2001. "Two Civilizations and Ethnic Conflict: Islam and the West." *Journal of Peace Research* 38:459–72.

Fox, Jonathan. 2004. "Is Ethnoreligious Conflict a Contagious Disease?" *Studies in Conflict and Terrorism* 27:89–106.

Fraenkel, Ernst. 1941. *The Dual State.* New York: Oxford University Press.

Frederickson, Barbara. 2000. "Extracting Meaning from Past Affective Experiences: The Importance of Peaks, Ends and Specific Emotions." *Cognition and Emotion* 14 (4): 577–606.

Freedom House. 1972–. *Freedom in the World.* Annual.

Freedom House. 2006. "Methodology." www.freedomhouse.org/template.cfm?page=35&year=2006, accessed October 5, 2006.

Freud, Sigmund. 1961. *Civilization and Its Discontents.* Trans. James Strachey. New York: Norton.

Friedländer, Saul. 1997. *Nazi Germany and the Jews.* New York: HarperCollins.

Friedländer, Saul. 2007. *The Years of Extermination: Nazi Germany and the Jews, 1939–1945.* New York: HarperCollins.

Gaddis, John Lewis. 1987. *The Long Peace: Inquiries into the History of the Cold War.* Oxford: Oxford University Press.

Gaer, Felice D. 1997. "UN-Anonymous: Reflections on Human Rights in Peace Negotiations." *Human Rights Quarterly* 19 (1): 1–8.

Gagnon, V. P., Jr. 1994–95. "Ethnic Nationalism and International Conflict: The Case of Serbia." *International Security* 19 (3): 130–66.

Gagnon, V. P., Jr. 2004. *The Myth of Ethnic War: Serbia and Croatia in the 1990s.* Ithaca: Cornell University Press.

Gartner, Scott Sigmund. 1997. *Strategic Assessment in War.* New Haven: Yale University Press.

Gartzke, Erik. 1999. "War Is in the Error Term." *International Organization* 53:567–87.

Gartzke, Erik. 2000. "Preferences and the Democratic Peace." *International Studies Quarterly* 44:191–212.

Gartzke, Erik, and Kristian Skrede Gleditsch. 2006. "Identity and Conflict: Ties That Bind and Differences That Divide." *European Journal of International Relations* 12:53–87.

Gates, Scott. 2002. "Recruitment and Allegiance: The Microfoundations of Rebellion." *Journal of Conflict Resolution* 46:111–30.

Gates, Scott, Håvard Hegre, Mark P. Jones, and Håvard Strand. 2006. "Institutional Inconsistency and Political Instability: Polity Duration, 1800–2000." *American Journal of Political Science* 50:893–908.

Gates, Scott, and Håvard Strand. 2006. "Modeling the Duration of Civil Wars: Measurement and Estimation Issues." Chap. 3 in Strand (2006).

Gaubatz, Kurt Taylor. 1999. *Elections and War.* Stanford: Stanford University Press.

Gault, Barbara, and John Sabini. 2000. "The Roles of Empathy, Anger and Gender in Predicting Attitudes toward Punitive, Reparative, and Preventive Public Policies." *Cognition and Emotion* 14 (4): 495–520.

Gaventa, John. 1980. *Power and Powerlessness: Quiescence and Rebellion in an Appalachian Valley.* Urbana: University of Illinois Press.

Geddes, Barbara. 2003. *Paradigms and Sand Castles: Theory Building and Research Design in Comparative Politics.* Ann Arbor: University of Michigan Press.

Geertz, Clifford. 1963. "The Integrative Revolution." In *Old Societies and New States: The Quest for Modernity in Asia and Africa,* ed. Clifford Geertz. New York: New Press.

Gellner, Ernest. 1983. *Nations and Nationalism.* Ithaca: Cornell University Press.

George, Alexander L., and Juliette L. George. 1964. *Woodrow Wilson and Colonel House.* New York: Dover.

Gerlach, Christian. 2000. "The Wannsee Conference, the Fate of German Jews, and Hitler's Decision in Principle to Exterminate All European Jews." In *The Holocaust: Origins, Implementation, Aftermath,* ed. Omer Bartov. New York: Routledge.

Ghobarah, Hazeem Adam, Paul Huth, and Bruce Russett. 2003. "Civil Wars

Kill and Maim People—Long after the Shooting Stops." *American Political Science Review* 97:189–202.

Gibson, James L. 2004. *Overcoming Apartheid: Can Truth Reconcile a Divided Nation?* New York: Russell Sage Foundation.

Gilbert, Daniel, Elizabeth Pinel, Timothy Wilson, Stephen Blumberg, and Thalia Wheatley. 1998. "Immune Neglect: A Source of Durability Bias in Affective Forecasting." *Journal of Personality and Social Psychology* 75 (3): 617–38.

Gilbert, Martin. 1989. *The Second World War: A Complete History.* New York: Henry Holt.

Glaser, Charles L. 1992. "Political Consequences of Military Strategy: Expanding and Refining the Spiral and Deterrence Models." *World Politics* 44:497–538.

Glaser, Charles L. 1997. "The Security Dilemma Revisited." *World Politics* 50:171–201.

Gleditsch, Kristian Skrede. 2002a. *All International Politics Is Local: The Diffusion of Conflict, Integration, and Democratization.* Ann Arbor: University of Michigan Press.

Gleditsch, Kristian Skrede. 2002b. "Expanded Trade and GDP Data." *Journal of Conflict Resolution* 46:712–24.

Gleditsch, Kristian Skrede. 2007. "Transnational Dimensions of Civil War." *Journal of Peace Research* 44:293–309.

Gleditsch, Kristian Skrede, and Michael D. Ward. 1997. "Double Take: A Re-Examination of Democracy and Autocracy in Modern Polities." *Journal of Conflict Resolution* 41:361–83.

Gleditsch, Kristian Skrede, and Michael D. Ward. 1999. "Interstate System Membership: A Revised List of the Independent States since 1816." *International Interactions* 25 (4): 393–413.

Gleditsch, Kristian Skrede, and Michael D. Ward. 2006. "The Diffusion of Democracy and the International Context of Democratization." *International Organization* 60:911–33.

Gleditsch, Nils Petter, and Håvard Hegre. 1997. "Peace and Democracy—Three Levels of Analysis." *Journal of Conflict Resolution* 41:283–310.

Gleditsch, Nils Petter, Peter Wallensteen, Mikael Eriksson, Margareta Sollenberg, and Håvard Strand. 2002. "Armed Conflict 1946–2001: A New Dataset." *Journal of Peace Research* 39:615–37. Current version is at http://www.prio.no/cwp/ArmedConflict/.

Glenny, Misha. 1992. *The Fall of Yugoslavia.* London: Penguin.

Goemans, Hein E. 2000. *War and Punishment.* Princeton: Princeton University Press.

Goldberg, David Howard. 1990. *Foreign Policy and Ethnic Interest Groups: American and Canadian Jews Lobby for Israel.* New York: Greenwood.

Golder, Matt. 2005. "Democratic Electoral Systems around the World, 1946–2000." *Electoral Studies* 24 (1): 103–21.

Goldstein, Joshua S., and John R. Freeman. 1991. "U.S.-Soviet-Chinese Relations: Routine, Reciprocity, or Rational Expectations?" *American Political Science Review* 85:17–35.

Goldstone, Jack A. 1991. *Revolution and Rebellion in the Early Modern World.* Berkeley and Los Angeles: University of California Press.

Gonzalez-Perez, Margaret. 2006. "Guerrilleras in Latin America: Domestic and International Roles." *Journal of Peace Research* 43:313–29.

Goodwin, Jeff. 1997. "State-Centered Approaches to Social Revolutions: Strengths and Limitations of a Theoretical Tradition." In *Theorizing Revolutions,* ed. John Foran. London: Routledge.

Goodwin, Jeff. 2001a. "Is the Age of Revolution Over?" In *Revolution: International Dimensions,* ed. Mark Katz. Washington, DC: CQ Press.

Goodwin, Jeff. 2001b. *No Other Way Out: States and Revolutionary Movements, 1945–1991.* Cambridge: Cambridge University Press.

Goodwin, Jeff, and Theda Skocpol. 1989. "Explaining Revolutions in the Contemporary World." *Politics and Society* 17 (4): 489–509.

Goreux, Louis. 2001. "Conflict Diamonds." Africa Region Working Paper Series No. 13, World Bank.

Gourevitch, Peter. 1979. "The Reemergence of Peripheral Nationalisms: Some Comparative Speculations on the Spatial Distribution of Political Leadership and Economic Growth." *Comparative Studies in Society and History* 21 (3): 303–22.

Grant, Andrew J., and Ian Taylor. 2004. "Global Governance and Conflict Diamonds: The Kimberley Process and the Quest for Clean Gems." *Round Table* 375:385–401.

Greene, Joshua D., R. Brian Sommerville, Leigh E. Nystrom, John M. Darley, and Jonathan D. Cohen. 2001. "An fMRI Investigation of Emotional Engagement in Moral Judgement." *Science* 293:2105–8.

Greif, Avner. 2005. "Commitment, Coercion, and Markets: The Nature and Dynamics of Institutions Supporting Exchange." In *Handbook of New Institutional Economics,* ed. Claude Ménard and Mary M. Shirley. Dordrecht: Springer.

Greif, Avner. 2006. *Institutions and the Path to the Modern Political Economy: Lessons from Medieval Trade.* Cambridge: Cambridge University Press.

Grieco, Joseph M. 1988. "Realist Theory and the Problem of International Cooperation: Analysis with an Amended Prisoner's Dilemma Model." *Journal of Politics* 50:600–624.

Grinker, Roy, and, John Spiegel. 1945. *Men under Stress.* Philadelphia: Blackiston.

Gross, Jan T. 2006. *Fear: Anti-Semitism in Poland after Auschwitz.* New York: Random House.

Gulick, Edward Vose. 1955. *Europe's Classical Balance of Power.* Ithaca: Cornell University Press.

Gurr, Ted Robert. 1968. "A Causal Model of Civil Strife: A Comparative Analysis Using New Indices." *American Political Science Review* 62:1104–24.

Gurr, Ted Robert. 1970. *Why Men Rebel.* Princeton: Princeton University Press.

Gurr, Ted Robert. 1981. "The Conflict Process: A Formal Model." *Journal of Conflict Resolution* 25:3–29.

Gurr, Ted Robert. 1986. "Forecasting Internal Conflict: A Competitive Evaluation of Empirical Theories." *Comparative Political Studies* 19:3–38.

Gurr, Ted Robert. 1988. "On the Outcomes of Violent Conflict." In *Handbook of Political Conflict: Theory and Research,* Ted Robert Gurr. New York: Free Press.

Gurr, Ted Robert. 1990. "Ethnic Warfare and the Changing Priorities of Global Security." *Mediterranean Quarterly* 1 (1): 82–98.

Gurr, Ted Robert. 1993a. *Minorities at Risk: A Global View of Ethnopolitical Conflicts.* Washington, DC: United States Institute of Peace Press.

Gurr, Ted Robert. 1993b. "Why Minorities Rebel: A Global Analysis of Communal Mobilization and Conflict since 1945." *International Political Science Review* 14 (2): 161–201.

Gurr, Ted Robert. 2000. *People versus States: Minorities at Risk in the New Century.* Washington, DC: United States Institute of Peace Press.

Gurr, Ted Robert, and Mark Irving Lichbach. 1979. "Forecasting Domestic Political Conflict." In *To Augur Well: Forecasting in the Social Sciences,* ed. J. David Singer and Michael D. Wallace. Beverly Hills, CA: Sage.

Gurr, Ted Robert, and Will H. Moore. 1997. "Ethnopolitical Rebellion: A Cross-Sectional Analysis of the 1980s with Risk Assessment for the 1990s." *American Journal of Political Science* 41:1079–1103.

Hall, Peter A., and Rosemary C. R. Taylor. 1996. "Political Science and the Three New Institutionalisms." *Political Studies* 44:936–57.

Hamilton, Alexander, John Jay, and James Madison. 1961. *The Federalist: A Commentary on the Constitution of the United States.* New York: Random House.

Haney, Craig, Curtis Banks, and Philip Zimbardo. 1973. "Interpersonal Dynamics in a Simulated Prison." *International Journal of Criminology and Penology* 1:57–73.

Haney, Patrick J., and Walt Vanderbush. 1999. "The Rope of Ethnic Interest Groups in US Foreign Policy: The Case of the Cuban American National Foundation." *International Studies Quarterly* 43:341–61.

Haney, Craig, and Philip Zimbardo. 1977. "The Socialization into Criminality:

On Becoming a Prisoner and a Guard." In *Law, Justice, and the Individual in Society: Psychological and Legal Issues,* ed. J. Tapp and F. Levine. New York: Holt, Rinehart and Winston.

Harbom, Lotta, Stina Högbladh, and Peter Wallensteen. 2006. "Armed Conflict and Peace Agreements." *Journal of Peace Research* 43:617–31.

Harbom, Lotta, and Peter Wallensteen. 2005. "Armed Conflict and Its International Dimensions, 1946–2004." *Journal of Peace Research* 42:623–35.

Hardin, Russell. 1995. *One for All: The Logic of Group Conflict.* Princeton: Princeton University Press.

Harff, Barbara. 2003. "No Lessons Learned from the Holocaust? Assessing the Risk of Genocide and Political Mass Murder since 1955." *American Political Science Review* 97:57–73.

Harff, Barbara, and Ted Robert Gurr. 1988. "Toward Empirical Theory of Genocides and Politicides: Identification and Measurement of Cases since 1945." *International Studies Quarterly* 32:359–71.

Harff, Barbara, and Ted Robert Gurr. 1998. "Systematic Early Warning of Humanitarian Disasters." *Journal of Peace Research* 35:551–79.

Harris, Geoff. 1999. "Peacebuilding and Reconstruction after War in Developing Countries." *Journal of Interdisciplinary Economics* 10:107–22.

Hart, Allen, Paul Whalen, Lisa Shin, Sean McInerney, Hakan Fischer, and Scott Rauch. 2000. "Differential Response in the Human Amygdala to Racial Outgroup vs. Ingroup Face Stimuli." *Neuroreport* 11 (11): 2351–54.

Hartlyn, Jonathan. 1993. "Civil Violence and Conflict Resolution: The Case of Colombia." In *Stopping the Killing: How Civil Wars End,* ed. Roy Licklider. New York: New York University Press.

Hartz, Halvor A., Laura Mercean, and Clint Williamson. 2005. "Safeguarding a Viable Peace: Institutionalizing the Rule of Law." In *The Quest for Viable Peace: International Intervention and Strategies for Conflict Transformation,* ed. Jock Covey, Michael J. Dziedzic, and Leonard R. Hawley. Washington, DC: United States Institute of Peace Press; Arlington, VA: Association of the United States Army.

Hartzell, Caroline. 1999. "Explaining the Stability of Negotiated Settlements to Civil Wars." *Journal of Conflict Resolution* 43:3–22.

Hartzell, Caroline A. 2004. "Civil War Settlements and Enduring Peace: A Test of the Wagner and Licklider Hypotheses." Paper presented at the Annual Meeting of the Midwest Political Science Association, Chicago.

Hartzell, Caroline A., and Matthew Hoddie. 2003. "Institutionalizing Peace: Power Sharing and Post-Civil War Conflict Management." *American Journal of Political Science* 47:318–32.

Hartzell, Caroline A., and Matthew Hoddie. 2007. *Crafting Peace: Power Sharing Institutions and the Negotiated Settlement of Civil Wars.* College Park: Pennsylvania State University Press.

Hayner, Priscilla B. 2001. *Unspeakable Truths: Confronting State Terror and Atrocity.* New York: Routledge.

Hechter, Michael. 1974. *Internal Colonialism.* Berkeley and Los Angeles: University of California Press.

Hegre, Håvard. 2000. "Development and the Liberal Peace: What Does It Take to Be a Trading State?" *Journal of Peace Research* 37:5–30.

Hegre, Håvard. 2003. "Disentangling Democracy, Development as Determinants of Armed Conflict." Paper presented at the Annual Meeting of the International Studies Association, Portland, OR, February 25–March 1. www.prio.no/files/file40692_ddcwwb.pdf.

Hegre, Håvard. 2004. "The Duration and Termination of Civil War." *Journal of Peace Research* 41:243–52.

Hegre, Håvard. 2005. "Development and the Liberal Peace." *Nordic Journal of Political Economy* 31 (1): 17–46.

Hegre, Håvard, Tanja Ellingsen, Nils Petter Gleditsch, and Scott Gates. 2001. "Toward a Democratic Civil Peace? Democracy, Political Change, and Civil War, 1816–1992." *American Political Science Review* 95:34–48.

Hegre, Håvard, Ranveig Gissinger, and Nils Petter Gleditsch. 2003. "Globalization and Internal Conflict." In *Globalization and Armed Conflict,* ed. Gerald Schneider, Katherine Barbieri, and Nils Petter Gleditsch. Lanham, MD: Rowman and Littlefield.

Hegre, Håvard, and Nicholas Sambanis. 2006. "Sensitivity Analysis of the Empirical Literature on Civil War Onset." *Journal of Conflict Resolution* 50:508–35.

Henderson, Errol A. 1997. "Culture or Contiguity: Ethnic Conflict, the Similarity of States, and the Onset of War, 1820–1989." *Journal of Conflict Resolution* 41:649–69.

Henderson, Errol A. 2005. "Not Letting Evidence Get in the Way of Assumptions: Testing the Clash of Civilizations Thesis with More Recent Data." *International Politics* 42:458–69.

Henderson, Errol A., and J. David Singer. 2000. "Civil War in the Post-colonial World, 1946–92." *Journal of Peace Research* 37:275–99.

Henderson, Errol A., and Richard Tucker. 2001. "Clear and Present Strangers: The Clash of Civilizations and International Conflict." *International Studies Quarterly* 45:317–38.

Heraclides, Alexis. 1991. *The Self-Determination of Minorities in International Politics.* London: Frank Cass.

Herbst, Jeffrey. 1989. "The Creation and Maintenance of National Boundaries in Africa." *International Organization* 43:673–92.

Hibbs, Douglas A. 1973. *Mass Political Violence: A Cross-National Causal Analysis.* New York: Wiley.

Hilberg, Raul. 1961. *The Destruction of the European Jews*. Chicago: Quadrangle Books.

Hilberg, Raul. 2003. *The Destruction of the European Jews*. 3rd ed. New Haven: Yale University Press.

Hill, Stuart, and Donald Rothchild. 1986. "The Contagion of Political Conflict in Africa and the World." *Journal of Conflict Resolution* 30:716–35.

Hill, Stuart, and Donald Rothchild. 1992. "The Impact of Regime on the Diffusion of Political Conflict." In *The Internationalization of Communal Strife*, ed. Manus I. Midlarsky. London: Routledge.

Hill, Stuart, Donald Rothchild, and Colin Cameron. 1998. "Tactical Information and the Diffusion of Peaceful Protests." In *The International Spread of Ethnic Conflict: Fear, Diffusion, and Escalation*, ed. David Lake and Donald Rothchild. Princeton: Princeton University Press.

Hironaka, Ann. 2005. *Neverending Wars: The International Community, Weak States, and the Perpetuation of Civil Wars*. Cambridge: Harvard University Press.

Hirsch, John L., and Robert B. Oakley. 1995. *Somalia and Operation Restore Hope: Reflections on Peacemaking and Peacekeeping*. Washington, DC: United States Institute of Peace Press.

Hitler, Adolf. 2000. *Hitler's Table Talk, 1941–1944: His Private Conversations*. Trans. Norman Cameron and R. H. Stevens. New York: Enigma Books.

Hobsbawm, Eric J. 1990. *Nations and Nationalism since 1780: Programme, Myth, Reality*. Cambridge: Cambridge University Press.

Hockenos, Paul. 2003. *Homeland Calling: Exile Patriotism and the Balkan Wars*. Ithaca: Cornell University Press.

Horowitz, Donald L. 1985. *Ethnic Groups in Conflict*. Berkeley and Los Angeles: University of California Press.

Horowitz, Donald L. 2001. *The Deadly Ethnic Riot*. Berkeley and Los Angeles: University of California Press.

Howard, Lise Morjé. 2008. *UN Peacekeeping in Civil Wars*. New York: Cambridge University Press.

Hroch, Miroslav. 1985. *Social Preconditions of National Revival in Europe*. Cambridge: Cambridge University Press.

Hufbauer, Gary Clyde, Jeffrey J. Schott, and Kimberly Ann Elliott. 1990. *Economic Sanctions Reconsidered*. Washington, DC: Institute for International Economics.

"Human Rights in Peace Negotiations." 1996. *Human Rights Quarterly* 18 (2): 249–58.

Human Rights Watch. 2006. "Funding the 'Final War': LTTE Intimidation and Extortion in the Tamil Diaspora." *Human Rights Watch Report* 18 (1): 1–47.

Human Security Centre. 2005. *The Human Security Report 2005.* Oxford: Oxford University Press.

Humphreys, Macartan. 2003. "Economics and Violent Conflicts." Unpublished manuscript, Harvard University.

Humphreys, Macartan. 2005. "Natural Resources and Armed Conflicts: Issues and Options." In *Profiting from Peace: Managing the Resource Dimensions of Civil War,* ed. Karen Ballentine and Heiko Nitzschke. Boulder: Lynne Rienner.

Huntington, Samuel P. 1968. *Political Order in Changing Societies.* New Haven: Yale University Press.

Huntington, Samuel P. 1991. *The Third Wave: Democratization in the Late Twentieth Century.* Norman: University of Oklahoma Press.

Huntington, Samuel P. 1993. "The Clash of Civilizations?" *Foreign Affairs* 72 (3): 22–28.

Huth, Paul K. 1998. *Standing Your Ground: Territorial Disputes and International Conflict.* Ann Arbor: University of Michigan Press.

Huth, Paul K. 2004. "Research Design in Testing Theories of International Conflict." In *Models, Numbers, and Cases: Methods for Studying International Relations,* ed. Detlef F. Sprinz and Yael Wolinsky-Nahmias. Ann Arbor: University of Michigan Press.

Huth, Paul K., and Todd L. Allee. 2002. *The Democratic Peace and Territorial Conflict in the Twentieth Century.* Cambridge: Cambridge University Press.

Iatrides, John O. 1993. "The Doomed Revolution: Communist Insurgency in Postwar Greece." *Stopping the Killing: How Civil Wars End,* ed. Roy Licklider. New York: New York University Press.

Iklé, Fred Charles. 1971. *Every War Must End.* New York: Columbia University Press.

International Commission on Intervention and State Sovereignty 2001. *The Responsibility to Protect.* 2 vols. Ottawa: International Development Research Center.

Ioanid, Radu. 2000. *The Holocaust in Romania: The Destruction of Jews and Gypsies under the Antonescu Regime, 1940–1944.* Chicago: Ivan R. Dee.

Isaacs, Harold R. 1970. *Idols of the Tribe: Group Identity and Political Change.* New York: Harper and Row.

Jäckel, Eberhard. 1981. *Hitler's World View: A Blueprint for Power.* Trans. Herbert Arnold. Cambridge: Harvard University Press.

Jackman, Robert W. 1993. "Rationality and Political Participation." *American Journal of Political Science* 37:279–90.

Jackson, Robert H., and Carl G. Rosberg. 1982. "Why Africa's Weak States Persist: The Empirical and the Juridical in Statehood." *World Politics* 35:1–24.

Jaggers, Keith, and Ted Robert Gurr. 1995. "Tracking Democracy's Third Wave with the Polity III Data." *Journal of Peace Research* 32:469–82.

Jakobsen, Monica Sofie. 1998. "Peace and Prosperity or Democratic Chaos? A Study of Political Transitions and Civil War 1945–92." Department of Sociology and Political Science, Norwegian University of Science and Technology, Dragvoll.

Janis, Irving, and Leon Mann. 1977. *Decision Making.* New York: Free Press.

Jarstad Anna K., and Timothy D. Sisk. 2008. *From War to Democracy: Dilemmas of Peacebuilding.* New York: Cambridge University Press.

Jelavich, Barbara. 1983. *History of the Balkans.* Vol. 2. Cambridge: Cambridge University Press.

Jenne, Erin K. 2004. "A Bargaining Theory of Minority Demands." *International Studies Quarterly* 48:729–54.

Jenne, Erin K. 2007. *Ethnic Bargaining: The Paradox of Minority Empowerment.* Ithaca: Cornell University Press.

Jenne, Erin K. Forthcoming. "How Ethnic Partition Perpetuates Conflict: The Consequences of De Facto Partition in Bosnia and Kosovo." *Regional and Federal Studies.*

Jenne, Erin K., Stephen M. Saideman, and Will Lowe. 2007. "Separatism as a Bargaining Posture: The Role of Leverage in Minority Radicalization." *Journal of Peace Research* 44:539–58.

Jeong, Ho-won. 2005. *Peacebuilding in Postconflict Societies: Strategy and Process.* Boulder: Lynne Rienner.

Jervis, Robert. 1978. "Cooperation under the Security Dilemma." *World Politics* 30:167–213.

Jervis, Robert. 1992. "Political Implications of Loss Aversion." *Political Psychology* 13 (2): 187–204.

Jervis, Robert. 1993. "The Drunkard's Search." In *Explorations in Political Psychology,* ed. Shanto Iyengar and William McGuire. Durham, NC: Duke University Press.

Johnson, Eric, and Amos Tversky. 1983. "Affect, Generalization, and the Perception of Risk." *Journal of Personality and Social Psychology* 45 (1): 20–31.

Jones, Bruce D. 2002. "The Challenges of Strategic Coordination." In *Ending Civil Wars: The Implementation of Peace Agreements,* ed. Stephen John Stedman, Donald Rothchild, and Elizabeth M. Cousens. Boulder: Lynne Rienner.

Judah, Tim. 2000. *The Serbs: History, Myth, and the Destruction of Yugoslavia.* New Haven: Yale University Press.

Junne, Gerd, and Willemijn Verkoren. 2005. *Postconflict Development: Meeting New Challenges.* Boulder: Lynne Rienner.

Jutikkala, Eino, and Kauko Pirinen. 1974. *A History of Finland.* Rev. ed. Trans. Paul Sjöblom. New York: Praeger.

Kahneman, Daniel. 2000. Preface. In *Choices, Values, and Frames,* ed. Daniel Kahneman and Amos Tversky. New York: Russell Sage Foundation; Cambridge: Cambridge University Press.

Kahneman, Daniel, Ed Diener, and Norbert Schwarz, eds. 2003. *Well-Being: The Foundations of Hedonic Psychology.* New York: Russell Sage Foundation.

Kahneman, Daniel, and Amos Tversky. 1979. "Prospect Theory: An Analysis of Decision under Risk." *Econometrica* 47:263–91.

Kahneman, Daniel, and Amos Tversky. 1984. "Choices, Values, and Frames." *American Psychologist* 39 (4): 341–50.

Kahneman, Daniel, and Amos Tversky. 1992. "Advances in Prospect Theory: Cumulative Representation of Uncertainty." *Journal of Risk and Uncertainty* 5 (4): 297–324.

Kahneman, Daniel, and Amos Tversky, eds. 2000. *Choices, Values, and Frames.* New York: Russell Sage Foundation; Cambridge: Cambridge University Press.

Kalyvas, Stathis N. 2004. "The Urban Bias in Research on Civil Wars." *Security Studies* 13 (3): 160–90.

Kalyvas, Stathis N. 2008. "Fear, Preemption, Retaliation: An Emperical Test of the Security Dilemma." In *Intra-State Conflict, Government and Security: Dilemmas of Deterrence and Assurance,* ed. Stephen M. Saideman and Marie-Joëlle Zahar. London and New York: Routledge.

Kang, Seonjou. 2008. "Post-Conflict Economic Development Sustaining the Peace." In *Conflict Prevention and Peacebuilding in Post-War Societies: Sustaining the Peace,* ed. T. David Mason and James D. Meernik. London and New York: Routledge.

Kang, Seonjou, and James Meernik. 2005. "Civil War Destruction and the Prospects for Economic Growth." *Journal of Politics* 67:88–109.

Kaplan, Robert D. 1993. *Balkan Ghosts: A Journey through History.* New York: Vintage.

Kaplan, Robert D. 1994. "The Coming Anarchy: How Scarcity, Crime, Overpopulation, Tribalism and Disease Are Rapidly Destroying the Social Fabric of Our Planet." *Atlantic Monthly,* February, 44–76.

Karklins, Rasma. 1986. *Ethnic Relations in the USSR: The View from Below.* Boston: Unwin and Hyman.

Katzenstein, Peter J. 1985. *Small States in World Markets: Industrial Policy in Europe.* Ithaca: Cornell University Press.

Katznelson, Ira. Forthcoming. In *Comparative Politics: Rationality, Culture, and Structure.* ed. Mark I. Lichbach and Alan S. Zuckerman. 2nd ed. Cambridge: Cambridge University Press.

Katznelson, Ira, and Helen V. Milner, eds. 2002. *Political Science: The State of the Discipline.* New York: Norton.

Katznelson, Ira, and Barry R. Weingast, eds. 2005. *Preferences and Situations.* New York: Russell Sage Foundation.

Kaufman, Stuart J. 1995. "The Irresistible Force and the Imperceptible Object: The Yugoslav Breakup and Western Policy." *Security Studies* 4 (2): 281–329.

Kaufman, Stuart J. 1996. "Spiraling to Ethnic War: Elites, Masses and Moscow in Moldova's Civil War." *International Security* 21 (2): 108–38.

Kaufman, Stuart J. 2001. *Modern Hatreds: The Symbolic Politics of Ethnic War* Ithaca: Cornell University Press.

Kaufmann, Chaim D. 1996a. "Intervention in Ethnic and Ideological Civil Wars." *Security Studies* 6 (1): 62–104.

Kaufmann, Chaim D. 1996b. "Possible and Impossible Solutions to Ethnic Civil Wars." *International Security* 20 (4): 136–75.

Kaufmann, Chaim D. 1998. "When All Else Fails: Ethnic Population Transfers and Partitions in the Twentieth Century." *International Security* 23 (2): 120–56.

Kaufmann, Chaim D. 2005. "Rational Choice and Progress in the Study of Ethnic Conflict: A Review Essay." *Security Studies* 14 (1): 178–207.

Keeley, L. 1996. *War before Civilization.* Oxford: Oxford University Press.

Kelley, Judith G. 2004a. *Ethnic Politics in Europe: The Power of Norms and Incentives.* Princeton: Princeton University Press.

Kelley, Judith G. 2004b. "International Actors on the Domestic Scene: Membership Conditionality and Socialization by International Institutions." *International Organization* 58:425–57.

Kennedy, Robert. 1969. *Thirteen Days: A Memoir of the Cuban Missile Crisis.* New York: Norton.

Keohane, Robert O., and Joseph S. Nye Jr. 1977. *Power and Interdependence: World Politics in Transition.* Boston: Little, Brown.

Kier, Elizabeth. 1998. "Homosexuals in the U.S. Military: Open Integration and Combat Effectiveness." *International Security* 23 (2): 5–39.

Kiernan, Ben. 1996. *The Pol Pot Regime: Race, Power, and Genocide in Cambodia under the Khmer Rouge, 1975–79.* New Haven: Yale University Press.

Kim, Woosang, and James D. Morrow. 1992. "When Do Power Shifts Lead to War?" *American Journal of Political Science* 36:896–922.

King, Charles, and Neil J. Melvin. 1999. "Diaspora Politics: Ethnic Linkages, Foreign Policy, and Security in Eurasia." 24:108–38.

King, Gary, Robert O. Keohane, and Sidney Verba. 1993. *Designing Social Inquiry.* Princeton: Princeton University Press.

Kirby, D. G. 1979. *Finland in the Twentieth Century.* Minneapolis: University of Minnesota Press.

Knight, Mark. 2004. "Guns, Camps and Cash: Disarmament, Demobilization and Reinsertion of Former Combatants in Transitions from War to Peace." *Journal of Peace Research* 41:499–516.

Knutson, Brian. 2004. "Sweet Revenge?" *Science* 305:1246–47.

Kohli, Atul. 2002. "State, Society, and Development." In *Political Science: The State of the Discipline,* ed. Ira Katznelson and Helen V. Milner. New York: Norton.

Kopstein, Jeffrey, and Mark Irving Lichbach. 2005. *Comparative Politics: Institutions, Identities, and Interests in Today's Small World.* 2nd ed. Cambridge: Cambridge University Press.

Körding, Konrad P., and Daniel M. Wolpert. 2004. "Bayesian Integration Is Sensorimotor Learning." *Nature* 427:244–47.

Kornprobst, Markus. 2007. "Dejustification and Dispute Settlement: Irredentism in European Politics." *European Journal of International Relations* 13:459–87.

Krain, Matthew. 1997. "State-Sponsored Mass Murder: The Onset and Severity of Genocides and Politicides." *Journal of Conflict Resolution* 41:1–24.

Krain, Matthew. 2005. "International Intervention and the Severity of Genocides and Politicides." *International Studies Quarterly* 49:363–88.

Krain, Matthew, and Marissa Edson Myers. 1997. "Democracy and Civil War: A Note on the Democratic Peace Proposition." *International Interactions* 23 (1): 109–18.

Krasner, Stephen D. 1999. *Sovereignty: Organized Hypocrisy.* Princeton: Princeton University Press.

Krause, Volker, and Susumu Suzuki. 2005. "Causes of Civil War in Asia and Sub-Saharan Africa: A Comparison." *Social Science Quarterly* 86 (1): 160–77.

Kumar, Radha. 1997. "The Troubled History of Partition." *Foreign Affairs* 76 (1): 22–34.

Kupchan, Charles A., ed. 1995. *Nationalism and Nationalities in the New Europe.* Ithaca: Cornell University Press.

Kuran, Timur. 1998. "Ethnic Dissimilation and Its International Relations." In *Ethnic Conflict: Fear, Diffusion, and Escalation,* ed. David A. Lake and Donald Rothchild. Princeton: Princeton University Press.

Kurlantzick, Joshua. 2006. "Global Gun Rights? How the National Rifle Association Is Promoting a Universal Right to Bear Arms." *New York Times Magazine,* April 17, 28.

Kurzban, Robert, John Tooby, and Leda Cosmides. 2001. "Can Race Be Erased? Coalitional Computation and Social Categorization." *Proceedings of the National Academy of Sciences* 98 (26): 15387–92.

Kydd, Andrew. 2006. "When Can Mediators Build Trust?" *American Political Science Review* 100:449–62.

Kymlicka, Will. 1998. *Theories of Secessionism.* London: Routledge.

Lacina, Bethany. 2006. "Explaining the Severity of Civil War." *Journal of Conflict Resolution* 50:276–89.

Lacina, Bethany, and Nils Petter Gleditsch. 2005. "Monitoring Trends in Global Combat: A New Dataset of Battle Deaths." *European Journal of Population* 21 (2–3): 145–66.

Laitin, David D. 1986. *Hegemony and Culture: Politics and Religious Change among the Yoruba*. Chicago: University of Chicago Press.

Laitin, David D. 1992. *Language Repertoires and State Construction in Africa*. Cambridge: Cambridge University Press.

Laitin, David D. 2001. "Secessionist Rebellion in the Former Soviet Union." *Comparative Political Studies* 34:839–61.

Lake, David A. 1992. "Powerful Pacifists: Democratic States and War." *American Political Science Review* 86:24–37.

Lake, David A. 2002. "Rational Extremism: Understanding Terrorism in the Twenty-first Century." *Dialogue-IO*, Spring, 15–29.

Lake, David A. 2003. "International Relations Theory and Internal Conflict: Insights from the Interstices." *International Studies Review* 5 (4): 81–89.

Lake, David A., and Matthew A. Baum. 2001. "The Invisible Hand of Democracy: Political Control and the Provision of Public Service." *Comparative Political Studies* 34:587–621.

Lake, David A., and Donald Rothchild. 1996. "Containing Fear: The Origins and Management of Ethnic Conflict." *International Security* 21 (2): 41–75.

Lake, David A., and Donald Rothchild, eds. 1998a. *The International Spread of Ethnic Conflict: Fear, Diffusion, and Escalation*. Princeton: Princeton University Press.

Lake, David A., and Donald Rothchild. 1998b. "Spreading Fear: The Genesis of Transnational Ethnic Conflict." In *The International Spread of Ethnic Conflict: Fear, Diffusion, and Escalation*, ed. David A. Lake and Donald Rothchild. Princeton: Princeton University Press.

Lang, Anthony F., Jr. 2003. *Just Intervention*. Washington, DC: Georgetown University Press.

Langlois, Jean-Pierre P., and Catherine C. Langlois. 2006. "Holding Out for Concession: The Quest for Gain in the Negotiation of International Agreements." *International Interactions* 32 (3): 261–93.

Laponce, Jean. 1987. *Languages and Their Territories*. Trans. Anthony Martin-Sperry. Toronto: University of Toronto Press.

Lasswell, Harold D. 1930. *Psychopathology and Politics*. Chicago: University of Chicago Press.

Lasswell, Harold D. 1948. *Power and Personality*. New York: Norton.

Lasswell, Harold D. 1950. *Politics: Who Gets What, When, How*. New York: P. Smith.

Lavy, George. 1996. *Germany and Israel: Moral Debt and National Interest.* London: Frank Cass.

Le Billon, Philippe. 2001. "The Political Ecology of War: Natural Resources and Armed Conflict." *Political Geography* 20:561–84.

Leeds, Brett Ashley, and David R. Davis. 1997. "Domestic Political Vulnerability and International Disputes." *Journal of Conflict Resolution* 41:814–34.

Leff, Carol Skalnik. 1999. "Democratization and Disintegration in Multi-national States: The Breakup of the Communist Federations." *World Politics* 51:205–35.

LeMay, Curtis R., with Dale O. Smith. 1968. *America Is in Danger.* New York: Funk and Wagnalls.

Levendel, Isaac. 1999. *Not the Germans Alone: A Son's Search for the Truth of Vichy.* Evanston, IL: Northwestern University Press.

Levi, Margaret. 1974. "Poor People against the State." *Review of Radical Political Economics* 6 (Spring): 76–98.

Levi, Margaret. 1981. "The Predatory Theory of Rule." *Politics and Society* 10 (4): 431–65.

Levi, Margaret. 1988. *Of Rule and Revenue.* Berkeley and Los Angeles: University of California Press.

Levi, Margaret, and Michael Hechter. 1985. "A Rational Choice Approach to the Rise and Decline of Ethnoregional Political Parties." In *New Nationalisms of the Developed West: Toward Explanation,* ed. Edward Tiryakian and Ronald Rogowski. Boston: Allen and Unwin.

Levin, Bernard. 1993. "One Who Got It Right." *National Interest* 31 (Spring): 64–65.

Levy, Jack S. 1988. "Domestic Politics and War." *Journal of Interdisciplinary History* 18:653–73.

Levy, Jack S. 1989. "The Diversionary Theory of War: A Critique." In *Handbook of War Studies,* ed. Manus I. Midlarsky. Boston: Unwin Hyman.

Levy, Jack S. 1992a. "An Introduction to Prospect Theory." *Political Psychology* 13 (2): 171–86.

Levy, Jack S. 1992b. "Prospect Theory and International Relations: Theoretical Applications and Analytical Problems." *Political Psychology* 13 (2): 283–310.

Levy, Jack S. 1996. "Loss Aversion, Framing, and Bargaining: The Implications of Prospect Theory for International Conflict." *International Political Science Review* 17 (2): 177–93.

Levy, Jack S, 1997. "Prospect Theory, Rational Choice, and International Relations." *International Studies Quarterly* 41:87–112.

Levy, Jack S. 2000. "Loss Aversion, Framing Effects, and International Conflict." In *Handbook of War Studies II,* ed. Manus I. Midlarsky. Ann Arbor: University of Michigan Press.

Levy, Jack S. 2002. "War and Peace." In *Handbook of International Relations,* ed. Walter Carlsnaes, Thomas Risse, and Beth A. Simmons. London: Sage.

Lichbach, Mark Irving. 1987. "Deterrence or Escalation? The Puzzle of Aggregate Studies of Repression and Dissent." *Journal of Conflict Resolution* 31:266–97.

Lichbach, Mark Irving. 1989. "An Evaluation of 'Does Economic Inequality Breed Political Conflict?' Studies." *World Politics* 41:431–70.

Lichbach, Mark Irving. 1992. "Nobody Cites Nobody Else: Mathematical Models of Domestic Political Conflict." *Defence Economics* 3 (4): 341–57.

Lichbach, Mark Irving. 1995. *The Rebel's Dilemma.* Ann Arbor: University of Michigan Press.

Lichbach, Mark Irving. 2009. "Thinking and Working: Discovery, Explanation, and Evidence in Comparative Politics." In *Comparative Politics: Rationality, Culture, and Structure,* ed. Mark Irving Lichbach and Alan S. Zuckerman. 2nd ed. Cambridge: Cambridge University Press.

Lichbach, Mark Irving, and Helma DeVries. 2007. "Mechanisms of Globalized Protest Movements." In *Handbook of Comparative Politics,* ed. Carles Boix and Susan C. Stokes. Oxford: Oxford University Press.

Licklider, Roy. 1988. *Political Power and the Arab Oil Weapon: The Experience of Five Industrial Nations.* Berkeley and Los Angeles: University of California Press.

Licklider, Roy. 1993. "How Civil Wars End: Questions and Methods." In *Stopping the Killing: How Civil Wars End,* ed. Roy Licklider. New York: New York University Press.

Licklider, Roy. 1995. "The Consequences of Negotiated Settlements in Civil Wars, 1945–1993." *American Political Science Review* 89:681–90.

Licklider, Roy. 2008. "Ethical Advice: Conflict Management vs. Human Rights in Ending Civil Wars." *Journal of Human Rights* 7, no. 4 (in press).

Licklider, Roy, and Mia Bloom. 2006. *Living Together after Ethnic Killing.* New York: Routledge.

Lijphart, Arend. 1975. *The Politics of Accommodation: Pluralism and Democracy in the Netherlands.* 2nd ed. Berkeley and Los Angeles: University of California Press.

Lijphart, Arend. 1977. *Democracies in Plural Societies: A Comparative Exploration.* New Haven: Yale University Press.

Lijphart, Arend. 1984. *Democracies: Patterns of Majoritarian and Consensus Government in Twenty-one Countries.* New Haven: Yale University Press.

Lijphart, Arend. 1999. *Patterns of Democracy: Government Forms and Performance in Thirty-six Countries.* New Haven: Yale University Press.

Lind, Jennifer. 2003. "Apologies and Threat Reduction in Postwar Europe." Paper presented at the Meeting of the International Studies Association, Portland, OR, March 1.

Linden, Ronald H. 2000. "Putting on Their Sunday Best: Romania, Hungary, and the Puzzle of Peace." *International Studies Quarterly* 44:121–46.

Linden, Ronald H., ed. 2002. *Norms and Nannies: The Impact of International Organizations on the Central and East European States.* Lanham, MD: Rowman and Littlefield.

Lindström, Ronny, and Will H. Moore. 1995. "Deprived, Rational or Both? 'Why Minorities Rebel' Revisited." *Journal of Political and Military Sociology* 23 (Winter): 167–90.

Linz, Juan J. 1980. "Political Space and Fascism as a Late-Comer." In *Who Were the Fascists? Social Roots of European Fascism,* ed. Stein U. Larsen, Bernt Hagtvet, and Jan P. Myklebust. Oslo: Universitetsforlaget.

Linz, Juan J. 2000. *Totalitarian and Authoritarian Regimes.* Boulder: Lynne Reiner.

Lipset, Seymour M. 1959. "Some Social Requisites of Democracy: Economic Development and Political Legitimacy." *American Political Science Review* 53:69–106.

Lipset, Seymour Martin, and Gyorgy Bence. 1994. "Anticipations of the Failure of Communism." *Theory and Society* 23 (2): 169–210.

Lischer, Sarah K. 2003. "Collateral Damage: Humanitarian Assistance as a Cause of Conflict." *International Security* 28 (1): 79–109.

Lischer, Sarah K. 2005. *Dangerous Sanctuaries: Refugee Camps, Civil War, and the Dilemmas of Humanitarian Aid.* Ithaca: Cornell University Press.

Lobell, Steven E., and Philip Mauceri, eds. 2004. *Ethnic Conflict and International Politics: Explaining Diffusion and Escalation.* New York: Palgrave Macmillan.

London, Louise. 2000. *Whitehall and the Jews, 1933–1948: British Immigration Policy, Jewish Refugees, and the Holocaust.* Cambridge: Cambridge University Press.

Lounsbery, Marie Olson, and Frederic Pearson. 2008. *Civil Wars: Internal Struggles, Global Consequences.* Toronto: University of Toronto Press.

Luong, Pauline Jones. 2002. *Institutional Change and Political Continuity in Post-Soviet Central Asia: Power, Perceptions, and Pacts.* Cambridge: Cambridge University Press.

Lustik, Ian S., Dan Miodownik, and Roy J. Eidelson. 2004. "Secessionism in Multicultural States: Does Sharing Power Prevent or Encourage It?" *American Political Science Review* 98:209–29.

Lust-Okar, Ellen. 2005. *Structuring Conflict in the Arab World: Incumbents, Opponents, and Institutions.* Cambridge: Cambridge University Press.

Luttwak, Edward. 1999. "Give War a Chance." *Foreign Affairs* 78 (4): 36–44.

Lyon, Alynna J., and Emek M. Uçarer. 2001. "Mobilizing Ethnic Conflict: Kurdish Separatism in Germany and the PKK." *Ethnic and Racial Studies* 24:925–48.

Lyons, Terence. 2005. *Demilitarizing Politics: Elections on the Uncertain Road to Peace.* Boulder: Lynne Rienner.

MacCoun, Robert, Elizabeth Kier, and Aaron Belkin. 2005. "Does Social Cohesion Determine Motivation in Combat?" *Armed Forces and Society* 32 (4): 1–9.

Mack, Andrew. 2002. "Civil War: Academic Research and the Policy Community." *Journal of Peace Research* 39:515–25.

Mack, Andrew. 2006. Human Security Brief. Human Security Centre, University of British Columbia. http://www.hsrgroup.org//images/stories/HS Brief2006/2006/index.html.

Mack, Raymond W., and Richard C. Snyder. 1957. "The Analysis of Social Conflict: Toward an Overview and Synthesis." *Journal of Conflict Resolution* 1:212–48.

Magaloni, Beatriz. 2006. *Voting for Autocracy: Hegemonic Party Survival and Its Demise in Mexico.* Cambridge: Cambridge University Press.

Malkki, Liisa H. 1995. *Purity and Exile: Violence, Memory, and National Cosmology among Hutu Refugees in Tanzania.* Chicago: University of Chicago Press.

Mamdani, Mahmood. 2001. *When Victims Become Killers: Colonialism, Nativism, and the Genocide in Rwanda.* Princeton: Princeton University Press.

Mandelbaum, Michael. 2000. *The New European Diasporas: National Minorities and Conflicts in Eastern Europe.* Washington, DC: Brookings Institution Press.

Mann, Michael. 2005. *The Dark Side of Democracy: Explaining Ethnic Cleansing.* New York: Cambridge University Press.

Mansfield, Edward D., and Jack Snyder. 1995. "Democratization and the Danger of War." *International Security* 20 (1): 5–38.

Mansfield, Edward D., and Jack Snyder. 2005. *Electing to Fight: Why Emerging Democracies Go to War.* Cambridge: MIT Press.

Manson, Joseph, and Richard Wrangham. 1991. "Intergroup Aggression in Chimpanzees and Humans." *Current Anthropology* 32 (4): 369–90.

Maoz, Zeev. 1990. "Framing the National Interest: The Manipulation of Foreign Policy Decisions in Group Settings." *World Politics* 43:77–110.

Maoz, Zeev, and Bruce M. Russett. 1993. "Normative and Structural Causes of the Democratic Peace." *American Political Science Review* 87:624–38.

Marashlian, Levon. 1999. "Finishing the Genocide: Cleansing Turkey of Armenian Survivors, 1920–1923." In *Remembrance and Denial: The Case of the Armenian Genocide,* ed. Richard G. Hovannisian. Detroit: Wayne State University Press.

Marcus, George. 2000. "Emotion in Politics." *Annual Review of Political Science* 3:221–50.

Marcus, George, Russell Neuman, and Michael MacKuen. 2000. *Affective Intelligence and Political Judgment.* Chicago: University of Chicago Press.

Markusen, Eric. 1987. "Genocide and Total War: A Preliminary Comparison." In *Genocide and the Modern Age: Etiology and Case Studies of Mass Death,* ed. Isidor Wallimann and Michael N. Dobkowski. New York: Greenwood Press.

Marrus, Michael R., and Robert O. Paxton. 1995. *Vichy France and the Jews.* Stanford, CA: Stanford University Press.

Marshall, Monty G., and Keith Jaggers. 2003. *Polity IV Project: Political Regime Characteristics and Transitions, 1800–2003.* www.cidcm.umd.edu/in scr/polity/index.htm.

Marx, Karl. 1964. *Class Struggles in France, 1848–1850.* New York: International Publishers.

Mason, T. David. 1992. "Women's Participation in Central American Revolutions: A Theoretical Perspective." *Comparative Political Studies* 25:63–89.

Mason, T. David. 1994. "Modernization and its Discontents Revisited: The Dynamics of Mass-Based Opposition in the People's Republic of China." *Journal of Politics* 56:400–424.

Mason, T. David. 2004. *Caught in the Crossfire: Revolution, Repression, and the Rational Peasant.* Lanham, MD: Rowman and Littlefield.

Mason, T. David, and Patrick J. Fett. 1996. "How Civil Wars End: A Rational Choice Approach." *Journal of Conflict Resolution* 40:546–68.

Mason, T. David, and Dale A. Krane. 1989. "The Political Economy of Death Squads." *International Studies Quarterly* 33:175–98.

Mason, T. David, Joseph P. Weingarten, and Patrick J. Fett. 1999. "Win, Lose, or Draw: Predicting the Outcome of Civil Wars." *Political Research Quarterly* 52 (2): 239–68.

Maynard, Kimberly A. 1999. *Healing Communities in Conflict: International Assistance in Complex Emergencies.* New York: Columbia University Press.

Mazur, Allan. 1968. "A Nonrational Approach to Theories of Conflict and Coalitions." *Journal of Conflict Resolution* 12:196–205.

McAdam, Doug. 1982. *Political Process and the Development of Black Insurgency, 1930–1970.* Chicago: University of Chicago Press.

McAdam, Doug. 1996. "Conceptual Origins, Current Problems, Future Directions." In *Comparative Perspectives on Social Movements: Political Opportunities, Mobilizing Structures, and Cultural Framings,* ed. Doug McAdam, John D. McCarthy, and Mayer N. Zald. Cambridge: Cambridge University Press.

McAdam, Doug, John D. McCarthy, and Mayer N. Zald. 1988. "Social Movements." In *Handbook of Sociology,* ed. Neil J. Smelser. Beverly Hills, CA: Sage.

McAdam, Doug, Sidney Tarrow, and Charles Tilly. 1996. "To Map Contentious Politics." *Mobilization* 1 (1): 17–34.

McAdam, Doug, Sidney Tarrow, and Charles Tilly. 2001. *Dynamics of Contention*. Cambridge: Cambridge University Press.

McDermott, Rose. 1998. *Risk Seeking in International Relations: Prospect Theory in American Foreign Policy*. Ann Arbor: University of Michigan Press.

McDermott, Rose. 2004a. "The Feeling of Rationality: The Meaning of Neuroscientific Advances for Political Science." *Perspectives on Politics* 2 (4): 691–706.

McDermott, Rose. 2004b. *Political Psychology in International Relations*. Ann Arbor: University of Michigan Press.

McDermott, Rose. 2004c. "Prospect Theory in Political Science: Gains and Losses from the First Decade." *Political Psychology* 25 (2): 289–312.

McGarry, John, and Brendan O'Leary, eds. 1993 *The Politics of Ethnic Conflict Regulation*. London: Routledge.

Mearsheimer, John J. 1983. *Conventional Deterrence*. Ithaca: Cornell University Press.

Mearsheimer, John J. 1990a. "Back to the Future: Instability in Europe after the Cold War." *International Security* 15 (1): 5–56.

Mearsheimer, John J. 1990b. "Why We Will Soon Miss the Cold War." *Atlantic Monthly*, August, 35–50.

Meernik, James. 2005. "Justice and Peace? How the International Criminal Tribunal Affects Societal Peace in Bosnia." *Journal of Peace Research* 42:271–89.

Melson, Robert. 1992. *Revolution and Genocide: On the Origins of the Armenian Genocide and the Holocaust*. Chicago: University of Chicago Press.

Melvin, Neil. 1995. *Russians beyond Russia: The Politics of National Identity*. London: Royal Institute of International Affairs.

Mendeloff, David. 2004. "Truth-Seeking, Truth-Telling, and Postconflict Peacebuilding: Curb the Enthusiasm?" *International Studies Review* 6 (3): 355–80.

Mendeloff, David. 2006. "The Psychological Impact of Post-Conflict Truth-Telling: A Critical Examination." Norman Paterson School of International Affairs, Carleton University, Ottawa, July.

Mercer, John. 1995. "Anarchy and Identity." *International Organization* 49:229–52.

Mercer, Jonathan. 2006. "Human Nature and the First Image: Emotion in International Politics." *Journal of International Relations and Development* 9 (3): 288–303.

Mershon, Robert F. 1992. *Revolution and Genocide*. Chicago: University of Chicago Press.

Meyer, David S., and Sidney Tarrow, eds. 1998. *The Social Movement Society:*

Contentious Politics for a New Century. Lanham, MD: Rowman and Littlefield.

Miall, Hugh. 1992. *The Peacemakers: Peaceful Settlement of Disputes since 1945*. New York: St. Martin's.

Midlarsky, Manus I. 1988. "Rulers and Ruled: Patterned Inequality and the Onset of Mass Political Violence." *American Political Science Review* 82:491–509.

Midlarsky, Manus I. 1998. "Democracy and Islam: Civilizational Conflict and the Democratic Peace." *International Studies Quarterly* 42:485–511.

Midlarsky, Manus I. 1999. *The Evolution of Inequality: War, State Survival, and Democracy in Comparative Perspective*. Stanford, CA: Stanford University Press.

Midlarsky, Manus I., ed. 2000a. *Handbook of War Studies II*. Ann Arbor: University of Michigan Press.

Midlarsky, Manus I. 2000b. "Identity and International Conflict." In *Handbook of War Studies II*, ed. Manus I. Midlarsky. Ann Arbor: University of Michigan Press.

Midlarsky, Manus I. 2003. "The Impact of External Threat on States and Domestic Societies." *International Studies Review* 5 (4): 13–18.

Midlarsky, Manus I. 2005a. "The Demographics of Genocide: Refugees and Territorial Loss in the Mass Murder of European Jewry." *Journal of Peace Research* 42:375–91.

Midlarsky, Manus I. 2005b. *The Killing Trap: Genocide in the Twentieth Century*. Cambridge: Cambridge University Press.

Midlarsky, Manus I. Forthcoming. *The Origins of Political Extremism*. Cambridge: Cambridge University Press.

Midlarsky, Manus I., Martha Crenshaw, and F. Yoshida. 1980. "Why Violence Spreads: The Contagion of International Terrorism." *International Studies Quarterly* 24:262–98.

Midlarsky, Manus I., and Kenneth Roberts. 1985. "Class, State, and Revolution in Central America: Nicaragua and El Salvador Compared." *Journal of Conflict Resolution* 29:163–95.

Milgram, Stanley. 1974. *Obedience to Authority*. New York: Harper and Row.

Milner, Helen. 1998. "International Political Economy: Beyond Hegemonic Stability." *Foreign Policy* 110 (Spring): 112–23.

Minow, Martha. 1998. *Between Vengeance and Forgiveness: Facing History after Genocide and Mass Violence*. Boston: Beacon Press.

Mintz, Alex, and Geva Nehemia. 1993. "Why Don't Democracies Fight Each Other? The Political Incentives Approach." *Journal of Conflict Resolution* 37:487–503.

Mishali-Ram, Meirav. 2006. "Ethnic Diversity, Issues, and International Crisis Dynamics, 1918–2002." *Journal of Peace Research* 43:583–600.

Moe, Terry M. 1980. *The Organization of Interests: Incentives and the Internal Dynamics of Political Interest Groups*. Chicago: University of Chicago Press.

Moe, Terry M. 2005. "Power and Political Institutions." *Perspectives on Politics* 3 (2): 215–33.

Moore, Barrington, Jr. 1966. *The Social Origins of Democracy and Dictatorship: Lord and Peasant in the Making of the Modern World*. Boston: Beacon Press.

Moore, Barrington, Jr. 1978. *Injustice: The Social Bases of Obedience and Revolt*. White Plains, NY: M. E. Sharpe.

Moore, Will H. 1998. "Repression and Dissent: Substitution, Context, and Timing." *American Journal of Political Science* 42:851–73.

Moore, Will H., Ronnie Lindström, and Valerie O'Regan. 1996. "Land Reform, Political Violence, and the Economic Inequality-Political Conflict Nexus: A Longitudinal Analysis." *International Interactions* 21 (4): 335–63.

Morgan, T. Clifton. 1984. "A Spatial Model of Crisis Bargaining." *International Studies Quarterly* 28:407–26.

Morgan, T. Clifton, and Kenneth Bickers. 1992. "Domestic Discontent and the External Use of Force." *Journal of Conflict Resolution* 36:25–52.

Morgan, T. Clifton, and Sally H. Campbell. 1991. "Domestic Structure, Decision Constraints, and War: So Why Kant Democracies Fight?" *Journal of Conflict Resolution* 35:187–211.

Morgenthau, Hans. 1948. *Politics among Nations*. New York: Knopf.

Morgenthau, Hans J. 1978. *Politics among Nations*. 5th ed. Boston: McGraw Hill.

Morrow, James D. 1991a. "Alliances and Asymmetry: An Alternative to the Capability Aggregation Model of Alliances." *American Journal of Political Science* 35:904–33.

Morrow, James D. 1991b. "Electoral and Congressional Incentives and Arms Control." *Journal of Conflict Resolution* 35:243–63.

Morrow, James D. 1993. "Arms versus Allies: Trade-Offs in the Search for Security." *International Organization* 47:207–33.

Morrow, James D. 1994. "Alliances, Credibility, and Peacetime Costs." *Journal of Conflict Resolution* 38:270–97.

Morrow, James D., Bruce Bueno de Mesquita, Randolph M. Siverson, and Alastair Smith. 2006. "Selection Institutions and War Aims." *Economics of Governance* 7 (1): 31–52.

Most, Benjamin A., and Harvey Starr. 1989. *Inquiry, Logic, and International Politics*. Columbia: University of South Carolina Press.

Most, Benjamin A., Harvey Starr, and Randolph M. Siverson. 1989. "The Logic and Study of the Diffusion of International Conflict." In *Handbook of War Studies*, ed. Manus I. Midlarsky. Boston: Unwin Hyman.

Mousseau, Michael. 2000. "Market Prosperity, Democratic Consolidation, and Democratic Peace." *Journal of Conflict Resolution* 44:472–507.

Mousseau, Michael, Håvard Hegre, and John R. Oneal. 2003. "How the Wealth of Nations Conditions the Liberal Peace." *European Journal of International Relations* 9:277–314.

Mueller, John. 2000. "The Banality of Ethnic War." *International Security* 25 (1): 42–70.

Mueller, John. 2004. *The Remnants of War*. Ithaca: Cornell University Press.

Mukherjee, Bumba. 2006. "Why Political Power-Sharing Agreements Lead to Enduring Peaceful Resolution of Some Civil Wars, but Not Others?" *International Studies Quarterly* 50:479–504.

Mullenbach, Mark J. 2005. "Deciding to Keep Peace: An Analysis of International Influences on the Establishment of Third-Party Peacekeeping Missions." *International Studies Quarterly* 49:529–55.

Mullenbach, Mark J. 2006. "Reconstructing Strife-Torn Societies: Third-Party Peacebuilding in Intrastate Disputes." In *Conflict Prevention and Peacebuilding in Post-War Societies: Sustaining the Peace*, ed. T. David Mason and James D. Meernik. London and New York: Routledge.

Muller, Edward N. 1985. "Income Inequality, Regime Repressiveness, and Political Violence." *American Journal of Sociology* 50:47–61.

Muller, Edward N., and Mitchell Seligson. 1987. "Inequality and Insurgency." *American Political Science Review* 81:425–51.

Muller, Edward N., and Erich Weede. 1990. "Cross-National Variations in Political Violence: A Rational Action Approach." *Journal of Conflict Resolution* 34:624–51.

Munck, Gerardo L., and Jay Verkuilen. 2002. "Conceptualizing and Measuring Democracy: Evaluating Alternative Indices." *Comparative Political Studies* 35:5–34.

Murdoch, James C., and Todd Sandler. 2002. "Economic Growth, Civil Wars, and Spatial Spillovers." *Journal of Conflict Resolution* 46:91–110.

Murdoch, James C., and Todd Sandler. 2004. "Civil Wars and Economic Growth: Spatial Dispersion." *American Journal of Political Science* 48:138–51.

Neumann, Franz. 1942. *Behemoth: The Structure and Practice of National Socialism*. New York: Oxford University Press.

Niou, Emerson, and Peter Ordeshook. 1990. "Stability in Anarchic International Systems." *American Political Science Review* 84:1207–34.

Niou, Emerson, and Peter Ordeshook. 1991. "Realism versus Neoliberalism." *American Journal of Political Science* 35:481–511.

Niou, Emerson, Peter Ordeshook, and Gregory Rose. 1989. *The Balance of Power*. Cambridge: Cambridge University Press.

North, Douglass C. 1990. *Institutions, Institutional Change, and Economic Performance.* Cambridge: Cambridge University Press.

North, Douglass C., and Robert Paul Thomas. 1973. *The Rise of the Western World: A New Economic History.* Cambridge: Cambridge University Press.

O'Connell, James. 1993. "The Ending of the Nigerian Civil War: Victory, Defeat, and the Changing of Coalitions." In *Stopping the Killing: How Civil Wars End,* ed. Roy Licklider. New York: New York University Press.

Oliver, Pamela. 1993. "Formal Models of Collective Action." *Annual Review of Sociology* 19:271–300.

Olson, Mancur. 1965. *The Logic of Collective Action: Public Goods and the Theory of Groups.* Cambridge: Harvard University Press.

Olson, Mancur, Jr. 1990. "The Logic of Collective Action in Soviet-Type Societies." *Journal of Soviet Nationalities* 1 (2): 8–27.

Olzak, Susan. 1992. *The Dynamics of Ethnic Competition and Conflict.* Stanford, CA: Stanford University Press.

Organski, A. F. K. 1958. *World Politics.* New York: Knopf.

Orr, Robert C. 2001. "Building Peace in El Salvador: From Exception to Rule." In *Peacebuilding as Politics: Cultyivating Peace in Fragile Societies,* ed. Elizabeth M. Cousens and Chetan Kumar with Karin Wermester. Boulder: Lynne Rienner.

Orren, Karen. 2004. *The Search for American Political Development.* Cambridge: Cambridge University Press.

Orren, Karen, and Stephen Skowronek. 1994. "Beyond the Iconography of Order: Notes for a 'New Institutionalism.'" In *The Dynamics of American Politics: Approaches and Interpretations,* ed. Lawrence C. Dodd and Calvin Jillson. Boulder: Westview Press.

Ottaway, Marina. 2003. "Promoting Democracy after Conflict: The Difficult Choices." *International Studies Perspectives* 4 (3): 314–22.

Pape, Robert. 1997. "Why Economic Sanctions Do Not Work." *International Security* 22 (2): 90–136.

Paris, Roland. 2004. *At War's End: Building Peace after Civil Conflict.* New York: Cambridge University Press.

Perito, Robert. 2004. *Where Is the Lone Ranger When We Need Him? America's Search for a Postconflict Stability Force.* Washington, DC: United States Institute of Peace Press.

Perriello, Tom. 2006. *The Special Court for Sierra Leone under Scrutiny.* Prosecutions Case Studies Series. New York: International Center for Transitional Justice.

Perriello, Tom, and Marieke Wierda. 2006a. *Lessons from the Deployment of International Judges and Prosecutors in Kosovo.* Prosecutions Case Studies Series. New York: International Center for Transitional Justice.

Perriello, Tom, and Marieke Wierda. 2006b. *The Special Court for Sierra Leone*

Under Scrutiny. Prosecutions Case Studies Series. New York: International Center for Transitional Justice.

Petersen, Karen K. 2004. "A Research Note: Reexamining Transnational Ethnic Alliances and Foreign Policy Behavior." *International Interactions* 30 (1): 25–42.

Petersen, Roger D. 2002. *Understanding Ethnic Violence: Fear, Hatred, and Resentment in Twentieth Century Eastern Europe.* Cambridge: Cambridge University Press.

Phelps, Elizabeth, Kevin O'Connor, William Cunningham, Sumie Funayam, Christopher Gatenby, John Gore, and Mahzarin Banaji. 2000. "Performance on Indirect Measures of Race Evaluation Predicts Amygdala Activation." *Journal of Cognitive Neuroscience* 12 (5): 729–38.

Pierson, Paul, and Theda Skocpol. 2002. "Historical Institutionalism in Contemporary Political Science." In *Political Science: The State of the Discipline,* ed. Ira Katznelson and Helen V. Milner. New York: Norton.

Pillar, Paul. 1983. *Negotiating Peace: War Termination as a Bargaining Process.* Princeton: Princeton University Press.

Pittman, R., and S. Orr. 1995. "Psychophysiology of Emotional and Memory Networks in Posttraumatic Stress Disorder." In *Brain and Memory: Modulation and Mediation of Neuroplasticity,* ed. J. Mcgaugh, N. Weinberger, and G. Lynch. New York: Oxford University Press.

Polanyi, Karl. 1944. *The Great Transformation.* New York: Rinehart.

Polvinen, Tuomo. 1986. *Between East and West: Finland in International Politics, 1944–1947.* Ed. and trans. D. G. Kirby and Peter Herring. Minneapolis: University of Minnesota Press.

Posen, Barry R. 1993. "The Security Dilemma and Ethnic Conflict." *Survival* 35 (1): 27–47.

Powell, G. Bingham, Jr. 1982. *Contemporary Democracies: Participation, Stability, and Violence.* Cambridge: Harvard University Press.

Powell, Robert. 1990. *Nuclear Deterrence Theory: The Search for Credibility.* Cambridge: Cambridge University Press.

Powell, Robert. 1991. "Absolute and Relative Gains in International Relations Theory." *American Political Science Review* 85:1303–20.

Powell, Robert. 1993. "Guns, Butter, and Anarchy." *American Political Science Review* 87:115–32.

Powell, Robert. 1994. "Anarchy in International Relations Theory: The Neorealist-Neoliberal Debate." *International Organization* 48:313–44.

Powell, Robert. 1996. "Uncertainty, Shifting Power, and Appeasement." *American Political Science Review* 90:749–64.

Powell, Robert. 1999. *In the Shadow of Power: States and Strategy in International Politics.* Princeton: Princeton University Press.

Powell, Robert. 2002a. "Bargaining Theory and International Conflict." *Annual Review of Political Science* 5:1–30.

Powell, Robert. 2002b. "Game Theory, International Relations Theory, and the Hobbesian Stylization." In *Political Science: The State of the Discipline*, ed. Ira Katznelson and Helen V. Milner. New York: Norton.

Price, Michael, Leda Cosmides, and John Tooby. 2002. "Punitive Sentiment as an Anti Free Rider Psychological Device." *Evolution and Human Behavior* 23 (3): 203–31.

Przeworski, Adam. 1985. *Capitalism and Social Democracy.* Cambridge: Cambridge University Press.

Przeworski, Adam. 1991. *Democracy and the Market: Political and Economic Reforms in Eastern Europe and Latin America.* Cambridge: Cambridge University Press.

Przeworski, Adam, Michael E. Alvarez, José Antonio Cheibub, and Fernando Limongi. 2000. *Democracy and Development: Political Institutions and Well-Being in the World, 1950–1990.* Cambridge: Cambridge University Press.

Putnam, Robert D., with Robert Leondardi and Raffaella Y. Nanetti. 1993. *Making Democracy Work: Civic Traditions in Modern Italy.* Princeton: Princeton University Press.

Putnam, Tonya L. 2002. "Human Rights and Sustainable Peace." In *Ending Civil Wars: The Implementation of Peace Agreements,* ed. Stephen John Stedman, Donald Rothchild, and Elizabeth M. Cousens. Boulder: Lynne Rienner.

Pye, Lucian W. 1964. "The Roots of Insurgency and the Commencement of Rebellion." In *Internal War: Problems and Approaches,* ed. Harry Eckstein. New York: Free Press of Glencoe.

Quinn, John James. 2004. "Diffusion and Escalation in the Great Lakes Region: The Rwandan Genocide, the Rebellion in Zaire and Mobutu's Overthrow." In *Ethnic Conflict and International Politics: Explaining Diffusion and Escalation,* ed. Steven E. Lobell and Philip Mauceri. New York: Palgrave Macmillan.

Rabushka, Alvin, and Kenneth A. Shepsle. 1972. *Politics in Plural Societies: A Theory of Democratic Instability.* Columbus, OH: Merrill.

Raknerud, Arvid, and Håvard Hegre. 1997. "The Hazard of War: Reassessing the Evidence for the Democratic Peace." *Journal of Peace Research* 34:385–404.

Raleigh, Clionadh, and Håvard Hegre. 2005. "Introducing ACLED: An Armed Conflict Location and Event Dataset." Paper presented at the IGCC Conference "Disaggregating the Study of Civil War and Transnational Violence," University of California San Diego, March 7–8. www.prio.no/files/file46564_ucsd_paper_final.pdf.

Reed, William. 2003. "Information, Power, and War." *American Political Science Review* 97:633–41.

Regan, Patrick M. 1998. "Choosing to Intervene: Outside Intervention in Internal Conflicts." *Journal of Politics* 60:754–79.

Regan, Patrick M. 2000. *Civil Wars and Foreign Powers: Outside Intervention in Intrastate Conflict.* Ann Arbor: University of Michigan Press.

Regan, Patrick M. 2009. *Sixteen Million One: Understanding Civil Wars.* Boulder and London: Paradigm.

Regan, Patrick M., and Aysegul Aydin. 2006. "Diplomacy and Other Forms of Intervention in Civil Wars." *Journal of Conflict Resolution* 50:736–56.

Reid, James J. 1992. "Total War, the Annihilation Ethic, and the Armenian Genocide, 1870–1918." In *The Armenian Genocide: History, Politics, Ethics,* ed. Richard G. Hovannisian. New York: St. Martin's Press.

Reif, Linda L. 1986. "Women in Latin American Guerrilla Movements: A Comparative Perspective." *Comparative Politics* 18 (2): 147–69.

Reiger, Caitlin, and Marieke Wierda. 2006. *The Serious Crimes Process in Timor-Leste: In Retrospect.* Prosecutions Case Studies Series. New York: International Center for Transitional Justice.

Reiter, Dan. 2003. "Exploring the Bargaining Model of War." *Perspectives on Politics* 1 (1): 27–43.

Reiter, Dan, and Allan Stam III. 2002. *Democracies at War.* Princeton: Princeton University Press.

Remak, Joachim. 1993. *A Very Civil War: The Swiss Sonderbund War of 1847.* Boulder: Westview Press.

Reynal-Querol, Marta. 2002. "Ethnicity, Political Systems, and Civil Wars." *Journal of Conflict Resolution* 46:29–54.

Richards, Michael. 1998. *A Time of Silence: Civil War and the Culture of Repression in Franco's Spain, 1936–1945.* Cambridge: Cambridge University Press.

Riker, William H. 1982. *Liberalism against Populism: A Confrontation between the Theory of Democracy and the Theory of Social Choice.* San Francisco: W. H. Freeman.

Riker, William H. 1996. *The Strategy of Rhetoric.* New Haven: Yale University Press.

Riker, William H., and Peter Ordeshook. 1973. *An Introduction to Positive Political Theory.* Englewood Cliffs, NJ: Prentice Hall.

Roe, Paul. 2006. "Which Security Dilemma? Mitigating Ethnic Conflict: The Case of Croatia." In *Living Together after Ethnic Killing: Exploring the Chaim Kaufmann Argument,* ed. Roy Licklider and Mia Bloom. London and New York: Routledge.

Roeder, Philip G. 1991. "Soviet Federalism and Ethnic Mobilization." *World Politics* 43:196–232.

Roeder, Philip G. 2001. "Ethnolinguistic Fractionalization (ELF) Indices, 1961 and 1985." February 16. http//:weber.ucsd.edu\~proeder\elf.htm>, accessed June 15.

Roeder, Philip G. 2003. "Clash of Civilizations and Escalation of Domestic Ethnopolitical Conflicts." *Comparative Political Studies* 36:509–41.

Roeder, Philip G., and Donald Rothchild. 2005. "Conclusion: Nation-State Stewardship and the Alternatives to Power Sharing." In *Sustaining Peace: Power and Democracy after Civil Wars,* ed. Philip G. Roeder and Donald Rothchild. Ithaca: Cornell University Press.

Rose, William. 2000. "The Security Dilemma and Ethnic Conflict: Some New Hypotheses." *Security Studies* 9 (4): 1–54.

Ross, Michael L. 2004a. "How Do Natural Resources Influence Civil War? Evidence from Thirteen Cases." *International Organization* 58:35–67.

Ross, Michael L. 2004b. "What Do We Know about Natural Resources and Civil War?" *Journal of Peace Research* 41:337–56.

Rothchild, Donald. 1991. "An Interactive Model for State-Ethnic Relations." In *Conflict Resolution in Africa,* ed. Francis Deng and I. William Zartman. Washington, DC: Brookings Institution Press.

Rothchild, Donald. 1997. *Managing Ethnic Conflict in Africa.* Washington, DC: Brookings Institution Press.

Rothchild, Donald, and Caroline Hartzell. 1993. "The Peace Process in the Sudan, 1971–1972." In *Stopping the Killing: How Civil Wars End,* ed. Roy Licklider. New York: New York University Press.

Rudé, George. 1964. *The Crowd in History, 1730–1848.* New York: John Wiley and Sons.

Ruggie, John. 1996. Comments at "The Security Dilemma within States" conference of the Institute of War and Peace Studies, Columbia University, May.

Rummel, Rudolph. 1997. *Power Kills: Democracy as a Method of Nonviolence.* New Brunswick, NJ: Transaction.

Rummel, Rudolph. 1998. *Statistics of Democide: Genocide and Mass Murder since 1900.* Münster: Lit Verlag.

Russett, Bruce M. 1964. "Inequality and Insurgency: The Relation of Land Tenure to Politics." *World Politics* 16:442–54.

Russett, Bruce M. 1967. "Pearl Harbor: Deterrence Theory and Decision Theory." *Journal of Peace Research* 4:89–105.

Russett, Bruce M. 1990. "Economic Decline, Electoral Pressure, and the Initiation of International Conflict." In *The Prisoners of War?* ed. Charles Gochman and Alan Sabrosky. Lexington, MA: D. C. Heath.

Saideman, Stephen M. 1997. "Explaining the International Relations of Secessionist Conflicts: Vulnerability vs. Ethnic Ties." *International Organization* 51:721–53.

Saideman, Stephen M. 1998a. "Inconsistent Irredentism? Political Competition, Ethnic Ties, and The Foreign Policies of Somalia and Serbia." *Security Studies* 7 (3): 51–93.

Saideman, Stephen M. 1998b. "Is Pandora's Box Half-Empty or Half-Full? The Limited Virulence of Secession and the Domestic Sources of Disintegration." In *The International Spread of Ethnic Conflict: Fear, Diffusion, and Escalation*, ed. David A. Lake and Donald Rothchild. Princeton: Princeton University Press.

Saideman, Stephen M. 2001. *The Ties That Divide: Ethnic Politics, Foreign Policy, and International Conflict.* New York: Columbia University Press.

Saideman, Stephen M. 2002. "The Power of the Small: The Impact of Minorities on Foreign Policy." *SAIS Review* 22:93–105.

Saideman, Stephen M. 2007. "Ties versus Institutions: Revisiting Foreign Interventions and Secessionist Movements." *Canadian Journal of Political Science* 40:733–47.

Saideman, Stephen M., and R. William Ayres. 2000. "Determining the Causes of Irredentism: Logit Analysis of Minorities at Risk Data from the 1980s and 1990s." *Journal of Politics* 62:1126–44.

Saideman, Stephen M., and R. William Ayres. 2007. "Pie Crust Promises and the Sources of Foreign Policy: The Limited Impact of Accession Processes and the Priority of Domestic Constituencies." *Foreign Policy Analysis* 3:189–210.

Saideman, Stephen M., and R. William Ayres. 2008. *For Kin or Country: Xenophobia, Nationalism, and War.* New York: Columbia University Press.

Saideman, Stephen M., Beth K. Dougherty, and Erin K. Jenne. 2005. "Dilemmas of Divorce: How Secessionist Identities Cut Both Ways." *Security Studies* 14:607–36.

Saideman, Stephen, David J. Lanoue, Michael Campenni, and Samuel Stanton. 2002. "Democratization, Political Institutions, and Ethnic Conflict: A Pooled Time-Series Analysis, 1985–1998." *Comparative Political Studies* 35:103–29.

Salehyan, Idean. 2007. "Transnational Rebels: Neighboring States as Sanctuary for Rebel Groups." *World Politics* 59:217–42.

Salehyan, Idean, and Kristian Skrede Gleditsch. 2006. "Refugees and the Spread of Civil War." *International Organization* 60:335–66.

Sambanis, Nicholas. 2000. "Partition as a Solution to Ethnic War: An Empirical Critique of the Theoretical Literature." *World Politics* 52:437–83.

Sambanis, Nicholas. 2001. "Do Ethnic and Non-ethnic Civil Wars Have the Same Causes? A Theoretical and Empirical Inquiry (Part 1)." *Journal of Conflict Resolution* 45:259–82.

Sambanis, Nicholas. 2002. "A Review of Recent Advances and Future Directions in the Quantitative Literature on Civil War." *Defence and Peace Economics* 13 (3): 215–43.

Sambanis, Nicholas. 2004. "What Is Civil War? Conceptual and Empirical Complexities of an Operational Definition." *Journal of Conflict Resolution* 48:814–58. Data at http://pantheon.yale.edu/~ns237/index/research.html#Data.

Sargent, Thomas J. 1993. *Bounded Rationality in Macroeconomics.* Oxford: Clarendon Press.

Sarkees, Meredith Reid. 2000. "The Correlates of War Data on War: An Update to 1997." *Conflict Management and Peace Science* 18 (1): 123–44.

Scarritt, James R., and Susan McMillan. 1995. "Protest and Rebellion in Africa: Explaining Conflicts between Ethnic Minorities and the State in the 1980s." *Comparative Political Studies* 28:323–49.

Schabas, William A. 2000. *Genocide in International Law: The Crimes of Crimes.* Cambridge: Cambridge University Press.

Schelling, Thomas. 1960. *Strategy of Conflict.* Cambridge: Harvard University Press.

Schimmelfennig, Frank, and Ulrich Sedelmeier, eds. 2005. *The Europeanization of Central and Eastern Europe.* Ithaca: Cornell University Press.

Schivelbusch, Wolfgang. 2003. *The Culture of Defeat: On National Trauma, Mourning, and Recovery.* Trans. Jefferson Chase. New York: Metropolitan Books.

Schneider, Gerald, and Nina Wiesehomeier. 2008. "Rules That Matter: Political Institutions and the Diversity-Conflict Nexus." *Journal of Peace Research* 45:183–203.

Schofield, Norman. 2006. *Architects of Political Change: Constitutional Quandaries and Social Choice Theory.* Cambridge: Cambridge University Press.

Schotter, Andrew, and G. Schwödiauer. 1980. "Economics and the Theory of Games: A Survey. *Journal of Economic Literature* 18 (June): 479–527.

Schultz, Kenneth A. 1998. "Domestic Opposition and Signaling in International Crises." *American Political Science Review* 92:829–44.

Schultz, Kenneth A. 2001a. *Democracy and Coercive Diplomacy.* Cambridge: Cambridge University Press.

Schultz, Kenneth A. 2001b. "Looking for Audience Costs." *Journal of Conflict Resolution* 45:32–60.

Schwarz, Norbert, and Gerald Clore. 1983. "Mood, Misattribution, and Judgments of Well-Being: Informative and Directive Functions of Affective States." *Journal of Personality and Social Psychology* 45 (3): 513–23.

Seligson, Mitchell A. 1996. "Agrarian Inequality and the Theory of Peasant Rebellion." *Latin American Research Review* 31 (2): 141–57.

Senese, Paul D., and John Vasquez. 2004. "Alliances, Territorial Disputes, and the Probability of War: Testing for Interactions." In *The Scourge of War:*

New Extensions on an Old Problem, ed. Paul F. Diehl. Ann Arbor: University of Michigan Press.

Shain, Yossi. 1994–95. "Ethnic Diasporas and U.S. Foreign Policy." *Political Science Quarterly* 109:811–41.

Shain, Yossi. 1995. "Multicultural Foreign Policy." *Foreign Policy* 100:69–87.

Shain, Yossi. 1999. *Marketing the American Creed Abroad: Diasporas in the U.S. and Their Homelands.* New York: Cambridge University Press.

Shain, Yossi. 2002. "The Role of Diasporas in Conflict Perpetuation or Resolution." *SAIS Review* 22:115–44.

Shain, Yossi. 2007. *Kinship and Diasporas in International Affairs.* Ann Arbor: University of Michigan Press.

Shain, Yossi, and Aharon Barth. 2003. "Diasporas and International Relations Theory." *International Organization* 57:449–79.

Shaw, Martin. 2003. *War and Genocide: Organized Killing in Modern Society.* Cambridge, MA: Polity.

Sheffer, Gabriel, ed. 1986. *Modern Diasporas in International Politics.* New York: St. Martin's Press.

Shepsle, Kenneth A. 2006a. "Old Questions and New Answers about Institutions: The Riker Objection Revisited." In *The Oxford Handbook of Political Economy,* ed. Barry R. Weingast and Donald A. Wittman. Oxford: Oxford University Press.

Shepsle, Kenneth A. 2006b. "Rational Choice Institutionalism." In *The Oxford Handbook of Political Institutions,* ed. R. A. W. Rhodes, Sarah A. Binder, and Bert A. Rockman. Oxford: Oxford University Press.

Sherif, Muzafir, O. Harvey, B. White, W. Hood, and C. Sherif. 1961. *Intergroup Conflict and Cooperation: The Robbers Cave Experiment.* Norman, OK: University Book Exchange.

Shils, Edward, and Morris Janowitz. 1948. "Cohesion and Disintegration in the Wehrmacht in World War II." *Public Opinion Quarterly* 12 (2): 281.

Sidanius, James, and Felicia Pratto. 1999. *Social Dominance.* New York: Cambridge University Press.

Signorino, Curt. 1999. "Strategic Interaction and the Statistical Analysis of International Conflict." *American Political Science Review* 93:279–98.

Simon, Herbert A. 1955. "A Behavioral Model of Rational Choice." *Quarterly Journal of Economics* 69 (1): 99–118.

Simon, Herbert A. 1976. "From Substantive to Procedural Rationality." In *Method and Appraisal in Economics,* ed. S. J. Latsis. Cambridge: Cambridge University Press.

Sisk, Timothy D. 1996. *Power Sharing and International Mediation in Ethnic Conflicts.* Washington, DC: Carnegie Commission on Preventing Deadly Conflict; United States Institute of Peace.

Siverson, Randolph M., and Harvey Starr. 1991. *The Diffusion of War: A Study in Opportunity and Willingness.* Ann Arbor: University of Michigan Press.

Skocpol, Theda. 1979. *States and Social Revolutions: A Comparative Analysis of France, Russia, and China.* Cambridge: Cambridge University Press.

Slantchev, Branislav L. 2003. "The Power to Hurt: Costly Conflict with Completely Informed States." *American Political Science Review* 97:123–33.

Slovic, Paul. 1999. "Trust, Emotion, Sex, Politics and Science: Surveying the Risk Assessment Battlefield." *Risk Analysis* 19 (4): 689–701.

Small, Melvin, and J. David Singer. 1982. *Resort to Arms: International and Civil War, 1816–1980.* Beverly Hills, CA: Sage.

Smillie, Ian. 2005. "What Lessons from the Kimberley Process Certification Scheme?" In *Profiting from Peace: Managing the Resource Dimensions of Civil War,* ed. Karen Ballentine and Heiko Nitzschke. Boulder: Lynne Rienner.

Smith, Alastair. 1995. "Alliance Formation and War." *International Studies Quarterly* 39:405–25.

Smith, Alastair. 1996. "Diversionary Foreign Policy in Democratic Systems." *International Studies Quarterly* 40:133–53.

Smith, Alastair. 1998. "Testing Theories of Strategic Choice: The Example of Crisis Escalation." *American Journal of Political Science* 43:1254–83.

Smith, Alastair. 2004. *Election Timing.* Cambridge: Cambridge University Press.

Smith, Alastair, and Allan C. Stam III. 2004. "Bargaining and the Nature of War." *Journal of Conflict Resolution* 48:783–813.

Smith, Anthony. 1986. *The Ethnic Origins of Nations.* Oxford: Blackwell.

Smith, Benjamin. 2004. "Oil Wealth and Regime Survival in the Developing World, 1960–1999." *American Journal of Political Science* 48:232–46.

Smith, Tony. 2000. *Foreign Attachments: The Power of Ethnic Groups in the Making of American Foreign Policy.* Cambridge: Harvard University Press.

Smuts, Barbara, Dorothy Cheney, Robert Seyforth, and Richard Wrangham. 1987. *Primate Societies.* Chicago: University of Chicago Press.

Snidal, Duncan. 1991. "Relative Gains and the Pattern of International Cooperation." *American Political Science Review* 85:701–26.

Snyder, Jack, and Karen Ballentine. 1996. "Nationalism and the Marketplace of Ideas." *International Security* 21 (2): 5–40.

Snyder, Jack. 2000. *From Voting to Violence.* New York: Norton.

Snyder, Richard. 1992. "Explaining Transitions from Neopatrimonial Dictatorships." *Comparative Politics* 24 (4): 379–400.

Snyder, Robert S. 1999. "The End of Revolution?" *Review of Politics* 61 (1): 5–28.

Solomon, Sheldon, Jeff Greenberg, and Tom Pyszczynski. 2000. "Pride and

Prejudice: Fear of Death and Social Behavior." *Current Directions in Psychological Science* 9 (6): 200–204.

Spzorluk, Roman. 1990. "The Imperial Legacy and the Soviet Nationalities Problem." In *The Nationalities Factor in Soviet Politics and Society,* ed. Lubomyr Hajda and Mark Bessinger. Boulder: Westview Press.

Stack, John F., Jr., and Lui Hebron, eds. 1999. *The Ethnic Entanglement: Conflict and Intervention in World Politics.* Westport, CT: Praeger.

Stanley, William. 1996. *The Protection Racket State: Elite Politics, Military Extortion, and Civil War in El Salvador.* Philadelphia: Temple University Press.

Stanley Foundation. 2000. *Creating the International Legal Assistance Consortium.* April. http://www.stanleyfoundation.org/publications/archive/ILAC00p.pdf.

Stedman, Stephen John. 1991. *Peacemaking in Civil War: International Mediation in Zimbabwe, 1974–1980.* Boulder: Lynne Rienner.

Stedman, Stephen John. 1993a. "The End of the American Civil War." In *Stopping the Killing: How Civil Wars End,* ed. Roy Licklider. New York: New York University Press.

Stedman, Stephen John. 1993b. "The End of the Zimbabwean Civil War." In *Stopping the Killing: How Civil Wars End,* ed. Roy Licklider. New York: New York University Press.

Stedman, Stephen John. 2002. "Policy Implications." In *Ending Civil Wars: The Implementation of Peace Agreements,* ed. Stephen John Stedman, Donald Rothchild, and Elizabeth M. Cousens. Boulder: Lynne Rienner.

Steinberg, Jonathan. 1990. *All or Nothing: The Axis and the Holocaust, 1941–1943.* London: Routledge.

Stouffer, Samuel, Arthur Lumsdaine, Marion Harper Lumsdaine, Robin Williams, Brewster Smith, Irving Janis, Shirley Star, and Leonard Cottrell. 1949. *The American Soldier.* Vol. 2, *Combat and Its Aftermath.* Princeton: Princeton University Press.

Stover, Eric. 2005. *The Witnesses: War Crimes and the Promise of Justice in The Hague.* Philadelphia: University of Pennsylvania Press.

Strand, Håvard. 2006. "Reassessing the Civil Democratic Peace." Ph.D. diss., Department of Political Science, University of Oslo and Centre for the Study of Civil War, PRIO. http://www.prio.no/files/manual-import/Strand_Thesis.pdf.

Strand, Håvard. 2007. "Research Design for Article on Democracy and Civil War." www.prio.no/cscw/datasets.

Strand, Håvard, Joachim Carlsen, Nils Petter Gleditsch, Håvard Hegre, Christin Ormhaug, and Lars Wilhelmsen. 2005. *Armed Conflict Dataset Codebook, Version 3–2005.* Oslo: Centre for the Study of Civil War, PRIO. www.prio.no/cscw/armedconflict.

Straus, Scott. 2006. *The Order of Genocide: Race, Power, and War in Rwanda.* Ithaca: Cornell University Press.

Suarez, S., and G. Gallup. 1979. "Tonic Immobility as a Response to Rage in Humans: A Theoretical Note." *Psychological Record* 89 (4): 315–20.

Suhrke, Astri, and Lela Garner Noble, eds. 1977. *Ethnic Conflict in International Relations.* New York: Praeger.

Svensson, Isak. 2007. "Bargaining, Bias and Peace Brokers: How Rebels Commit to Peace." *Journal of Peace Research* 44:177–94.

Tabb, William K. 2004. *Economic Governance in the Age of Globalization.* New York: Columbia University Press.

Tajfel, Henri. 1978. *Differentiation between Social Groups.* New York: Academic Press.

Tajfel, Henri., M. Billing, R. Bundy, and C. Flament. 1971. "Social Categorization and Intergroup Behavior." *European Journal of Social Psychology* 1 (2): 149–78.

Talentino, Andrea Kathryn. 2007. "Nation Building or Nation Splitting? The Links Between Political Transition and Violence." Department of Political Science Department, Drew University, Madison, NJ.

Tamm, Ingrid J. 2004. Dangerous Appetites: Human Rights Activism and Conflict Commodities. *Human Rights Quarterly* 26 (3): 687–704.

Tanner, Marcus. 1997. *Croatia: A Nation Forged in War.* New Haven: Yale University Press.

Tanner, Marcus. 2001. *Croatia: A Nation Forged in War.* 2nd ed. New Haven: Yale University Press.

Tarrow, Sidney. 1989. *Democracy and Disorder: Protest and Politics in Italy, 1965–1975.* Oxford: Clarendon Press.

Tarrow, Sidney. 1994. *Power in Movement: Social Movements and Contentious Politics.* New York: Cambridge University Press.

Tarrow, Sidney. 1998. *Power in Movement: Social Movements and Contentious Politics.* 2nd ed. New York: Cambridge University Press.

Tarrow, Sidney. 2005. *The New Transnational Activism.* Cambridge: Cambridge University Press.

Taylor, Christopher. 1999. *Sacrifice as Terror: The Rwandan Genocide of 1994.* Oxford: Berg.

Taylor, Michael. 1976. *Anarchy and Cooperation.* New York: John Wiley.

Taylor, Michael. 1988. "Rationality and Revolutionary Collective Action." In *Rationality and Revolution,* ed. Michael Taylor. New York: Cambridge University Press.

Thaler, Richard. 1980. "Toward a Positive Theory of Consumer Choice." *Journal of Economic Behavior and Organization* 1 (1): 36–90.

Thaler, Richard. 1999. "Mental Accounting Matters." *Journal of Behavioural Decision Making* 12:183–206.

Thucydides. 1959. *History of the Peloponnesian War*. 3 vols. Trans. T. Hobbes. Ann Arbor: University of Michigan Press.

Tiech, Mikulas, and Roy Porter, eds. 1993. *The National Question in Europe in Historical Context*. Cambridge: Cambridge University Press.

Tilly, Charles. 1974. "Town and Country in Revolution." In *Peasant Rebellion and Communist Revolution in Asia*, ed. John W. Lewis. Stanford, CA: Stanford University Press.

Tilly, Charles. 1975. "Reflections on the History of European State-Making." In *The Formation of National States in Western Europe*, ed. Charles Tilly. Princeton: Princeton University Press, 1975.

Tilly, Charles. 1978. *From Mobilization to Revolution*. Reading, MA: Addison Wesley.

Tilly, Charles. 1990. *Coercion, Capital, and European States, AD 990–1990*. Cambridge, MA: Basil Blackwell.

Tilly, Charles. 2006a. *Regimes and Repertoires*. Chicago: University of Chicago Press.

Tilly, Charles. 2006b. "Why and How History Matters." In *Oxford Handbook of Contextual Political Analysis*, ed. Robert E. Goodin and Charles Tilly. Oxford: Oxford University Press.

Tilly, Charles, and Sidney Tarrow. 2007. *Contentious Politics*. Boulder: Paradigm.

Tiryakian, Edward A., and Ronald Rogowski, eds. 1985. *New Nationalisms of the Developed West: Toward Explanation*. Boston: Allen and Unwin.

Tocqueville, Alexis de. 1955. *The Old Régime and the French Revolution*. Trans. Stuart Gilbert. Garden City, NY: Doubleday. (Orig. pub. 1856.)

Todorov, Tzvetan. 2001. *The Fragility of Goodness: Why Bulgaria's Jews Survived the Holocaust*. Trans. Arthur Denner. Princeton: Princeton University Press.

Toft, Monica Duffy. 2002–3. "Indivisible Territory, Geographic Concentration, and Ethnic War." *Security Studies* 12 (2): 82–119.

Toft, Monica D. 2003. *The Geography of Ethnic Violence: Identity, Interests, and the Indivisibility of Territory*. Princeton: Princeton University Press.

Toft, Monica Duffy. 2006a. "Issue Indivisibility and Time Horizons as Rationalist Explanations for War." *Security Studies* 15 (1): 34–69.

Toft, Monica Duffy. 2006b. "Peace through Security: Making Negotiated Settlements Stick." John M. Olin Institute for Strategic Studies, Harvard University.

Toft, Monica Duffy. 2006c. "Religion, Civil War and International Order." Belfer Center Discussion Paper, Harvard University, July.

Toft, Monica Duffy. 2007a. "Getting Religion? The Puzzling Case of Islam and Civil War." *International Security* 31 (4): 97–131.

Toft, Monica Duffy. 2007b. "Population Shifts and Civil War: A Test of Power Transition Theory." *International Interactions* 33 (3): 243–69.

Toft, Monica Duffy. 2009. *Securing the Peace: The Durable Settlement of Civil Wars*. Princeton: Princeton University Press.

Tooby, John, and Leda Cosmides, eds. 2002. *Evolutionary Psychology: Foundational Papers*. Cambridge: MIT Press.

Treier, Shawn, and Simon Jackman. 2008. "Democracy as a Latent Variable." *American Journal of Political Science* 52 (1): 201–17.

Trumbore, Peter. 2003. "Victims or Aggressors? Ethno-Political Rebellion and Use of Force in Militarized Interstate Disputes." *International Studies Quarterly* 47:183–201.

Turner, John, R. Brown, and Henri Tajfel. 1979. "Social Comparison and Group Interest in Ingroup Favoritism." *European Journal of Social Psychology* 9 (2): 187–204.

Tversky, Amos, and Daniel Kahneman. 1986. "Rational Choice and the Framing of Decisions." *Journal of Business* 59 (4): S252–S254.

United Nations Institute for Disarmament Research. 2003. *The Scope and Implications of a Tracing Mechanism for Small Arms and Light Weapons*. Geneva: UNIDIR, Small Arms Survey.

Urdal, Henrik. 2005. "People vs. Malthus: Population Pressure, Environmental Degradation and Armed Conflict Revisited." *Journal of Peace Research* 42:417–34.

U.S. Army and Marine Corps. 2007. *The U.S. Army/Marine Corps Counterinsurgency Field Manual*. Forewords by David H. Petraeus and James F. Amos and by John A. Nagl. Chicago: University of Chicago Press.

Vachudova, Milada Anna. 2005. *Europe Undivided: Democracy, Leverage, and Integration after Communism*, Oxford: Oxford University Press.

Valentino, Benjamin A. 2004. *Final Solutions: Mass Killing and Genocide in the Twentieth Century*. Ithaca: Cornell University Press.

Van Belle, Douglas A. 1996. "Leadership and Collective Action: The Case of Revolution." *International Studies Quarterly* 40:107–32.

Van Evera, Stephen. 1990. "Why Europe Matters, Why the Third World Doesn't: American Grand Strategy after the Cold War." *Journal of Strategic Studies* 13 (2): 1–51.

Van Evera, Stephen. 1994. "Hypotheses on Nationalism." *International Security* 18 (4): 5–39.

Vanhanen, Tatu. 2000. "A New Dataset for Measuring Democracy, 1810–1998." *Journal of Peace Research* 37:251–65. Data available at www.prio.no/jpr/datasets.

Van Houten, Pieter. 1998. "The Role of a Minority's Reference State in Ethnic Relations." *Archives Européennes de Sociologie* 39:110–46.

Varshney, Ashutosh. 2002. *Ethnic Conflict and Civic Life: Hindus and Muslims in India.* New Haven: Yale University Press.

Vasquez, John A. 1992. "Factors Related to the Contagion and Diffusion of International Violence." In *The Internationalization of Communal Strife,* ed. Manus I. Midlarsky. London: Routledge.

Vasquez, John A. 1997. "The Realist Paradigm and Degenerative versus Progressive Research Programs: An Appraisal of Neotraditional Research on Waltz's Balancing Proposition." *American Political Science Review* 91:899–913.

Vasquez, John A. 2000. "Reexamining the Steps to War: New Evidence and Theoretical Insights." In *Handbook of War Studies II,* ed. Manus I. Midlarsky. Ann Arbor: University of Michigan Press.

Vreeland, James Raymond. 2008. "The Effect of Political Regime on Civil War: Unpacking Anocracy." *Journal of Conflict Resolution* 52 (3): 401–25.

Wagner, Robert Harrison. 1993. "The Causes of Peace." In *Stopping the Killing: How Civil Wars End,* ed. Roy Licklider. New York: New York University Press.

Wagner, R. Harrison. 2000. "Bargaining and War." *American Journal of Political Science* 44:469–84.

Walt, Stephen M. 1996. *Revolution and War.* Ithaca: Cornell University Press.

Walt, Stephen M. 1999. "Rigor or Rigor Mortis? Rational Choice and Security Studies." *International Security* 23 (4): 5–48.

Walter, Barbara F. 2002. *Committing to Peace: The Successful Settlement of Civil Wars.* Princeton: Princeton University Press.

Walter, Barbara F., and Jack Snyder, eds. 1999. *Civil Wars, Insecurity, and Intervention.* New York: Columbia University Press.

Waltz, Kenneth. 1959. *Man, the State, and War: A Theoretical Analysis.* New York: Columbia University Press.

Waltz, Kenneth. 1964. "The Stability of a Bipolar World." *Daedalus* 93: 881–909.

Waltz, Kenneth. 1979. *Theory of International Politics.* New York: McGraw-Hill.

Wantchekon, Leonard. 2004. "The Paradox of 'Warlord' Democracy: A Theoretical Investigation." *American Political Science Review* 98:17–33.

Ward, Michael D., and Kristin Bakke. 2005. "Predicting Civil Conflicts: On the Utility of Empirical Research." Paper presented at the conference "Disaggregating the Study of Civil War and Transnational Violence," University of California Institute of Global Conflict and Cooperation, San Diego, March 7–8.

Ward, Michael D., Randolph M. Siverson, and Xun Cao. 2007. "Disputes, Democracies, and Dependencies: A Reexamination of the Kantian Peace." *American Journal of Political Science.* 51:581–601.

Wasserstein, Bernard. 1999. *Britain and the Jews of Europe, 1939–1945.* 2nd ed. London: Leicester University Press.

Wayland, Sarah. 2004. "Ethnonationalist Networks and Transnational Opportunities: The Sri Lankan Tamil Diaspora." *Review of International Studies* 30:405–26.

Weber, Max. 1968. *Economy and Society.* 2 vols. Trans. Hans H. Gerth and C. Wright Mills. Berkeley and Los Angeles: University of California Press.

Weiner, Myron. 1971. "The Macedonian Syndrome." *World Politics* 23: 665–83.

Weiner, Myron. 1978. *Sons of the Soil: Migration and Ethnic Conflict in India.* Princeton: Princeton University Press.

Weiner, Myron. 1996. "Bad Neighbors, Bad Neighborhoods: An Inquiry into the Causes of Refugee Flows." *International Security* 21 (1): 5–42.

Weingast, Barry R. 1995. "The Economic Role of Political Institutions: Market-Preserving Federalism and Economic Development." *Journal of Law, Economics, and Organization* 11 (1): 1–31.

Weingast, Barry R. 1997. "The Political Foundations of Democracy and Rule of Law." *American Political Science Review* 91:245–63.

Weingast, Barry R. 2002. "Rational-Choice Institutionalism." In *Political Science: The State of the Discipline*, ed. Ira Katznelson and Helen V. Milner. New York: Norton.

Weisman, Steven R. 2004. "Crisis in Sudan Resists Simple Solutions." *New York Times*, August 8, N6.

Weitz, Eric D. 2003. *A Century of Genocide: Utopias of Race and Nation.* Princeton: Princeton University Press.

Werner, Suzanne. 1996. "Absolute and Limited War: The Possibilities of Foreign Imposed Regime Change." *International Interactions* 22 (1): 67–88.

Werner, Suzanne. 1999. "The Precarious Nature of Peace: Resolving the Issues, Enforcing the Settlement, and Renegotiating the Terms." *American Journal of Political Science* 43:913–34.

Werner, Suzanne, David Davis, and Bruce Bueno de Mesquita, eds. 2003. "Dissolving Boundaries." Special issue of *International Studies Review* 5 (4).

Wheeler, M., and Susan Fiske. 2005. "Controlling Racial Prejudice: Social Cognitive Goals Affect Amygdala and Stereotype Activation." *Psychological Science* 16 (1): 56–63.

Wickham-Crowley, Timothy. 1992. *Guerrillas and Revolution in Latin America: A Comparative Study of Insurgents and Regimes since 1956.* Princeton: Princeton University Press.

Wilkinson, Steven I. 2006. *Votes and Violence: Electoral Competition and Ethnic Riots in India.* Cambridge: Cambridge University Press.

Winer, Jonathan M. 2005. "Tracking Conflict Commodities and Financing." In

Profiting from Peace: Managing the Resource Dimensions of Civil War, ed. Karen Ballentine and Heiko Nitzschke. Boulder: Lynne Rienner.

Wintrobe, Ronald. 2006. *Rational Extremism: The Political Economy of Radicalism.* Cambridge: Cambridge University Press.

Wittman, Donald. 1979. "How a War Ends: A Rational Model Approach." *Journal of Conflict Resolution* 23:743–63.

Wolf, Eric R. 1969. *Peasant Wars of the Twentieth Century.* New York: Harper and Row.

Wolf, Eric R. 1982. *Europe and the People without History.* Berkeley and Los Angeles: University of California Press.

Wolffsohn, Michael. 1993. *Eternal Guilt? Forty Years of German-Jewish-Israeli Relations.* New York: Columbia University Press.

Woloch, Isser. 1994. *The New Regime: Transformations of the French Civic Order, 1789–1820.* New York: Norton.

Wood, Elisabeth Jean. 2001. *Forging Democracy from Below: Insurgent Transitions in South Africa and El Salvador.* New York: Cambridge University Press.

Woodward, Susan L. 1995. *Balkan Tragedy: Chaos and Dissolution after the Cold War.* Washington, DC: Brookings Institution Press.

Woodward, Susan L. 2002. "Economic Priorities for Successful Peace Implementation." In *Ending Civil Wars: The Implementation of Peace Agreements,* ed. Stephen John Stedman, Donald Rothchild, and Elizabeth M. Cousens. Boulder: Lynne Rienner.

Woodwell, Douglas. 2004. "Unwelcome Neighbors: Shared Ethnicity and International Conflict During the Cold War." *International Studies Quarterly* 48:197–223.

Wrangham, Richard. 1999. "Evolution of Coalitionary Killing." *Yearbook of Physical Anthropology* 110:1–30.

Wrangham, Richard, and Dale Peterson. 1996. *Demonic Males: Apes and the Origins of Human Violence.* New York: Houghton Mifflin.

Wyman, David. 1985. *Paper Walls: America and the Refugee Crisis 1938–1941.* New York: Pantheon.

Zacher, Mark W. 2001. "The Territorial Integrity Norm: International Boundaries and the Use of Force." *International Organization* 55:215–50.

Zagare, Frank C. 1977. "A Game-Theoretic Analysis of the Vietnam Negotiations: Preferences and Strategies, 1968–1973." *Journal of Conflict Resolution* 21:663–84.

Zagare, Frank C. 1990. "Rationality and Deterrence." *World Politics* 42:238–60.

Zagare, Frank C., and D. Marc Kilgour. 2000. *Perfect Deterrence.* Cambridge: Cambridge University Press.

Zanger, Sabine C. 2000. "A Global Analysis of the Effect of Political Regime

Changes on Life Integrity Violations, 1977–93." *Journal of Peace Research* 37:213–33.

Zartman, I. William. 1985. *Ripe for Resolution: Conflict and Intervention in Africa.* New York: Oxford University Press.

Zartman, I. William. 1993. "The Unfinished Agenda: Negotiating Internal Conflict." In *Stop the Killing: How Civil Wars End,* ed. Roy Licklider. New York: New York University Press.

Zartman, I. William. 2001. The Timing of Peace Initiatives: Hurting Stalemates and Ripe Moments. *Global Review of Ethnopolitics* 1 (1): 8–18.

Zevelev, Igor. 2000. *Russia and Its New Diaspora.* Washington, DC: United States Institute of Peace Press.

Zimbardo, Philip G. 2008. *The Lucifer Effect: Understanding How Good People Turn Evil.* New York: Random House.

Zimmerman, Warren. 1995. "The Last Ambassador." *Foreign Affairs* 74 (2): 2–20.

Zuccotti, Susan. 2000. *Under His Very Windows: The Vatican and the Holocaust in Italy.* New Haven: Yale University Press.

Zucker, Bat-Ami. 2001. *In Search of Refuge: Jews and US Consuls in Nazi Germany, 1933–1941.* Portland, OR: Vallentine Mitchell.

Index